First Edition
isbn 978-2-915723-94-6

Pursued by Bishops

Edwin Apps's other publications:

L'abbaye de Maillezais
Geste Editions, 2002

•

Maillezais
the story of a French abbey
Geste Editions, 2002

Edwin Apps

Pursued by Bishops

Durand-Peyroles

2013

For Barnaby

Contents

—

FOREWORD

—

B ishops, and other species of clergy, have loomed large in my life. In France, where I live now, I am known for my paintings of bishops in unconventional situations; and my name is chiefly associated with "*All Gas and Gaiters*", which Pauline Devaney and I wrote between 1965 and 1972.

It was the first television comedy series about the Church of England that struck a chord with viewers, both in Britain and elsewhere. There had been several earlier attempts that failed due to lack of understanding and knowledge of that singular institution, and there have been others since. When the journalist, Miriam Maisel, interviewed us in December 1967, she wrote that she had:

> "... Expected to find a middle-aged, rather hearty couple. I even expected a clerical background on one side or the other and a couple who had spent most of their lives in the country.
>
> What I actually found was a couple of young, sophisticated and highly decorative actors who live in a flat in Blackheath. And as for a bishop in the family – neither Edwin nor Pauline had actually met one."

In fact we neither of us went to church and we were married in a registry office. And yet bishops and the clergy had figured in my life due to an unexpected event, or rather several unexpected events. But my whole life seems to have been composed of unexpected events, some of which have proved more fruitful than others.

I have written at some length about my family background because I believe that we, like trees, have as much of us underground as above it and that our roots colour and shape everything we do. In my case, I have come to see that everything I have done, the way I have reacted to events, even where I have lived, have all been influenced not only by my background and my childhood, but by much that occurred before I was born.

It happened that I was separated from my parents for long peri-
ods from an early age and that contact was maintained by regular
correspondence. Almost all these letters have survived and they have
enabled me to check my memory of events against accounts written
at the time. Even allowing for the fact that writing to parents involves
a certain amount of presentation, I have been surprised how often
my memory of events has been at odds with these contemporary
witnesses.

Digging back along the path I have travelled, I have been forced to
turn over some of its stones and reveal certain things I should have
preferred to have left where they were. But for better or worse it has
been my path, so, spade in hand, let me begin.

* * *

CHAPTER ONE

—

"Be happy in the moment, take no thought
For hidden things beyond, be firm to test
And turn the edge of troubles with a jest,
For bliss unmixed was never earthly lot."

From Edward Marsh's translation
of Horace's Ode XVI Book II

Two o'clock in the morning and I am still painting. For many years I have worked into the early hours, the hours when everyone is asleep, the telephone is silent and there are no distractions. On this particular night I am working on one of my bishop paintings. Since I came to live in France almost forty years ago and began to paint seriously, bishops have been one of my principal themes.

There is a ruined cathedral in the next village whose bishop at the time of the Renaissance had François Rabelais as his chaplain. I like to imagine the two of them still riding round the marsh together, the bishop on a horse with Rabelais beside him on a donkey, figures seen fleetingly in the mist, by the light of the early morning sun.

I break off for a moment and look at my watch, thinking there might be a late news bulletin on the television. I have a television set in the studio that is tuned to English speaking stations, as we only have French stations in the house.

When the set warms up, an old black and white film is just ending. The credits roll and I notice a name, John Loder. *Loder,* I think, *Loder,* and my memory stirs, as did Marcel Proust's when he tasted the madeleine that took him back to the world of his childhood.

For me, seeing the name John Loder on the television in the corner of my studio has the same effect: it takes me back instantly to the first time I went to the cinema.

We drove to Canterbury in the Lanchester with my mother driving, my father sitting beside her and Gladys Pepper, my nursemaid, and me, seated behind. The cinema was called *The Friars* and my father, who knew the manager, had organised the expedition. We parked the car and, holding Gladys's hand, I followed my parents along the pavement and up the steps into the vestibule. The manager came to greet us and, looking at me curiously, led us through the doors into the darkened hall. There on the screen was the enormous face of a man with a moustache. My mother turned to the manager:

"Is that him?".

"Yes" he replied.

"Look, darling," said my mother "That's Loder."

"It's not." I said "That is not Loder."

"But it is," they all insisted, "That is Loder."

"It is not," I shouted "That is not Loder – he doesn't look a bit like that".

It was my first glimpse of the unbridgeable gap between reality and the world of the imagination.

As an only child in the country with no one to play with, I had invented an imaginary friend called Loder. Nobody knew where the name came from, but I would endlessly recount his life, his troubles with his wife and his many children, his lack of money and much else besides. Surrounded by adults, it was a way of keeping my end up. While they might not want to hear the opinions of a child, I found that when I began my sentence with "Loder thinks" or "Loder says" or "That's just what Loder feels", I was more readily listened to. So, Gladys, Edith the cook, Attaway the gardener, Mrs Pepper, Gladys's mother who came in to clean each day and even Tutt, the back-door-boy who cleaned the shoes, brought in the logs and ran errands, as well as my parents, were familiar with the sayings and doings of Loder.

I am not sure whether I discussed Loder with my other two friends, Old Bill and Measday.

Bill Sheaff, known as 'Old Bill' to distinguish him from his son, 'Young Bill' who drove the tractor, was the farm bailiff who lived with his wife in a late Victorian redbrick house at the top of the lane. He rode a red bicycle that had once belonged to a postman. Although adept at getting on and riding, he had never mastered the art of getting off and so would collapse into the hedge or onto the bank at the side of the lane. His other form of transport was a dung-cart drawn by a fat little horse called Topsy. When I got older I would spend happy hours seated beside him on the front of the cart as he smoked his pipe and we made our way slowly up the hill to Hearts Delight. There we loaded up the cart with wurzels from the clamp and brought them back to Wenderton, the scent of shag mingling with the peppery smell of the wurzels. Sometimes he would let me hold the reins, "Gee up, Topsy". Topsy would take no notice and we would continue at the same leisurely pace.

Measday was the stockman and I would help him mix the mash for the pigs while he would tell me about the last night's radio programmes. He was a keen listener and his favourite programme was "In Town Tonight" which included a sketch each week with Richard Goolden as Old Ebenezer the night watchman. I was allowed to stay up and listen to this on Saturday nights and the following week we would endlessly dissect last week's episode, quoting lines and imitating the quavering voice of Richard Goolden.

Monday was market day at Sandwich and my father, in breeches, boots and gaiters, his market coat and trilby hat, would drive off early with Mr Fordham, his clerk, to conduct the sales of pigs, sheep and cattle. Monday was also washday and Dash, the old black and white Clumber Spaniel who lived in the backdoor porch beside the kitchen, would look more than usually lugubrious, knowing that not much fun was to be had that day.

Saturday was market day at Canterbury and in the afternoon my mother, Gladys and I would do the weekly shopping in Canterbury ending with tea at Lefevres, Canterbury's department store. On one of these trips I was taken to the hairdressing saloon as it was felt I should have a real haircut. When the assistant arrived dressed all in white with a white sheet to put over me, I screamed the place down and had ignominiously to be led out, so it was back to Gladys wielding the scissors in the nursery.

Another visit to the cinema several years later was no more successful. The film chosen was Hitchcock's "The Lady Vanishes".

All went well until Margaret Lockwood appeared smothered in white bandages. Again I had to be led out.

The theatre proved more satisfactory. I was taken to see the Canterbury Amateur Dramatic Society's production of "The Pilgrim's Progress" in the Cathedral Chapter House. This was a seminal experience and resulted in my spending days trudging round the kitchen table in a pair of my father's boots with a pack on my back, imagining myself to be the Pilgrim.

Dressing up was my favourite occupation; my father's old uniforms, my mother's riding coat, two early nineteenth century wigs that had belonged to an ancestor, which I'd found in the attic, and a Father Christmas outfit with a hook-on beard, allowed me to be practically anyone I chose, from Nelson to the old man with the white beard and black homburg hat who lived in one of the farm cottages along the lane. On one occasion I was dressed in the riding coat with the beard and a hat, imitating his walk with his two sticks in the middle of the lawn when I saw him walking past the gate. I fled into the house.

Beside the house was the hop-garden, which in winter presented the spectacle of bare rows of poles held together by stretched wires. In the spring, beside each hop-plant, strings were tied to the bottom wires and attached to the top wires by men on stilts. Up these strings the tendrils known as bines climbed, putting out leaves and finally forming the fruit, until the hop-garden was transformed into parallel alleys of overhanging dark green leaves.

Picking time was the big event of the year. The pickers came from London on special trains and were housed in primitive huts, a hut to each family. Picking, too, was organised by families, each family being allotted an alley. The grandmother would sit at the end with the big basket, and a man with a knife on the end of a pole would cut bines down for the members of the family, who, seated on stools or upturned boxes, would drape the bines across their knees and pick the hops into smaller baskets which, when full, they would carry to the grandmother. Hops, to anyone not familiar with them, are pale green and feather light.

The grandmother's job – one might say her art – was to pour the hops into the big basket with such care that they took up the maximum of space so that the basket would be filled with the least possible effort on the part of the pickers.

Young Bill, temporarily separated from his tractor, was the tallyman who kept count of who had picked what and saw that the baskets, when full were emptied into the loosely woven sacks or 'green-bags,' which were then loaded on to the wagon and taken by the wagoner to the oast to be dried. An internecine war was waged between Young Bill and the grandmothers, with frequent loud disputes as to whether or not the baskets were full. His favourite tactic was to accidentally kick the basket as he walked past which made the hops settle at a lower level. At this, there would be a roar of rage from the grandmother, sometimes followed up by a physical attack. On one occasion he was seized by an irate group of pickers, pushed head first into a basket and left struggling with his legs in the air.

The arrival of the hop-pickers was looked upon with mixed feelings in Wingham village. While the publicans and shop-keepers might be glad of the increased trade, the drunken brawls, break-ins, missing poultry and general upset caused by an influx of cockneys in holiday mood unfamiliar with the country and its ways, meant that people locked their doors, kept them locked and stayed behind them.

There was always a moment after the novelty had worn off, when the pickers went on strike. Young Bill would plead with them to go back to work and when this failed, Old Bill would arrive on his red bicycle and, collapsing against the wagon, would get off and tell them that it was impossible to pay more. Finally, when they still refused to continue picking, my grandfather would arrive impressively in the black Hillman with Kelk, his uniformed chauffeur, and, after a heart rending speech in which ruin was seen to be stalking East Kent, would offer a farthing a bushel more, which was always accepted -except for one year when they threatened to overturn the car and he was so taken by surprise he offered a halfpenny.

When the time to go to school came, I was sent to Reed Barn School in the neighbouring village of Ash. Two sisters, known as 'The

Miss Elgars', kept it. Miss Edith, the elder, was the dominant partner, the stern headmistress, while Miss Gracie was more approachable and only to be feared when leaning over one's shoulder to see what one had written when a fine spray of saliva was emitted as she talked. The Miss Elgars lived at Wingham and drove daily to their school in a capacious black car, which gradually filled with children on the way. Each morning Gladys would take me up the lane to the turnpike road where we would await their arrival.

School was my first experience of being with other children. The nearest children at home had been those of the farm workers, but I was not allowed to play with them for fear that I might pick up a common accent or "catch something" so I remained a solitary prisoner in my garden surrounded by its tall yew hedge. At one point, a boy from the cottages took pity on me and came to chat through the hedge. This Pyramus-and-Thisbe friendship was too limited to last long, so school was something of a shock.

I was not unlike one of Conrad Lorenz's geese; having always been surrounded by adults, I considered myself to be one, and found the children childish. Unused to playing with others, I had none of the skills such as throwing and catching balls, and absolutely no sense of competition, which made me a perfect butt for the school bully. I could read and soon learned to write, I enjoyed drawing and painting, daydreaming and inventing stories because although solitude had left me physically retarded, it had developed my imagination.

Although I was solitary I was far from unhappy. Wenderton House and garden were the perfect setting to develop the imagination of a child. The house was an accretion dating from the fourteenth century. The main part was seventeenth century, refaced with stock bricks and a slate roof in the middle of the nineteenth century. An additional Regency bow-windowed wing had been added earlier and the whole had been topped off with a late Victorian gothic front porch sometime in the 1870s. The garden consisted of an upper and lower lawn, a wilderness, leading to a rose garden and, beyond, a pond on which were semi-wild ducks. An orchard and a big kitchen garden stretching down to the marsh succeeded this in turn. Tall clipped hedges surrounded each part of the garden, so that one had the impression of discovering one secret place after another.

On the upper lawn, opposite the front door, was a weeping ash. In the hall, a yellowing photograph showed my great-great-great aunt, Sarah Anne Minter, wearing a bustle, and her brother, William, with mutton chop whiskers standing in front of the same tree when it was half grown sometime in the 1860s. Now its branches touched the ground all round, so that when it was in leaf it formed a dark green room to play in. At the side of the house was a yew tree between three and four hundred years old, which it was believed, had been planted to provide wood to make bows in the days of the English archers. In the wilderness, an ancient mulberry tree said to date from the time of James I, who had encouraged their planting to breed silkworms, twisted in every conceivable direction and was perfect for climbing.

Then there were the attics, which contained the books and toys that had belonged to my father and his seven brothers and two sisters. My mother, for whom books were dust-traps, had consigned them there. The attics, strictly out of bounds because of the accumulated dust and dirt, were naturally my favourite part of the house. There, amidst dust and dead flies, I lived a vicarious late-Victorian boyhood, full of such wonders as the magic lantern, an imposing machine with a chimney for the oil lamp which fitted inside it and by whose flickering light it projected glass slides showing Adam and Eve naked in the garden of Eden, scenes from the Holy Land and, best of all, a wooden slide of a kaleidoscope with a small handle which when turned made the colours on the screen move in and out of each other. Books included the works of Dickens, "Masterman Ready" by Captain Marryat, "Coral Island", Southey's "Life of Nelson" and a long run of bound copies of the first Strand Magazines, with the "Adventures of Sherlock Holmes".

My father's family had all been fond or reading and he himself often read to me. His favourite book was "The Pickwick Papers"; a copy of which he had carried with him throughout the First World War and which he claimed had never failed to cheer him up in his darkest moments. I was five years old when he first read it to me and at eight I read it for myself. I don't suppose I understood much at five, but his enjoyment was infectious and when I read it today, I hear his voice. He successfully read all sorts of books to me. Two favourites were "Winnie the Pooh" and "The Wind in the Willows, both of which we read so often I knew them almost by heart. The only time we admitted defeat over a book was when he bought a copy of "Uncle Remus". The Southern drawl in which it is written proved too difficult for both of us and he took it back to the shop the next day.

My father's family lived at Tenterden in the Weald of Kent. 'Apps' is a Flemish name and it is probable that the family came to England as weavers. The grazing land of Romney Marsh, renowned for its sheep and their wool, surrounds Tenterden and the neighbouring town of Cranbrook, and the area was the centre of a major weaving industry in the Middle-Ages. In 1336, Edward III invited Flemish weavers to come to work in England under Royal Protection and the family may well have come at that time.

In any case, by 1890, when my father was born, they were well established as one of the oldest families in the town where they had a prosperous ironmonger's business, which had survived several generations. Ironmongery at that time was not simply a matter of selling ready-made products as it is today; everything was designed and made on the premises by a workshop of tin-smiths and the distribution system entailed delivery vans and a stable of horses. Grandfather Edwin was a Town Councillor and Churchwarden, as his father, Edwin Percival, had been before him. He had married Margaret Edwards, the eldest daughter of Obadiah Edwards, who owned the Tenterden Brewery and possessed no less than thirteen pubs. Edwin and Margaret lived in a rambling old house, called Beach House next to the Baptist Chapel. Not that Edwin had any time for Baptists – if he saw the minister approaching, he would cross to the other side of the street. The family was staunchly Church of England and all the boys sang in the choir. In all, Margaret gave him ten children, two girls followed by eight boys of whom my father was the third. He was christened Bertram Robert and was sent to school at Thanet College, a private school on the Isle of Thanet, where he enjoyed games, especially cricket, and was good at maths. In the holidays he was a favourite of grandfather Obadiah, who took him with him visiting his farms in his pony-trap; he had several farms for grazing his dray-horses.

Obadiah was the image of a prosperous mid-Victorian; he had first bought the brewery at Tunbridge Wells and then sold it to buy the brewery at Tenterden, which he had turned into the major employer of labour in that part of Kent. He had twice been mayor and was a justice of the peace (although he refused to sit on the bench on Mondays, saying he could not sit in judgement on people who had drunk too much of his beer the previous Saturday night) and had been instrumental in bringing the railway to the town. During those drives in the pony cart he no doubt sought to instil ambition in his grandson.

My father's other influence was his Uncle Bob, Robert Edwards, who owned the first motor car in Tenterden, was a member of the Fire Brigade and who taught him to shoot. Shooting was his passion and it was when he got home after a day's shooting with his Uncle Bob during the school holidays, at the age of fifteen, that Edwin told him he had been articled to Mr Judge, the auctioneer and land-agent, and would start work the next day.

That year, my father had passed the Oxford Local Examination in "Writing from Dictation, Arithmetic, Religious Knowledge, History; Grammar, Literature, Essay; Geography and Mathematics", with right answers to such posers as–

'Where are the chief coal-fields of Scotland and what important towns are situated upon them?'

'Distinguish the four classes into which the hearers of the Word are divided in the explanation of the parable of the Sower'.

'Find the rent of a farm 25 acres, 3 roods, 16 perches in extent at £1. 16s. 8d. an acre.'

'What happened at the following places? Bannockburn, Acre, Bretigny, Falkirk, the New Forest, Alnwick'.

His eldest brother, Harry, was training as an engineer, and the next brother, Arthur was learning the ironmonger's business, while there were the twins, Charles and Leonard as well as Fred and Stuart still to be educated, not to mention Gordon aged two.

Considering he had no choice in his career, my father was a round peg in a round hole. His four years as an articled clerk passed off well; he helped Mr Judge with weekly sales in Ashford market, farm sales, private house sales, and the annual Kent lamb sales, which was the usual routine of a country auctioneer at that time.

At the end of his articles, as he was looking for a firm to join as "an improver", a friend suggested that Arthur Marchant at Ash was looking for someone. They were introduced to each other in Ashford market and the deal concluded; so at the age of eighteen, my father went to work with his future father-in-law.

As Grandfather Apps died before I was born and Grandmother Apps when I was only four, I knew neither of them. Nor, until much later, did I know my father's brothers, who had married and moved away from Tenterden. Thus it was my mother's family, the Marchants and in particular my grandmother's family, the Goodsons, that I came to identify with in my childhood.

The Marchants were as un-bookish as it is possible to be. At Guilton, my grandparents' house, the only books I ever saw were, "The Compleat Farrier", R.S. Surtees' "Handley Cross" and "Jorrocks' Jaunts and Jollities" by the same author. Horses were everywhere, from the stables to the drawing room. Pictures of them covered every wall, furniture was made wherever possible to resemble them and, once dead, ashtrays made from their hooves prolonged their memory. My grandfather, Arthur Marchant, in spite of being six feet tall and enormously fat, was an intrepid fox-hunter "No five-barred gate ever stopped me" he would declare in old age. That it was not an idle boast, I learned years later when I found a copy of the memoirs of Harry Selby-Lowndes, who had been the master of the East Kent, the local hunt during the 1920s. In it he recounts how, with hounds running, he found himself between my grandfather and Troward Spanton, another farmer of similar girth, approaching the level crossing on the Sandwich road;

"Without hesitating, these two heavyweights jumped over the first six-foot gate, on to the line and straight out over the other," adding, "being the Master, I felt bound to follow."

My mother's brother, uncle John, was an amateur jockey and my early memories of him are of his being continually in hospital with broken bones. His greatest success was when he won the Stock Exchange Plate, but he was a familiar figure at the local point-to-points, where he frequently came in first on a horse called Jack Frost.

Later, when I went to school, I met a boy who told me he had systematically put his pocket money on Jack Frost and never regretted it.

A friend of Uncle John's, who was veterinary surgeon to the Jockey Club, had often asked if he might have Jack Frost's front legs to dissect when he died. The request was of course agreed to, but the melancholy event occurred in the first year of the war while my uncle's friend was in the United States and unable to return. So Jack Frost's legs were preserved in formaldehyde in a milk churn, which stood beside the backdoor of Guilton throughout the rest of the war.

My mother was the eldest of the three Marchant children and totally horse-obsessed; the despair of her mother, she was rarely seen out of the stables. Hunting was her passion where she was known as "The Leading Hound". Riding astride at a time when it was not considered suitable for women, her greatest regret was that her parents would not let her compete in point-to-points

After her marriage my mother no longer hunted, but this did not stop her following the hunt on foot. She had a remarkable sense of how the hunt was going, where the fox would break cover and so on. She could smell a fox and, walking in a wood, would suddenly say, "There's a fox here". On one occasion she was following the hunt by car with me aged five when she suddenly stopped, shouted "Come on!" picked me up and half carried me across a field, arriving just as the hounds killed. When the master, huntsmen, whippers-in and the rest of the field rode up, there was general laughter. I was blooded, the ceremony of wiping blood on the forehead of someone at his first kill, and, whereas the tradition was to give the brush to the first person to arrive, the mask to the second and the pads to the others, all these gruesome trophies were given to my mother.

At my birth, the doctor had handed me to her with an exhortation not to use the currycomb on me, and it always seemed that in bringing me up she was guided less by books on baby-craft, than by her favourite treatise on stable management. My horsemanship was considered a foregone conclusion and from the earliest days I was lifted on to horses whenever possible and there was a good deal of talk about my having a natural seat. A rocking horse was early acquired for the nursery and at the age of four, my first pony, a Shetland. Once in the saddle, I promptly fell off. "Get up, get up and get back on at once!" cried my mother. Feeling safer on the ground I felt a reluctance to obey and I'm ashamed to say this reluctance has tended to persist.

My mother's pelvis had been deformed by riding, which meant that my birth was something of a trauma with my struggles to see the light lasting over twenty-four hours, during which my father claimed he had walked round the hop-garden several hundred times. The situation had not been helped by the fact that, once pregnant, my mother had ceased all physical activity and "eaten for two" – with the result that may be imagined.

My birth had been so traumatic that the doctor warned her not to have another child because it was too dangerous. When she immediately became pregnant again, she went to him in a panic, but he had changed his opinion and assured her everything would be all right.

In those days hospitals were viewed with suspicion. If anyone in the family needed an operation, a London surgeon was brought down and the operation performed on the dining-room table, while in the kitchen a gargantuan luncheon was prepared for the distinguished guest. However, on this occasion, the doctor refused all demands from the family that he bring down a gynaecologist to help him and the second birth, thirteen months after mine, again took place at home with only himself and a midwife in attendance. I had been a big baby, but my brother was bigger and the doctor crushed him. Thus my mother, who had always wanted six sons, had to make do with me.

I believe that after the loss of her baby, my mother suffered a depression although it was not called that. She spent a lot of time in bed and I remember being taken in to see her. In any case I spent most of my time with my nurse and saw relatively little of my parents.

Until I was five, I had my meals in the kitchen sitting between Gladys and Edith, Gladys in her uniform of white mob-cap, blue and white striped dress, with a white bib and apron, starched collar and cuffs, and Edith in a cream cap and dark blue dress. I listened entranced to their conversation about their families and from time to time the bell would ring and they would go to wait on my parents who were having lunch in the breakfast room. When I was five, the moment came when I was considered sufficiently civilised to eat with my parents. I remember feeling rather nervous and very grown-up. As I was a thin child, I was given a mug of beer with my lunch to strengthen me and later, as the beer did not seem to have had much effect, this was changed to a glass of port. I have never liked beer, but I still enjoy a glass of port.

At about that time I was sent with Gladys to stay with my mother's grandmother, Harriet Goodson, who, widowed in 1920, had moved out of Upton, the Goodson family home near Broadstairs, into the original little mediaeval farmhouse which had been modernised for her. It was called Little Upton and she lived there with her cook and gardener, Caley. My chief memory is of the custards her cook made and going down to the beach with Gladys and the cook armed with bucket and spade.

When I was a little older, I was sent without Gladys to stay with Aunty Peggy, my Mother's younger sister. She had married Uncle George Stevens who was the managing director of a family firm, on the Isle of Sheppey, which made glue and artificial manure. Uncle George's grandfather, who had seen possibilities in the barges bringing rags and bones down the Thames from the rapidly growing capital, had founded the company. The business had prospered and Uncle George, although he had set his heart on going into the Navy, had been constrained to become the Managing Director. His hobby was making models of all kinds and he made me a model castle that opened up and had rooms and stairs inside. Uncle George had a Peter Pan quality, a sense of never having really grown up, which made him a matchless uncle. He and Aunty Peggy lived in a mock-Elizabethan house, called Little Guilton near Sittingbourne, which he had designed. It was built from old ship's timbers. Aunty Peggy, who greatly resembled my grandmother, was fanatically house-proud and the house, like Guilton, was over-cleaned and over-polished.

The stink engendered by Uncle George Stevens' factory was not appreciated in Queenborough, the principal town on the island, so to avert public hostility it had been the family tradition that a member of the family should be the mayor. Uncle George's father had handed on the charge to him soon after his marriage when he was thirty and Aunty Peggy was eighteen. They were thus the youngest mayoral couple in the country and led a full social life as a result. Aunty Peggy was even more austere and disciplined than my grandmother and when my stay came to an end I was glad to get home.

Among the figures of my childhood Great-aunt Maggie, my grandmother's younger sister, held pride of place. Maggie was drenched in moral turpitude, had a lively sense of humour and brought a much-needed breath of fresh air to the prevailing respectability. Disowned by the rest of the family and disinherited by her uncle, G. M. Goodson, who was rich and unmarried; ("a mother who deserts her child will get nothing from me!") she remained my mother's favourite aunt and our most frequent visitor.

The moral turpitude was hardly her fault; married at eighteen to a man who gave her syphilis and himself died of it a few years later, she had fled the family home, leaving her baby son behind her to be brought up by her sister-in-law. After the divorce, she kept house for her unmarried brother Frank until her brother George found her a second husband, the son of a Lincolnshire parson, but he turned out to be gay. Finally, determined to choose for herself, she lived unmarried with the young man who delivered the vegetables. He was twenty years younger than she, and they were blissfully happy.

They had a farm at Headcorn and Gladys and I used to go to stay with them. It was by far the happiest house I knew in my childhood. Maggie gave everyone nicknames, so I was Baboo, she was Yaya and Harold, her companion, was OK, short for OK Chief. He had an old grey van, (probably the same in which he had delivered his seductive vegetables) which seemed to me the acme of motorised transport. I did not like cars and deeply regretted that I had been born too late for horse-drawn transport that was obviously preferable, but I made an exception for OK's van. It rattled and banged and you had to hold on tight; driving became an adventure, just as it should be.

Yaya herself had a baby Austin which she drove wearing a pair of sheep's wool backed gauntlets, with a cigarette in the corner of her mouth, eyes half closed because of the smoke and the window wide open. She would come to Wenderton and take Gladys and me for a drive round the villages and through the marsh, shouting "Bumpety bump, Yaya" every time we went over one of the little hump-backed bridges.

At school we were doing a play, "Father Christmas Comes to Supper", and I was to play Father Christmas. I had to climb up steps at the back of the stage and come in through the window with my sack and distribute the presents. Dressed in a red robe with a big hook-on beard, I was in my element and the day of the performance, when everyone clapped, was wonderful. Not that anyone would have dreamt of my becoming an actor; my future was already mapped out. I was to be a farmer and auctioneer following my father into the business; the cards were dealt. Nevertheless, things had been happening at home, which were to change the hand.

I suppose the first inkling I got that something was wrong, was when I was told I must not go on to the farm and asking why, was told that grandfather would not like it.

Then, one day when I was dressed as Nelson, with a patch over one eye and an arm inside my father's old tunic, I came into the breakfast room and found my parents talking seriously together.

"We should ask him", said my father, turning to me. "We are

trying to decide if I should start my own auctioneering practice, or take a farm"

"Be a farmer," I said without hesitation.

It was sound advice, and had he taken it, our lives might have been very different. In fact what had happened, as I was to learn later, was that there had been a falling out between my parents and the rest of the family. My father had joined my grandfather in 1908 and, apart from the war, they had been together ever since and built the business up together. Throughout the twenties he had never taken a holiday and when times were bad, as they often were, left part of his salary in the business. It had long been agreed that my grandfather was to make him a partner. A deed had been drawn up and was waiting at the solicitors to be signed. It continued to wait.

The problem was that relations between my father and Uncle John had become strained. My father had joined the firm the year John was born, he had watched him grow up, bought him his first air-gun, taught him to shoot and generally been a sort of unofficial uncle. But one grows out of uncles and John, in his early twenties, anxious to experiment, headstrong and ambitious, saw my father now in his forties, with his war experience and a cautious approach to life, as an obstacle. Moreover John was conscious of being his father's son and found it intolerable to have his ideas questioned and to be treated as a mere boy by someone who was only a son-in-law. In short they had become incompatible. All the members of the family took sides, and the atmosphere became poisonous and could not continue. A final family conference in the dining room at Guilton, resulted in my father agreeing to leave but demanding to be repaid the money he had left in the firm over the years, a sum not easy to find in the mid-thirties when farming was in great difficulty. After this, my parents left shaking the metaphorical dust from their shoes.

The first thing my father did was to take an office in Wingham and set up his practice, selling in the Canterbury and Sandwich markets in direct opposition to grandfather and uncle John. This put the clients in the difficult position of having to choose between people they knew and liked. Many of them solved the problem by going to other firms, so that both sides lost.

It was at this time that tomatoes came into our lives. Farming being in difficulty, my parents were tempted by the idea, becoming popular at the time, of growing tomatoes under glass. They rented part of Betteshanger Park, the seat of Lord Northbourne, where they constructed glasshouses and, as their knowledge of the subject was limited, engaged a manager to run it, while my mother, determined to play a part, rushed about being busy in a small van with "Betteshanger Nurseries" painted on the side.

Suddenly Kent was in the grip of a Foot-and-Mouth epidemic. After staying a weekend with Yaya and OK at Headcorn, we drove home through a countryside lit by fires on which the cattle were being burnt. All the markets were closed and remained closed, eliminating at a stroke the main source of my father's income.

Happily there were still the tomatoes, but curiously, although the crop looked promising, the harvest was meagre and, as the glasshouses were not paid for, the situation began to be worrying. Economies were needed and Edith Weller, our cook, had to go. The morning she left, I went to say goodbye and found her in the dining room, in front of the sideboard polishing the silver. She was crying and bent down to kiss me; I can still remember the feel of her wet cheeks against mine.

The markets remained closed and the tomatoes continued to give disappointing results. Much later it was learned that the manager had cheated. When the lorry came to the front door of the glasshouses to collect the boxes for Covent Garden, the manager's lorry came to the door at the other end and took a lion's share of the crop.

The relations with the family at Guilton had by no means been improved by my father's setting up in opposition in the markets. Wenderton House was part of the farm and my parents rented it from grandfather, who now began the process of ejecting them. Uncle John took matters in hand and turned off the water. My grandmother objected that there was a child in the house, so the water was turned back on. But the incident decided my parents that it was time to move.

I can remember visiting several empty houses in the district at that time.

"How would you like to live here?"

"I shouldn't. We can't leave Wenderton –it's our home."

"We may have to."

"Why?"

"Grandfather says so."

One of my favourite books at that time was "Little Lord Fauntleroy" with whose hero, Cedric, I closely identified, both of us having cruel and unfeeling grandfathers. He, however, had managed to charm his grandfather but I could not see much hope of charming mine, as I watched him drive past, sitting in the back of his car, not so much as looking in my direction. As for the reconciliation with 'Dearest', Little Lord Fauntleroy's gentle mother, that looked even more improbable given the hunting-field expletives that my mother emitted whenever her father's name was mentioned.

The bank foreclosed and Betteshanger Nurseries ceased to exist, leaving my father with debts that weighed him down for the rest of his life and a great many boxes of printed stationery that had been ordered in a fit of optimism and that were to remain with us as a reproach for many years to come.

CHAPTER TWO

—

This, our family drama, was being played out against the backdrop of a far greater European drama. My father had long been convinced that another war was inevitable and some time at the end of 1937 he applied to join the Air Ministry as a Lands Officer. His having been a pilot in the war and being a qualified Valuer and Land agent fitted him for the job, and he was accepted. My mother stoutly refused any suggestion that she should move to London, the idea of living in a town being quite out of the question, so began a daily ritual of my mother driving him at dawn to Adisham station where he caught the train for Charing Cross, returning late in the evening. Occasionally my mother went with him and they stayed the night in London, leaving Gladys and me together. Since Edith had left, Gladys no longer slept up in the maid's room as they both had, but with me in the twin beds in the spare room. She was a very pretty girl and when she came to bed, I would pretend to be asleep and watch her undress and sit at the dressing table looking at her self in the mirror. I can still remember the mole on her back. It was my first erotic experience.

On the 29th September, Mr Chamberlain went to Munich to meet Adolf Hitler and came back waving a piece of paper. We listened to his assurance that there would be peace in our time on the Pye portable radio in the lounge, but my father shook his head, convinced otherwise. Winston Churchill, he said, was the only one who had the right idea. A friend of his, with whom he had been involved in several projects over the years, was Osborne Dann, a wealthy businessman who lived at Wateringbury Place where we used to go to tea and admire his black swans on the lake. Several years earlier, Mr Dann had had Mr Churchill to dinner to discuss the possibility of forming a new political party. It was at a time when Mr Churchill was neither popular with his fellow MPs nor with the country, but Mr Dann had been very impressed and, when he saw my father the next morning, said he was convinced Mr Churchill would one day be Prime minister.

At school we were fitted with gas masks. These were made of black rubber that smelled unpleasant. They were housed in square cardboard boxes, which were carried by means of a string, over the shoulder. Decorative covers for them soon appeared on the market and they became a sort of fashion accessory. We were supposed to keep them with us at all times.

One result of the family quarrel was that we saw more of my grandmother's brother, George Goodson and his wife Aunty Hilda, who lived at Frognal farm Wickhambreaux. My grandmother was on bad terms with all her brothers and sisters since she had brought a high court action against them over the inheritance of some family furniture. She had lost the case and been told by the judge that the she was a jealous and grasping woman for her pains.

Great-uncle George Goodson was my favourite uncle. When he came to dinner, he would come and sit on my bed and tell me stories about the family. Of the time when his great-aunt, Sarah Ann Minter, and her brother, William Wraith Wood Minter, lived at Wenderton, their initials were carved into the brickwork above the front porch, while their brother, John Minter, a huntsman who had been a local celebrity, lived in a caravan in the Wenderton woods with a pack of beagles. John had played cricket for the Gentlemen of Kent in 1843 with some success (he made twenty three runs).

His hunting clothes had all been preserved and great uncle George gave his hunting cap to my Mother. I still have it, a high domed black cap, typical of the 1840s. Their sister, Kezia Minter, had married William Goodson and they lived at the neighbouring farm of Deerson. They had a daughter, Anne, who was the centre of attention of both her mother and her aunt. When Anne died suddenly on the 15th September 1847 aged ten, Kezia and Sarah Anne were devastated. Kezia turned to religion and for the rest of her live, dressed in black, she haunted churches and graveyards. She and William Goodson had no more children until 1854 when my great-grandfather, Edward

Stephen Goodson was born, followed in 1860 by the birth of his brother, George Minter Goodson.

At the death of his uncle, Stephen Goodson in 1874, my great grandfather inherited the family home at Upton.

There was a strain of eccentricity in the Minter family, which great-uncle George had inherited. He disliked change to such a point that everything around him, including his clothes had to be old.

"I've had this suit thirty years! Wouldn't wear anything I hadn't had for thirty years". He said to me reproachfully when I went to see him in the early sixties and was rather too fashionably dressed for his taste.

Once he engaged a farm hand, the man was sure to have a job for life. Every morning he would get on his horse and ride round the farm.

"Morning, Godden."

"Morning sir"

"You know what to do?"

"Yes, sir"

"Right, carry on!"

Then he would return to the house, have a cup of coffee and read "The Field". The farm, like Wenderton, had long been connected with the Minter family and had been given to him by his father as a twenty-first birthday present. It was planted with fruit, chiefly Cox's Orange Pippin, and was always immaculate with everything freshly painted white. It lay back from the road and was approached by a long drive that he had divided into two parallel drives; one marked "Trade" and the other "Private". My mother, who was something of a favourite with him, loved teasing him and would intentionally drive down the wrong drive to be told off, "You're not Trade, you're Private, You'd better go back and come in again"

Entering the house, which was Queen Anne, one was greeted by the smell of wood-smoke and beeswax. On the walls were the family portraits in oils. These were not portraits of people but of their horses.

The Minter's father, William Minter of New Place Ickham, had bred racehorses at the time of the Regency. I have a print of a painting of one of his horses with the inscription:

"WALTER GAY by Pincher. Dam, Maid of the Valley. Bred by Mr Minter of Ickham. Trained by Richard Sherrard of Bridge.

"Performed twenty miles and jumped twenty one hurdles within the hour having one minute and three quarters to spare for 100 guineas.

"Ridden by the owner, Toke James Simmonds Esq. of Canterbury at Romney, Kent, 30th January 1840."

William Minter's grave is at the entrance to Ickham church and bears the inscription: "In life respected, in death lamented." An unbeatable epitaph, I have always thought.

In front of Frognal House was a lawn laid out for clock golf, for although great uncle George had a withered leg as the result of polio as a child, it didn't stop him hunting or playing golf. There was, however, one touch of modernity at Frognal as I was to discover one day when he and I were in the garden. Pointing to the wall, which ran round the front lawn, he indicated an old oak door with a squint cut in the wall beside it. "Know what's behind there?"

I shook my head. "Have a look" I opened the door to reveal a sparkling, modern and perfectly equipped lavatory. "My refuge," he chuckled "had it built especially so I can escape the vicar when he calls and watch him go".

Aunty Hilda was a placid, rather beautiful woman who took his eccentricities and wild statements in her stride, saying gently, "Don't be a fool, G" They had two daughters, Betty and Nina; Betty was married and lived in Lincolnshire. It was on a visit to her that great uncle George discovered Woolworth's. At that time the American chain store had recently opened in England and everything for sale was sixpence. He was enchanted and seeing a tray of spectacles, tried a pair, decided he saw better with them, paid sixpence and wore them for the rest of his life.

Nina, who had not long left school, lived at home and would ride

over to see us on her fat little brown and white pony. I have a photo
of myself sitting on it.

1938 turned into 1939. The bully having left, I was beginning
to enjoy school. A French teacher arrived who had just returned
from France. She explained to us that in France they spoke another
language and they didn't call bread "bread" like we did, but *"pain"*.
I was fascinated and decided there and then that I must learn this
language, though at first, at least, it seems I found it difficult. My
end of term report for the Easter term 1939 gave me a "C" and noted
"Fair, finds great difficulty though he is anxious to learn", whereas
for "Picture study and architecture" I got an "A" "A careful observer,
he describes well", while "Painting and Drawing" a "B" "Does
original work and is very keen" I also got "A s" for Bible lessons"
for "Recitation," "Memory work fairly good, try to keep the voice
more even" and for "Reading" "A fluent good reader", but a "C" for
Arithmetic, "E" for writing and "D" for needlework, "rather slow"
and finally, "a well-mannered gentlemanly little boy"

Soon afterwards, it was decided that for Parents Day we were to
do a play, a real play, "Midsummer Night's Dream", and I was cast
as Bottom the Weaver. I was terribly excited, but my excitement was
short lived as there was an epidemic of chickenpox and the school
was closed after the first reading.

Meanwhile at Wenderton, Attaway the gardener and Tutt the
back-door-boy had gone and the garden was beginning to look sad.
Weeds flourished on the gravel drive and in the flowerbeds, while the
yew hedges remained unclipped and an air of neglect began to hang
over the place. Then the unthinkable happened: I went out one day
and when I came home, Gladys was not there.

"Where's Gladys?"

"She's left."

"But she can't have. Where is she, I must see her."

"You can't."

My world fell apart. Gladys was the person I loved the most, she
was my best friend, my rock: a cushion between my parents and me.
We had been inseparable for as long as I could remember, I relied on

her practical good sense for everything and suddenly she had left without even saying goodbye: a feeling of abandonement and betrayal was followed by a rush of guilt; it must be my fault, something I had done, but what?

I decided to investigate and, without telling my mother, I cycled down to Wingham and went to the Peppers' house and rang the bell. Gladys's mother came to the door. She looked at me oddly.

"What do you want?"

"Please may I see Gladys?"

"No, you can't, she's not here," and she closed the door.

I returned home and for days mooned about the house feeling a terrible sense of loss. What was – what could be – the explanation? "You'll understand when you're older" was all my mother would say when pressed.

It was several years before I learned the truth; a family friend, who had recently qualified as a gynaecologist, had come to tea with my mother. As Gladys brought in the tea he looked at her intently and when she had gone he asked my mother if she knew that Gladys was pregnant. He seemed so certain, that when he had gone my mother taxed Gladys with it at which she broke down.

Gladys at that time must have been about twenty-eight or nine. It had long been understood that she would marry Young Bill Sheaff, but recently he had surprised everyone by suddenly marrying an unknown woman "from London" who was older than he. In her disappointment, Gladys, on her day off, went to Dreamland, the funfair at Margate, where she met a sergeant who talked of marriage but who, as she discovered too late, was already married.

My mother asked her what she wanted to do and encouraged her to stay, but she insisted she leave immediately.

A new maid arrived, Frances, but it wasn't the same. Nothing was the same; they had all gone, Edith, Attaway, Tutt and now Gladys. The world was falling apart.

Working at the Air Ministry, my father had begun to meet some of his former colleagues from the Royal Flying Corps, some of whom, having stayed in the service, had reached dizzy heights of promotion.

Britain had been caught totally unprepared for a war; there were not enough aeroplanes, not enough pilots, nor even enough aerodromes. Something had to be done and done quickly, so the Aerodrome Board was formed to requisition the necessary sites. One of my father's former colleagues, now an Air Marshal, proposed him as a member and he was appointed. Asked what rank he wanted, he replied, that he would prefer a bowler hat rather than risk having to deal with someone of superior rank. His request was granted and so began an extraordinary episode in his life. Alone, or driven by my mother, and furnished with draconian powers, he toured the British Isles looking for suitable sites for aerodromes and bombing ranges and incidentally causing panic among the landed classes.

"What? You mean the fellow wants to put a runway through the park?"

If he did, no one could gainsay him. Later, when Mr Churchill became Prime minister, the authority of the Aerodrome Board was reinforced. It was then that invitations to shoot over some of the best shoots in the country and dine in ducal mansions were showered on my father. After the disasters of recent years, it must have been an agreeable respite. Two of my father's letters to my mother from that time have survived. They give an insight into the frenetic atmosphere of those late summer days just before the declaration of war. The first is from the Station Hotel Chesterfield and postmarked 24th August 1939;

> "Darling, I have just arrived here – last minute rush to do an urgent job – left the office at 5.30 to catch the 6.0/c train at St. Pancras, no idea where I was going to stay until I arrived here – it's a nice clean hotel – I have really no idea where I am or what Chesterfield is like, shall know more tomorrow – Have got to look at a property here and then I go to Buxton to look at another site – I will get back as soon as I can and get in touch when I'm back in London.
>
> The news looks pretty serious – am wondering what Lord Halifax said over the wireless tonight.
>
> Everyone is being recalled at the Ministry and they fear the

worst. I don't think anything will happen until after Hitler's speech on Sunday...."

The second, from The Strand Palace Hotel, where he always stayed when in London, as it was convenient for his office at Bush House, is postmarked 30th August 1939:

"Darling, I have just had dinner – got back from Leighton Buzzard at 7.30 Euston – went to the office left my papers and rang up here for a room – Hope you got my wire alright – I couldn't ring up as I was so rushed... It has been frightfully hot and sticky all day feels very stormy ... Had the loan of a Rolls today with chauffeur complete never felt so rich in my life – should love you to have seen me – It belonged to a Jew – had to kick him out of a house I felt very sorry for them – they were very decent about it ... Of course you have heard the news – I have just read Chamberlain's speech – nothing in it and the position is about the same – I have a feeling Hitler won't strike – at the same time I cannot imagine what else he can do except commit suicide ..."

Towards the end of August, my cousin Bibby came to stay. She was the daughter of my father's brother, Uncle Arthur. Bibby was seventeen and had just left the convent where she had been educated by an order of French nuns. She was waiting to go to the Royal College of Music. We all liked her, though my mother disapproved of the fact that she spent so much time reading, "That girl has always got her nose in a book".

War was looking more and more inevitable; women and children were being evacuated from London – then, on the 1st September, Germany invaded Poland. The next day the call-up began and the day after it was war.

It was a Sunday, my mother and father had gone to London leaving Bibby and me in the charge of Frances. At eleven o'clock we went into the lounge to hear Mr Chamberlain who was due to speak to the Nation.

The wireless with its moving-iron loud speaker, although

technically portable, for it contained a large glass battery that my mother used to take to the garage in Wingham to be charged each week, was large and heavy. It had a highly polished rectangular wooden case with a sunburst fretted on the side and the control panel let into the front. This brown metal panel, with its two knobs resembling eyes and its semi-circular aperture for tuning like a down-turned mouth had a lugubrious expression perfectly suited to the gloomy voice of Mr Chamberlain as he announced that all his hopes were shattered and we were at war with Germany. When he had finished, Frances turned off the wireless and went to get lunch. Bibby and I decided to go for a walk. We went out of the gate along the lane past the farm. As we were passing the row of cottages, a sound filled the air, an unearthly wail that rose and fell and turned your stomach over. We looked at each other in a panic; it was the air raid warning. A man came out of the cottages with a terrified look on his face, "Get back, Get back" he shouted to us looking up at the sky as though he expected bombs to fall at any second, then he disappeared shutting the door violently. We turned tail and fled back to the house.

It was a false alarm and one that echoed round Britain causing panic. My parents were just arriving at Charing Cross as the siren sounded. As they were walking up the platform, the guard followed the crowd of passengers and, as was the custom, slammed the carriage doors shut as he passed. My mother, convinced it was a stick of bombs falling behind her, had to be restrained from lying flat on the platform.

That evening, when they got home, I went out to meet them and announced dramatically that all my hopes were shattered.

CHAPTER THREE

—

"Mr Langton one day asked him how he had
acquired so accurate a knowledge of Latin, in
which, I believe he was exceeded by no man
of his time; he said "My master whipt me very
well. Without that, Sir, I should have done
nothing".

James Boswell's *"Life of Johnson"*

I was to go to boarding school and the search was on for a suitable establishment. My parents took me with them to visit several prep schools and then one day we went to a school on a hill overlooking Canterbury. Unlike the prep schools, which were ordinary red brick houses, it was a gothic, stone building and seemed to me terribly old and romantic. I was not able at that time to distinguish between mediaeval gothic and nineteenth-century gothic; St Edmunds was barely ninety years old. We were welcomed by Mr Powers the headmaster of the Junior School, who played golf with great-uncle George who had himself organised our visit. Mr Powers took us along echoing stone-flagged corridors to the headmaster's house to meet the Reverend Henry Balmforth, a clergyman dressed in a black cassock. He took us to meet his wife, a lady who was bedridden, in a large gothic room with long windows looking onto the terrace and across the city of Canterbury. A prominent feature of the room was an altar, which seemed to me even more romantic and, as we drove out of the gates, I announced that this was the school I wanted to go to.

Summer turned into autumn and winter. It was the phoney war. We spent Christmas with Yaya and OK at Headcorn and Father Christmas brought me an airgun. My father left immediately afterwards for Scotland, where he was to spend several weeks, and Mother and I returned to Wenderton. Frances had gone to her parents for Christmas and not yet returned. It began to snow; it continued to snow; it went on snowing and soon we were snowed-in. Wenderton is in a valley and the snow was soon seven feet deep. Days passed; weeks passed; the snow remained. Finally Uncle John came with six men who dug us out. I described the situation in a letter to my Father:

"Please excuse bad spelling

24th January 1940

My dear old Daddy,

No water, no paraffin, no coke that is the state Mummy and I were in so we decided to go to Guilton and here we are I enjoy every minite of the day. Only wish you were here. Uncle John and I play cards every night I go out with Clayson the carpenter from dawn to dusk and learn a lot about carpentering pluming and being a blacksmith I do hope you are keeping warm in some places there is seven feet of snow Clayson made me a very nice toboggan and I gave him a pacit of sigerets and he saved all the ends and put them in his pipe and smoked them again because he had not got any tobacco. Well I must say good bye now because here comes mummy to lay the tea. Oh by the way thank you very much for the letter and sigeret cards.

With love and wishes

From Teddy"

I can remember writing this letter and my anxiety to reassure my father, as I knew that he would be less than pleased at our being rescued by Uncle John. While in Scotland, my Father became ill with the 'flu which delayed his return. A second letter shows that we remained at Guilton for some time.

"Feb 6 1940

My dear Daddy,

I do hope you are all right I am glad you are better when you come home I shall be very happy yesterday we started school and Miss Elgar was in a good temper wich pleased me no end please write to me soon I do love your letters. Mummie has gone over to Wenderton with Fraces and Granny and Esme are ironing and im writing to you from the breakfast room and at school today we had French History wich is very intresting well

I suppose I shall have to close down so good by old fellow see
you soon I hope
    Love from, Teddy"

Esme was one of my grandmother's maids who proved more
resistant that most; she left several times but always came back.

It is from this period that my memories of Guilton date. The
house, a double-fronted Queen Anne house built by an army major
returning from Marlborough's wars, faced on to the road at the
entrance to the village of Ash. Along the side of the house stretched
a high garden wall and beyond was the main entrance which led in,
round the side of garden, to the stable yard, the farm, out-houses and
backdoor. It was a hive of activity.

My grandfather did not come from a farming family; the Marchants
were drapers and had been for generations. Around 1850, his father,
Joseph Marchant, founded Marchant and Tubb, a wholesale business
making and selling workingmen's clothes with a shop in Maidstone.
Arthur was his thirteenth and youngest child and was educated at
Dulwich College. When Joseph Marchant died, his widow, with the
other children off her hands, moved to Weddington a small country
house at Ash where Arthur was articled to a firm of auctioneers.

He qualified in 1900 and in 1903, soon after his marriage, he took
a lease on Guilton farm, which belonged to St John's College Oxford,
and set up as an auctioneer and farmer. He was a likeable, sociable
man, shrewd and hard working. His business prospered.

Farming in Britain had been in difficulty since the 1860s, when
cheap food began to be imported from the United States whose slave
economy could easily outmatch British farmers with wages to pay.

Britain had seen the rise of industry and a massive exodus from
the country to the towns. These new town-dwellers did not care
where the food came from so long as it was cheap, and it was up to
British farmers to compete with the Americans or go under.

My grandfather's five farms amounted to about a thousand acres.
They lay several miles apart and were autonomous, each being run
by a bailiff and separate work force of fifteen to twenty men. Guilton
was the home farm with its own carpenter, blacksmith and mechanic

– even its own petrol pump. For those days, the business was modern and efficient.

The office stood in the middle of my grandmother's garden, a big garden that was essentially mineral, consisting of stone paths and rockeries without a blade of grass. I was to learn that there had been lawns but that my grandfather had once remarked on the noise of the mower, whereupon my grandmother had taken offence and ordered their destruction. The garden was one of many battlefields my grandparents had fought over since their marriage in 1903.

The backdoor led into "the barn" a long flag stoned room which had once been a barn, but which now served as a cloakroom and outer kitchen. At the end, steep steps led up to a massive door with large bolts behind which lay the kitchen. Two doors led from the kitchen, one into the breakfast room, a small room overlooking the cattle yard, from where my grandfather could watch his cattle, a sight he insisted was far more beautiful than a flower garden.

The other door from the kitchen led out past the dining-room, along the hall to the front door, on the left of which was my grandmother's drawing-room, painted white with a pale blue carpet, blue and white chintz curtains and chair covers, blue and white china ornaments and her baby grand piano. On the other side of the hall was the lounge, a dark room with heavy brown velvet curtains, massive worn leather settee and deep leather armchairs, horse brasses, hunting prints, and a strong smell of pipe, cigar smoke and snuff of which my grandfather was inordinately fond, pinching it from an elegant silver snuff-box and sneezing loudly in a vast and colourful silk handkerchief. A door from the lounge led out into a sunroom known as the veranda, where there was another vast leather armchair where he sat in the summer.

The bedrooms above had powder-closets reminding one that the original owners had worn powdered wigs.

The house was over-cleaned and over-polished. In contrast to her husband, my grandmother was slim, and fiercely self-disciplined. What she expected of herself, she expected of others and whereas the family tradition was that people who worked for you were part of the family and should be treated as such, my grandmother did not see it like that, with the result that visitors to Guilton rarely saw the same maid twice.

Grandmother was the eldest daughter of Edward Goodson of Upton St Peters at Broadstairs on the Isle of Thanet. While Arthur was a newcomer to the district, the Goodsons were an old East Kent farming family who had farmed Upton without interruption since the 1590s. Broadstairs was a quiet fishing village, but when Charles Dickens bought a house there, it soon became a smart little seaside resort, several notches socially above neighbouring Ramsgate. The village of Upton St Peters was owned by Edward Goodson and by the sale of cottages and land for building, he amassed a comfortable fortune.

At 18, Joan was attractive, smartly dressed, with a slim tall figure and, as 'Miss Goodson', the eldest of the five children, she was used to having her own way. She had been educated at Bartram Gables, a school for young ladies kept by Miss Bartram, where she had learned to play the piano and the organ competently and to have a high opinion of herself. She and Arthur had met at a private dance and she had thought him handsome. He was always well dressed and Dulwich College had given him an easy social manner. Although already corpulent, he danced extremely well. The attraction must have been reciprocated, because he invited her to tea at his lodgings. When she arrived with her chaperone, she was shown into a waiting-room and, it not being as clean as she felt it should be, as she told me herself, she wrote 'SLUT' in the dust on the table.

Soon after the marriage, her younger sister, Maggie, then aged twelve, went to spend a week with the young couple. The first evening after returning home, her father, who was a churchwarden at St Peter's, was out at a Parish Council meeting.

Maggie began to fidget and kept asking her mother when he would return until finally Harriet asked what the matter was. "Well" she blurted out "Will he be all right?" After a week of her new brother-in-law's drunken homecomings, she could be certain of nothing.

Auctioneering in those days entailed long hours standing in the open in all weathers selling, followed by long drives home on cold nights in a horse and trap. A warming glass of something was almost a necessity, and usually more than one. Then there was the public relations side of the business, which meant a good deal of drinking in pubs with the clients. At twenty-nine, Arthur was an alcoholic.

I never felt comfortable at Guilton. My grandmother was kind to me and seemed to like me, but I never felt at ease with my grandfather. Almost colliding with him at the backdoor one day while we were staying there, he looked down at me and said, "I hear you are to become a public school man" Not understanding; I stammered uncomfortably, "Am I, Grandfather?" At which he laughed and walked on. Then there was Mr Hincks, the man who had replaced my father. I did not like Mr Hincks; he had an ingratiating manner, a way of saying "Yes, Mr Marchant and No, Mr Marchant" that reminded me of Uriah Heep. I was pretty certain that my dislike was reciprocated; for while he treated me with smiling solicitude when others were present, when we were alone he behaved as though I was not there. Altogether, although I was the only grandchild, I felt out of place and unwanted. This feeling led to the need to try to make people like me, a habit that has lasted all my life.

Preparations for boarding school were in full swing and included an all-important visit to London to Daniel Neal's, the school outfitters, to buy the uniform. This meant a train journey, my first experience of public transport. I found it thrilling, and felt very grown-up sitting surrounded by strangers, the heaving and puffing of the engine, clanking of the carriages, porters shouting out the names of the stations; it all seemed new and exciting.

In fact steam engines were dirty and the carriages not only smelled of soot, but a fine film of it covered the doors and window ledges. If you put your head out of the window there was a risk of getting smuts in your eyes and at the end of even a short journey your collar would be black. These facts tend to be forgotten in the romantic haze which envelopes the memory of steam travel today.

At Daniel Neal's my mother took one look at the dark grey suits, which were the official uniform and pronounced them badly made and too expensive. She took a sample of the cloth and decided our family tailor could produce the same thing better and cheaper.

In the afternoon we went to a matinee of "Iolanthe" by the D'Oyly Carte Company at the King's Hammersmith. It was magic and the Lord Chancellor's Nightmare Song was a favourite that I eventually learned by heart.

I left Miss Elgar's with a final Report giving me an "A" in Literature, "It is surprising how much he understands" and an "A" in Painting and Drawing, still doing "Original work", but a "D" in French "Too inattentive to learn much but can do quite well when he wants to" and a final remark that "He is an intelligent worker and has got on well. He should do well in his new school"

At the beginning of May, just before my ninth birthday, the time had come to go to St Edmund's. We had received an impressive list of clothes needed, six of this, twelve of that, all of which my mother had got together and packed in her own old school trunk and my new overnight case, a present from my grandmother, with my initials, B.E.G.A. stamped on it; initials, which were to cause amusement to my school fellows and lead me, at certain low points in my life, to wonder at the prescience of my godparents.

As my father was away harassing landowners and throwing people out of their houses, Uncle John took us. He had himself been to Brighton College and gave me a list of dos and don'ts, which I tried to memorise. Mr Powers welcomed us, told them I would be all right, my mother kissed me, Uncle John shook hands and they left.

Suddenly I was overwhelmed by the enormity of the situation, the realisation that I was surrounded by total strangers; I felt the need to be alone and remembering a lavatory Powers had shown us on the staircase leading to the dormitory, I hurried to it and locked myself in. Through the gothic slit window I had a view of the playground, an asphalt yard surrounded by a wooden fence. It was a mass of boys who all seemed to be shouting and hitting each other.

I had recently read "ViceVersa", Anstey's novel about Paul Bultitude, a boy who does not want to go back to school. He finds a magic wishing-stone in the garden. His father takes it from him and, with it in his hand, says he wishes he could go to school in Paul's place and is instantly transformed into a schoolboy. He gives the stone to Paul telling him sharply to wish the spell undone, but Paul wishes to be his father, and is transformed into a pompous middle-aged city gent, so poor Mr Bultitude is sent to school where he finds himself at the mercy of a lot of little ruffians who take him for one of themselves. At that moment I identified completely with Mr Bultitude.

Realising I couldn't stay in the lavatory indefinitely, I went down to the classroom Mr Powers had shown me as being mine. As I walked along the corridor, a big man loomed up in front of me. "Who are you?" he asked. "Teddy Apps" I replied.

"No you're not, you're Apps here". Someone giggled and I remembered that I had been warned never, never to reveal my Christian name. The ideal to strive for, Uncle John had insisted, was to be known by ones initials, so I was B.E.G. Apps, and when I eventually left school years later no one should be any the wiser as to what those initials stood for.

"I'm Mr Brand" he said, not unkindly, and moved on.

Feeling shaken at having made a blunder so early on, I found the classroom and went to the locker I had been allotted. There was tall, thin boy with glasses in front of it. "That's my locker", I said. "No it isn't".

I looked at him and something about him, his glasses, his supercilious manner, irritated me and, with the pent up emotion of recent events, I hit him. He hit me back and we had a fight. People separated, us, we calmed down and so began a friendship that has lasted all our lives.

His name, I discovered, was B.G. Rhodes. He was a new boy, like me, and he came from Yorkshire. He was a foundationer.

St Edmund's School, with its armorial shield bearing three Suns, and its motto, "Ecclesiae Filii", had been founded in the eighteenth century by the Clergy Orphan Corporation to educate the fatherless sons of Church of England clergy, so the Board of Governors read like a page from Crockford's and was well laden with archdeacons and bishops, while the President was the Archbishop of Canterbury in person. The school was run as a public school and when I went to the Junior School I was one of a handful of boys who were known as "non-foundationers" which meant that our fathers were neither necessarily dead nor parsons and that they paid school fees. Most of the boys, however, were fatherless and were on the receiving end of a charity. The typical case history was that of an underpaid and over-worked parson or curate with a young family, housed in a rambling, draughty parsonage resistant to any form of heating he could afford, who had succumbed to pneumonia or a similar disease leaving his widow destitute. On the day of the funeral, the Bishop had politely pointed out that he needed the parsonage as soon as possible, so the widow had returned to her parents or gone into lodgings and the children had been taken away from their schools and the boys shipped off to Canterbury and the Girls to the sister school, St Margaret's Bushey. All this meant that they were more or less traumatised and probably explains a level of nervous tension that always seemed to characterise the place.

Apart from Rhodes, there were two other new boys, B.L. Comyns, who came from Devon and W.E. Harries from Wales, otherwise known as Little Harries as his brother, already at the school, was Big Harries. Both were foundationers. Naturally, religious observance was a priority and much time was spent in the school chapel, which was considered to be the centre of school life.

This presented me with a difficulty because, apart from my baptism, of which I remembered nothing, I had hardly ever been to church and was unfamiliar with its rites and ceremonies.

No one at Guilton went to church except for weddings and funerals and my grandfather even avoided the latter when possible, on the grounds that he could not do any good. However, my father, who came from a staunchly Church of England family and had, like all his brothers, sung in the choir, insisted when they married that he and my mother say their prayers each night, kneeling at the bedside. I, too, had been taught to do so; it went with cleaning your teeth. But going to church was another matter. On the first Sunday after their marriage, he had taken my mother to Wingham church, but she said she felt everyone was looking at her and decided not to go again, a decision she stuck to. In this she would seem to have followed a family tradition, for the Marchant family seems always to have been resistant to religion. When Luke Marchant, son of Richard, was baptised at Mayfield on the 14th May 1629, the vicar found it necessary to add a note:

> "Luke Marchant, son of Richard being about one year old was baptised with the consent of John Elliott of Rotherfield who was grandfather unto the said infant by the mother's side, the parents both obstinately refusing".

At Miss Elgar's, we had said prayers every morning round the piano and sung a hymn. A favourite was "All things bright and beautiful" whose second verse;
"The rich man in his castle,
The poor man at his gate,
He made them high and lowly
And ordered their estate".
Generally omitted today, was never questioned by us. Social mobility was a thing of the future. In those days it was still considered normal to know your place and keep it.

Chapel at St Edmund's was a very different affair. Every morning after breakfast, we had to line up in the corridor and walk in file, youngest leading, along to the chapel. We, the four new boys, went to the front pew and each of us bowed to the altar before taking our places. Behind us came the bigger boys, then the Senior School who seemed to us giants, and when everyone was in place, the organ blasted forth and the choir in cassocks and surplices, some, who were masters, wearing their academic hoods, red for Oxford, white for Cambridge, two abreast, mounted the choir steps, bowed and peeled off left and right to fill the choir. Behind them came the headmaster in full canonicals.

As anyone unfamiliar with religious practice soon learns, the trick is to sit at the back and watch what the rest of the congregation does. Sitting in the front pew, this help was denied me. What is more, I was exposed not only to the gaze of those behind, but also to that of the choir in front. Luckily, my companions, being foundationers, knew exactly what to do and I was able to follow them out of the corner of my eye in their arcane antics of standing up, sitting down, kneeling and intoning responses, and thus to pass unnoticed.

On Fridays we had the Litany. This meant that instead of going into the choir, Mr Balmforth knelt at a prayer desk placed between the two front pews and began intoning:

"From all evil and mischief; from sin, from the crafts and assaults of the devil; from Thy wrath, and from everlasting damnation –"

And we intoned, "Good Lord deliver us"

"From all blindness of heart; from pride, vain-glory, and hypocrisy; from malice and all uncharitableness –"

"Good Lord, deliver us"

"From fornication, and all other deadly sins, and from all deceits of the world, the flesh and the devil –"

"Good Lord, deliver us".

"From lightning and tempest; from plague, pestilence and famine; from battle, murder and sudden death –"

Good Lord, deliver us".

We intoned, and so on through sedition, privy conspiracy, rebellion, not to mention heresy and schism, on and on, through pleas to keep the king on the right track, illuminate bishops, priests and deacons, endue all the nobility with grace, wisdom and understanding (a tough number that, one would have thought, even for the Almighty). The Litany droned on for what seemed like hours until eventually, with stiff knees, we staggered out of the chapel.

I was beginning to congratulate myself on how well I was managing to remain unnoticed, when two disasters struck. The first was that people started to realise that my suit was not like everyone else's. Although our tailor had found a cloth closely resembling that of Daniel Neal's, it was of noticeably better quality and the suit having been made for me, actually fitted. This caused me great embarrassment for if there is one thing that small boys dislike, it is to be in any way different from the others.

However this paled as a disaster beside the second, which occurred in the first week. It was Mr Balmforth's practice personally to take the juniors for Divinity in order to show the importance placed on this discipline. We were warned in advance what an honour it was to be taught by the headmaster in person and everyone was agog with anticipation. We stood up as he swept into the room in cassock and gown and, settling himself at the tall master's desk, invited us to sit and take out our bibles. There was the noise of desktops being lifted and the rustle of books followed by desks being closed. Mine, however remained open, as it did not contain a bible.

"Please, sir, I don't have a bible."

"What do you mean?"

"I don't have one."

"But you must have, boy, go and get it!"

"Please, sir, I don't. I think my mother must have forgotten to pack one";

There was an awful silence.

Mr Balmforth's face took on an expression resembling Dante's when he peered into the sixth circle of hell, and in a voice combining horror and pity, he asked rhetorically;

"Is it possible that there is a boy whose mother sends him to school without a bible?"

I thought of my mother with her dislike of books and felt in all probability there was. Everyone looked at me and I wished the ground would swallow me up and felt the sensation only too familiar from Guilton; the feeling that I did not belong.

Apart from Divinity, the most important subject was Latin. We were given worn copies of two books familiar to schoolboys over many generations. Kennedy's Latin Primer, with its light brown cover on which the title was invariably amended by two inked-in lateral strokes on the L and the addition of a final G, to read Kennedy's Eating Primer. This loathsome volume contained the nouns and their cases, the verbs and their tenses together with lists of irregular nouns and verbs, all of which had to be learned by heart. The other was a blue book of exercises containing phrases to be translated into Latin.

The hero of this work, a certain Labienus, was forever wounding the barbarians with arrows and performing similar feats, which required grammatical ingenuity.

In all the years I struggled with Latin, I do not remember anyone attempting to explain why we should learn it. It had been the essential requirement for entry to the professions or any sort of social advancement since the Middle Ages and, in the nineteen-forties, not only did its teaching date from that time but also the manner in which it was taught. Mr Balmforth had not long replaced Canon Burnside, a headmaster for whom the birch was an essential piece of teaching equipment. Carol Powers used the cane.

He would come into class holding it, put it firmly on the table and then, pointing to some quaking individual, demand that he recite whatever had been the subject of prep the previous evening.

Carol Powers also took us for English. Here, he did not bring a cane in with him because the classes were held in another classroom where the canes were already in place. He would announce a page of the text and one by one we would stand up and read a passage. Luckily for me, reading aloud was my strong point, so I was less troubled in these classes. It was the boys from Wales who suffered; one of them had barely spoken English until he arrived at Canterbury, and the others all had accents considered unacceptable. This situation gave Powers' latent sadism a field day. He would demand menacingly how the word was pronounced and if the stammered answer were wrong, he would summon the wretch with a movement of his forefinger, then open his desk and produce a series of canes with names like "chocolate biscuit" or "Lemon Sponge" and invite the victim to choose.

We dreaded Latin and English lessons, but music lessons were worse. For these we stood round the grand piano, sheets of incomprehensible music in hand, while Mr Pullen-Baker, the school organist and music master, played. Suddenly he would stop, get up and prowl round the circle menacingly, before stopping in front of someone and saying, "Tell me, boy, what was the last note I played?" If the answer were unsatisfactory, he would take the boy's ear, between his forefinger and thumb, and twist it, at the same time pushing the boy off balance and jerking him upright by his ear. R.E. Jones, a small fair-haired boy from Shrewsbury, had his ear torn so that it bled at the back. He showed it to us after the lesson and we all crowded round to look.

The lesson we enjoyed most was Geography taught by Mr Coates, a young master in his twenties whom we all liked. History was taught by a First World War shell-shock victim, the Reverend Captain Becher, who was unpredictable. With us his unpredictability was limited to entering the classroom by the window rather than the door, though whether this was the result of an eccentric sense of humour, or of having been deprived of windows in the dugouts of the Western front, no one could say.

Carol Powers' use of the cane was not limited to the classroom. The threat of it was a constant feature of our lives. He had been to school at Westminster and thence to Cambridge in the 1890s, had arrived at St Edmund's in 1903 and been in charge of the Junior School ever since. Golf was not the only passion he shared with great-uncle George; he too hated change and had managed to keep the junior school totally free from it, with the result that the place was in a time warp circa 1900.

The school uniform was an indication, for while most prep school boys in the late thirties were wearing light grey flannel shorts and blazers with grey flannel shirts with collars attached, we were in dark grey suits with long trousers and Eton collars.

For anyone unfamiliar with it, the Eton collar is a conical shaped instrument of torture attached to the shirt band back and front by two studs. The tie is then inserted and when the jacket is put on, the Eton collar and tie are hoisted up over it, so that the sharp edge meets the neck at an angle of between 30° and 40° depending on the rise of the shoulders, the discomfort being thus increased according to the shortness of the neck. Luckily for me, I have a long neck, but some boys suffered visibly.

We were issued with clean collars every Sunday and Wednesday morning. When they are clean, they are starched rigid, including the holes for the studs, so every Sunday and Wednesday morning, we sat on our beds chewing the ends of them to make it possible to get the studs through, or dipping them in the washbasins. These washbasins were a line of wooden washstands that ran up the middle of the dormitory. There was no running water, so they were filled and emptied each day by a servant. He filled them in the evening giving the water plenty of time to cool down before we washed our faces in the morning. Once a week we had a bath. The bathroom contained four baths and Miss Chaffer, the matron, presided with a lavatory brush with which she gave indiscriminate and painful scrubs on the backs of the four occupants.

The junior dormitory was a long room with beds lining each side. At the far end was Carol Powers' bedroom in which was a wardrobe containing yet another cane. If anyone were caught talking after lights out, he would be hauled out of bed, bent over and beaten, as would his neighbours on either side for good measure. One of our "dares" was to go into his bedroom, open the wardrobe and look at the cane. We would stand together, looking at it with horror spiced with fascination.

Each morning when the bell rang we got up, dressed, went down to the boot-room to clean our shoes and then to the playground and out through the gate for a run along the pavement to a distant lamp-post and back. As each of us returned, he had to stand in the corner until the next boy took his place, and so on until the last boy who, with no one to relieve him, had to stay there until the breakfast bell. Never fast at the best of times, I spent a lot of time in the corner.

One afternoon a week, we were allowed to go to the tuck-shop. This was an undertaking heavy with decision. First of all we went to Carol Power's study where, in the role of banker, he let us draw on our pocket money. This was the sum of ten shillings which our parents gave us at the beginning of term and which, failing windfalls, such as birthdays, had to last until the end of term. So deciding whether to draw out threepence or fourpence, needed careful calculation. But the die once cast and the money clutched in our hands, we hurried to the tuck-shop.

Situated in the senior school, this comprised a window at the side of the cricket pavilion through which a cornucopia of tempting delights could be seen and bought from the wife of the groundsman. Here, the problem was to decide whether to go for something known and tried, such as boiled sweets or liquorice all-sorts, or to risk disappointment in trying something new. The decision had to be made rapidly owing to the press of the queue behind.

Once the purchase had been made for better or for worse, there followed the problem of getting the goods safely home, for, as we had discovered to our cost on our first tuck-shop visit, a group of bigger boys would be waiting at the entrance to the playground and, with cries of "Contraband Control," would relieve us of half our treasure. Any attempt to hide it about one's person was futile, as it would be revealed by a none-too-gentle body search. The only safe course was to walk slowly back to the playground while eating as much of the tuck as you could, as fast as possible, and hope you would not be sick.

The great social event of their first term for new-boys was tea with Mrs Balmforth. We were issued into the room with the altar and the long gothic windows where she reclined in bed, her long greying hair hanging down romantically like an ageing Elizabeth Barrett Browning. We sat beside the bed while she poured tea and made us welcome. Suddenly, in the middle of the conversation to our astonishment, she skipped out of bed to get something and then jumped back in again which left us wondering about the exact nature of her illness.

On Sundays there were two full services, morning and evening in the chapel complete with sermons. On one occasion the Bishop of Dover came to preach. It was my first glimpse of a bishop in full fig with his robes and mitre, carrying his crook. I had never seen anything so magnificent – it out-classed everything in my dressing-up box and made a profound impression on me.

In the afternoon we went for a walk. For these expeditions, straw hats with the black and red school hatband and gloves, worn or carried, were obligatory, as, led by Carol Powers, we followed in a crocodile two abreast round the country lanes.

Later, after supper, we changed into pyjamas, dressing gowns and slippers and went into his study and sat on the floor, while, from a capacious basket chair, he read us several chapters of a novel. The novel was John Buchan's "Prester John". Reading aloud was still a major home entertainment in those days before television, when even the radio was considered too new to be wholly acceptable.

It was an art that people studied and practised and Carol Powers, a master of it, made Sunday evening the high spot of the week.

The war had now been on for eight months, but nothing much had happened and we were beginning to get used to it, when suddenly the Luftwaffe began making desultory night raids over the Kent coast, dropping bombs here and there. At each of these unwelcome visits, all the air-raid sirens began to wail and we had to put on our dressing-gowns and slippers and go down to the cellar where we sat on benches while Miss Chaffer, the matron, handed round a box of biscuits. They were those that have shiny icing on one side with the outline of animals. I had enjoyed them at children's parties, but faced with them at four o'clock in the morning, they lost most of their appeal.

Soon after this, an event occurred which finally put an end to any hopes I retained of passing unnoticed. It is described in "A Sneak at St Edmund's" (published in 2005) written by George Harries, the W.E. Harries who was my fellow new-boy, the significance of whose initials remains a mystery to this day:

"In the summer of 1940, (...) Apps, the youngest boy in the school, was about a fortnight short of his ninth birthday. With the usual routine getting under way, athletic heats and sports day had to be completed before cricket could begin. Everyone had to compete.

If you were new ... your mind would centre on the last event of the afternoon. It was a race for all those who had not gained any points in the sports, "the pot of jam race".

Great excitement; it was very easy to understand and every-one got a prize. The first home got the jam. Lying on the grass in wait for the coming stampede were sweets of all kinds in a tube, bar or packet. To be in such a charge was exhilarating and we grabbed our share of the spoils. In the rush somebody noticed that the race had not finished. A lonely figure was about halfway round and proceeding as if the whole day was at his disposal. We all watched the drama unfolding, enjoying every second. What was going to happen? No one could tell. Powers bellowed, boys shouted, all to no apparent effect. Could the headmaster let Apps carry on like this?

The headmaster did his headmasterly stuff and Apps continued without any visible acceleration, while the spectators were being marshalled ready to depart. Those of us, who were worried about being the last in everything, were now confident we could scratch athletics off the list".

We had been told we could invite our parents to Sports Day and, of the letters I wrote home that month, the only one to survive is this invitation. It is in an envelope postmarked 21st May 1940 and reads:

> tuesday
> "My dear Mummy,
> please will you
> come to the sports on thursday it
> will be very nice so please come
> if daddy will come I would
> like him to come to if you
> come come at half past two im sorry
> its such a quick note
> love from
> Teddy"

My Mother came to the sports day. She was wearing her fur coat and was dressed as for a point-to-point complete with field glasses. I hate to imagine how galling it must have been for her to see her horse run so ingloriously. However she didn't let me see her disappointment and greeted me warmly. She gave me the once-over, without actually opening my mouth and looking inside, turned me round to inspect my hind quarters and in so doing let out a cry of horror; "your neck!"

In the whole three weeks since term began, it had never occurred to me to wash it and it had become "Black, absolutely black" she exclaimed as she marched me up to Carol Powers and stuck it under his nose. Retrospectively I must feel sorry for Powers. For nearly forty years he had been a surrogate father for orphaned boys and had had the upper hand with their mothers, widows only too conscious of being at the receiving end of a charity. And here he was suddenly in the role of a hunted fox with the Goddess Diana bearing down on him. He stammered apologies and called for Miss Chaffer, who came running. My neck was minutely examined and there was a great deal of cluck-clucking and head shaking.

That evening I was given a bath and Miss Chaffer, with the aid of the lavatory brush, recovered her self-esteem as, in every sense, I got it in the neck.

*

During those first three weeks of May 1940, news from the outside world got worse and worse; Mr Chamberlain resigned and Mr Churchill became Prime minister forming a National government, Hitler invaded Holland, Luxembourg and Belgium. On my ninth birthday which was Ascension Day and a holiday (we had a picnic in the woods) we learned that the previous day, Mr Churchill had made a great speech in the House of Commons when he had said he had nothing to offer but blood, toil and sweat. News of this cheered everyone up as we began to feel the country at last had a leader. But on that same day, the Dutch army surrendered and the German army turned the line of the Albert Canal and pierced the French defences near Sedan. A week later, on the 21st, they captured Amiens and Arras.

Sports Day had been on the 22nd and the following morning we were woken by Carol Powers coming into the dormitory and clapping his hands:

"Wake up, wake up! You are all going home!"

There was a stunned silence.

"We are going to be evacuated to Cornwall," he explained

"Get up and dress, go down to breakfast and then I will give you your tickets and pocket money."

We broke into cheers, scrambled out of bed and began dancing round the dormitory.

Home! It was a word we had been trying to forget, with the long summer term stretching out for weeks and weeks before us. Now, all was changed and we were actually going home, not in a few weeks, not next week, not tomorrow even, but today.

With my overnight case packed and a letter of explanation from Powers to my mother, I caught the bus outside the school, which took me down St Thomas's Hill to the bus station beside the Westgate Towers. There I caught the bus to Sandwich getting off in Wingham village.

I began walking up the steep incline of Preston Hill but it was a hot day and my overnight case was getting heavier and heavier and I was just beginning to wonder what to do, when I was overtaken by the milkman on his milk float. "Are you going to Wenderton?" I asked

He nodded, "Could you take my case?

"I'll take you as well, jump up!"

So, after only three weeks at boarding school, I arrived home at 11 o'clock in the morning with the milkman.

CHAPTER FOUR

—

My Mother immediately decided I had been expelled. Apparently no mention of an evacuation had been made during her visit the previous day.

"What have you done? What have you been up to?" she asked anxiously.

I tried to explain that we were going to Cornwall, gave her Carol Powers' letter and eventually got her to calm down and read it. In fact what had happened was that, with the Allied armies falling back towards the coast, the invasion of England looked distinctly possible. Canterbury was badly placed for this eventuality and the school authorities hunted desperately for a solution. It came from the King's School, the ancient public school centred round the Cathedral, which, in the same predicament, had managed to secure two hotels at Crinnis Bay, near St Austell.

The problem was that the hotels were too big for the school alone and with billeting officers and a government department set up with draconian powers to organise evacuation on a national scale, Canon Shirley, the headmaster, fearing he would be forced to take in a grammar school or worse, decided that clergy orphans were at least respectable and the best of a bad job. So it was decided the schools should amalgamate. The King's School was already *in situ* and we were to meet at Paddington on the 6th June and catch the Cornish Riviera to join it. In the meantime we had two whole weeks at home in the glorious month of May. Perhaps the war wasn't such a bad thing after all.

I went up to my bedroom, took off my school uniform and put on some of my old clothes. How friendly and comfortable they felt. I went into the nursery where, to my amazement, everything was just as I had left it. How could I have changed so much, been through so many new and often unpleasant experiences, while all the while, in this quiet room, nothing had changed? There was my Teddy Bear,

Pooh, and all my other stuffed animals, my toy farm with the headless farmer and his wife. The harmonium, presented to a church by my great-great grandmother, which had returned it when an organ had been bought. Nobody had known what to do with it, so it had been given to me to practise on. The wind-up gramophone with the record of Richard Tauber singing "You are my heart's delight", something I had never understood because the farm at the top of the lane was called "Hearts Delight" and you couldn't be a farm. All these things completely untouched by all I had been through.

I went downstairs and out into the garden. It was getting more and more overgrown, but the important thing was that it was still there and oh, how glad I was to see it!

One of the first games I played after my return home, and child psychologists may make of it what they will, was to line up all my stuffed toys, find a cane and threaten to beat them with it.

The fear of invasion was being taken seriously in East Kent. One of the measures taken with the intention of confusing invaders was to remove all the signposts. As that part of Kent is a mass of interweaving lanes, it was not only potential invaders who were confused.

From that fortnight, one image has stayed indelible in my memory. My mother and I were staying at Guilton and one evening with my grandmother we drove to Dover, to see the troops being landed from Dunkirk. The troops we saw were French; bearded, bedraggled, exhausted some bandaged, limping, being helped along; the very picture of a defeated army. It was a grim sight and it brought the reality of the war closer, reminding us that it was being fought only twenty-five miles from where we were standing and that only a thin strip of water, the English Channel, was protecting us from the Wehrmacht and the Hitlerian Blitzkrieg.

*

On the third of June, with my overnight case repacked, I went to London with my father and we took a taxi to Paddington station.

Accustomed to the green of the Southern Railway, the cream and brown of the Great Western was the first surprise. The second was the splendour of the Cornish Riviera Express, one of its most prestigious trains. I recognised some people from the school and saw Mr Brand, who showed us the carriage reserved for the school and ticked my name on the list, "*Apps B.E.G.*" With a sinking feeling in the pit of my stomach, I said goodbye to my father, and climbed on board. The whistle blew and, as the train began to move, I leaned out of the window and waved to him and went on waving until he became a distant dot on the platform and disappeared.

Arriving at Par early that evening, we were met by buses that took us through a landscape dominated by large white pyramids formed from the detritus of the china clay mines, the chief industry of the region, and brought us along dusty white roads to the two hotels which faced each other across the cliff road. On one side, with its back to the sea, was a grandiose semi-circular white building with a central tower-like entrance. This was the four-star Carlyon Bay Hotel that had served in the thirties as the trysting place for the future King Edward VIII and his American mistress, Mrs Simpson. This was to be the Senior School. On the opposite side of the road, facing the sea was a more modest, pebbledash building with "Bayfordbury Hotel" in large letters over a colonnaded entrance that was to be the Junior School. Here we were greeted by Carol Powers and shown to our dormitories.

The Junior King's School had got there first and taken all the best rooms, so we found ourselves on the top floor, in the maid's rooms, under the eaves. Nevertheless we had nothing to complain about in the exchange with the junior dormitory at Canterbury. Instead of all being in one long room with its row of Victorian washstands, we were in bedrooms with washbasins and hot and cold running water. True, they had taken out the carpets and the comfortable beds and replaced them with our iron bedsteads, but the low ceilings and the fact of being only four to a room gave a sense almost of cosiness.

We trooped downstairs to the hotel dining room. Light and airy, it faced across the cliffs to the sea. The King's School's boys were already in place, and we presented a strange contrast; for the Junior King's School, known as Milner Court, was a thoroughly modern prep-school. The boys were in grey flannel shorts, grey shirts with attached collars and blazers. We, in our late nineteenth century uniforms, must have appeared very odd in that setting; we were welcomed by Mr Juckes.

The form the amalgamation took was that in the Senior School Canon Shirley, the Headmaster of the King's School became Warden, while Mr Balmforth took the title of Headmaster. In the Junior School, Ralph Juckes, the Headmaster of Milner Court, was in overall charge and Carol Powers, although also a headmaster was reduced effectively to being the housemaster of St Edmund's, which, as a much smaller school, was really little more than a house in what was now known as The Canterbury Schools.

Mr Juckes was a gentleman farmer *manqué*. He dressed like one, in roomy sports coat and baggy corduroy trousers, and spent his days fiddling about with ponies, chicken, geese and various bits of machinery. He didn't appear to do much if any teaching, but ran the place efficiently with a relaxed authority and a supportive wife who one suspected was the real organiser.

Miss Chaffer and her lavatory brush had been left behind in Canterbury and we encountered a new and gentler race of matrons. Pullen Baker, the dreaded music master, had also fallen by the wayside, (it would be nice to think he had been thrown out on his ear) and Powers, for the moment at least, seemed subdued.

One of the first and most merciful dispensations was the abandoning of Eton collars and dark suits; replaced by shirts with soft collars, blazers and flannel trousers. Classes were in a row of garages behind the hotel, or in the dining room or the cocktail bar; not many people can claim, as I can, to have learnt Latin in a cocktail bar. In the afternoon we had a glass of milk and a doughnut on the front lawn so, what with the sea air, and a general air of relaxation, we were all beginning to think Hitler had come up trumps, when, on Sunday, Powers got us back into the Eton collars and, in the afternoon, with hats and gloves, took us for the customary walk. The scenery was different; the fertile Kentish lanes replaced by pine woods and dry, white roads with, from time to time, a large black slag-heap thrown up in a previous mining operation.

Halting at a clearing in front of one of these, he gathered us round him and asked what we thought of our new home. A dozen voices assured him that we thought it was a definite change for the better, at which he looked gloomy and said "I don't, I think it's awful"

So, of course, from that moment, we, too, thought it was awful.

Clearly for someone as set in his ways and opposed to change of any sort as Powers, being uprooted and seeing his school suddenly and without warning thrust into the middle of the twentieth century must have represented everything he had fought against for the previous forty years. But with hindsight it was foolish of him to reveal his feelings to us, because up to that moment we were integrating happily with Milner Court and the amalgamation looked like being a real success. His words changed all that, from that moment we had the sense that any attitude on our part other than hostility was a betrayal of him and of St Edmund's.

Shortly after our arrival, the Canterbury Cathedral Choir School joined us. Housed some miles away in a café at St. Blazey, they arrived daily for lessons in a bus driven by their headmaster, the reverend Clive Pare, a minor canon of Canterbury, accompanied by Gerald Knight, the Cathedral organist, who left our ears alone and was in every way a great improvement on Pullen Baker. The younger masters, Mr Coates and Mr Brand, had left to join the services, (the nice Mr Coates was killed early in the war) so Mr Knight took us for Geography. Whether it was due to his not knowing the subject, or simply because railways interested him, he taught us the railway system and which parts of the country are served by which London stations and made us learn them by heart. Years later, as a touring actor, I often had cause to be grateful to him for those lessons.

None of my letters from that first term in Cornwall survive, and while the first three weeks at Canterbury are engraved on my memory in minute detail, the only thing I remember from the rest of that long summer term was the measles.

Parents were warned that there was an epidemic. My mother telephoned immediately to say I must be inoculated. This was done and I promptly went down with a very severe bout of the illness and felt terrible. The treatment in those days included being in the dark, so the curtains were drawn making it impossible to read. I was in a sick room with several older boys who were far less ill and they soon became extremely bored and began amusing themselves by throwing things at me and making me get out of bed to pick them up at the risk of being caught out of bed by Matron. On the 27th of July, the term at last came to an end and we caught the Cornish Riviera at Par for Paddington, where I was met by my mother with the news that I had a new bicycle and her sister, my aunt Peggy, had had a baby boy. For me, the first piece of news totally eclipsed the second.

At home, the Battle of Britain was getting into its stride. The German plan was to bomb London and the Southeast hard, to soften it up for the invasion. We were in the flight path and several times a day, we would hear the dreaded sound of German bombers and watch formations of them pass overhead. We became expert at recognising their sounds and could tell the difference between a Messerschmidt and a Heinkel. They did not pass unopposed, but were attacked by Spitfires and Hurricanes, whose sounds we could also differentiate. There would be the scream of engines as planes climbed and dived, the rattle of canon-fire and it was a common sight to see a plane going down with black smoke pouring from it and the pilot eject, his parachute open and watch him float slowly down.

One of my father's trophies from the First World War was a German Mauser rifle and a box of dum-dum bullets. These flat nosed bullets that spread out and cause terrible wounds are forbidden under the Geneva Convention. The Germans had denied using them and he had kept this box as proof of their perfidy. Now he brought them out and, standing in the porch, with the Mauser in hand, fired them at the German bombers overhead.

I was disappointed not to see a plane or two drop out of the sky, but I thought the gesture splendid.

Each evening we listened eagerly to the news to hear how many

German planes had been shot down and each day the numbers increased. The battle reached its climax on August 15th. The summer of 1940 was very hot, and on that day, which was a Sunday, it was decided to have tea in the garden. A folding table was laid with a crisp white tablecloth, teacups, the silver teapot, plates of bread and butter and paste sandwiches, biscuits and cakes on the lawn opposite the front door and we sat down, waited on by Frances in her uniform. We had barely started, when we heard the drone of approaching aircraft and in a short time, the sky above us was black with wave after wave of German bombers passing overhead. Attacked by the Spitfires and Hurricanes, they seemed to be coming down all round us as we sipped our tea, took another sandwich and said, "Oh, look, he's baled out!" "There's another!" "Look, *he's* on fire!" At one point we counted five parachutes descending slowly all round us. Finally, my father said, "Its getting rather hot, perhaps we should go in," so we finished our tea indoors. That evening it was announced on the radio that 180 German bombers had been shot down.

Hop picking was in full swing and at Guilton Uncle John had moved into the oast personally to supervise the drying. My father had begun the practice in the twenties when the business's survival depended on the quality of the hops, and Uncle John had continued it.

I was visiting him when we heard a plane flying low overhead and a Messerschmidt crashed into one of the hop gardens. The pickers had only moved out of that garden a few hours before and as we looked at the scene of devastation, with the tangled mass of wires and poles and the swathe the plane had cut through them, it was terrible to think what a carnage it would have been had the pickers still been there. For several days, we dared not approach the smoking wreck as from time to time bullets continued to explode. When we did approach, I recovered the rocker arm, a souvenir I kept for many years.

While at Guilton, I continued to spend as much time as possible with Clayson, the carpenter, and it was there that an event occurred that made a profound impression on me. Going into his workshop one day I found him making a long box. I asked what it was and he explained it was a coffin, adding that one of the hop-pickers had died, a grandmother. I asked where she was and he said they had put her in a stable on trestles.

It so happened that the grandmother of a neighbouring farming family, the Questeds, had died a few days previously and the funeral was to be that afternoon. For this, blinds were down in all the houses in the village and shops shut as the hearse, magnificent with floral tributes, followed by mourners in cars and on foot, proceeded slowly along the High street.

The contrasting ways in which these two grandmothers were treated struck me forcibly. Clayson was a socialist and no doubt he brought it to my notice. In any case it was an important moment in my political education and it was certainly from Clayson that me awareness of social inequality first came.

Although the Battle of Britain had peaked, and the threat of invasion receded, the bombing of London had intensified. My father's daily trips became increasingly hazardous, with trains and the line frequently bombed. On one occasion, returning in the evening, the train got to Chatham and everyone was told to get out. Asking how to continue the journey, the passengers were told that it was impossible and when they pressed the matter, pointing out that the train was there and the line had not been bombed, it was explained that the problem was the lack of a driver. My father then took command of the situation, asked where the nearest driver lived, went to his house, knocked him up and persuaded him to take the train to Dover. When, together, they arrived on the platform and he announced the news, they were given a round of applause.

The six weeks of the summer holiday passed all too quickly and it was back to Paddington and the train to Par. It was a long journey, made longer by the policy of confusing the enemy by taking all the names off the stations, so we never knew where we were.

The only letter that has survived from that winter-term is one to my Mother from Carol Powers. It is postmarked 14th November 1940.

November 13   *Bayfordbury Hotel*
                                 St Austell

Dear Mrs Apps

Teddy is looking very well and seems perfectly happy – he gets on with all the boys as far as I can see and he is a very good boy in every way.

As for his lessons, well there is no getting away from it that he is very slow – he is not altogether stupid, though he seems so at times, just because he is so slow –give him time he generally manages, but it does take a long time; he is apt to dream and get flustered. We are very peaceful here, but the weather has been awful lately, rain, rain and gale, and then rain again – though with short fine intervals. I hope you are not having it too hot and strong at Wingham.

Kindest regards,
Yours sincerely,

Carol Powers".

It must have been reassuring for my parents to know that I was "not altogether stupid", even if I clearly gave that impression. As for being flustered, it was difficult not to be with the threat of the cane hanging over every answer you gave.

Unfortunately Power's canes were not among the things left behind in Canterbury. They were now housed in the hotel wardrobe of his study, a room beside the dining-room, from where we would from time to time emerge, with lacerated buttocks and a face burning with a mixture of anger, humiliation and shame to be invited by one's friends to lower ones trousers so that they could appreciate the extent of the damage. Boys who were good-looking tended to be held back to be kissed and fondled, something I fortunately escaped. Caning sessions were announced after morning prayers and executed after lunch. I remember seeing Powers after one of these sessions enjoying a cigarette on the lawn outside his study and being struck by how satisfied and relaxed he looked.

Powers' Latin lessons (of which there many in the curriculum) remained, for me, the black spots of the week. French with Clive Pare was altogether more agreeable, as was English, even though it was with Powers. The King's School chaplain, Mr Brooke, known as 'The Tank'; a bulky figure rendered bulkier by his voluminous cassock, taught Divinity and was the butt of many jokes. It was, for instance noticed that he came to tea in the Junior School and then returned to the Senior School for a second tea. He was first cousin to Rupert Brooke the romantically beautiful young poet of the first war, but one could discern no family likeness. The Tank's sermons were an endless source of fascination because their subject was always the same: the evils of masturbation; the fascination came in wondering how and at what point the subject would be introduced. You knew it would be introduced at some point, but never when or how: in that the Tank showed great ingenuity.

Meanwhile the amalgamation was running into difficulty at its head. The problem lay with the character of Canon Shirley. The King's School Canterbury, which dates from the middle ages and was re-founded in the reign of Edward VI, claims to be the oldest public school in the country and counts many famous men among its past pupils. However in the twenties and early thirties, numbers had dropped dangerously and its reputation had sunk to an all-time low. The Cathedral Chapter, the governing body, felt that drastic action was needed in the form of a new and dynamic headmaster. The Reverend Fred Shirley had built a formidable reputation for pulling round failing schools, and the Chapter made approaches to see if he would accept the post. It was said that he drove a hard bargain that included the gift of a canonry. In any case, he became a canon of Canterbury when he was appointed and set about the task of putting the school back on the map with enthusiasm and a flair for publicity. He revived (some said invented) ancient customs. The school monitors were dressed in Court dress with knee breeches and purple gowns – something mothers found irresistible. Influential old boys were approached, and even those like Hugh Walpole and Somerset Maugham who had committed to print their hatred of their school days were cajoled into making handsome donations. In a comparatively short time numbers were up, new school houses with names recalling famous old boys were opened, and the schools' reputation soared.

It was clear from the start that the gentle, unworldly Mr Balmforth was no match for such a scintillating figure. Canon Shirley had his own way in everything and St Edmund's was defenceless. The situation could not continue and in 1941 Mr Balmforth resigned and went off to be head of Ely Theological College and Canon of Ely, eventually becoming Canon and Chancellor of Exeter where he died in 1973.

He was replaced by one of the school governors; the Reverend F.S. Williams, the retired headmaster of Eastbourne College. Aged 70, slim and upright, this wily old bird proved a bulwark against the devices and desires of Canon Shirley's heart. Each new scheme however deviously or charmingly proposed, was blocked with the same short reply: "No, Fred." Shirley would try again and again, but each time, the same answer: "No, Fred." It was thanks to Mr Williams that St Edmund's returned to Canterbury as a school and not as another of the King's School's houses, as Shirley had frequently proposed.

Each of my letters has, in the right hand top corner, a note of the exact number of days left before the holidays and although they are clearly written with the idea of reassuring my mother that I am well and happy, there is a sort of under swell of longing for home and the truth is that I lived for the holidays, for Wenderton, the farm, my pony, "Greynose", a New Forest pony who had reconciled me to riding, and the company of Old Bill, Measday and Walters, the shepherd; that was the real world, and school simply something to be endured.

I was no longer the youngest boy in the school, for when we left Canterbury, the younger brother of Mount, a boy whose family were farmers at Harbledown, a village close to Canterbury, joined us. T.H. Mount was only eight and because he was younger than everyone, was known as Tommy Mount, the only boy ever to be known throughout his schooldays by his Christian name. The Mounts were a large family all of whom seemed to own farms round Canterbury, leading to the saying that Canterbury lies in a hollow surrounded by Mounts. Our grandfathers and parents were friends and he and I became friends, making a small group with Rhodes and R.E. Jones, his ear completely healed. Not interested in games, we amused ourselves in other ways and, probably through my influence, in writing and performing plays. Rhodes's father had died three days after he was born (he would often say they were never on speaking terms) and his widowed mother worked as secretary to a charitable society, which existed to give annual holidays to deprived children in Leeds. As a result he was familiar with secretarial affairs and so we formed a dramatic society called "The United Players" with a slogan, "Up with the U.P.". Much time was spent with a primitive printing-set making posters and programmes. We worried less about the text of the play, usually making it up as we went along.

*

The summer holidays of 1941 were a high spot in my childhood. No longer forbidden by my grandfather, I roamed the farm and the woods on my pony. The Wenderton woods seemed to me wonderfully romantic, for not only did they contain memories of John Minter who had been the great family huntsman in his caravan with his pack of beagles, but there were also the ruins of a seventeenth-century country house, itself built on the ruins of a former palace of a fourteenth-century Archbishop of Canterbury. Little was left of either, but pushing through the undergrowth one came across cellars and remains of walls in moss-covered brick.

My father had preserved the woods as a shoot in the twenties and early thirties, and had had a game-keeper called Sammy Tutt who lived in the game-keeper's cottage with his young wife and a large family of little Tutts of whom our erstwhile back-door boy was one. A path led through the woods down to a wooden bridge over a gently flowing river on to the marsh. This river held considerable attraction for the miners from the local colliery. They came to bathe in the river and poach the game, much to the chagrin of Sammy Tutt, who saw the pheasants he had carefully nurtured disappearing prematurely.

He waged a guerrilla war against the miners without success, until finally my father had a large board put up at the entrance to the wood on which was written, "Beware of poisonous snakes". This proved to be a simple and effective deterrent.

During the holidays, we often went to see great-uncle George at Frognal. He had become a member of the Special Police and had a tin hat to prove it. Nina, his younger daughter, had become engaged to a bomber pilot, David Maltby. They married that autumn. My parents went to the wedding, which they described as being like a wake, with a sense of foreboding hanging heavy in the air. Maltby was soon to distinguish himself as one of the Dam-Busters, in fact the one who dropped the fatal bomb that burst the dam. Sadly he and his crew were killed returning from another raid some months later, leaving Nina with a ten-week-old baby son called Johnny. David Maltby's body, the only one recovered, is buried in the churchyard at Wickhambreaux.

Towards the end August, my father was on holiday, the only holiday I had ever known him take. There was an abundant crop of apples in the orchard and together we picked them and sent them to Convent Garden, a shared activity we both enjoyed, inventing a contraption on a pole to pick those on the high branches, we called it "the progger".

At the beginning of September, as the end of the holidays began to loom up, I dreaded more and more the day when I would have to go back to school. But the dreaded day arrived as dreaded days do, and it was time to say goodbye to the house and garden, to Old Bill and Measday, to my pony, to Bess the old liver-and-white Springer Spaniel, and get in the car for the drive to the station, the train to Charing Cross, the taxi to Paddington, where the Cornish Riviera was waiting like a tumbrel, with the carriages reserved for the school full of boys who seemed to be idiotically cheerful. I stood miserably on the platform beside my parents who had met other parents they knew and were chatting in what seemed to me a very unfeeling way. The whistle blew, a last kiss and handshake, I climbed on to the train, the hiss of steam as it slowly began to move, then with my head out of the window waving, waving until they disappeared, and the knowledge that it would be months and months, Christmas even, before I saw them again.

Back at the Bayfordbury Hotel we had a new school captain: he was from Wales. There were a number of Welsh boys at the school, many of them from remote parts where the parson was rarely much richer than his parishioners who were often among the poorest in the British Isles. Whatever his background, I quickly realised that this particular Welshman did not like me. The school captain and the other monitors sat each at the head of a table. As bad luck would have it, I was on his table, which gave him the chance to torment me at every meal, a chance that he exploited to the full. A school captain in that little world wielded considerable power; moreover, he was a good-looking boy and a great favourite with Carol Powers (who was much given to having favourites among the good-looking). He was also popular with the other boys and soon turned them against me, so that I became the school pariah.

There is a well-known study done with rats, in which one group was put in a cage where whenever they touched anything, including their food, they got an electric shock. Another group was put in an exactly similar cage where they too had to submit to shocks whenever they touched anything including their food, but this group enjoyed the addition of a small cage into which they could retire and escape the shocks. The result showed that while the first group went into depression and eventually died under the strain, the second group resisted.

My situation was that of the first group. There was no escape: at table, in the dormitory, wherever I went I was at the school captain's mercy. I needed a second small cage and eventually found one in the sickroom, or "sicker" as it was called.

The passport to the sicker was a temperature. You could be at death's door; if you did not have a temperature it was a spoonful of cod-liver oil and back to school. I don't know how I managed to acquire a temperature, probably the stress of the situation produced one naturally, but however it happened, the matron accepted me into that haven of peace. Once there I was confronted with a problem. Clearly I could not stay there indefinitely and at some point I would have to return and the nightmare would start all over again. What could I do? Should I write to my parents and ask for help? It was hardly a course to be undertaken lightly, for it meant breaking the great schoolboy rule of not sneaking.

I remember lying in bed, ten years old, in that quiet room surrounded by empty beds, as I was the only occupant, and thinking through the situation. What had I to lose? The school captain had already turned everyone against me: I was stuck here hundreds of miles from home for the next three months; Carol Powers would think less of me – but he did not think much of me anyway because I was no good at games. So I decided to write.

The letter has survived and it's writing, compared to my usual hand, shows the stress I was under.

I heard nothing, my temperature dropped and I was considered well enough to return to school. When I did so, I was told to go and see Powers. He said he was aware of what had happened and that there would be no more of it, but that I should not be a baby.

From then on the school captain left me in peace and I gradually ceased to be the most unpopular boy in the school.

There is a sequel to this event that occurred sixty-five years later. I was invited to speak at the Old Boy's annual dinner. There were few people of my age there, but one of them was the school captain. In his seventies he was still good looking, very well dressed and had spent his life in the financial industry and been successful. Someone introduced us and he said he remembered me because my mother had come to sports day wearing a fur coat. It was, he said, the first time he had seen a fur coat, for in the poor village where he had lived in Wales, where his father had been the incumbent no-one had anything of the sort.

We went into dinner and I made my speech and afterwards everyone wandered about chatting. At this point he came up to me again, congratulated me on my speech and said, "You know I have often thought about the way I treated you. I don't know why I did it. Even at the time, I felt it wasn't me doing it."

He added that Powers had caned him; the only time he had ever caned a school captain. It was clear that the event had marked him and that the memory of it had hurt and puzzled him ever since.

I tried to reassure him by saying that there were certainly boys to whom I had not been very nice, but it was immediately clear why he had done it; it was all the fault of my mother's choosing on the afternoon of the 22nd of May 1940, with her husband away, to bolster her waning morale by wearing her fur coat.

I had barely recovered from this trauma when a letter arrived from my parents telling me that they had left Wenderton. This was a real shock, for although there had been talk of leaving earlier, recently it had seemed that the danger had blown over. Now it was suddenly presented as a *fait accompli*.

In fact, as I was to learn later, the Aerodrome Board, its mission accomplished, had been disbanded and my father's job had come to an end. He could have returned to his previous job as a lands officer, but the daily five-hour journey in the blackout, the stress of trains cancelled and the risk of bombing, and the long separations from my mother, made him, at the age of fifty-one, look for a quieter life.

Through friends he was advised that the family firm of G.H. Dean at Bapchild near Sittingbourne was looking for a land agent to run its thirteen farms. The Chairman was Leslie Doubleday who had inherited the business from his grandfather, the original Mr Dean who had been a brick-maker in the Victorian era, when London was expanding fast and bricks were needed. He had bought up land at Sittingbourne, excavated the brick earth, and when that was exhausted, had planted the land with fruit trees, principally cherries, and built a jam factory. The business had prospered and was a considerable affair with several satellite companies.

The war had transformed agriculture. With German submarines sniffing at their shores, the British found that cheap imported food was no longer available, and that they needed the long neglected home industry after all. The government, as governments do, set up a ministry with experts to go and tell the long-suffering farmers which crops to plant. These agricultural advisers, strong on theory, were often more of a hindrance that a help. They knew better and said so, thus when a farmer protested that a certain field would not grow a certain crop, that it had been tried in his father's time on several occasions and always failed, they overrode him with predictable results.

But in spite of these problems farmers prospered, as they had not for the previous eighty years. G.H. Dean was no exception and there were plans to buy more farms. Mr Doubleday's son was away at the war, and help was needed.

It happened that Mr Doubleday and his wife were friends of my grandparents with whom they had been on a cruise in the twenties. At that time my mother and my Aunt Peggy were at a private school in Thanet called Glyn House. The Doubledays had two daughters and were looking for a school. My grandmother offered to speak to the headmistress, a ferocious snob, called Miss Perks. This was arranged and the Doubledays went to see the school and liked it. But when she next saw my grandmother, Miss Perks expressed some hesitation, "were they", she wondered "quite?" She had heard, she confided "that they ate mutton on Sundays." It was of course a well-known fact that the best families ate beef on Sundays.

It seems my grandmother was able to reassure her about the Doubleday's social credentials, for both girls were accepted at Glyn House.

If this family connection was not sufficient, there was also the fact that, when during the 14-18 war, Mr Doubleday had been in the trenches and had been wounded during an assault and left lying on no-man's-land, it had been great-uncle George's brother-in-law who had risked his own life to go over the top and bring him to safety.

My parents went to Bapchild to see him and he showed them the farmhouse they would eventually have but which was currently let. However the Old Vicarage at Tonge situated close to the estate office, had been vacated by its owner for the duration of the war, and, by storing her furniture in certain rooms, we could manage for the time being. So it was arranged that my father would take over the running of the farms for a salary considerably less that he had received at the Air Ministry, but it promised a quieter life, less expense and an end to the separations.

In the letter telling me of the move, my father made much of the attractions of our new home. An admiral had lived there and there was a cutlass on the wall that looked as if it had belonged to a pirate. Moreover there was an organ in the dining room.

My letters for the rest of the term are full of questions.

When I eventually saw it, the Old Vicarage proved to be all that he had cracked it up to be. Surrounded by cherry orchards, it had belonged to the Reverend Joseph Apperley, who had married late in life a lady considerably younger. He had been dead for many years and his widow was now herself old. They had an only daughter married to an admiral. The house, which was late Regency, was furnished in a manner typical of a cultivated clergyman in the second part of the nineteenth century. It was approached by a circular carriage drive round a lawn with a large baobab in the centre. The front door opened on to a lofty hall with the main staircase. A dining room (which did indeed contain an organ) was on the left, and a typically late Regency drawing room with French doors on to the garden lay ahead, with the study, which led to the conservatory, beside it. The garden had a large monkey-puzzle tree and a croquet-lawn bordered by a shrubbery with the kitchen garden behind. Beyond the staircase to the right a glazed door led to the kitchen and scullery with the servants' quarters above, reached by a second staircase rising from the kitchen. The backdoor led on to a cobbled yard with the coach-house and stables, while beyond them, lay an orchard of apples and plums and a paddock. The walls were hung with paintings by Victorian Academicians and the study was lined with glass-fronted bookcases containing theological and literary works and, as I was to discover as a nosey eleven-year-old, one or two books of "special interest".

This was to be our home for the next four years

CHAPTER FIVE

—

Back at school, we were to do a play for the fifth of November about the gunpowder plot and I was to play Catesby, one of the conspirators. It was a good part and I was very excited about it. I had been cast as the result of a poetry recital the previous term, in which I had had some success in reciting "The Mad Dog of Islington."

Another member of the cast was Adam Gielgud. Adam's father was Val Gielgud, the head of BBC Drama and his uncle was the actor John Gielgud. His family tree also included Ellen Terry, Henry Irving's leading lady.

This meant that great interest surrounded his first stage appearance. Adam was a nervous and emotional boy and those who expected to see the emergence of a new star were disappointed. All I can remember of his performance was his pointing above the heads of the audience and shaking with emotion as he described the moon as "hanging like a cheese in the sky." I cannot remember the name of the author of the piece, which is perhaps just as well.

I don't know if it was on this occasion or another that Adam's father came down to see him. His visit caused great excitement and I wrote home in a letter dated the 11th May 1941:

"Last evening Geilgud came in (he had been out for the day) with no less a person than Val Gielgud himself he is quite a hansom chap with a black beard."

Val Gielgud was not the only celebrity to visit us in Cornwall; Canon Shirley saw to that. Among those he persuaded to make the pilgrimage were the Duke of Kent, then an R.A.F. officer, who came down only shortly before he was killed in a flying accident, and General Montgomery who arrived fresh from his victory over Rommel at El-Alamein. He had spent a term in the Junior King's School while staying with his grandfather the then Dean of Canterbury, on the strength of which Shirley persuaded him to inspect the school.

We lined up in military formation and the figure in battle-dress with the beret and its two badges, so familiar from press photographs, walked slowly past us looking us up and down. Afterwards he gave a talk in the former hotel garage which had become the assembly room, with chapel at one end and a lecture hall at the other (depending on which way the chairs faced). Of his lecture I remember only two things: the first was his saying, "Everyone keeps asking when we are going to open a second front. I don't understand what they mean, there are already three"; and the second was when the Americans, who were camped nearby practising landing on the beach with their amphibious tanks, started the engine of one of these monsters in the vicinity while 'Monty' was speaking. He gave a quick nod towards the elegant staff major who accompanied him, the major slipped discreetly out of the hall, silence fell instantly and the major was back in his place before you could say 'high-command'.

When Hitler invaded Russia and it became an ally, we began to be visited by Dr Hewlett Johnson, the Dean of Canterbury. In the Church of England, the prime minister, on behalf of the Crown, appoints deans and bishops for life. Ramsey Macdonald had formed the first Labour Government in June 1929. It had not lasted long, but long enough for him to appoint Dr Hewlett Johnson, an enthusiastic Communist and friend of Joseph Stalin, to the Deanery of Canterbury. By any standard a bizarre appointment, it led to difficult situations, such as the extremely conservative Archbishop, Dr Geoffrey Fisher, refusing to speak to the Dean. But with Stalin our ally, no one could refuse the Dean and he came regularly to speak to us of the advantages of Communism and to explain what a civilized and agreeable country communist Russia was.

Although my religious education had got off to a bad start under Mr Balmforth, it had made a spectacular recovery and I even found myself winning the seven-and-sixpenny book token that comprised the Musgrave Divinity Prize. This was due less to any excessive religiosity on my part than to my appreciation of good strong stories and my ability to remember them. Divinity was taught by the Tank who was a keen supporter of an institution called "The Bible Reading Fellowship" a religious society that issued monthly pamphlets indicating bible passages for daily reading with a suitable commentary. These he handed out to us individually with our names written in the top corner. I don't know how many pupils read them, but I was certainly not of their number, nor were most of my friends – although to the frequently asked question "Have you been reading your Bible Reading Fellowship?" we invariably answered "Yes, sir". On one occasion, arriving late for a Divinity lesson, I found the entrance to the class blocked by the massive form of the Tank; "Apps, have you been reading your Bible Reading Fellowship?" "Yes, sir" "Well, that's a very funny thing because I've just found it on the floor!" and he produced the crumpled remains covered in footprints and with my tell tale name written on the front. This took some explaining and in spite of my best efforts, the Tank looked disappointed and regarded me with suspicion for a long time afterwards.

The culmination of these lessons was confirmation. This rite of passage took place normally at the age of thirteen. As my birthday fell in May, I was always at the younger end of the group and only twelve when our year was due to take the plunge. Doubts were expressed about my maturity, but Powers gave the green light and I joined the group that was being prepared by the Headmaster, Mr Williams.

Naturally at St Edmund's confirmation was taken with great seriousness. For several days leading up to the ceremony we were cloistered in the church of the neighbouring small port of Charlestown, under the aegis of the Bishop of Dover, who put great stress on the mystical significance of the laying on of hands, and what we should feel at that moment, so that we were all in a highly emotional and susceptible state of mystical enthusiasm.

So important was the event considered to be, that our parents were invited. Widowed mothers came from Wales and even from Yorkshire, in spite of the expense, and my own parents made their only visit during the whole time I was at school in Cornwall.

Staying in a boarding house on the quay at Charlestown, they arrived the evening before the ceremony and as it was a nice evening, walked from Charlestown to the hotel. I was anxiously waiting for them and I see them now, as they appeared, walking along the cliff path towards me.

"Well, my boy, how are you? Enjoying yourself?" asked my father in his firm deep voice. "I remember when I was confirmed we had a lot to eat."

With that phrase he undid all the work of the Bishop of Dover. Suddenly I was jolted back into the ordinary world and the following day when the bishop laid his hands on my head I felt nothing but their weight.

Over the years I have become increasingly grateful to my father for his words. He saved me from an experience that might have proved disastrous and even led to my becoming a religious enthusiast, a fate reserved for certain of my contemporaries. As it was he put my feet back on the ground and I am glad to say they have stayed there.

The following term we moved across the road to the Senior School, a minor move geographically but major in all other respects.

CHAPTER SIX

—

Life at the Old Vicarage confirmed something I had begun to believe, namely that we were no longer "modern" and that the age of modernity had ended in 1938.

"Modern" had been the buzzword of the 1930s. While I was growing up, "modern" had been the most complimentary adjective on offer, women were modern, cars were modern, everything was modern or about to be modernised. When my parents took Wenderton they modernised it; putting hand basins with hot and cold water in the bedrooms, and electric light run from a series of glass batteries installed in an outhouse with a petrol engine and dynamo. In 1938 my grandmother bought a refrigerator, which was installed in the china pantry at Guilton, enabling cold beer to be served in summer and an endless supply of ice cubes. In that same year, my grandfather changed his black car for a Hillman that was brown and cream and Kelk had a new brown uniform to match, which everyone agreed was truly modern.

Since then, I had been to St Edmund's which was anything but modern, and now we were living in the Old Vicarage with gas lamps downstairs and candles and paraffin lamps upstairs which was not at all modern. Moreover, and this was something I was delighted about, because of petrol rationing, my mother now drove a gig drawn by a cob. We sat with rugs wrapped round our knees, my mother holding the reins and with a flick of the whip we were bowling silently along the lanes with just the clip-clop sound of the horse's shoes on the macadam. It was wonderful – but it was certainly not modern.

In other respects life was not so very different from Wenderton. We had a gardener, Phipps, who had worked for the Apperleys for many years and must have been in his late fifties or early sixties. He had a stammer, which he treated in a most original and effective manner. When he couldn't get a word out, he would try two or three times then, while never taking his eyes off his interlocutor, his hand would swing up unseen from his side and give his cheek a resounding smack, literally knocking the offending word out of his mouth. The stammer was noticeable at the beginning of a conversation, but after a couple of false starts and smacks on the cheek, it didn't seem to bother him unduly.

Phipps knew all the local gossip and was full of stories especially about "the ol' vicar". It seems Mr Apperley had owned the first motorcar in the district but never became proficient at driving it. As a result he had been a public danger on the roads and, Phipps claimed, had at one time or another run down almost half his parishioners.

"Kept 'avin' to go to court, he did, and in the end the magistrate took it away from 'im, he did. Weren't allowed to drive it no more, nor weren't he. That pleased us, I can tell you. Didn't feel safe walking, we didn't, not with him comin' round the corner at you all over the place".

Many local people confirmed Phipps's story, and it could be said that while the Reverend Joseph Apperley had been dead for many years, his parishioners had not forgotten him.

One big difference between this and our former life was that to my great joy my father was at home and I could go with him as he drove round the farms and walked the fields. The Lanchester being under wraps in the garage because of lack of petrol, my father used an old Morris Ten belonging to the firm for his work. Up till now my mother, who enjoyed driving and was good at it, had driven me. My father neither enjoyed it nor was good at it. He drove slowly, hanging on to the wheel and peering over it as though expecting the worst to happen, as it frequently did. On one occasion we found ourselves in a minor traffic jam in Sittingbourne high street. Suddenly we lurched forward and bumped into the car in front. The driver turned round angrily and my father immediately reversed and bumped into the car behind. I began to laugh.

"Don't laugh, don't laugh," he said anxiously, "you'll upset them." No damage was done but I did begin to wonder whether there wasn't something about living at the Old Vicarage that was inimical to road safety.

One of the farms included several acres of marshland and when he visited this, my father let me drive along the private roads, so that I got used to changing gears and handling a car, an experience that proved invaluable when I did eventually learn to drive.

During one of the early holidays at the Vicarage, when I was about eleven, my grandmother came to tea. Petrol rationing and the absence of Kelk, who had been drafted into war work, meant that the only means of transport was the bus, a journey with several changes. We met her at the end of the lane and walked to the Vicarage, where tea was laid in the drawing room. My father was of course absent, but, in the middle of tea, the door opened and in he came. "Hullo, Joan!" he said.

My grandmother was sitting in an armchair by the fire with her back to the door, my mother opposite her and I was on the sofa behind the tea table. I saw my grandmother turn white and with a violent movement of her head look into the fire, holding up her hand as though to protect her self.

"Tell that man to leave the room!" she said. My mother rose in distress muttering something about it being my father's house and he had a right to be in it. My grandmother rose, my father withdrew, my grandmother demanded her coat and we walked with her down the road in silence where, as luck would have it, a bus came almost immediately.

Soon after, my mother received a letter from Uncle John accusing her of humiliating their mother.

I certainly felt humiliated. The scene played and replayed in my dreams for many years. It was something I kept to myself, something I could not share with my friends. It showed me the mysterious and unexpected depth of hatred that lay at the heart of the family quarrel, something I brooded over but was not to understand till much later.

We were of course camping out in the Old Vicarage, in the sense that we were only using the drawing room, study, kitchen and scullery downstairs and two bedrooms upstairs. The rest of the rooms were piled up with Mrs Apperley's things and ours, jumbled together. I was not supposed to go into them, but the temptation was too strong.

I had enjoyed the attics at Wenderton and this was better, far better. There was the organ in the dining room, which knocked my harmonium into a cocked hat. It had stops you could pull out, with words like "diapason," which altered the noise you made. I would pedal away and pretend to be Mr Knight. There was a violin in its case and then, in an upstairs room over the kitchen, I found a box of oil paints. This was a turning point in my life.

Before the first war, my father had known the East Kent painter, Dan Sherrin, a colourful figure who had anticipated the "happening" by half a century, with such gestures as installing himself in a coffin in a shop window in the middle of Canterbury or walking down the street shaking hands with people and slipping a kipper into their hand at the same time. My father's association with Sherrin had given him some notion of the technique of oil painting and this enabled me to make a start so that, at the end of the holidays, I took the box back to school and announced to Mr Stainer, the art master, that I did oil painting.

Mr Stainer was a dear, gentle man and instead of telling me to stop talking nonsense and join the class like everyone else, he put me in a corner with my oil paints and from time to time came to give me advice. For this I remain forever in his debt. My preferred subjects were stables with horses being groomed (no doubt inspired by the horse paintings at Frognal) and landscapes with cows. When the horses and cows got too difficult, Mr Stainer would do them for me. He never told me what to paint, only how to paint, leaving me to develop in my own way and above all helping me to gain confidence.

During the holidays I spent a lot of time painting and, one day seeing a postcard of Wingham, I decided to paint the village pub, the Red Lion, which stands at the top of the village street and is one of several similar constructions, originally part of a college of secular canons founded in 1282 by Archbishop Peckham. He intended it to become a university, but the project failed to prosper and after a chequered career, which included housing the magistrate's court, the building became a pub at the end of the eighteenth century. Picturesque, with leaded windows and a flight of stone steps leading up to a central massive oak front door, it was neither this, nor its unusual history, that constituted its fascination for me. Among the family tales great-uncle George had told me as he sat on my bed at Wenderton, had been that of one of the Minters who, in the 1850s had fallen down those same stone steps to his death.

Immensely impressed by this romantic end of an ancestor, I had asked my grandmother if it were true. She had confirmed it, adding that he could not have been drunk or he would have "fallen soft". The resulting painting was considered by everyone to be a success and Uncle John was so impressed he took it to the landlord and sold it to him for £5, a colossal sum in those days and much too big for me to be allowed to enjoy it, for I had the mortification of seeing it disappear immediately into my savings account. It was to be forty-two years before I sold another painting.

One day at about this time my father cleared his throat, went red in the face and said to me "You may perhaps have noticed that I had you circumcised" I admitted that it had come to my attention. In fact since I was eight I had regularly been in the showers naked with the other boys and we had long ago classed ourselves as cavaliers and roundheads. The reason was, he explained, "that when I was in the desert, the sand was a problem, so I thought like that you would be able to go in the desert whenever you wanted to". I thanked him.

A little later, it must have been the Easter holidays of 1944, one evening my mother seemed very anxious that he and I should go for a walk. Unusually reluctant, because he was a keen walker, he eventually agreed and we set out through the cherry orchards. He seemed ill at ease, and I gathered that he had been deputed to tell me the facts of life. His embarrassment was palpable and I waited all agog to hear what he had to tell me that I did not know already. It had been a major topic of discussion in the junior dormitory when I was nine, but when a boy had explained the principle of human sexual congress we had refused to believe it on the grounds that no one could imagine the King and Queen doing such a thing and they had two daughters. Now, as we continued our walk among the cherry trees, we came across a ewe in the middle of lambing. As we watched the lamb's struggles to emerge, my father said; "Well, there you see that's how it is, in any case I expect you know more about than I do" and, relieved and cheerful, he led the way home.

In fact all the Apps uncles were equally prudish. My cousin Christopher Apps told me that when his wife was pregnant with their first child and it began to show, each time she entered the room, his father would blush with embarrassment, Stuart was the uncle who had been in the trenches and lost a leg in the war.

Now that I was twelve, my father let me use his small-bore 4.10 shotgun, sometimes referred to as a 'garden gun'. I would sit for hours at my bedroom window waiting for a pigeon to perch in the monkey puzzle tree, or creep round the hedges in the evening to catch an unsuspecting rabbit out nibbling the grass. With food rationed, any rabbits or pigeons I managed to kill were a welcome addition to the larder.

Once the game season opened we sometimes went shooting with Mr Doubleday. On these occasions he regularly gave me a half-crown piece. At that time he was elected High Sheriff of Kent for the year, an honorary position, which includes among its duties that of sitting with the presiding judge at the County Assizes. I went to his house on the first morning to see him drive off in his court dress and sword.

Among the cases heard was a man tried for murder. Found guilty, he was condemned to be hanged. The High Sheriff was not obliged to be present at the execution. That was left to the Under Sheriff, a civil servant, but he was obliged to go to Maidstone prison the night before the execution, meet the hangman, look at the prisoner through a spy hole and watch a rehearsal where the hangman 'executed' a sack of the same weight as the prisoner to judge whether the drop would be sufficient to break his neck. The experience had a traumatic effect on Mr Doubleday; he did not sleep for nights. "It was," he said, "the casual way the hangman kicked the lever that released the trapdoor" that he couldn't get out of his mind.

My father had a reputation as a good shot and was consequently invited to other shoots. It was on one of these occasions that I shot a pheasant. Our party consisted of the owner of the estate, his two sons, both older than me and at Eton, and the gamekeeper. We were in a wood and the dogs went into a thicket, there was the whirring sound of a pheasant rocketing into the air, I took aim and just as it hesitated before changing direction, the keeper shouted, "Now!" I fired and the pheasant fell to the ground amidst general congratulations. I did not shoot another pheasant, nor did I see the two boys again; one became an opera singer and the other Governor of the Bank of England.

—

CHAPTER SEVEN

Going from the Junior School to the Senior School was not dissimilar from passing from this world to the next in so far as many people one had known had made the journey but none had returned to tell the tale. There were differences of course, for while in the latter case sightings are rare, we could see our departed almost daily across the road. But the frustration remained the same and there lurked the nasty suspicion that if they, like the ghost of Hamlet's father, were able to speak about their situation they "could a tale unfold whose slightest word would harrow up our souls and freeze our young blood."

Happily, the Senior School turned out to be far more agreeable than the Junior, at least as far as I was concerned. In my first letter home dated 20th January 1945, I am able to reassure my mother that:

"I am getting on very well. We have done some lessons and I have got on O.K. The food is pretty foul compared with Junior School but it is edible and I have not died yet!! Otherwise I really prefer this place to the Junior School...... We have a frightful form room in an old garage as cold as hell is hot: brrrruh!! But I put on my coat and it wasn't too bad. It seems I may go to a higher form for Latin but I doubt it as I am not good enough".

We come home on March 23rd, 9 weeks 2 days. What a term!

"If you have a kitchen knife & fork & spoon please send as they are all rusty and dirty here......I unpacked and got out my suit. It is in good condition and I put it straight on a hanger, so it ought to be O.K. We arrived at school at 7.30 p.m. after the worst journey I was terribly bored and the carriage was FILTHY."

A second letter written two days later says:

"I have quite settled in and am very happy. The atmosphere here is very nice and friendly... The only thing that is wrong is that my classroom is outdoors and is just like an ice-well. So would you please send me a nice big warm scarf no matter what colour! Now here is a "Strange but True" (like you have in the Sunday paper).

There was actually a heavy fall of snow on Friday night and on Saturday there was about 3 inches of snow on the ground and it is still with us!!! If that doesn't beat the band what does?

I do not find that I get so tired here as I did in the Junior School. We had some fun on Saturday. There is a nasty master who takes German and looks like one! His name is Mr Minns. Well this bloke was taking a class in the garage which had a bust window so someone got the bright idea and chucked a snowball in through the window. Well! Old Minns came out shaking his fist and cursing and as soon as he appeared 5 more snowballs hit him on his face, neck and body and all his form cheered and he went purple in the face (you'd have roared!) then he went back and more balls came through the window and at the end of the period when he came out he had to pretty well run to the school and was pelted the whole way.

Well cheerio and don't worry as I'm getting on fine. Love from Teddy;"

Poor Mr Minns was one of those unfortunate teachers who cannot discipline a class. As a result classes tended to get out of hand – on one occasion a boy set fire to his desk – at which Mr Minns would panic and hand out punishments that were out of all proportion. For this he was generally disliked and the boys were not slow to take revenge. At the end of one term, a group of them opened the revolving doors at the main entrance to the hotel and carried his car up the entrance steps into the hall, closing the doors after them. How Mr Minns recovered his car we never knew.

He was in fact a gentle, mild man, congenitally absent-minded. He used to lunch daily in a restaurant in St Austell. One day he got back to school and realised he had forgotten his hat. Returning to the restaurant, the manager told him that there were several in the backroom and suggested he go and find it. Mr Minns emerged some minutes later saying that they were all his.

Another of the King's School's masters, Mr Harris, invited him and his wife to lunch. A few weeks later, Minns went up to Harris in the master's common room and said that he and Mrs Minns would be pleased if Mr and Mrs Harris would lunch with them the following Saturday, adding "and do bring your children"

"But, Minns," said Harris, "we don't have any children."

"Then whose were those when we lunched with you the other day?"

"They were yours."

Writing on the 4th February 1945,

"Thanks very much for parcel containing pears (very nice) butter, cheese (jolly good) and last but not least a cake!! They gave me a uniform on Thursday it is quite a good fit but mighty uncomfortable! We had to go for a four mile run the other day gosh! It was a fag!!"

After explaining how I had been talking with "Mr Stainer (my art master)" about Kent I had discovered that he knew a friend of my parents, I continued;

"I am study fagging this week, I've got to get up at 7.0 a.m. and sweep out the monitor's study and clean his shoes and tidy up the place it's a bit grim but you've got to take the rough with the smooth and I prefer the senior to the junior school"

On the 26th of the same month;

"I have done quite a nice painting this term it is of a farm but quite a different kind to my last and it has a lovely Hereford (underlined) with a white face plumb in the foreground... Jones' sisters have come up to scratch over the senior school and he gets a lot of cakes and so I give him some of mine and he gives me some so when you don't send any I still get some! I had a bit of sport today (Sunday.) I went to Charlestown in the afternoon and coming back (about 2.30) I saw a bloke setting some nets and he had a 4.10. Well you know me. I went up to him and asked him if he was doing a bit of ferreting he said he was, so

I had a look at his gun – it was a poacher gun just like mine. Anyhow, he is an awfully nice bloke and I went ferreting with him and we got a rabbit (he shot it) I thoroughly enjoyed it. Please will you go into my room and you will see a picture of some partridges at sunset. Take it out of its frame and take out the glass and send the frame to me!! as I have done a portrait of old Bess and send some tacks with it. Now please don't forget! I received a cake!! Thank you and a bag of sweets which was awfully kind of you. They don't seem to have found my clothes yet. I like this place much better than the Junior School we are so nice and free."

"Old Bess" was my father's liver-and-white Springer Spaniel.

The Carlyon Bay Hotel was much bigger than the Bayfordbury, but here again the King's School, having got there first, had secured all the best parts of the building so that our dormitories were again in the servants' quarters on the top floor. Only the monitors and the sixth form had studies, the rest of us lived in the houseroom. The St Edmund's houseroom (St Edmund's counting numerically for no more than a single house) was in the billiard-room, a semi-annexe with a flat roof attached to the front of the building. It had a small anteroom, which served as a locker room through which one passed on to the dais at the entrance before stepping down into the well of the room where the billiard table had presumably stood. Our desks were arranged round the perimeter of this lower part of the room.

The tone of the houseroom was set by an easy-going, tall fair-haired, untidy boy called Potts who had a passion for wild life and in particular falcons and falconry. Potts must have been about sixteen or seventeen at the time, old to still be in the houseroom, and only kept there by his lack of academic achievement. However he made up for this by all sorts of unexpected skills. One of these was farting. He would regularly enter the houseroom on a fart, which without, as it were, drawing breath would continue at the same intensity until he reached his desk in the far corner of the room. Much admired and attempted by many yet equalled by none, his talent was remarkable.

Had he wished he could in all probability have made a career on the music-hall stage to rival that of the celebrated French artist, *Le Pétomane*, but he decided perhaps wisely to follow his father into the army where he was mentioned in dispatches in Korea in 1951 and retired with the rank of Major.

I liked Potts and we got on well both being from the same sort of background and having similar interests in country pursuits.

The summer term was our last in Cornwall and the high spot of my schooldays.

Writing after my birthday (May 14th);

"Wasn't it nice to be able to speak over the telephone? I had a lovely birthday..... I found a magpie's nest."

I was a keen egg-collector;

"I've got three seagulls this term, also I have my eyes on a whitethroat and wood wren. I missed a thrush. I may (mark the fact I say may) take a jackdaw from his nest and try to bring him up. The tennis and fishing are going fine (no catches yet)."

I remember fishing but cannot imagine that at any time in my life I played tennis.

On June 6th;

"I received "The Gamekeeper" and Kent paper, thanks awfully, I like reading about what is happening... It was a real treat to have some real milk chocolate... I got a magpie last Sunday, he was a fine fellow and I kept him out in an out-house (nobody knew about him) but as luck would have it I went out there on Monday and there had been rain and he was standing in 3" of water. Well, I dried him and he seemed alright and by Tuesday he looked O.K. so I gave him his first lesson in perching. He sat on my hand and got quite tame. But I went back on Wednesday and he was dead."

The major event of the term was that I made a new friend, Sherlock. He was at the King's School, a couple of years older than me he had a slightly sulphurous reputation, the cause of which I never discovered. Slim and dark with black eyes and hair he seemed to exude danger and I fell completely under his spell. Friendships between the schools were frowned on, but I didn't care. With Sherlock life became more exciting.

I don't remember how we met, perhaps in the art class where he spent hours making careful copies of seventeenth century Dutch landscapes. We discovered that we were both interested in falconry and decided to find a kestrel's nest and rear a couple and train them. Behind the Bayfordbury hotel lay a pine forest known as Crinnis woods and there we located a nest with several young. I broke the news to my parents on June 12th;

"I am doing rather well with birds. I know of 5 kestrel's nests, 1 buzzard and 1 sparrow hawk. I may (with a big 'M') be keeping a hawk! Anyhow a friend of mine (a boy in King's) is and I am going to help him look after it. Please could you get a little box and go to the potting shed and get 3 mole traps and 3 gins (you will find the gins in the garage on top of a white cupboard I will bring them back!!"

On the 25th June it was;

"My friend in King's and I have known for 5 weeks about a kestrel's nest in an old ruin. It was about 30 feet up, well this bloke, as far as climbing is concerned, has no nerves at all. He will go anywhere. Well, we got two poles and strapped them together and we got up to the nest, at least I say we, I mean he did. He is about the best climber in both schools. Well, we have not told a soul of what we knew and this afternoon we told Potts who is the hawk expert. He came with us. There were 4 in the nest. I have one, my friend has one and Mount has one. I would be pleased if you would send 3 or 4 preferably 4 gins and 3 or 4 mole traps. THIS IS URGENT AS IT MAY MEAN LIFE OF DEATH TO MY BIRD. Please send"

The last letter is addressed to my Father from The Carlyon Bay Hotel 27th June 1945;

"Dear Daddy, You have heard from my last letter all about my Kestrel. He is a little topper. I think I shall call him "Thunderbolt". I expect you know all about kestrels, they are the hawks which are well known for their hovering. At the moment he is just a little ball of fluff, like a little goose except for a pronounced hawk beak. I am having rather a job to feed him. We have got 4 break-backs (you know, they are like over grown mouse traps) we have 3 gins, 32 snares and 1 mouse trap. On Monday morning we got up and found a massive rat in one gin, in the course of the day we got another rat, 2 small robins and some tits that was just enough. On Tuesday we got 1 very small mouse, oh dear, anyhow Sherlock, that is the name of my friend, went and got some young gulls which we fed them on, in the course of the day we got a rat. They are very fierce (I mean the birds) but they eat themselves and we do not have to stuff it down their throats. I hope I am not boring you about them, but I thought you might be interested. It is rather interesting as a coincidence that we saw the haggard (parent bird) wearing jesses and we find that it is one a boy tried to tame 2 years ago but it got away, isn't that funny!!

Prepare for the shock (this is heavily underlined)

I am bringing my bird HOME IF it lives. I shall be able to feed it with stuff caught in the garden and with luck I may be able to teach it falconry. We had a boy here last year who got a sparrow-hawk to kill partridges at 400 yards.

You will not be the only person who has to face a shock; Michael Mount intends to bring his back too. IF they live. I hope you have sent off the gins and mole traps!!!

Potts, the boy who I sold the cartridges to, has been an absolute brick he is helping me with food and has an air gun. He is actually keeping two hawks, a kestrel and a sparrow hawk, he is about the best falconer we have.

By the way I met my friend with the ferret on Sunday he has offered to shoot me rabbits for Thunderbolt if I get the cartridges so if you could pack up a few I would be grateful as it would help matters considerably (4.10 bore) love from Teddy".

Potts had an air-gun at the school which was as against the rules as were most of his activities; this he kindly lent me and I remember keeping it under my mattress, getting up at 5 a.m., creeping out with it through the hotel kitchens and going down to the beach to shoot seagulls and anything that might appeal to young kestrels, then creeping back before the rising bell.

The last correspondence from Cornwall is a postcard. The postmark is obscured but it must have been early July.

"Carlyon Bay Hotel St Austell, My dear Mummy, I do not know what part of the train I shall be in on Monday. So you had better wait up by the Engine as I shall have my Gladstone bag + kestrel and I shall not travel very fast, so don't bring any baggage as you'll be required to carry bag".

"Nutty" as he was eventually called, proved a great success. I had made him a hood and he had jesses, leather throngs that are attached to the legs of hawks which are in turn attached to a lead when he is sitting on the gloved fist (a thick leather glove is necessary for, while the beaks of hawks look ferocious, they kill with their talons). I taught him to fly and return to the lure (a bunch of feathers attached to a leather thong which I whirled round my head while at the same time whistling to attract him) and we were inseparable throughout the long summer holidays. I was just beginning to wonder what to do with him when I had to go back to school, when the tragedy occurred; Nutty suddenly flew off while still attached to his lead and was last seen flying with the lead trailing below him over the cherry orchards. The cherry trees were still in leaf and although I spent my days searching, I could not find him. When the leaves fell that autumn, the gamekeeper found the remains of Nutty hanging upside down attached to a branch by his lead.

CHAPTER EIGHT

—

Returning to the neo-Gothic flint of Canterbury (in spite of adult insistence that we were "lucky to be home") was like a cold shower. Worse, for among the school tradition gratefully left behind in 1940 and now being revived, was The Early Morning Bathe.

This unwelcome rite involved the newly demobbed Sergeant Major O'Leary ringing a hand-bell at seven o'clock in the morning, whereupon we had to put on slippers and dressing gowns, descend the two flights of stone stairs, cross the open courtyard and go into a shed containing the swimming bath. There, in musty cabins, we stripped naked while the veteran roared, "Two lengths this morning!" and saw that no one escaped.

When it is remembered that St Edmund's School is built on the crest of the hill which overlooks Canterbury from the West, facing across East Kent to the North Sea and the plains of Northern France (the Geography Master was often heard to say that there was nothing between us and the Urals), readers may judge for themselves how enjoyable that swim was on a January morning.

It was said that the tradition had been in existence for over seventy years and that it originated in a wish to discourage unhealthy sexual desires among adolescent boys. In this it was, in my experience, totally successful – at least until lunchtime when life began to return to our loins.

During the war numbers had dwindled – the younger clergy serving in the armed forces were no doubt having their lives prolonged by better food and housing. In any case at the return to Canterbury we numbered only twenty-six in the Senior School and although certain of us had been there before the war, none had been in the senior school. This meant that the traditional minefield of 'dos' and 'don'ts' that make the public school boy's life a burden and prepare him for English social life had to be recreated and the monitors and others of a conservative turn of mind set about the task with enthusiasm. For those of us who had enjoyed the anarchy of Cornwall, shades of the prison house were indeed surrounding the growing boy. Moreover, as The Rev. F.S. Williams wanted to return to retirement, there was also a new headmaster.

From the school's foundation the post had always been filled by clergymen, but the governors now decided to break with this tradition and appoint a layman, their choice falling on a master at Blundells, Mr W.M. Thoseby.

We had first seen him when he was presented to us in the houseroom in Cornwall by the Rev F.S. Williams and all of us had been struck by his uncanny resemblance to Tommy Handley, the star of the very popular radio comedy show, "Itma", which we sometimes managed to listen to after Lights Out under the bedclothes on home-made cat's whisker and crystal sets. Later we were to discover that Mr Thoseby was comic without being funny.

In 1940 all the young masters had been called up so that during the war we had become used to being taught by masters over forty and some considerably older. An elderly Colonel who was almost deaf and nearly blind had coached us in Latin in the Junior School. Coaching took place in his room where he seemed to be perpetually making tea on a primus stove. Our chief amusement had been to pop sacharrin tablets (used at that time to replace sugar which was rationed) down the spout of the kettle when he wasn't looking. The Colonel detested sweet tea and his expression of disgust and puzzlement each time he sipped another cup of inexplicably sweetened tea, gave us endless pleasure. He had previously taught at Repton and a boy from there assured me that during a lesson someone had cooked a kipper on a primus stove at the back of the class without the Colonel noticing.

Although we had returned from Cornwall with few beds and fewer pupils, we had only lost one master to the King's School. The four pillars of the school, all of whom had been there longer than anyone could remember, had all stuck with it. They were a remarkable quartet.

All of them spent their entire professional lives teaching at St Edmund's and they certainly did not do so with an idea of becoming rich. The sense of vocation was very strong in those days. Apart from Carol Powers, there was Walter Stephen-Jones, known as *"the Buffer"* who taught the classics and whose hawk-like appearance and ferocious manner belied a gentle naturalist, the kindest of men. Giles Kedge, who taught maths and science and was rarely seen out of the lab. Finally there was G.P. Hollingworth, known as *"Holly"* or *"The Man"*, who taught English and French and produced the school plays.

While I was still in the Junior School, he had produced "Macbeth" from a mixed cast of King's and St Edmund's. A stage had been erected in the garage/chapel/lecture hall and we had formed part of the audience. I had found it absolutely thrilling, especially the last scene when the two sixth-form rugger-playing heavyweights clashed swords together.

During my two terms in the Senior School in Cornwall, I did not have any contact with him, but once back at Canterbury I met him for the first time when he took us for English. In his early forties, stocky, good looking with a high colour, prematurely grey, untidily dressed and wearing a tattered gown apparently made up entirely of patches and repairs with which he cleaned the blackboard, he exuded energy. Holly had charisma and I fell totally under his spell.

The first school play we did was Oscar Wilde's "The Importance of Being Earnest and I was cast as Canon Chasuble. Holly had produced it in the early 30s, when Michael Goodliffe, who was now a successful West-end actor, had played the part of Jack. I had seen him playing Banquo to Michael Redgrave's Macbeth. He had been taken prisoner at Dunkirk and had organised plays in the prison camp, notably a production of Hamlet, in which he played the Dane, which had been widely reported in the English press. He came to Canterbury to talk to us about his experiences and I remember his saying how he had detested people trying to escape because the first thing the Germans did was shut down the theatre.

I was very excited at the thought of being produced by Holly after all I had heard about him and I was not disappointed. He could conjure up the essence of a character or the purpose of any particular scene in a way that showed you immediately how it should be played.

He taught us how to pick up cues, the importance of pace, how to wait for laughs: all the rudiments of stagecraft. Playing a clergyman at St Edmund's meant that I had a great deal of professional advice to fall back on. The chaplain took a great interest in my costumes and even lent me his clerical evening dress. The play was deemed a success and the notice in the school magazine, written by the Headmaster, when speaking of the performances began

"Apps must become a bishop".

Now that we were back in Kent it meant that I could go home between chapel services on Sundays and at half term, something that had been impossible while we were in Cornwall. Unfortunately this privilege did not last long, because after one term my father's job came to an end. Relations between him and Mr Doubleday had deteriorated. Years later my Father told me that the problem had been brought to a head by Mr Doubleday asking him to put his name to some accounts for the Inland Revenue which were incorrect. My father refused and pointed out that as Mr Doubleday was a Commissioner of Inland Revenue, he should not have suggested it. After this it was only a matter of time before he was asked to leave. The excuse was that Mr Doubleday's son was returning from the war so he was no longer needed. Added to this, Mrs Apperley wanted her house back. Something had to be done and done quickly.

The Government had decided to revalue all properties in the British Isles for tax purposes and as a result the Inland Revenue was looking for Valuers. My father applied and was posted to Gloucester as assistant to the District Valuer. Houses to rent were very difficult to find in the period just after the war and it was sometime before anything suitable could be found. In the meantime my father was living in digs in Gloucester and my mother under siege in the Old Vicarage. Mr Doubleday brought a court action against my father to evict him in which he described him as a farm bailiff, a small reckoning of accounts for which he had to pay by five uncomfortable minutes in the witness box when he was cross examined by Mr Mowll, my father's solicitor.

My mother told me all this in the kitchen at the Old Vicarage the evening of my return from School at the end of the term. She was clearly upset by it and for me, aged fourteen, that anyone could describe my father, as a farm bailiff was devastating. Already unstable socially as a result of the family quarrel, our move and the ever-widening gap between the standard of living of my parents and that of the rest of the family, I felt I had to do something to repair the family honour. I had just had a success with a sketch I had written and produced at school and it was then and there that I decided I would be an actor.

At last my father found a house and my parents moved there. So, at the end of the Easter term 1946 I went to stay with Yaya and one morning, we got into the baby Austin, she lit a cigarette, pulled on the sheep's wool backed gauntlets, opened the window and we set out for Gloucester. It was a long drive and we did not arrive until late in the afternoon. When we found it, Alexandra Road, was a road of late Edwardian redbrick houses. No 21 was semi-detached, with a small front garden behind a privet hedge. I looked at it in consternation "Is that our home?"

Yaya nodded. "You have to go where your bread and butter is" she said. My father had heard the car and came out into the street to greet us. He saw my face and looked defensive.

Something about him had changed; I noticed he had a new watchstrap.

My mother welcomed us at the door and began saying at once what a lovely house it was. I sensed immediately that she was worried that my father might think she was not grateful to him for having found us a home. We went in. The house was decorated through-out with dark brown paint and lugubrious Victorian-style wallpaper with a motive of unidentifiable flowers. The front door had two stained-glass panels, and the bay window of the living room had a stained-glass surround. Two narrow windows each side of the dark brown painted fireplace were also filled with stained glass. The stair-case faced the front door and the passage, tiled with heavily decorated tiles, led to the dining room, which overlooked a small walled garden with a garage at the end. A door opposite the stairs led to the kitchen quarters. Upstairs there were two main bedrooms, the one at the front of the house having a dressing room, and another smaller bedroom and bathroom with a separate lavatory. Another staircase led to the floor above where there was a large room and two smaller ones.

Any reasonable person would have found 21 Alexandra Road a pleasant house in a nice street where the neighbours were all from the professional classes; barristers, solicitors, architects, engineers. To me it was quite simply a prison, a morgue, a tomb. How could one live surrounded by red brick and tarmac, without trees, or fields, not an animal in sight, no cows, no sheep, no pony and no gun? What was the point of having a holiday if one had to spend it in such a place?

For the time being we occupied ourselves with arranging our furniture and hanging pictures with the help of Yaya, who did all she could to keep our spirits up.

Gradually we began to make the rooms look less gloomy, but our country-house furniture and hunting and racing prints looked out of place in such an urban setting. The four years at the Vicarage had shielded us from the truth that was now staring us in the face. We had come down in the world.

My parents had met the neighbours in the adjoining house; Jimmy Taylor, a Scotsman, was the county vet. They had four sons, my parents said, so I would have someone of my own age. We met, but they were all rugger enthusiasts and the current did not pass between us. I mooned about, reading and painting until it was time to return to school.

Now that my parents were in Gloucester, I would occasionally take the bus out to Guilton on Sundays. Uncle John had married. My mother had received an invitation, but as it did not include my father, she declined it. Uncle John and his bride were living temporarily at Heart's Delight before moving to Wenderton. After we had left, the house had been let to Admiral Sir Dudley Pound, the First Sea Lord. He did not spend much time there but his son and daughter-in-law did. His son was in the Navy and away in his ship when Billy Sheaff went excitedly to Uncle John one day and announced that Mrs Pound had got a 'fancy man', "saw him coming out of the house early in the morning, big chap with a beard". Great was his disappointment when it was discovered that the 'fancy man' was her husband who had grown a beard while he was afloat.

These Sundays spent with my grandparents followed the same routine. As I got off the bus, my grandmother would be at the front gate looking out for me, upright and elegant, still with her hair put up in the Edwardian style. "Hullo Lad!" I was always 'Lad' while Uncle John was 'Boy'. She led me into the hall with its shining copper and brass, richly coloured Afghan rugs and the staircase with the collection of Swiss cowbells hanging along its length that rang if you touched them with your shoulder.

It was much later that I was to learn the origin of the cowbells. In the twenties, my grandfather's drinking had become an acute problem and as my grandmother had always insisted that no drink was kept in the house, he would disappear for several days and would be found eventually in the back parlour of a village pub, in an advanced state of alcoholic decay. Smuggling him back to the house and explaining his absence became increasingly difficult and finally my father suggested that it would be perhaps be wiser to keep drink in the cellar. This worked except for the fact that my grandfather would get up in the night and creep down to the cellar where he would be found the next morning in the same state. It was then that my grandmother got the idea of the cowbells, which would sound as soon as he brushed against them. With his great bulk there would seem to be little chance that he could ever navigate past the bells in the dark, yet, it seems that, with the cunning of the true alcoholic, he devised a way and managed occasionally to get to the cellar unhindered and to be found there the next morning.

Once in the hall, my grandmother would say, "Go and see your grandfather while I get lunch," opening the door of the lounge and ushering me in. As she did so I was greeted by the overwhelming smell of pipe and cigar smoke. There, reclining in a massive, worn leather armchair was the tweed-encased bulk of my grandfather. He looked at me, his beady eyes glinting over his gold-rimmed spectacles.

"Well, what have you got to say for yourself?" I explained that I was back at school after the holidays. He asked after my mother but not, of course, my father, and went on to tell me how he had been to Richborough where he owned grazing land, to see his cattle. They were doing well, he assured me. After that, conversation flagged.

I looked for a topic and saw the picture on the wall behind him, a large framed painting of a huntsman with a pack of hounds. I asked him about it, "I knew every one of those hounds by name," he said, "No five-barred gate ever stopped me."

Again, conversation flagged until my grandmother announced that lunch was ready.

He rose with difficulty and shuffled out of the room. He had been ill in 1942 and had heard of a miraculous cure offered at Ruthin Castle in North Wales. When he had suggested to his doctor that it might be the solution, the reply had been; "If you go there, Arthur, you'll come home in your box." Nevertheless he decided to go. Petrol rationing precluded going by car, so Uncle John took him to London and put him on the train. Changing trains at Crewe, he felt too weak to walk and persuaded the porter to let him sit on the front of his trolley. The cortege did not pass unnoticed and the rumour began to circulate that the cherubic-looking old gentleman sitting on the trolley with a cigar was Mr Churchill. People began applauding and my grandfather, never at a loss, gave them the "V" sign to more applause.

The cure had been a success and he returned to his former life and business, although limiting his intake of Johnny Walker to half a bottle a day. Now, however, it was 1946 and, as he shuffled out of the room, it was clear that his riding days and drinking days were over. At 74 he was looking every day of his age.

Lunch was in the breakfast room. The dining room was hardly ever used now and, it being Sunday, there was no Esme. We sat at a round oak gate-legged table on tall-backed rush-seated chairs. Below the window we could see his cattle in the yard. My grandfather carved at the sideboard. The vegetables were on the table in blue and white willow-pattern dishes. My grandparents hardly spoke during the meal. He sat, craning forward with lowered head in an effort to convey the food from the plate to his mouth across the expanse of his stomach without dropping it. She sat bolt upright and watched him with an expression that did not suggest indulgence. If, as frequently happened, a morsel fell on his waistcoat, there would be a sharp intake of breath from my grandmother and a muttered apology from him as he hastily tried to repair the damage with his napkin. If they did speak, they addressed each other as "Mother" and "Father".

At the end of the meal he thanked her courteously and, taking his coffee cup and saucer in a none-too-steady hand, shuffled back to the lounge. I sensed that I was witnessing the last round in a match – or rather a mismatch – that had lasted since their marriage in 1903 and that Granny had got him on the ropes.

Alone, my grandmother seemed to relax. I chatted away and she listened benignly. Her brothers and sisters, her children and her servants had found her a difficult woman, but, to me, her grandson, she was everything a grandmother should be. She had wanted me to be a musician, had paid for me to have piano lessons but it had become clear that I had no talent. I was interested in painting and she was as enthusiastic as I was. She had an account at Goulden's the stationers, in Canterbury. I was to go and buy the oil paints and canvases I needed. She went further and, in an antique shop, found a tin canister full of brushes.

For my birthday she told me to go to Goulden's and buy an easel. "Buy a good one!" I went; there were two, one was evidently better than the other, but more expensive. I hesitated, and not wanting to abuse her generosity, I settled for the second. I still have it today. It has never been wholly satisfactory and I have often regretted that I did not take her at her word and buy the good one. The reason was, of course the family quarrel that meant that however kind she, or anyone in the family were, I viewed them all with a sense of reserve, hearing my Father say, as he frequently did, "God gives you your relations, luckily you can choose your friends," or "If you are in difficulty, never, never, ask help from the family."

When it was time to go, my grandmother would send me into

the lounge to say goodbye to my grandfather. It was the moment I dreaded.

"I've come to say goodbye, Grandfather."

He would look up from his book and the glasses would glint.

"I suppose you want some pocket money?" He would say without enthusiasm, then, sighing and with evident reluctance he would put his hand in his pocket and take out some coins, choose one and hand it to me. "Here."

Deeply embarrassed, I would take the coin, thank him and make my escape. But it was not over; for once out of the room; my grandmother would ask what he had given me. I would show her and if she considered it insufficient, she would, against my protests, go into the room and tell him it was not enough. He would grumble, his hand would go back into his pocket, the coins would be brought out and another handed to me with even greater reluctance. "All right, all right, here then" More embarrassed than ever I took the coin, thanked him and escaped, my grandmother coming with me to the bus stop.

On one occasion we missed the bus. I can't remember why, probably my grandfather took longer than usual pulling the coins out of his pocket.

I was in a panic; to be late for roll call on a Sunday evening was unthinkable.

The chauffeur lived in Sandwich and did not work on Sundays, so my grandmother went across the road to the cottage where George Davidson, the farm mechanic lived and persuaded him to leave his tea and drive me back to school. He was a big, kindly Yorkshireman with a large black moustache who had worked for my grandfather for over thirty years. Davidson was thorough and did everything with deliberation – including driving.

"Oh, hurry, Davidson, do hurry", I cried in anguish as the Hillman lumbered slowly along.

"Going as fast as I can," was the only reply I got. We just made it and I slipped into the hall as my name was called, "Apps?" "Adsum" I shouted, sweating with relief.

Some weekends I would go and see Yaya and OK. They had moved from Headcorn back to Thanet, where OK was working his family's farm for his mother. Yaya had rented a small cottage called "The Studio" standing in the middle of a meadow. Built in the thirties by a lady artist, it had a vaguely bohemian air that perfectly suited their *ménage*. These Sundays were a whole lot more fun than those at Guilton.

In the summer term we were allowed to have our bicycles at school and I took to cycling to Guilton rather than taking the bus. On one of these occasions, as I went through Littlebourne, I met great uncle George driving through the village. As usual the hood of his car was down; great uncle George believed in fresh air (at Frognal, windows and door were left permanently open) if it were cold, he would simply put a second overcoat over his first and wrap a rug round his knees, driving exactly as he had in a horse and trap. He seemed pleased to see me "Are you coming to see us?" he asked, smiling. When I said I was going to see his sister, he stopped smiling, "Hope you enjoy youself", he said and drove off.

Relations between my grandmother and her brothers and sisters had dropped to a new low due to a recent bequest they had received: The father of William Minter of Newplace Ickham, (the racehorse breeder), himself another William Minter, had married Sarah Wraith, the aunt of two brothers, John and Samuel Wraith who lived in Canterbury. They had a prosperous business and owned property and farms. Neither of them had children, so when they died in the 1850s, they left a trust for their Wraith descendents. The last of these, an old unmarried lady living in Eastbourne, had recently died and it was discovered that the brothers had named Edward Goodson (1805-1878), my grandmother's grandfather, as the eventual heir. Thus my grandmother, great uncle George, great uncle Frank and Ya-ya, as his surviving descendants, were informed that the money was to be divided beween them. But as usual, my grandmother began to make difficulties, as she had over the division of the furniture. This caused the solicitors to go more deeply into the matter where they discovered that the Edward Goodson in question was not their grandfather (born 1805), but their great grandfather (born 1773), who was also called William. This meant that the money had to be shared with the brothers and sisters of their grandfather and their descendents, of whom there were a surprising number, which considerably reduced the sum – a fact that did nothing to endear my grandmother to her siblings.

On another occasion, cycling through Wingham village, I decided to branch left up Preston Hill – rather than continue on the turnpike road to Ash – and go and look at Wenderton. My grandfather had bought the farm from the Marquis of Conyngham at the end of the war. The house was empty Uncle John and Aunty Betty had not yet moved in. It was difficult to see much from the lane because of the yew hedge, so I went round to the farmyard. As it was Sunday, there was no one about so I went into the barn from where, across the stockyard, I could see the kitchen and the window of my nursery. Suddenly memories flooded back, I felt like Mole in "The Wind in the Willows" returning to his old home. For there, with the house, lay my childhood, my identity, the days when I was "Master Teddy" and my future lay clearly traced before me. As I looked across at the familiar windows, I asked myself the question – if I were no longer "Master Teddy" who was I and what was my future? It was a question for which I could find no immediate answer.

*

The move to Gloucester and the fact of no longer living in the country meant that my interests and values were of necessity ceasing to be those of a country boy. It did not happen overnight. At school I continued to go fishing, collecting bird's eggs and trying unsuccessfully to bring up jackdaws. But gradually painting, the theatre, acting and writing and producing sketches for the revues that we put on regularly, together with reading, took up more and more of my interest, particularly acting; I began to read the lives of famous actors and the history of the theatre. My friends changed too. Jones who had been my bosom friend from the junior school ceased to be so,

Rhodes, who had always been a friend became even more of one. We found that we had much in common; we detested organised games, enjoyed walking and talking and had long conversations on all sorts of subjects on these walks. Tall and thin, with big feet and hands, he would stride along with his head thrown back and I would struggle to keep up. His grandfather had a parish in Norfolk and while we were in the junior school, he had played the organ for services during the holidays. "What hymns did you play? I asked. "Oh, "Ub", he replied. What's "Ub" I asked. "You know "Ub- ide with me" he replied. He was himself destined for the church.

We now had studies that we shared with three other boys. Rhodes was in the study next to mine. There were two gas rings and some primitive cooking equipment at the end of the study corridor and we both took up cooking with enthusiasm.

We were joined by a new boy who was our age but had only just arrived at the school, Paul Balmforth whose father, a clergyman in Worcester, had only recently died with the result that Paul had been taken away from the Worcester Grammar School and sent to Canterbury. The three of us got on well, the only difference being that Balmforth played cricket. He was a big, fat ungainly figure, not at all what one imagines a cricketer to be, but he was a redoubtable bowler. He would lumber up to the crease, stop dead and swing his arm over his head like the sail of a windmill, the ball would streak down the field as though it had been fired from a cannon and woe betide anyone who got in its way. The St Edmund's cricket team used him as a sort of secret weapon and their successes greatly increasing with his presence.

One Sunday in 1946 I had made an attempt to cycle to Smallhythe, the village beside Tenterden, to see Ellen Terry's house which had become a museum, but it proved to be too far and I had to turn back so as not to be late for roll-call. At the end of June 1947 I made another attempt. This time I did not go alone:

"On Sunday I had another shot to get to Smallhythe. Well one bloke had two punctures before we got the other side of Canterbury and when we got out of Canterbury I started having them and we got to Chilham and I have got one I can't mend so we had to come home. I think I shall have to get a new inner tube. They are only 3/1d and I've had this one for seven years, at present it looks like a patchwork quilt! I'd like to go by bus but it costs about 5/-."

I continued;

"I'm having a lovely term. The time is flying. They say that schooldays are the happiest time of your life – and if I'm ever as happy again I shall be very agreeably surprised".

The chief reason for this was that I had found an ally and friend in Mr Hollingworth. At the end of May I had written:

"I was up in the masters' wing last night and Hollingworth met me and asked if I could spare a minute and he took me into his room and showed me all his books on production and acting and told me I could borrow any I liked so I'm most excited as he's got some smashing books"

P.S. I'm working HARD!

And on the 17th June;

In the evening I went up to see Mr Hollingworth to change my book and we got talking – he is in the Canterbury Drama Festival in the Cathedral. They have it every year. This year it's called "Peasant's Priest" (it has been specially written) and he's playing the Earl of Kent, a big part. While talking I told him I'd only ever been in the Chapter House once and that was to see "Pilgrim's Progress" (you remember with Miss Elgars) and he told me he was the bloke who played Christian (the lead) – rather interesting. I told him how it inspired me to put on Dad's boots- and walk round the kitchen table with a sack on my back aged 6."

"The Peasant's Priest" by Laurie Lee, the Gloucestershire poet, was about John Ball, who led the Kentish Peasant's Revolt in the MiddleAges. Bernard Miles played the part of John Ball and I remember him, an impressive figure, with his strong Hertfordshire accent proclaiming,

When Adam delved

And Eve Span,
Who was then the gentleman?

Writing on the 25th June, I again assure my parents that I am working hard, adding that I nearly know Macbeth by heart
     "and what I don't know about the perishing Acts of the Apostles and St Mark isn't worth knowing!!!"
Then;
     "Oh you'll never guess, The Rev. Mr Stapley is getting married. Sister told me a fortnight ago. I've never laughed so much. So is Dr Kahn!! Honestly! We heard a rumour and I was laughing and telling Ball before a period when in came Mr Hollingworth to take the period so I went and sat down – still laughing and he looked at me and smiling asked what the Joke was – so of course I laughed all the more and said "Nothing, Sir" Then he made a remark about it being strange to laugh at nothing, so I said "Well, sir, we've just heard that Dr Kahn is getting married!" With that everyone howled with laughter and old Hollingworth (grinning away) asked if I saw any reason for ribald mirth in it and that it was true. (That was on Saturday) so yesterday when we were starting German, and old Khan had picked up his book to begin, I stood up and said;
     "Sir, I should like to take this opportunity, on behalf of the form, to congratulate you and wish you every happiness in your new venture". Old Khan went as red as a cricket ball and bowed and smiled. You'd have howled if you'd been there."

Mr Stapley who was the acting chaplain, was in fact the chaplain to St Augustine's Theological College where his future bride was a deaconess. In his fifties, he was kind to me and lent me his bike from time to time. On one occasion I had tea with them both at St Augustine's. The news had been announced of a new ecclesiastical appointment, and they were eagerly looking up the newcomer in Crockford's, the Church Registry. It was the first time I had been privy to a conversation among church professionals and it fascinated me.

Henry James famously wrote that; "the minimum of valid suggestion serves the man of imagination better than the maximum" by which he meant, as he explained, that someone walking past St James Palace and catching a glimpse through the open window of the Guards officers relaxing and hearing snatches of their conversation, would be in a better position to write a novel about their life than were he to spend several years in the Guards. My tea with the chaplain and the deaconess was a copybook example of the truth of this theory, for years later, writing "All Gas and Gaiters", the memory of it was always at the back of my mind as a reference.

Dr Kahn, the gentle, ex-professor of Heidelberg University, who had narrowly escaped from the Nazis, was our German master. He was a cultivated, serious scholar who should not have had to teach adolescent boys and be teased by them. He, too, was in his fifties and his bride was Lottie, another refugee from Hitler. I lost sight of the Stapleys, but the Khans lived happily for many years and boys and old-boys were always given a warm welcome at their house.

At the end of term when I arrived home, my Mother took me into my bedroom, saying she had some bad news. It seemed that my Father had been having pains in his chest. They had seen a specialist who had diagnosed *angina pectoris*, the hardening of the arteries of the heart. In those days before the introduction of heart surgery there was no cure for this disease. The specialist had explained that exertion or even emotional excitement could bring on attacks any one of which could be fatal.

Wenderton House.

Gladys at the front door.

The Lanchester.

Caricature of my father
in Canterbury market
by Syd Jordan, 1933.

Hop picking.

OK in front of his van.

On cousin Nina's pony.

Sarah Ann Minter and her brother in front of the weeping ash in the 1860s.

The master with hounds outside Wenderton.
Me in the pram and YaYa beside me.

On Young Bill's tractor.

Staying at Little Upton with
my great grandmother and her
gardener, Caley.

On my first pony.

Going to a family
wedding at St Peter's
Broadstairs
with my parents.

My father (right) with his parents and his elder brother Harry in 1904.

Grandfather Edwin Apps as mayor of Tenderden
(with chain of office) annoucing the accession of George V^th.

Headcorn stock sale.

My mother "the leading hound".

My mother,
rarely seen out of the stables.

Uncle John drawing ahead on Jack Frost.

Obadiah Edwards, my great
grandfather who refused to sit
in judgement on those who had
drunk too much of his beer.

My grandfather with my mother behind, in 1914.

My grandmother
and my father with
a motoring friend,
circa 1913.

My father on
his motorbike

The *Star* in 1912 with
my grandmother behind
and Uncle John next
to the chauffeur.

My father (on the right)
before take-off.

My father as a newly commissioned
captain looking surprised.

My father (right) and the observer with Lewis
gun. The "dinner plate" clearly visible.

Major Michin.

Letter dropped by the ennemy, 1917.

My father recovering
from his accident.

At Frognal in 1940 wearing Uncle George's
tin hat with my mother and Aunty Hilda..

Carol Powers.

Going to school.

St Edmund's school.

School group in 1880. In 1940 little had changed
apart from the staff being clean shaven.

The dormitory.

The Bayfordbury
Hotel.

The Rev. F.S. Williams (left)
and Canon Shirley
with General Montgomery.

My first (and only) pheasant.

CHAPTER NINE

—

Talking to my father always made me feel everyone interesting had died before I was born.

"It's a pity you didn't know old so-and-so," he would say, looking over the top of his tortoiseshell pince-nez and the 'Farmer and Stockbreeder'.

"He was a real character. You don't see people like that about today – do you?" turning to my mother who was knitting.

"You certainly don't," she'd reply firmly.

She had taken the specialist's warning to heart and now agreed with everything my Father said on principle, a principle that I was finding hard accept, though the realisation of how precarious our life had become was gradually sinking in.

They were sitting in the thickly upholstered armchairs bought at the time of their marriage and now clad in covers made from a grey, prickly material that my Mother considered she had been lucky to find. For, although the war had been over for nearly two years, these were the years of Austerity.

I was sitting on the sofa, which was similarly clad, with a book from the Gloucester Public Library. I was on holiday from school and as my school fees were consuming a major part of the family budget, the Public Library being free, was my chief, indeed my only place of entertainment during the holidays.

The problem of lack of money was compounded by the fact that I had no friends.

My parents knew hardly anyone either, apart from their immediate neighbours, and an old man my father had met one evening walking the dog.

Carey Pitt, a retired seed-merchant in his eighties with a rubicund face and a shock of white hair, was, as far as my father was concerned, one of the rare exceptions to the rule that no one interesting was still alive.

What was more, it turned out that they had known each other during the First World War, when my father in a fervour of patriotism and with the help of considerable string-pulling had got himself commissioned into the Royal Army Service Corps with the rank of captain and posted to Gloucester as the District Provisioning Officer for Gloucestershire, a job that involved requisitioning corn and hay for the army in France.

"When I think" he would say as we waited for the bus in Northgate Street to take us to the Midland Bank on the Cross - petrol rationing still making it impossible to use the car except for official business, "When I think that the last time I walked these streets I was booted and spurred."

The habit of requisitioning had stayed with him. He never seemed, for example, to catch buses like other people, but to requisition them. On one occasion, after a long wait, when the bus eventually arrived our entry was blocked by the conductor who announced that it was a workers' bus.

"We are all workers today!" said my father in requisitioning mood, pushing past him and sitting down.

The conductor might be forgiven for his mistake, my father, dressed in his customary breeches and stockings, tweed shooting-jacket and waistcoat with a blue and white spotted bow, the whole topped off with a trilby hat, and carrying a walking stick, hardly resembled the typical worker.

My parents never stopped saying how happy they were at having left Kent and got away from the family, but their protestations rang false. In reality, I think, they saw the move to Gloucester as a shipwreck. Europe at that time was full of Displaced Persons and they too, were in their way D.P.s

It was the street that my mother found difficult. She had lived in the country all her life and the idea of walking out of the house on to a pavement went against the grain.

Happily, at the end of the garden there was a door leading on to a lane that enabled her to sustain the illusion that she was not in a town. During the fourteen years my parents lived in Alexandra Road, Gloucester, I hardly ever remember my mother using the front door.

It was during these holidays in Gloucester that I began slowly to piece together the background to the family drama that had led to the break between my parents and the rest of the family.

When, in 1908, my father arrived in Ash, he took lodgings in Sandwich. Photographs of that time show him smartly, even a little too smartly dressed, laughing, clowning and pulling funny faces with his future mother-in-law only a few years older than he, tall and elegant, laughing in the background.

People have told me that my father at that time was full of high spirits and a great practical joker. I used to be shown the marks on the wall of Cave's café, the sedate old coffee-shop opposite the entrance to Canterbury Cathedral, where the clientele included a high proportion of clergymen, marks that the owner told me had been made many years before by my father and his friends who had a meringue fight. It seemed hard to believe.

He certainly entered into the social life of the district, becoming an umpire for the Wingham Cricket Club, where he risked social ostracism by declaring 'out, LBW' Lord Harris of Belmont, purported to be Kent's best batsman – his Lordship was, it seems, not wholly willing to accept the verdict – and being made Secretary of the Sandwich Fat Stock Show, a local event held under the presidency of Lord Northbourne of Betteshanger Park. He also bought himself a motorcycle and it was on this that, hearing that Bleriot was to make an attempt to fly across the channel he managed to be in the field as Bleriot landed.

"Not that we saw much," he would add. "A policeman kept us back."

Although he and my grandfather worked well together, he appears to have been worried by Arthur's alcoholism, because a letter from William Wynch, the friend who originally introduced them, is clearly a reply to a letter showing he was thinking of leaving because of it.

However, he did not leave and he became a favourite with the family, which he seems to have adopted as his own. When she had first seen him, Molly, with the confidence of her four years, had announced that he was the man she was going to marry. She and John became fond of their 'Uncle Bertie', while Joan saw him as an ally in her attempts to stop Arthur drinking, the business was expanding and they took on several more farms including Wenderton.

My grandmother was especially pleased at this because it had long been connected with the Minters and she had known it as a child when her great-aunt, Sarah-Ann Minter, had lived there. The farm belonged at that time to the Marquis of Conyngham and had been acquired by his ancestor, Lord Albert Conyngham, when he was Member of Parliament for Canterbury and took it in to his head that he would like to walk to the sea over his own land. His mother had been that Lady Conyngham, mistress of George IV, of whom it was said that when she left Windsor after his death, she was accompanied by thirteen wagonloads of loot.

The farms in East Kent, which is known as 'the garden of England,' were often owned by absent landlords, or by syndicates. The land is very rich and in spite of being tenants, the farmers fully justified the verse in "The Ingoldsby Legends", written, incidentally, at Wingham, which claims that:

> "A knight of Cales,
> A gentleman of Wales,
> A laird of the North countree:
> A yeoman of Kent
> With his annual rent,
> Will buy them up, - all three."

Hop growing in England is believed to have begun near Canterbury in 1520 and one of the reasons given is that the farmers in the area, being the richest in the country, could afford the considerable investment needed.

Suddenly it was 1914 and war was in the air. The country was mobilising and my father was keen to volunteer. With the help of Lord Northbourne's brother, the Hon. Cuthbert James, a Colonel in the Marines, who had noticed the efficient secretary of the Sandwich

Fat Stock Show, he was given an introduction to a Colonel Morgan at the War Office.(They were not afraid of calling a spade a spade in those days, no mealy-mouthed Ministries of Defence) and so, catching the train from Canterbury straight after the market still in his boots and gaiters, he presented himself at Whitehall and was commissioned into the Army Service Corps, with a handsome document to prove it, signed by the King himself, immediately gazetted in the rank of captain and posted to Gloucester as District Purchasing Officer to buy hay for the British Expeditionary Force in France. He was twenty-four.

I have a photo of him in his uniform, seated, with his older but equally inexperienced second-in-command, Lt. Lacy, standing beside him. They both look extremely surprised.

The posting of newly commissioned Purchasing Officers throughout the country led to difficulties. A man might know the price of hay at home but have little idea of it at the other end of the country. At one point a question was asked in the House of Commons.

However, my father seems to have come out of it well, for when he left Gloucester he received a letter from H.Q. congratulating him and saying that his accounts were the best kept of any in the service. (It was, incidentally, to the man who wrote that letter, who had become the head of the Inland Revenue, that he owed his move to Gloucester).

Suddenly finding himself a captain in the army was certainly agreeable to my father (when Arthur Marchant heard the news of his young assistant's vertiginous promotion, he said he supposed, had he volunteered, they would have made him a General) but a comfortable war spent in Gloucester was not what he was looking for and he immediately asked to be posted to France. This was granted and after a brief course at the Cavalry School he was sent to France in time for the Battle of the Somme. His job was to take the convoys of munitions and rations up to the front line, during which they were the target for shelling which left horses and men struggling in the mud.

The day after the battle, hearing that his brother, Harry, a lieutenant in the Royal Engineers, was near he rode over to find him and they spent an hour together walking and talking behind the lines.

While he was in France, Molly baked cakes and sent them to him. His letter of thanks is written in pencil:

> *"France, May 2 / 16*
> My dear Bib,
>
> I am sorry I have not written before to thank you for that lovely chocolate cake you made me – it was good – I really wanted to eat it all myself but I live with three other officers, I had to give them some of it – they all said they had not tasted such a good cake before and they were very keen on knowing who made it, but I would not tell them – I told them they wanted to know too much.
>
> Now just fancy your going away to school! You lucky girl, you will have a good time – with lots of other girls to play with and make friends of – When I come home I will come and take you out to tea – Oh won't the other girls talk – also you must write to me and tell me all about your school – now don't forget – We poor boys out here are only too glad to receive letters. When the postman comes we nearly knock him over to see if he has any letters in his bag for us.
>
> This is a funny old place out here. I am living in an old farm house with earthen floor and not even bricks – sleep on the floor in my blankets – oh you would laugh to see us- anyway we don't have to brush carpets and polish floors chairs and tables like Mummy does because there are not any to polish except chairs, but they are nearly all broken – When you see me again I expect you will say I'm untidy. Well how is everybody at Guilton? Father, Mummie, John and Peggy also Aunty Maggie – all quite well I hope – Tell John to make haste and learn his lessons as we shall soon want him in the army.
>
> Goodbye old girl, take care of your-self – I am now going to write to Mummie.
> With love from
> Uncle Bertie"

At the time Molly was eleven and John nearly eight. There is no mention in the letter of the rats that ran over him in the night, nor of being woken one morning by the sound of a firing squad executing a deserter behind the house.

*

Winston Churchill, who had been First Lord of the Admiralty, resigned over the landing in the Dardanelles. It is now known that Churchill took the blame for Admiral Lord Fisher, but at the time he was seen as being solely responsible for the tragedy. Taking the rank of Major, he went to serve in France and my father and another officer were standing by the side of the road in a village as the columns of soldiers marched up to the front, Churchill appeared marching at the head of a column. They both turned to face the wall so as not to have to salute "that bugger Churchill."

Flying had always fascinated my father, he had not forgotten the excitement of seeing Bleriot land, and now he applied to join the Royal Flying Corps. On the strength of having owned a motorcycle, he was accepted, although it meant coming down a rank to Lieutenant, but he got a second commission. This one, however, was signed not with the King's signature, but with a stamp. The Royal hand was getting weary after three years of war.

After a theoretical course at Jesus College Oxford, he was posted to Hendon Aerodrome to learn to fly. The posting came earlier than expected during a week when the D'Oyly Carte Opera Company was playing at the Oxford theatre. My father, a Gilbert and Sullivan enthusiast, who had booked for every performance, now had reluctantly to return his tickets. But after waiting in a long queue at the box-office the booking clerk refused to give him a refund. As though to prove he had not forgotten his pre-war profession, my father climbed the steps leading to the theatre and from that vantage point conducted an auction sale interrupted by the furious protests of the clerk, craning his head through the window.

"You can't do that!" shouted the clerk.

"I am doing it," replied my Father calmly, as he knocked the tickets down at rather more than he had paid for them.

Hendon aerodrome at that time boasted one hangar and a wind sock which, when it moved only slightly in the breeze, meant an end to flying for the day. The first aeroplane on which he learned, known as 'The Rumpety', had no seat and the pilot sat on an upturned Tate and Lyle sugar box. The instructor was an irascible Frenchman, 'Ruffy' Beauman, who was paid one hundred pounds for each British officer he taught to fly. He seems to have been a resourceful man, because one of the pupils who had suffered from his temper decided to teach him a lesson. At the end of the course, each pupil had to do a flight with the instructor, the pupil in the front cockpit and the instructor behind. Once in the air, this pupil put the plane into a nose-dive and in spite of the instructor's shouts from behind, refused to pull out intending to leave it till the last moment to give him a fright. He was able to do this because if the front joystick was engaged, the person behind had no control of the aircraft. But he had underestimated the instructor, who unscrewed his joystick and hit him over the head knocking him senseless before replacing it to land the plane.

My father had arrived at Hendon on the 16th November 1916 and from his Pilot's Flying Log Book, it is clear that the windsock was extremely active in that and the following month, so that between the 16th of November and the 22nd of December, he only managed to do 54 minutes dual in the air. *'Too windy'*, *'No Flying'* continues almost daily and was probably the cause of his being sent to finish training at Heliopolis Aerodrome in Egypt.

Staying in Cairo at Shepheard's Hotel, he was in the bedroom next to Lawrence of Arabia and was fascinated to see that two Arabs slept outside his door. Coming face to face with Lawrence in the hotel foyer, my father said, "Colonel Lawrence, I believe – may I shake you by the hand?"

Lawrence remained a hero for him all his life.

His training finished, my father graduated flying officer on the 15th May 1917 and was posted to the 47th Squadron on the first of June. It was based at Janes Aerodrome in Macedonia. Strategically it was the dump for the Divisions operating on the Doiran front in the war against the Bulgars. The 47th Squadron was involved chiefly in photographing behind the enemy lines to direct the artillery, bombing and aerial combat. The machines flew at 60 m p. h. and the combat technique was to get as high as possible above the enemy and swoop down while the observer in the rear cockpit fired a Lewis machine gun. The ammunition for these guns was, as my father described it, like a dinner plate that sat on top of the gun and revolved when fired. On one occasion, he had got well above the enemy plane and begun to dive down when he heard his observer shouting "pull out, pull out". The 'dinner plate' had fallen overboard and there was nothing for it but to run for home.

A more successful sortie is described in "Over the Balkans and South Russia, being the history of No 47 Squadron Royal Air Force" by H.A. Jones, M.C.

"On the morning of the raid over Janes Aerodrome, Lieutenant B.R. Apps and Lieutenant A.S. Clark, observer, on an A.W.12, were taking photographs over Bogorodica. They were attacked by two enemy scouts, one was sent down out of control, and the other, after receiving several bursts from the observer's gun at 50 yards range, gave up the uneven combat. In the afternoon, 2nd Lieutenant J.C. Nelson, with Lieutenant A.J. Pick, observer, went out to photograph the machine which had been sent down out of control by Apps and Clark in the morning".

In the same book my father has underlined a passage reading,

"It is true that the types of machines which 47 possessed were slow and much inferior to those flown by the Royal Flying Corps on the western front."

On one occasion, a visiting General came to inspect the squadron. One of the pilots had been in his regiment, where the General was unpopular. The planes were due to leave on a bombing raid and the General stood on a podium at the salute as, one after another, they taxied, took off and went into circuit round the airfield. When it came to this pilot's turn he taxied, took off and, as he went into circuit, dropped his bombs on the edge of the airfield. The General was the first person to lie flat on his face. Later when asked for an explanation, the pilot simply said that the release device had not worked properly. This device was a new invention, before that they had simply dropped the bombs over the side.

A chivalrous code of conduct existed between the British and German flying men, who would drop messages informing about the dead and wounded and asking if their things could be dropped for them.

Among my father's papers is the faded photo of a letter, dated 11.7.17, which reads:

"For the friends of Mr. Vautin.
I send you our photograph.
Mr Vautin has himself wellfelt.
He is a very kind man [1] yesterday
I have shoved to him Jerusalem.
In the next days I will write to his
father and send to him our photo.

We hope that you will dropp soon
his things four Mr V.
Very sportly
salutations
F.
Capt. Brook is buried
with military honour"

My father was with the 47th Squadron for six months almost to the day during a period when the policy was to harass the enemy, who were well armed and comfortably dug-in among the mountains, day and night. It is clear from his Log Book that, except for two bouts in hospital with malaria, there was scarcely a day when he was not over enemy lines at heights ranging between 4000 and 11000

---

1. And of course a gentleman.

feet, on a 'shoot', 'reconnaissance', 'distraction shoot,' 'photography', offensive patrol' or 'bomb raid'.

The mortality rate among pilots was extremely high, so at the end of the six months the faces in the mess had changed several times and he found himself to be an almost solitary survivor.

One evening at dinner, after an abortive but costly raid, when a more than usual number of chairs stood empty, the commanding officer, Major Minchin, not himself a flying man, but a career officer, remarked affably that he had been on to H.Q. and they were delighted with the day's work. My father, looking at the empty chairs, remarked that he had always understood discretion to be the greater part of valour. He already had a difficult relationship with Minchin, and for this he was posted to Suez, to the 58th Training Squadron, as an instructor. Major Minchin seems to have been generally disliked, because a letter from one of the other officers, "The Doc", on the 22nd May 1918, says that, to every one's relief, Minchin has been posted to France. It goes on to talk about the future, with the Doc saying that he has decided not to join the RAF (which was then being formed) for fear he might land up with Major Minchin again. The Doc's other worry is best expressed in his own words;

"...among the "new delights" are Australians[1] they are rather funny to get on with. However I manage in a sort of way. Not long ago I was away at the base quite near the aircraft park as you know just about the spot. There it was done old son and the "bluddy" F.L [2] burst. Poor old Doc thinks he's in the soup...".

A week after his arrival in Suez, my father was instructing in an Avro that had the new rotary engine. They had barely taken off with his pupil in the front cockpit and himself behind, when the engine cut out and the machine, being nose-heavy, plunged into the ground. Instructors who had seen much active service did not generally bother to fasten their safety belts and my father was no exception. The result was that while his pupil walked away unhurt, his face hit

1. Australian nurses.
2. French letter or condom.

the dashboard breaking his jaw. He remembered getting out of the plane; feeling angry with him self, waving away the ambulance and noticing, as he walked to his tent, that something was hanging down and hitting the top of his chest. It was, he realised, his chin. He threw himself on to his bed and was unconscious for ten days.

His Pilot's Flying Log Book ends;

Summary of hours flown:	hours	minutes
Graduation	20	23
Service flying in Salonika	148	35
Instructing	10	0

"Crashed on Avro while instructing
and admitted to hospital 27. 12. 17.
Washed out for flying by Medical Board."

The news of my father's accident reached Tenterden in a War Office telegram:

"The Kentish Express January 5th 1918:

FOR THEIR KING AND COUNTRY

Tenterden Flying Officer injured

"Councillor and Mrs Apps of Beach House, Tenterden, received the following wire on Saturday evening from the War Office: – Regret to inform you that the Government Hospital at Suez reports, December 28th, Lieutenant B.R. Apps, Royal Flying Corps, Training Squadron, dangerously ill with concussion of the brain and fractured jaw Lieutenant Apps was articled to Mr Harry Judge, auctioneer of Tenterden and for several years was with Mr Arthur Marchant, auctioneer, of Ash, near Canterbury. When war broke out he joined the R.A.S.C. and obtained his captaincy.

When volunteers for the Royal Flying Corps were asked for he threw up his captaincy in the Army Service Corps and joined the R.F.C. as lieutenant. After a short training he went out to Salonica and only a few days before his parents received the wire he had moved to Egypt".

My grandparents had six sons on active service, "one on every front and one in the air", as Edwin used to say, and the stress was beginning to tell, but the war was drawing to its close and everyone was thinking about returning to civilian life.

Once recovered from his accident, my father was posted to the 144th Squadron as adjutant but he too was beginning to think about his future. He could stay on in the Royal Air Force, as it was now called, return to the army or accept a post he had been offered with the Egyptian Police, but while he was considering these possibilities, a letter arrived from Joan imploring him to return to Guilton, saying that Arthur was drinking more than ever and they needed him to save the business. My father did not hesitate and returned to England to be demobbed.

At Tenterden, Edwin had bought a Union Jack on a white flagpole and, as each of his sons came home, this was hung out of a bedroom window over the front door. Miraculously, they all returned, the only casualties being my father and Stuart, the youngest of the brothers to be involved in the war. Stuart was in the trenches where, commissioned in the field when all the officers were killed, he lost a leg when a shell exploded beside him only ten days before the armistice.

Although he was still in his twenties, photos of my father taken at that time show him looking considerably older and far from well. Two bouts of malaria and his accident had left him in poor shape physically and the stress of flying had taken its toll.

Joan invited him to move in and live with them at Guilton, an offer he accepted. Thus the three of them, Arthur, Joan and my father were all living under the same roof. My grandparents had separate bedrooms and the children were away at boarding school. The full implication of this only struck me many years later.

Perhaps it was because Carey Pitt had known my father when he was booted and spurred that their friendship flourished. They would return visits and go to tea or supper with each other regularly. Carey Pitt was a widower who lived with his unmarried daughter Mary in a house called 'Clovelly' in Denmark Road. On these occasions, my father and Mr Pitt would discuss politics, current agricultural prices and the latest goings on in "The Archers" to which they both listened regularly.

It was after listening to "The Archers" early in the 1960s that Carey Pitt died. Mary took in his tea. He was sitting in his high-backed armchair by the fire. "Is everything all right, Father?" she asked.

"No," he replied, "I've just listened to "The Archers. It's not as good as it was." and he fell forward dead.

But that was later. For the moment I am on holiday from school, reading books from Gloucester Public Library, painting in oils in my bedroom under the reproachful eye of my mother who fears for the carpet and spending hours in the attic experimenting with theatrical make-up – because I am going to be an actor.

Although I had made my decision that evening in the kitchen of the Old Vicarage, I had still not dared tell anyone. It was Giles Kedge, "Daddy Kedge" as everyone called him, who broke the ice. I liked Mr Kedge and would often go into the lab' to chat to him. I was hopeless at maths, the moment people started talking in numbers my eyes glazed over, (they still do, I have never grasped how *a* can equal *b* over something or other). Giles Kedge tried hard to help me but it was to no avail. Then one day when we were talking, I was fourteen at the time, he said "I think you should give up maths, if you live to be a hundred you'll never understand it, besides" he added, "it is obvious you are going to be an actor". Today it may come as a surprise that a responsible maths master should advise a pupil to give up the subject at fourteen, but it must be remembered that maths and science were considered to be of less importance at that time than Latin, Greek or even modern languages. One hopes that it would not equally be a cause for surprise that a schoolmaster could take so much interest in his pupils that he could understand them better than they did themselves.

I loved him for those words; the fact that a grown-up could seriously consider the idea that I could become an actor, that it was not just a silly, childish dream. From then on the question was settled in my mind, the only thing now was how to convince other people.

In 1947 I took School Certificate and failed, and so had to spend the next year doing it all over again. The situation was made more galling by the fact that I had missed it by a very narrow margin. There were three categories; pass, credit and distinction. I had credits in English language, English Literature, French and Divinity but had failed to pass in history, which left me with one subject too few. The failure in history was especially irritating because it was a subject I had always liked and done well in. Unfortunately the programme that year was nineteenth-century governments, which amounted to a boring succession of opposing politicians regularly replacing each other in battles over such fascinating subjects as the Corn Laws and the Schleswig-Holstein Question, of which Lord Palmerston is supposed to have said that, beside himself and two other people, no one in the world had ever understood it, adding that, of those other two, one was dead, another had gone mad while he himself could no longer remember.

At that time we did not have a regular Art Master, but a student from the Canterbury School of Art who came one afternoon a week. Talking to him, I discovered that it was possible to take Art as a School Certificate subject. There were two papers, one on the history of Art and another that involved drawing. I asked him if he would help me and he agreed, so I went to see the Headmaster to ask his permission.

Thoseby welcomed me frostily. Since my failure I was not among the elect. It was eleven o'clock in the morning and there was a hint of whisky fumes in the air.

"The school," he told me in his harsh Northern voice, "provides adequate teaching on the subjects necessary for passing the Oxford and Cambridge School Certificate. If you are not satisfied and want to study something that is not on the curriculum, you must do it in your own time. There is to be no question of using normal school hours. Do you understand?"

I said I did. He continued to stress the point ending by saying he thought it unnecessary and even absurd. I thanked him and escaped.

The Art Teacher gave me a book on Art History. I began to read it and could not put it down; suddenly not only painting showed itself in a new light, but history too. Where endless battles and governmental struggles had failed to touch my imagination, the history of artists, the changing taste of society and the evolution of costume, suddenly brought the past to light as nothing else had done. I discovered Rubens, El Greco, the German expressionists, Hogarth, Reynolds and Gainsborough beside whom Gladstone, Disraeli and Lord Palmerston seemed poor company.

At Christmas 1947 the school play was J.B. Priestley's "Laburnum Grove". I played the part of Uncle Bernard, the brother-in-law, back from the East, who is sponging off the family. A feature of Uncle Bernard is that he continually eats bananas. Due to the German submarines we had barely seen a banana since 1940 and supplies were only just trickling back. The cry went out for staff and parents to give us their bananas, which they did, so that on the three nights on which we performed the play I could eat my way through more bananas than anyone had seen in seven years and was the envy of the whole school. I remember, in obedience to the script, at one point taking a couple of bites and throwing the rest into the wastepaper basket and feeling a wave of almost palpable resentment from the other side of the footlights.

Gradually I let it be known that I wanted to be an actor. The news was received without enthusiasm, but, to my relief, there was no putting down of feet or outright refusal. My father remarked that as we now had a socialist government nobody would ever again be able to make money, so I might as well do something I enjoyed. He himself loved the theatre, as did all the Apps family. Grandfather Apps had been an admirer of Ellen Terry, who lived close to Tenterden at Smallhythe, and who gave him a handsome signed photograph when he was Mayor. He never missed any of the Lyceum productions in which she starred with Henry Irving.

At Guilton, I passed my grandfather in the hall. "I hear you are going to Hollywood," he chuckled, and walked on.

A memorable event at that time was the Anglican Convention, which was held at Canterbury. All the bishops of the Anglican

Church attended a service in the Cathedral. The sight of them in their robes and mitres processing two abreast all-round the Close, made a great impression on me.

Early in 1948 my grandfather became ill again and decided to return to Ruthin Castle and, as Gloucester was not too far from Wales, it was decided to go and see him. My parents had recently bought a car, a small blue 10 h.p. Hillman, and in it we set out for North Wales. It was the first time I had been to Wales. On the way we stopped to buy·something in a village. As I went into the shop, the woman behind the counter looked at me suspiciously. There were several people ahead of me and I waited for them to be served but just as it got to my turn, some more people came in and, looking behind me, she asked what they wanted and served them. Barely had they left and I was again approaching the counter, when more people came in and the same thing happened. Only when there was no one else in sight, did she turn to me and ask what I wanted.

When we arrived at Ruthin Castle, my father stayed in the car and my mother and I went in search of grandfather. We found him in a wooden cabin in the grounds seated beside his bed in pyjamas and dressing gown. His dressing gown was open and, through the opening of his pyjamas one could clearly see his testicles. I was fascinated; they seemed enormous: I could not take my eyes off them.

Of the conversation I only remember his saying that you don't appreciate good health until you lose it, a phrase that my mother repeated as we drove home; adding that it would be difficult to find someone who had abused his health more than he had.

Unfortunately for my grandfather, Ruthin Castle failed to work the miracle twice and, although he did not come home in his box, as his doctor had foretold on the first occasion, he returned far from well and in the Spring of 1948 became ill again;

"20th March 1948: "very sorry to hear about Grandfather and I think your idea would be a very nice gesture. But I can't very well give up my London project as Jolley's mother has booked the rooms for us".

Francis Jolley and I were planning a night in London to see a play and visit the National Gallery on the way home.

"I can't let him down at this stage of the proceedings, but I could go up there very cheaply as I shall be going up on the 6.47 from Canterbury East and I may be able to buy a workman's ticket. So what I could do is to have my two days there and then return to Guilton and spend a week or so with Granny."

Then, on the next page of the letter:

"I'm not awfully anxious to go to Guilton, but if you think Granny would like it I will".

My mother was obviously feeling guilty about not being with her mother herself and intended sending me instead. I was frequently used in this way when contact with the family was needed. In the end I did not have to go, but went on the first Sunday after the Easter holidays.

My grandfather was in the Veranda where they had installed his bed. This time my grandmother was with him so there was no question of his testicles being exposed to view. He looked pale and weak. We had a desultory conversation and thankfully there was no talk of pocket money. It was there that he died early one morning a few days later.

Aunty Peggy rang me at school to tell me the news.

My mother came to the funeral. Aunty Peggy and Uncle George picked me up from school and we went to meet my mother at Canterbury station.

Considering that my grandfather made it a principle not to go to funerals because he could not do any good, it was surprising to see how many people came to his. The church was crammed. Afterwards friends and family came to Guilton where tea was served in the Veranda. At the backdoor, Wellard, the backdoor boy, who had cleaned my grandfather's shoes every day for thirty years, was gently crying.

My mother and my aunt asked Uncle John when the Will was to be read. He replied that he had thought there was no need for a formal reading and had asked the solicitors to send copies to them. He was very busy, flitting here and there and neither of them got a chance to talk to him. In the car on the way back to Canterbury, we discussed it and everyone felt that it was rather unusual not to read the Will.

Since my parents had moved to Gloucester, relations between my mother and grandfather and especially her relations with Uncle John had greatly improved. They were remarkably similar and in their teens had been close, spending long days hunting together while she had prepared the horses he rode at point-to-points. Seeing them together it was obvious that she had more in common with him than with either her mother or her sister.

The arrival of the copy of the Will changed all that for good. It was immediately clear why Uncle John had wanted to avoid a reading; my grandfather had left him everything. Aunty Peggy was to receive one thousand pounds and my mother the same sum 'if she becomes a widow". In the event of Uncle John's premature death, my grandmother was to inherit, and in the event of her not being alive, Aunty Peggy and her children. My mother was totally excluded and so was I. I had always felt that my grandfather did not like me, but it was a shock to feel his dislike reaching out to me from the grave.

We subsequently learned that during my grandfather's last illness, my grandmother had read the Will and presented to him that it was unjust. He grudgingly agreed and his solicitor was summoned to his bedside and he dictated a codicil in which his daughters were each to get a third share of the family furniture after my grandmother's death. The solicitor took it back to Sandwich to be typed, but before it could be returned for his signature, my grandfather died. My grandmother asked Uncle John to honour his father's last wish. He agreed but even so it did little to ameliorate the sense of injustice.

In looking for reasons why my grandfather had left such an unkind Will, I could not help wondering if Mr Hincks had not played a part in persuading him to do so, because if the estate had been divided between the three children, the business would have needed to be broken up. With Uncle John inheriting everything the business remained intact – as did Mr Hincks's job.

The Will was proved at twenty thousand pounds, which my father estimated to be a fraction of the true value of the business. Then as now, accountants usually managed to underestimate the value of an inheritance to reduce death duties.

For my mother and aunty Peggy it was a blow. Aunty Peggy's husband was a relatively rich man and she was far from being in need, but she had hoped to be independent financially and not to have to be reliant on her husband for every penny. My parents, on the other hand, with my school fees to pay and the prospect that I might go to university, were stretched to the limit and it was only by very careful management that my father's salary was keeping us going. Moreover, we were all three aware that it could end at any time should his state of health deteriorate further. He was already finding it difficult to keep up with the owners as they showed him round their farms and estates. He told me he had developed a technique for dealing with the problem which was that when he felt an attack coming on, he would stop, look into the distance and say "What a fine view you have here!" and continue to admire it until he felt capable of going on. It was one of many techniques and subterfuges that he developed as the disease worsened over the years.

During the war all contact with the continent had been impossible, but now we began to have an intake of foreign boys at school. The first to arrive was a Greek, Gerolymatos, his family were ship-owners who had sent him to England for protection for, as he told us graphically, "The Communists cut my brother's throat with a piece of glass" Dark and thickset, he looked nearer thirty than fourteen which had been given as his age. Our housemaster, Stephen-Jones, was frequently seen looking at him while shaking his head and muttering, "Fourteen?"

Officially it was said that people from the Latin countries developed much earlier than those from northern climes. When we heard that a second Greek was due to arrive, we became apprehensive in case he might be a communist. Fortunately, Bazinas was the son of an Athens Surgeon and the two Greeks became friends. Then in 1948 a French boy, Armand Desenclos, arrived from Calais. He spoke hardly any English at first and I enjoyed trying out my French on him.

All three of them had lived under the Nazi occupation and were street-wise in ways of which we in the naivety of our monastic isolation had no notion. We needed a pass signed by our housemaster even to go to Canterbury for the afternoon and when we got there, the cinema was strictly out of bounds. Thus the discovery that Gerolymatos, when he went to London, frequented prostitutes and that Armand, who as a Roman Catholic was allowed to go to Canterbury to worship, managed in no time to fix himself up with a married woman as a mistress, gave us a glimpse of adult life that we had hardly imagined.

Shortly after the death of my grandfather, I plucked up courage one evening and went to the master's wing and knocked on Holly's door. He invited me in and asked what I wanted. I told him I wanted to ask him whether he thought I had enough talent to become a professional actor. He sat me down by the fire and offered me a glass of Dubonnet – an unheard of privilege.

We sat in silence for some minutes while he thought about it. Then he said that he saw no reason why not. "There is going to be more work with this new television that is starting up," he said, pointing out that while he did not see me as a star, he thought I should be able to make a decent living as a character actor, adding "Yes, you could be an actor, you are not too intelligent." At first I thought he was joking, it was typical of him to bring people down to earth in that way, but I came to realise that his remark was serious. What he meant was that I was not too intellectual, because he understood that intellectuals rarely make good actors; acting needs spontaneity and gut feeling rather than too cerebral an approach.

Some weeks later Holly sent for me and when I entered the room I saw a man sitting by the fire. "This is Apps, who wants to be an actor," he said and introduced me to Mr Deering, who was an actor-manager who ran repertory companies. He and Holly had been at school together. Rex Deering was an imposing figure in a well-cut double-breasted suit with an old-style theatrical manner. He was friendly and seemed to take my desire to be an actor seriously and, when I asked what I should do to prepare myself, advised me to read plays.

Holly had also told me to write to Michael Goodliffe, which I had done, and he had replied inviting me to go and see him on my way home from school. When I got to London, I rang him and he invited me to supper. He and his wife, Peggy, had a mansion flat near Paddington. They were very welcoming and Michael tried gently to warn me as to what I was letting myself in for in wanting to go on the stage. During the evening, the conversation turned to his years as a prisoner of war and he told me that when he was eventually released, and sitting in the plane on the way home, thinking to himself, "home, home at last!" It suddenly struck him that he did not have a home. His mother had died while he was a prisoner and he had no other relations. He went to London and the first night he met Peggy. They became engaged and married soon after. Peggy was the daughter of a Canadian Judge and in the ATS. Now they had a baby son and seemed very happy.

June saw the beginning of the exam season and my second attempt at the School Certificate. When the time came for me to take the Art History paper, it was in a master's study and the headmaster was the invigilator. I was late and when I arrived, he was fuming and continued to fume throughout the hour. However I decided to ignore him and set to work. I found the subjects interesting and enjoyed writing about them. At the end he collected my papers and swept out. The practical examination was more relaxed, the Art student invigilated and I felt at ease as I drew the still life he had set up for me.

My friendship with Armand Desenclos had continued and just before the end of the term he asked me if I would like to go and stay with him in Calais. My parents gave the green light and my father sent me five pounds. I applied for a passport; I have it still. It begins with the impressive phrase; "We, Ernest Bevin ..." I went to Guilton until it was time to cross the channel; Uncle John asked how much money my father had given me. I told him and he said it would not be enough and he lent me another five pounds. On the day, I took the bus to Canterbury, from there to Dover and boarded the ferry.

When we arrived at Calais the first thing that I noticed was the smell, the unforgettable smell of France. Unkind people have said it is due to the drains, but if that is so, it is a pity English drains do not smell as sweet.

Armand and his parents were there to meet me. His mother was an affectionate, generous woman, his father a down-to-earth, businessman. He had a garage and she a hat shop.

As I was used to being reprimanded for each and every grammatical fault I made, it was some time before I dared speak. When I did hesitantly utter my first phrase in French, they all applauded. They then took me to their house. It was in the typical red brick of Northern France. When we went into the dining room for lunch, they suggested I take off my jacket and make myself comfortable. I was enchanted for at home I had always had to put my jacket on for meals; I sensed I was going to like France. Armand's grandmother, a little old lady who smiled a lot and did the cooking, waited on us but did not sit with us.

We explored Calais and they took me in the car along the coast. The bomb damage was terrible. When I mentioned it and criticised the Germans, they replied that they were English bombs that had done the damage.

They decided to show me Paris, and we took the train from Calais. It was my first experience of continental trains. How different they seemed, the fact you had to climb up steps to get into them; the platform, being at ground level, brought back memories of films like "The Lady Vanishes" (not a reassuring memory). The seats were not upholstered like English trains, but as English trains seemed not to have been cleaned since the war and the upholstery stank of soot, this was not altogether a bad thing. In any case they were not uncomfortable and I shall never forget the excitement of seeing the suburbs of Paris for the first time and arriving at the Gare du Nord. The Desenclos had a flat at Bonne Nouvelle and we took the metro. I thought Paris the most exciting and wonderful city I had ever seen:

the bistros with the high ceilings, the bars, the restaurants, the narrow streets, the peeling paint, and the wide boulevards. My knowledge of French history at that time was limited to Dickens' "The Tale of Two Cities" and Baroness Orczy's "The Scarlet Pimpernel", both of which I had read and, more recently, had seen the film of the latter with Leslie Howard's unforgettable performance as Sir Percy Blakeney. I do not know exactly what I expected, but for me, as I suspect for most English people, the Revolution of 1792 was foremost in my mind and my sympathies were firmly with the Royal family and the oppressed aristocrats. I don't say I expected to see the guillotine still dominating La Place Royale, but I should not have been surprised. As the Desenclos took me around I began to see that the history of France had not ceased with the Revolution. They took me to the Louvre, to Les Invalides to see Napoleon's tomb, to the Eiffel Tower, to Versailles. In those days the wounded and handicapped from the First World War were still a very visible part of the Paris population. Seats were reserved for them on buses and in the metro and they had been found jobs as guides to the National Monuments. I especially remember the guide at Versailles, with his uniform, his medals and his wooden leg. We, the public, would enter each room and wait while he slowly stumped across to the other side with his wooden leg. Once there, he would stop, turn slowly and in a stentorian voice begin his text; *"Alors voyez ici la chambre à coucher de la Reine Marie-Antoinette"* an impressive pause *"regardez le plafond, ... etc"* every detail picked out at the same rhythm and with the same measured delivery. Then on to the next room, the wait, the slow progress, thump, thump, thump, the stop, the turn and *"Alors voyez ici ..."* That evening they took me to the theatre to see Sardou's *"La Maréchale sans Gène"* at the Châtelet, with live horses on the stage. Tired after a day spent going round Versailles, I found it difficult to follow the dialogue and had difficulty keeping my eyes open. But I enjoyed being in the theatre and the sound of the girls selling refreshments, *"Désirez des bonbons, des glaces, des bonbons, des glaces ..."* in a lilting sing-song that rose and fell, as I struggled to stay awake.

     We returned to Calais for several days and one evening went to a ball at the Town Hall with Madame Desenclos' shop assistant, a pretty, slim dark haired girl. She asked me to dance, I was hesitant because I had hardly ever danced, but she insisted. We went on to the floor and she held me close and suddenly I felt her body through her thin dress close to mine, it was something I was to remember for a long time.

Suddenly I felt acutely homesick for England and told Armand I must go. He tried to persuade me to stay, but the homesickness was over-whelming. I caught the boat the next morning. They had given me a bottle of wine to take home and on the boat I became worried about the problem of Customs. I went into the bar and got talking to a tall man in a raincoat and trilby who told me he was a chauffeur. I asked him what one was allowed to bring in and, looking at me suspi-ciously, he asked what I had got. I said I only had a bottle of wine and he said that should be all right. When we got to customs, I suddenly felt several pairs of eyes on me and sensed that I was a centre of inter-est. I went to one of the officers and then it began, he opened my case and went through it item by item, made me take off my coat and went through all my pockets. Finding nothing, he reluctantly let me go. I walked out mentally thanking my friend the chauffeur who had obviously given the Customs men the tip.

Once back in England I felt foolish that I had run away from France so precipitously. After all, homesickness was a problem I had got over many years before. What had got into me?

I decided it was the strangeness of everything and the continual sound of a foreign language as unaccustomed background music. I had to admit that I felt a sense of relief when we arrived at Dover and the background music became English again. All the same I knew that my relationship with France was by no means over, rather it was to be filed as "unfinished business".

When I returned to Gloucester and gave my father the bottle of wine, his face fell. "Didn't you get any cognac?" I had to point out that five pounds for ten days in France would not extend to a bottle of Cognac. I had, of course, returned Uncle John's loan.

The first thing I did was to sit down and write a letter in my best

French to try and express to Mme Desenclos and her husband my gratitude for all their kindness. I had barely finished when the fatal envelope arrived with the results of the School Certificate. I had passed with the same credits in French, English Language, English Literature and Divinity (when he was told, Holly said it proved the first time had not been a fluke) plus, this time, a pass in history and a distinction in Art.

When I got back to School on the first day of the new school year, I had hardly arrived when people surrounded me saying the head-master wanted to see me. I went to his study, "Come in Apps", he said with more affability that I had ever known." I want you to meet the new Art Master". And there, smiling was the Art Student.

No doubt Thoseby's reasoning had been that if an idiot like me could pass School Certificate with the help of Art, there must be something in it.

Now that I was in the sixth form, Holly had suggested to my father that it might be a good idea for me to stay on and take the Higher Certificate and try for a place at Durham University to do English. But I had had enough of school, I was seventeen and I was beginning to find the cloistered life irksome. I begged to be allowed to leave and my father, no doubt thinking with relief of the end of school fees, agreed.

But the feeling of being free, entering the adult world and hope-fully becoming an actor, was tempered by the awful prospect of conscription. Now euphemistically called National Service, the period of eighteen months in the armed forces was obligatory.

I was due to be called up in August, and if there was one thing I had really detested at school, it was the JTC: having to spend every Monday afternoon dressed in a prickly uniform stamping my feet and crawling about in the mud while Sergeant-Major O'Leary barked orders. In fact my relationship with him was not a happy one. If I did not like organized games, I disliked gym even more. Climbing ropes, jumping over the horse and all related activities found me at my most inadequate. To Sergeant-Major O'Leary I presented a chal-lenge and it was one to which he rose. He did everything he could to galvanize me, from anger to ridicule. At one point he made me show my stomach to the class to illustrate how it lacked muscle, something for which I am not sure I have forgiven him even now.

Things came to a head one day when we were doing P.T. and having to run round in a circle. As usual I was conserving my energy for other things, when I noticed him looking at me in a way that was less than reassuring. At the end of the class he said, "Everyone can go except Apps" Then, when everyone had gone, he went to the door and locked it, a move that I felt boded no good. Next he went into his office and came out carrying two pairs of boxing gloves. He threw a pair at my feet and said, "Put them on" and began to put the other pair on himself. Sergeant-Major O'Leary was, as his name suggests, an Irishman and the Irish are known for their hot temper. Looking at him, I could see that his was at boiling point and it struck me that if I didn't want to end up in hospital, I had to do something and do it quickly. Trying to sound as calm as possible, I refused to put the gloves on. This seemed to make him even angrier. "Put them on, put them on!"

"No", I said, "I'm not going to. What would it prove? It's obvious you can knock me about, but then what? If you do you'll lose your job. Think of your wife and children!"

There was a moment when I thought he was going to hit me anyway, but he suddenly flung down the gloves shouting, "Get out!" I did, and fast.

The thought of spending eighteen months in company with a lot of Sergeant-Major O'Learys, clouded the future.

CHAPTER TEN

—

It was the 21st January 1949; I was on my way to Southport to join Rex Deering's Crown Players in a repertory season at the Casino Theatre. Open on my lap was French's Acting Edition of "George and Margaret" with the part of Dudley underlined. As the train puffed its way northward from Gloucester, I leaned back against the dusty, acrid-smelling upholstery and thought of all that had happened in the last month.

To begin with, the school production of James Bridie's "Tobias and the Angel" in which I had played the archangel Raphael with some success. Then there had been the "carrying" – a rite of passage in which those boys who were leaving the school were carried by their peers up and down the cricket pitch while everyone sang, "For He's a Jolly Good Fellow", and the staff looked on benignly.

In reality this touching ceremony was a blood-thirsty settling of accounts, in which those who had suffered at the hands of the leaver in question would get in underneath him as he was stretched out on the shoulders of his friends and stab at his unprotected buttocks with a sharp instrument, usually a compass, while his cries were drowned by the singing. Popularity was gauged by how many times one was carried back and forth. This enabled those who had a big account to settle to shout "Again, Again!" and thus prolong the torture, while the watching staff remarked that they had not realised that So-and-so was so popular.

Carrying was a great leveller. Monitors who abused their power would be politely asked if the were leaving at the end of the term and the downtrodden would be buoyed up by the thought that the day of reckoning was not far off. I had been a house monitor during my last term and so was apprehensive that I might have been thought unjust. But if so, the victims were forgiving and the ceremony left my buttocks intact.

Then there had been the business of saying goodbye to the staff and friends and in particular the highly-charged goodbye to the boy on whom all my burgeoning-emotional life had been centred during the preceding two years, a fact of which he was quite unaware.

The journey home, with a night in London to see John Gielgud and Pamela Brown in "The Lady's not for Burning", had been a treat sanctioned and paid for by my parents. Christmas had brought with it uncomfortable questions about what I was going to do before my call-up in August, to which I could think of no adequate reply. Then, in the first days after Christmas, a telegram from Holly came telling me to start rehearsals for "George and Margaret" at Southport the following week to play the part of Dudley and to be the assistant stage manager, or A.S.M., for £4 a week.

Southport! I hurried to an atlas and saw that it was in Lancashire on the coast near Liverpool. My father muttered something about it being the Brighton of Liverpool, but as I had never been to Brighton I was none the wiser.

There had followed a rush of preparations; I was adamant that my school suit was not sufficient, so with reckless disregard for future emergencies, the family's clothes coupons were expended on a new suit from the Gloucester departmental store, 'The Bon Marche'. Admittedly the choice was not great and, after eight years of school uniform I was understandably eager for something brighter, but the rather-too-loud check that I insisted on against my mother's advice, I was to live to regret.

Repertory actors had in their contract a clause demanding that they "dress well on and off" and the details of the wardrobe they must provide. This list included; a suit, flannel trousers and sports jacket, dinner jacket and, where possible, tails. These last items were easy. My father had both and could no longer get into either, so with a selection of cast-off shirts from Uncles George and John, my holiday sports coat and trousers all packed into my school trunk, I was more or less equipped and felt that I was really an actor, although very conscious that my school trunk was a let-down. It should of course be a skip, one of those large laundry baskets that accompanied every provincial actor wherever he went.

I had to change at Crewe and the train arrived just in time for lunch. In the dining room, an elderly waiter with flat feet and a tail suit green with age, served me with steak and kidney pudding making me feel like Nicholas Nickleby on his way to Dotheboys Hall.

I changed again at Liverpool and arrived at Southport, where I was met by Rex Deering in person. It was our second meeting and I was slightly apprehensive because at our first in Holly's room, he had advised me to read as many plays as possible, advice I had not followed because I found plays difficult to read. Now, he was standing on the platform to greet me, an impressive figure, with a large, red face and black hair, greying at the temples and worn long for those days, brushed back and hanging over the shirt collar. He was splendidly dressed in the same double-breasted black and white suit as before. I was to see a lot of that suit in the next few months.

He greeted me warmly with an elaborate old-fashioned theatrical courtesy and, arranging for my trunk to be delivered to the theatre, led me to my digs. They were with Miss Hinton at 9, Portland Street. The house was in a tree-lined road that led off Lord Street and Miss Hinton was a rubicund woman with white hair and a pleasant, motherly manner. She showed me to my room and explained that the only other lodger was Mr Critchley, a retired clergyman, and that we would be having meals together in the dining room, a large room with heavy Victorian furniture.

As we left the house, Rex looked worried, "A retired clergyman," he mused, "You'll have to watch him." I assured him that I could defend myself from any inopportune ecclesiastical manoeuvres. Our next stop was the theatre.

I cannot imagine that any stage-struck boy of seventeen could have his dream of a theatre better fulfilled than mine was by the Casino Theatre Southport. Standing at the entrance to the pier, it was a perfect little wooden Victorian theatre with a rounded proscenium arch, and a balcony decorated in gold stucco with red plush seats and a red plush curtain. Rex showed me round and then suggested I go home and have tea and meet him later at Yates' Wine Lodge, a pub in the road leading up to the pier where we were to rehearse.

Back at the digs, I met my co-lodger, Mr Critchley. He was a spare, bald man in his sixties with a dried up, bony appearance. He had been the incumbent in a parish on the south coast and when I told him I had been to school at the clergy orphanage, his approval was evident.

Afterwards, at Yates' Wine Lodge, Rex bought me a beer and introduced me to the producer, Michael de Barrass and his wife, Sylvia. Michael was tall, in his late thirties or early forties, with the sort of dark good looks much in vogue in the forties and usually described as saturnine. Sylvia, his wife, was small, neat and pretty. They had worked for Rex before, when he had a string of small repertory companies. Recently they had been in management on their own account at Redcar, where, I gathered, things had not gone well. This impression was later confirmed by their appearing in play after play in the same clothes complaining loudly that their skip had been stolen and with clothes being rationed they were unable to replace their wardrobe. Clothes rationing was a God-given excuse for actors on hard times.

Rex, for whom things had not been going well either, had managed to persuade the owner of the Casino Theatre to give him a lease and finance him, and he had formed a company from people he had worked with before. All this, of course, I was to find out later. At the time I had to keep pinching myself to realise that I was in the company of real, professional actors.

We chatted for a bit and then Rex said he had a request, he was going to the Garrick Theatre, Southport's touring theatre, to hand out playbills to the members of the audience as they emerged after the show. Would I accompany him? I didn't have to, he would quite understand if I refused. I said of course that I should be delighted and after I had drunk another half pint, and he another double whisky, we set off.

Among the many, many things I learned about the theatre in my first season at Southport, I have often thought that the experience of handing out playbills on the first evening was one of the most valuable. It taught me that even before you begin rehearsing a play, the first and most important requirement is to be sure it will have an audience.

On the Sunday I met John Lewis and his wife Doreen. John was the scenic artist and Doreen the stage manager whose assistant I was to be. John was a raw-boned, quick-tempered, sentimental Welshman whom I liked immediately and Doreen, a down-to-earth, pleasant, fair-haired woman, several years younger than John, with whom he was clearly besotted. They made a good couple and I liked them both.

Walking into Yates' Wine Lodge at half-past nine on the Monday morning, I was struck by the smell of stale beer and tobacco smoke that characterises pubs in the morning. It was a smell I was to get to know well and to associate ever after with rehearsals. Even today, if I pass the open door of a pub in the morning, that smell gives me a little feeling of excitement.

Michael de Barrass had told me to be there at half past nine and I arrived on the dot to find Doreen already there setting out chairs and tables to represent the furniture according to the plan of the London production in French's acting edition of "George and Margaret".

In weekly rep there was no time for a preliminary reading of the play; work began on plotting the moves immediately. Soon after, Rex arrived and Michael and Sylvia, then; towards ten o'clock, the other members of the company made their appearance – or rather their entrances, for provincial actors in the late forties were conscious of their status. They exuded a distinct air of apartness, and let it be known that they considered they were doing any town in which they chose to appear a distinct favour by gracing it with their presence.

So much has changed in the theatrical life of Britain over the last sixty years, that it is hard to revive the attitudes of that time. It was the world before television; today it is common to see several plays in the course of an evening, but then many people had never once seen a play, and even the most enthusiastic playgoers, those who bought a season ticket for their local rep, only saw one play a week. So there was a *naïveté* about their reaction which included the total confusion of the actor and his part; when I returned to my digs after the first-night of "An Inspector Calls" in which I played the son who gets the girl, the victim of the play, "into trouble", Miss Hinton looked at me fiercely and said, "I would not have thought it of you," and she meant it and treated me with suspicion for the rest of the week. Many people thought we made the plays up as we went along. Actors were mysterious, a subject of fascination, and to see real live actors walking the streets of the town, gave people a feeling of excitement. The profession carefully nurtured this attitude; no actor would ever let himself be seen by the public in costume and make-up except on the stage; to be spotted at the stage door or in the wings was to break a fundamental taboo.

The first members of the company to arrive were Isobel (pronounced *"eyesobel"*) Grist, the juvenile, and Catherine Harding, the leading lady. Isobel, a black-haired, plump girl, was artistically dressed in a dirndl, and Catherine Harding, in her mid-twenties, tall and fair with a rich, dark voice, had been to a London theatre school and was neither impressed nor pleased to be working in weekly rep.

Ken Morey, in his thirties with a Clark Gable moustache, a belted raincoat and what was obviously his demob hat (people leaving the forces were each given a hat as part of their civilian wardrobe) made his entrance in a manner that showed his attachment to Hollywood films.

Work began at once on plotting the play, with everyone carefully writing in any changes to the moves that were printed in the book. Doreen sat at a table with the prompt copy in which she wrote down all the moves – the prompt copy being the official version and arbiter of any disputes during the rest of the rehearsals.

As assistant stage-manager or ASM, my job (when I was not actually on the stage) involved sitting beside Doreen and making a list of any props that were needed, prompting, helping her to change the position of furniture between scenes and making coffee for the break. The plotting went fast and was over by one o'clock when we broke for lunch. In the afternoon and the afternoons that followed, Doreen and I would go round the town either separately or together trying to borrow the furniture and props, offering publicity in the programme as bait.

This being the first week of the season, we had the evenings free and more time than usual for 'study,' as learning the lines was called. In the normal course of events the rhythm of weekly rep was to say the least dense. The plotting of the following week's play took place on Tuesday morning, after the Monday first night of the current play. Tuesday evening saw the second performance of the current play and Wednesday morning the rehearsal of the first act of the next play without books, which meant that everyone was expected to know his lines. If there was a mid-week matinee, it would mean doing the current play that afternoon, and again in the evening, leaving little time to learn the second act that would be rehearsed on Thursday morning without books. Friday morning the third act would be rehearsed without books and on Saturday morning the whole play would be run, in what was the final rehearsal before the dress rehearsal on Monday. The rest of Saturday was taken up with a matinee or early house followed by the last performance, after which the 'strike' when the stage management would take down the set and clear the stage.

On Sunday the actors would be free to read the next play, sort out their wardrobe for the dress rehearsal and draw breath. The stage management would spend the day putting up the new set and preparing furniture and props. Preparations continued on Monday morning and the dress rehearsal began at two o'clock and went on until curtain up. After the first night there would be notes from the producer before getting back to the digs for supper and bed.

At the first rehearsal of "George and Margaret" it was a topic of general rejoicing that the season did not include mid-week matinées

As I was engaged as the "juvenile" as well as the ASM, I frequently had a lot of lines to learn which meant that, as my afternoons were taken up with hunting down furniture and props, I often had to sit up half the night in order to be "DLP" (dead letter perfect) for the morning's rehearsal. The odd thing is that I don't remember ever being tired and I even managed to go to the cinema some afternoons.

I shared a dressing room with Ken Morey and one evening he said he had seen a film that afternoon and recommended it. I said I was saving up to buy a new jacket and could not afford it. "Oh", he said, "we don't pay!" and went on to explain that all I had to do was to go to the box-office and say, "Do you extend the courtesy of the house to the profession?" at which I would be given a complimentary ticket. I got him to repeat the phrase several times and the following afternoon, a Friday, when Doreen and I were free having already begged and borrowed everything required for the next play, I went with some trepidation to the box office of the local cinema wondering whether the woman behind the glass was as familiar with the magic phrase as Ken suggested. "Excuse me," I said, clearing my throat, "do you extend the courtesy of the house to the profession?" Without a word the woman reached for a stamp, stamped a ticket and handed it to me. I took it thankfully and made my way into the darkened cinema.

While we were rehearsing "George and Margaret", John Lewis was busy in the scene-dock painting the scenery and I would spend my free moments watching him as he sloshed the thick water paint on to the flats and grumbling endlessly in his strong Welsh accent about practically everything. "The bloody this... and the bloody that..." But he was a competent scenic artist and the sets were generally well done.

On Sunday morning when we put up the set, I learned the art of "throwing a line". Scenery is made up of a series of tall canvases known as "flats" stretched on wooden frames on the same principle as an artist's canvas. At the back on each side they have two cleats, one at the top and one at the bottom and a length of sash-cord known as a "line". The canvases are placed side by side and pulled tightly together by the line being thrown up over the top two cleats, pulled down round the lower two and tied off. The flats are then held upright by struts hooked on-to the back and attached to the floor of the stage by nails or the weight of sandbags. Doors and windows are made in the same manner and incorporated as and where they are needed. The theatre had two sets of flats so that one was in use while the other was being painted. In weekly rep. in those days this was a luxury; many scenic artists had to repaint the same set each Sunday.

I was to learn later that "throwing a line" the "dock" and many other expressions that have a maritime flavour owe their origin to the fact that, in the eighteenth and nineteenth centuries, the scene shifters in the London theatres were sailors earning extra money between voyages.

On the Monday morning Doreen and I dressed the set and prepared the props, and in the afternoon we dress-rehearsed almost until the curtain went up. On the first night of "George and Margaret" I was too busy to be nervous and the play went well with Rex, as the absent-minded father, getting most of the laughs. However, when I got back to the digs after the performance I found Miss Hinton and Mr Critchley waiting for me. They both congratulated me, but I got the distinct feeling that they were not impressed. They hinted, even that they were not too sure I had chosen the right profession.

The press, however, was enthusiastic. The Southport Guardian saying that;

"The ovation of the audience of 350 left no doubt that the company's debut had been a great success. The acting and easy manner with which the players presented this hilarious domestic comedy by Gerald Savory won complete favour."

It went to praise Rex Deering's playing of the Father and Catherine Harding's "charming portrayal" of the Mother, ending with;

"Other parts well played include those by Edwin Apps, Sylvia Kelly, Ken Morey, Michael de Barrass who also produced, Isabel Grist and Vera Williamson."

in other words; everyone.

I got a more individual, if rather back-handed notice in "The Southport Visitor" which said that;

"Edwin Apps, as the younger brother, behaves as one expects a younger brother to behave"

The second play was J.B. Priestley's "An Inspector Calls". I had had the script of "George and Margaret" for longer than a week and all my evenings free to learn the part. "An Inspector Calls" was different; I was given the script on the Saturday and we were playing every night. Suddenly it was weekly rep with a vengeance.

Looking back on the productions of those weekly rep companies, the surprising thing is how good some of them were, better often than the companies that had twice the time to rehearse. A play produced in a week is like a sketch for a painting and in the same way that sketches can be more alive and interesting than the final painting, so in a weekly rep production, as there is no time for extraneous detail, the company is forced to go for the essentials of the story and if the play is a good play with a good story and if the actors are reasonably well cast, their nervous energy will give the production a vibrant quality that is often missing when a more leisurely rehearsal schedule has given the actors time to go into their characters more deeply, but not quite deeply enough. The advantage is of course ephemeral. The moment the actors begin to relax, the lack of real preparation becomes evident and the production falls to pieces.

I don't remember much about "An Inspector Calls", or "Lover's Leap", a comedy by Philip Johnson, in which I played Poynter, the butler (I got the part because I had tails) nor "Suspect", a thriller by Edmund Percy and Reginald Denham in which I played Robert Smith, but the next play, J.B. Priestley's "Eden End" was a turning point for me. In the first four plays of the season I had been cast as a young man of more or less my own age, but in J.B.Priestly's "Eden End", I was cast as the elderly Dr Kirby, whose favourite daughter has run off to go on the stage, married an actor and comes home pretending to be successful but is discovered to be anything but.

To play someone resembling your self is difficult and calls for an objectivity and self-assurance that few young actors have and I certainly did not when I was seventeen. An old theatrical adage claimed that no one could be a convincing juvenile while he still had his own hair and teeth. In my case, although not quite so drastic, it was almost another ten years before I could play a young man and feel comfortable in the part. But I could play old men. I had lived among them, been surrounded by them, studied them and, in an odd way, longed to be one myself. Dr Kirby was right up my street.

This of course was my opinion and, as I soon realised, not one shared by the other members of the company who grumbled at the idea of an important character part being given to an inexperienced boy. Catherine Harding was especially vexed at having to play her major scene with a seventeen-year-old-father. Rehearsals went well and my playing of the part seemed to meet with approval even from Catherine Harding, but mutterings continued about the fact I looked so young.

My costume, a grey worsted suit with a wing collar and stock, together with a wig, had been ordered from Samuels in London. When it arrived, Michael handed it to me saying "You'll have to try and make-up as well as you can, do you need help? I said I thought I could manage.

Before the dress rehearsal, I got into my dressing room early and once there, all the experimenting I had done with make-up in the attic at Gloucester began to pay off.

Originally, the need for actors to use make-up had been due to the use of candlelight when candles had floated in a trough at the actors' feet and cast unnatural shadows on their faces. When gaslight replaced candles, the same footlight system was used and the problem had not been rethought in the change to electricity. Today, of course, stage lighting is highly sophisticated and comes at you from every point of the compass except the feet so there is practically no need for make-up, but in the theatre of the 1940s, the art of make-up was a matter of tradition, a tradition handed on from generation to generation like the art of painting icons in Russia.

Leichner grease paint came in sticks that were numbered. For a straight make-up, numbers 5, a yellow, and number 9, a brick red, were rubbed over the whole face and neck with the red concentrated on the cheekbones. The eyes were outlined with a dark blue liner and, as a finishing touch, bright red dots of carmine were placed on the inside corner of each eye and on the outside corner of each nostril so that, close to, the actor resembled nothing so much as a freshly painted rocking-horse.

For character parts, the face was covered with No 5, the yellow grease paint, only. The forehead was heavily lined and lines were drawn down each side from the nose. Crow's feet were drawn in on the sides of the eyes. All these lines were done with a lake liner, a deep violet red. The effect of this on young faces was to suggest some serious skin disease rather than age.

My interest in painting had led me to look at the problem afresh, to see the face in terms of highlights and shadows, with the object of showing, in T.S. Eliot's words "The skull beneath the skin". The wig that Samuels provided had the usual cotton forehead piece to cover the actor's hair with the thinning grey hair starting further back. The idea was to put the wig on first and cover the cotton with the same colour as the rest of the face. At that point it was usual to paint horizontal lines over the wig-join to disguise it, but this only accentuated the join. My approach was to treat the forehead vertically by sharpening with highlights the bones of the skull leading up from above the eyebrows, shading the sides of the forehead, and in that way disguising the wig-join by going up and down rather than along. For the rest of the face I threw the eyes into shadow and put highlights on the lids, highlighted the cheekbones and sunk the cheeks a little with shadows, sharpened the nose with a highlight on the ridge and shadowed the sides, with more shadow under the chin. A white moustache made from crêpe hair covered the mouth.

When I looked in the glass I saw Dr Kirby looking back at me. Satisfied, I finished dressing with the upright wing-collar and stock covering my neck, put number 5 on the backs of my hands and went out on to the stage to join the other actors. The effect was most gratifying, people looked, looked away and looked back quickly, not having at first realised who I was. Michael muttered that it was amazing and Catherine Harding began to look more cheerful.

Acting is essentially a matter of imagination. When Ellen Terry was asked what she considered to be the most important requisite for an actor, she replied, "Imagination, imagination, I put it first years ago!" The problem is, of course, how an actor sparks his imagination to the point that he believes himself to be the character so strongly that the other actors and the audience come to share his belief. It happens in different ways and at different times, sometimes early on in rehearsal and at others much later, sometimes not until the first night. What sparks it depends on the individual; it can be finding the right shoes, the right coat or simply getting the walk right. With Dr Kirby it was the make-up, from that moment I was Dr Kirby and I gave the first proper performance of my career. Actors are generous and they like nothing better than to see someone succeed and the Crown Players were very generous to me. Suddenly I felt I was accepted as a pro, an impression reinforced a few weeks later when I was made a member of Equity, the actor's trade union.

One pleasing result was that Catherine Harding suddenly seemed to take me seriously. She warned me that if I stayed in weekly rep I would pick up bad habits and insisted that I must go to a theatre school. I listened to her advice as I had come to respect her as an actress. In difficult circumstances she gave some excellent performances. After that season our paths never crossed again and I have often wondered what became of her.

During these weeks I had of course been returning to Miss Hinton's for my meals with Mr Critchley. Rex would often ask me about him with a slightly worried air. In fact we got on rather well at first. I think he enjoyed being vicariously part of a repertory company, and I gradually pieced together his history. He told me how he had lived on the south coast – Weymouth, if I remember correctly – and how he had a young friend of whom he was very fond, but whom he was no longer able to see. He showed me, with an air of sadness, a photo of a boy of about 14 in bathing shorts, and I got the impression that there had been some sort of scandal and that he had come to Southport under duress. He hinted from time to time that he was from a very grand family, but the figure that infused all his reminiscences and appeared in his conversation like Mr Dick's King Charles's head was "My old bishop, the Bishop of London, Dr Winnington-Ingram", repeated like an incantation. It was "My old bishop, The Bishop of London, Dr. Winnington-Ingram used to say" or "As I said to my old bishop, The Bishop of London, Dr. Winnington-Ingram" or "One day when I was walking with my old bishop, The Bishop of London, Dr. Winnington-Ingram" for breakfast, lunch and tea. Nevertheless, we got on quite well and he even made me a present of a nicely bound set of 19th-century poets, which I still have. However, the incompatibility between his retired life and my intense activity meant that I became restive under the endless accounts of the doings and sayings of Dr. Winnington-Ingram and he got tired of my obsession with my work. The situation became strained and one day Miss Hinton informed me that he found that my coming in late and making a noise disturbed him and that either I must go or he would. As he was paying more than I was, I must leave at the end of the week.

It was a blow as my room was comfortable and I enjoyed Miss Hinton's cooking. Then, too, at the bottom of Portland Street there was a rank of horse-drawn cabs and on wet nights I had enjoyed the luxury of being driven to the theatre amid the homely smell of straw and stable, leaning back on the seat feeling like Henry Irving on his way to the Lyceum.

When I broke the news at the theatre, Rex seemed relieved and suggested I go to Mrs Rimmer at 43 West Street, where several of the others were staying and he thought there might be room. Mrs Rimmer did have a room; what was more, it was five shillings cheaper than Miss Hinton's so, returning to collect my things, I moved in immediately. The contrast between Miss Hinton's and Mrs Rimmer's was, from my point of view, totally in favour of Mrs Rimmer's. Whereas Miss Hinton's had been a respectable boarding house, Mrs Rimmer's was a real theatrical digs. Miss Hinton had left me a cold supper after the show, which I ate alone, but at Mrs Rimmer's we all sat down to a relaxed and warming supper and a great deal of theatre chat and gossip. It was heady stuff and in leaving Mr Critchley behind, I felt I had at last left school and was living *la vie bohème* and I couldn't get enough of it.

It was about this time that someone got hold of a copy of

Stanislavsky's "An Actor Prepares" and it was passed round the company with everyone eagerly reading it. Stanislavsky, the founder of the Moscow Art theatre and first producer of the plays of Anton Chekhov, caused a revolution in the theatre at the end of the nineteenth century with his theories about the art of acting. His basic premise was that acting should not be superficial, but that it called for a profound study of the character to be portrayed, to enable the actor to present it from the inside and not comment upon it from the outside. To achieve this end, the Moscow Art Theatre rehearsed for many months and explored all sorts of different approaches before finally presenting the production before an audience. Stanislavsky encapsulated his ideas in two books, "My Life in Art" and "An Actor Prepares".

Although he had worked with Ellen Terry's son, the theatre designer, Edward Gordon Craig, Stanislavsky's ideas did not reach our shores in any significant way until the 1930s when John Gielgud and a few brave spirits began to try to put them into practice. The war brought theatrical experiment, like much else, to an end and it was only in the late forties that these ideas trickled down to the ordinary actor. "An Actor Prepares" is a book that every actor should read, but the best moment for doing so is not when one is playing a part in, say, "The Girl Who Couldn't Quite" in a weekly rep season in a seaside resort.

"An Actor Prepares" hit the Crown Players like a tsunami and with a similarly devastating effect. We always knew where it had got to and who was in the middle of reading it because of its repercussion on their current performance. Suddenly, without warning, in the middle of a slick comedy scene which depended on pace for its success, the actor or actress would unaccountably slow down. An intense and dreamlike expression would come into their eyes as they entered the spiritual life of the character, while their movements, subjected to a deep inner scrutiny as to their authenticity, would make them suddenly appear to be moving under water. The scene would go down the drain but the actor, once in the wings, would say in an awed voice, "It's incredible, I really felt the character tonight".

Time heals everything and eventually everyone had read the book and things got back to normal. Easter weekend was the occasion of my first getting drunk.

Rex, whose matrimonial life had been eventful (I once met him sloping into the post office ("got to wire some blood-money" he said in a low voice) had recently married Vera Williamson, a singer from Manchester. Vera was in her early thirties and they had just had a son, Howard. As it was Easter, they had arranged for Howard to be christened on the Sunday and they kindly invited me to the evening party. It was a very jolly affair. Vera's mother and sister were there and Michael de Barrass and his wife, Sylvia Kelly. It was my first experience of a theatrical party and I found it a great contrast to the parties I had been to with my parents. When they asked me what I would like to drink, I remembered that at home I had been allowed to drink a glass of dry sherry on occasions, so I plumped for that. The party got going and glasses were refilled, mine included, and by the end I had drunk a bottle of sherry and was in no state to walk back to my digs, so, with much giggling, Vera and her sister put me to bed on the sofa. I woke up the next morning feeling that my head would burst. As it was a Monday, there was a dress rehearsal and first night. How I got through it I shall never know, but it gave me a healthy respect for alcohol.

After "Eden End" the rhythm continued with "Meet the Wife", The Girl who Couldn't Quite", "Acacia Avenue", "The Shining Hour" (I am battling with an enormous part in the "Shining Hour") "Fly Away Peter" and "Peace Comes to Peckham". At that point, it being the Easter school holidays, Holly came to join us. It had been agreed, the rules about employing amateurs being less strict in those day, that he should play the part of the solicitor in Terrence Rattigan's "The Winslow Boy." I was of course overjoyed to see him and reassured when he told me he thought I had greatly improved and that Rex thought I was doing well. He acquitted himself well as Desmond Curry, though he admitted to finding the pace of weekly rep. a bit of a shock. Then it was "Spring-time for Henry" which gave me my first rest, there being no part for me, but I was still A.S.M. and the prop list that week presented a special problem as it included a pregnant cat. The next play was "The Poltergeist" by Frank Harvey in which I played an old farmer. I based the character on Old Bill Sheaff, the Wenderton bailiff, which gave me another chance to do an interesting make-up.

> "My part as the old farmer was well received and I got a round on my exit which, on a Monday night, is good going. I will get a photo taken – it is a good make-up, I have blacked out two teeth for the occasion and a red jolly face."

There follows a sketch.

Getting a round on your exit was something everyone hoped for and many were the devices used by the old actors to encourage the audience to do its duty in this regard. They would say part of their last line in the middle of the stage, move rapidly to the door, open it, turn, say the last part of the line to the audience, and exit quickly, shutting the door after them and at the same time stamping a foot hard on the stage. The idea was that the audience would hear the noise, think it was someone beginning to clap and join in. The practice was frowned upon, being considered unsporting, rather like shooting a sitting bird, but I often saw it done, sometimes with success.

The same letter begins with the news,

> "I have heard from Holly this morning saying that Christopher Hassall can use me as Assistant stage manager and small part in the Canterbury Festival and I have just written to Mr Hassall myself."

On the 22nd of May, my parents arrived for a long weekend for my eighteenth birthday. I had booked them into the Scarisbrick Hotel

> "the garage of which backs on to my digs"

and the plan was that they were to see the last performance of "Fools Rush in" and the first night of "The Two Mrs Carrolls". They enjoyed Kenneth Horne's "Fools Rush In," in which I played the bridegroom, the bride being played by a newcomer to the company. Jean was twenty-five, attractive with a sense of humour, and we hit it off at once. What's more we were in the same digs, which made for greater intimacy, especially when everyone else had gone to bed. Briefly, I was having a very enjoyable initiation into adult life and it was absorbing my thoughts.

In the plays of those days the characters did a great deal of smoking which meant cigarette boxes and match boxes were distributed on tables all over the sets, a match being carefully wedged half out of each box so that the actor could pull it out easily and not have to open the box, thus averting the danger of scattering matches due to first-night nerves. It was my job to check cigarettes and matches before each performance and again in the intervals. On the first night of "The Two Mrs Carrolls" the second act opened with a scene between me as Pennington and an elderly character actress who had joined the company for that production, Zaza Mottram, as my Aunt, Mrs Latham. As the curtain went up, I noticed that her hands were shaking.

Early in the scene she had the line,

"I think I'll have a cigarette, Pennington".

"Of course, Aunt" I replied "Let me get you one."

I went to the cigarette box only to discover that it was empty. I had not checked the props as I should have done before the play and, as the scene was played in evening dress and I had been busy in the Interval struggling into my dress shirt and white tie, I had not done the second obligatory check either.

"Oh dear, Aunt, I'm afraid there don't seem to be any. Perhaps in this box over here," as I crossed the stage to another box only to find that it, too, was empty. I looked across at my "aunt" and saw that she was in a bad way. I heard stirrings as panic spread behind the scenes. "I'll just look in the dining room" I hurried off leaving her on the stage alone with nothing to do, something I felt instinctively she would not enjoy. In the dark of the wings, someone thrust a cigarette into my hand and I re-entered; "Here you are, Aunt, let me light it for you. Oh, the matches don't seem to be..." and so I struggled on. Finally we got the cigarette alight and began to try to save the rest of the scene. When the curtain came down I had to face the fury of Michael de Barrass threatening to sack me, the reproaches of Doreen and worst of all having to beg forgiveness from Zaza. She was kind and forgiving, but treated me with obvious suspicion for the rest of the week. All this with my parents out front who had come many miles to see how well their son was succeeding in his chosen profession.

Not checking the props was by no means the only mistake I made that season. On another occasion, as the curtain came down after the curtain call, it was my job to rush into the prompt corner and put the National Anthem on the panatrope. I did so, there was the roll of drums, the audience stood up and the band played "Land of Hope and Glory" to laughter and cheers from the audience. I had put the record on the wrong side. Having no ear for music I didn't realise anything was wrong until I felt Michael de Barrass bearing down on me in a fury. I was again threatened with the sack.

After "The Two Mrs Carrolls", the last play of the season was "The Sacred Flame". While we were playing it, as there were no more rehearsals, we took a day off and went to Liverpool and saw a matinee of Pinero's "The Magistrate" at the four-weekly Liverpool Playhouse, considered to be one of the best repertory company in the country Cyril Luckham played the magistrate and I was bowled over by his grace and skill.

On the Saturday night the curtain fell for the last time and we made our tearful farewells, exchanged addresses and promised undying friendship. We did the strike and I returned to the digs where Jean and I had a delicious last moment, the company left for Portrush in Ireland where they were to do a summer season and I took the train back to Gloucester.

As the train pulled out of Southport station on that Sunday morning the 6th June, I thought of all that had happened since my arrival on the 15th January, barely five months before; I had become a professional actor, played eighteen parts without getting the sack and the company had even wanted me to go with them to Portrush. What was more, I had not only become a paid-up member of Equity, but I had ceased to be a virgin. Not a bad start, I thought, not bad at all.

*

When I got back to Gloucester, a letter was waiting for me from Christopher Hassall telling me that the company was rehearsing in London, but he wanted me to go straight to Canterbury and help Dorothy Sayers, who was overseeing the Canterbury end of the project, so I quickly unpacked, repacked and set off.

The Canterbury Festival owed its origins to Bishop Bell of Chichester who, in the 1920s, while he was Dean of Canterbury, wishing to bring Drama back into the Church, started a scheme whereby leading writers were commissioned to write plays to be performed in the Chapter House under the auspices of the Friends of the Cathedral. Authors had included Lawrence Binyon, Christopher Hassall and T.S. Eliot, whose "Murder in the Cathedral", about the death of Beckett, had become a classic. These plays were all in verse and they had begun a vogue for verse plays that continued.

When I got to Canterbury, I went straight to Guilton where it was arranged I should stay and commute daily. I found my grandmother shooting rats. The stockyard below the breakfast-room window was empty, the cattle being out to grass for the summer, and a quantity of rats could be seen drinking at the water tank. Armed with a 4.10, my grandmother was busy picking them off and shouting to Wellard to go and pick them up. She seemed very pleased to see me, but when I began to tell of my experiences and use some of the freer theatrical expressions I had become accustomed to, I felt a wave of disapproval and had to quickly readjust.

The following morning I went to meet "D. Sayers" or "the Sayers", as she was known.

Dorothy L. Sayers was, not only, a distinguished scholar, feminist and author of ground-breaking detective fiction, but she had written a popular radio series about the life of Jesus of Nazareth called "The Man Born to Be King" which had had a huge impact in those pre-television days. I had listened to it with my parents a few years previously during the Easter holidays and we had been moved and impressed by the force and modernity of the work. She was currently working on what was to be her major opus, a translation of Dante's Divine Comedy. The play we were now to do, "The Zeal of Thy House" was the story of William of Sens who, after the disastrous fire of 1174, designed and built much of the Cathedral including the great choir, but who, when he was hauled up to see the placing of the keystone, fell to the ground and was paralysed for life. The contemporary chronicler, Gervase the monk, describes the accident and attributes it to "either the Vengeance of God or the Envy of the Devil". Dorothy Sayers pounced on these words to tell the story of a great artist who, in his excessive pride, seeks to rival God, which leads to his downfall. The play was in verse and had been written just before the war for the 1937 festival. Now it was to be revived. Apprehensive at the thought of meeting someone so very famous, I made my way to the Cathedral and asked where I could find her; "You'll find her in the shed", I was told, "she has just reduced a journalist to tears." The shed was a temporary building erected on a bombed site of which there were a great many in Canterbury at that time.

Wondering if I, too, was about to be reduced to tears, I approached the shed and went in. At the other end I saw a stout figure bending over a table, busily involved with paper and glue. I announced myself. Dorothy looked up; she wore thick glasses, her hair was brushed over to one side and cut short in a masculine style and she wore a double-breasted coat and skirt with a very distinctive gold pendant, which I never saw her without. She greeted me warmly and explained that she was making angels' wings and please would I help.

In "The Zeal of Thy House" the four Archangels, Michael, Raphael, Gabriel, and the recording angel, Cassiel, formed the chorus and commented on the action. Their costumes included a pair of huge folded wings that rose, high above their heads in one direction and almost touched the ground in the other. These wings, made on wooden frames, Dorothy Sayers and I spent the week covering with feathers made of folded paper torn from old copies of The Christian Science Monitor, of which there seemed to be an endless supply. Once they had been glued on and the glue had dried, we painted them with gold paint and all the time she chatted and I listened. She talked on many subjects. One, I remember, which resonated with me then and has done since was that she drew a contrast between work and employment, saying that work was something you did in which you could take pride, but employment was something you did only to earn a living. It was important, she insisted, that we got back to a world where people worked.

At lunchtime each day we went to a restaurant and I noticed that when the bill came, she regularly took out a pencil and did the calculation so as to give a tip of exactly ten per cent. She was a wonderful companion, forthright, down to earth, and very funny. At one point she said we must go and see how the ladies of Canterbury were getting on with sewing the costumes. I followed her into another shed where the ladies were sitting in a semi-circle with their heads bent over their needlework. Dorothy looked at what they were doing in silence until one lady, holding up her work, asked what she thought of it. Dorothy peered at it, looked up and said, "Well, if you don't mind my saying so, you've properly buggered it up." A frisson went round the circle and heads bent lower. Such language had never been heard in the shadow of the Cathedral.

One morning she arrived in great distress "I've lost the keys of the Detection Club!" The Detection Club was the club for crime writers of which she was President (she was succeeded after her death by Agatha Christie.) "I must ring my husband", so we went to find a telephone. "You've got to find them," she told him "they can't get in. Tell them I can't come, I'm making angels' wings". I wondered what the members of the Detection Club would make of her alibi.

The "Friends of Canterbury Cathedral" had been founded some years earlier by Miss Margaret Babington who, always to be seen on her bicycle, was a familiar figure in Canterbury. Miss Babington considered the "Friends of Canterbury Cathedral" to be hers and, by extension, the Festival to be hers as well, an attitude that had led to several sharp exchanges with Dorothy, the details of which Dorothy had told me while we folded and glued.

To save my having to go back and forth to Guilton every day, I had been invited to stay with Mrs Vera Findlay who lived in Burgate Street, which backs on to the Cathedral Close. Mrs Findlay had been on the stage in her youth and was considered to be the official representative of the profession in Canterbury. No theatrical event was complete without her presence and any theatrical figure coming to the city, was officially welcomed by her. I knew her because she had helped us with the school plays, doing make-up for the boys who played the girls' parts and generally bringing a professional air to the proceedings. I had always liked Mrs Findlay and now I was a professional, we got on better than ever. On the Friday she suggested that I invite Dorothy for a drink when we had finished our angels' wings. I passed on the invitation and at about six o'clock we went to the house.

It was still difficult to get hold of any form of alcohol, but Mrs Findlay had managed to procure a bottle of sherry, which she proudly produced. Seeing it, I was reminded of the Deering's christening party and decided to be careful, but Dorothy brightened visibly and settled down comfortably in a big armchair. Whether it was because the angels' wings were at last finished, or the prospect of a welcome glass of sherry, Dorothy was in a relaxed mood and there was a great deal of gossip and laughter with Miss Babington and her bicycle as the main target. Mrs Findlay wondered whether when 'Babs' went to heaven she would take the bicycle with her, and Dorothy supposed that when she got to the gate and St Peter asked her who she was, she would reply; "I am Miss Margaret Babington of the Friends of Canterbury Cathedral."

The conversation then turned to what it was like living beside the Cathedral and Mrs Findlay told us that it could be eerie at night. She said she had often felt presences there and instanced one night when she and her daughter were going through the Dark Entry and her daughter felt something take her by the shoulder and pull her back; she screamed and they both ran. Dorothy listened and talked about well-known sightings of ghosts, while helping herself liberally from the bottle, which was eventually discovered to be empty. She was staying with Gerald Knight, the Cathedral organist, who had composed the music for the play. His house was in the Close and she was about to leave by the front door, when Mrs Findlay suggested she take the short cut through her garden and across Canon Crumb's garden, adding that his house had been destroyed in the bombing and the site was empty.

Canon Crumb was an authority on stained glass and it was said that, during the Canterbury blitz, he spent the night on his knees in front of the altar praying, "O Lord, please spare our stained glass, but Lord, if some must be broken, let it be the nineteenth-century glass and not the twelfth-century". The Lord had answered his request and the stained glass remained intact, but clearly the Canon had omitted to ask the same privilege for his house.

I offered to accompany Dorothy, which she accepted. Night had fallen and it was dark as we made our way out of Mrs Findlay's garden and into what had been Canon Crumb's. Dorothy was ahead of me and watching her walk, I got the impression that in the cold air the sherry was taking its toll. Suddenly there was a loud shriek and she disappeared from view. I had a moment of panic thinking the Cathedral ghost had made off with her, before I realised she had fallen into a bomb crater.

I rushed to pull her out, but the crater was deep and Dorothy was no light weight; I heaved and tugged, Dorothy struggled and pushed until suddenly, like Pooh being pulled out of Rabbit's hole when he had lost weight, she came out quicker than expected and I fell on my back with Dorothy Sayers on top of me. We picked ourselves up and she thanked me, adding that she would be all right from there on and, giving herself a shake and throwing her shoulders back, she marched off into the dark. Hoping there were no more craters in her path, I returned to the house.

The next day being Saturday, the cast were due to arrive. The stage manager, John Brebner, whom I was assisting, had arrived the day before and it was arranged that we should both go to the station to meet them and organize transport to their hotels. I had met and worked with rep actors; now, for the first time I was to meet real West End actors.

The first person I met on the platform was Christopher Hassall. The stage manager introduced me and Christopher, smiling, asked how I was getting on with Miss Sayers. I told him we had finished the angels' wings and he said Dorothy must be relieved as she set great store by them. Himself a poet and actor, Christopher Hassall was best known as Ivor Novello's lyricist. Ivor Novello was the actor-composer who had composed the popular song of the First World War, "Keep The Home Fires Burning" and all through the thirties and forties, his romantic musicals (usually concerned with Royal life and loves in Ruritania) with titles like "Careless Rapture" and "The Dancing Years" were a huge success, with their songs, ("We'll Gather Lilacs in the Spring Again") on everyone's lips.

Christopher, who had come to notice while he was an undergraduate, as Romeo in an OUDS production of "Romeo and Juliet" produced by John Gielgud with Peggy Ashcroft as Juliet, had been extremely good-looking as a young man. Now, in his forties, he was putting on weight, but had a lively and intelligent air and a beautiful voice and was much in demand as a reader of poetry, both his own and other people's. I had often heard him on the Third Programme, the cultural channel of the BBC. With him was Jill Balcon, daughter of Sir Michael Balcon, the film producer and herself a poetry reader who often read with Christopher. The other members of the company collected round us and we moved out to where the taxis were waiting. In the taxi I noticed a small, rather serious-looking man. He sat quietly saying little, but everyone seemed to respect him. His name, I learned, was George Benson.

Michael Goodliffe who was to play William of Sens and Joseph O'Conor, the Archangel Michael, had come down separately and we did not see them until the first rehearsal.

That first rehearsal was an eye-opener. From the moment Joseph O'Conor, with his huge voice and splendid presence began effortlessly;

"I am God's servant, Michael the Archangel
I walk in the world of men invisible,
Bearing the sword that Christ bequeathed His Church
To sunder and to save."

I realised at once that these actors were in another league from the Crown Players and I would need to work hard to get to their level.

I was to play the small part of Geoffrey, a workman, and I had short comedy scene with George Benson. By the way Christopher treated him, it was clear that he was considered to be a specialist in comedy. We had lunch together at Lefevres in the same tearoom where I had so often had tea with my Mother and Gladys in what seemed now a distant world.

During lunch several people congratulated George Benson on a radio comedy series he was currently doing with Joyce Grenfell. As we talked, I gathered that he had just returned from Broadway where he had been playing Desmond Curry in the American production of "The Winslow Boy".

Final rehearsals went well and the play opened to enthusiastic audiences. The only problem was that on the First Night there was an undignified scramble for seats. This was due to Miss Babington's telling everyone to "Hurry along!" Dorothy was furious and insisted on taking charge of the seating. She ordered that the queue of people should be halted at the entrance to the cloisters and that she, in the Chapter House, would send a runner when she was ready for more. She was very keen on this idea of the runner, and we were all expecting to see someone young and active, so it was a surprise when a very old gentleman made his appearance and told us he was "Miss Sayers' runner".

In the part of Geoffrey I again drew on the Wenderton characters and their broad Kentish accents and did a make-up based again on Old Bill Sheaff. Christopher Hassall seemed pleased. When I was having lunch one day with him and George Benson, the two of them asked me what I intended to do.

I told them I had to do National Service. They had both been in the war and commiserated with me. Then, remembering Catherine Harding's advice, I said I was thinking of going to a theatre school. They both seemed to approve and Christopher said, "It won't make you a better actor but it will make you better theatrically educated"

As we talked, it became clear that they were old friends. They told me that they had met on a tour of Australia at about the time I was born. The tour had been led by Athene Seyler and her husband

Nicholas Hannen; Athene Seyler was a major figure in the theatre of the twenties, thirties and forties and famous for her comedy technique. She had written a book, "The Craft of Comedy," in the form of a dialogue with the promising young actor, Stephen Haggard, who had died in the war. She had taught at RADA where George Benson had been her star pupil and had subsequently married her daughter. The marriage had failed and it was to recover from this that he had gone to the States. Now, he was about to begin rehearsals for the 1949 Old Vic season at the New Theatre.

I asked them which school I should try for, and it turned out that Christopher was the Master of the Voice at the Old Vic School. Started just after the war, it had a reputation for being the most innovative of the schools and students from it formed The Young Vic Company, a new and exciting classical company. The school's head was Glen Byam Shaw and the staff included Michel St Denis the famous French director. Christopher suggested I audition and George added that if I wanted a bed when I was in London he could put me up. It all seemed too good to be true.

Playing the small part of "The Fair Lady" was a professional actress, Pamela White. It turned out that she had agreed to do it as she was staying with her mother who lived near Canterbury. I noticed that she and George Benson seemed to spend a lot of time together.

At the end of the week, there was a party in a hotel, which ended with us all round Dorothy who talked about her translation of Dante. It was fascinating and I was mortified when I had to leave to catch the last bus out to Ash.

While I had been staying with my grandmother, I had found her far from contented. Living alone in the house, she was virtually a prisoner because, although she still had the Hillman, she could not drive and when she asked Uncle John if someone could drive her to do her shopping, his answer always seemed to be that everyone was busy. If she asked him to get her things he forgot, and altogether she had the sense of being neglected.

In my grandfather's Will, it was stipulated that my grandmother should have the contents of the house during her life on condition she kept it "in good repair and condition and insured against loss or damage by fire to the full value thereof."

In other words she was condemned to stay for the rest of her life at Guilton polishing furniture. I had noticed that in the rebuilding of Canterbury a block of neo-Georgian flats had just been built in Burgate Street, and I now suggested to her that she had no reason to stay at Guilton and comply with the conditions of the Will and that she would be more comfortable in one of the flats. The notion appealed to her and in the following months she moved. The move was a success, she enjoyed living in the town and it enabled her to see her friends more easily. On one occasion when I was staying with her, she announced that she had some schoolgirls coming to tea. Surprised, I waited for an invasion of gym-slips, only to see her greet several old ladies with whom she herself had been at school, including her great friend, Dossie Noote. The Nootes had been the Goodsons' neighbours at Upton St Peters, and Dossie, now Lady Somebody and a widow, was living in Canterbury. I noted her surname, which I was to make use of some years later.

But my grandmother's move to Canterbury did not please Uncle John, as it left him with the empty house on his hands and no one to look after it. Besides, my grandmother had been useful to him as she had answered the telephone at weekends and greeted clients in his absence. This led to a breach between them and as a result she became closer to my aunt and my mother.

It was about that time that a curious chance event occurred: my father had to go to Worcester one day to negotiate with the head of a family firm of auctioneers and land agents. After the negotiations they lunched together and the man remarked on my father not having a west-country accent. When he explained that he came from Kent, the man said that they had had a chap who had moved to Kent. "My father caught him fiddling the books and gave him twenty-four hours to get out of Worcester," he said. "We heard that he joined a firm near Canterbury," adding "His name was Bernard Hincks".

My mother did not hesitate to inform grandmother of this and the result was that she renewed relations with my father and began to visit them in Gloucester and my parents would stay with her in Canterbury. On these occasions I was surprised to see how well she and my father got on, she would ask his advice on everything and seemed to depend on him from then on. Seeing them together, I got the impression that they were very old friends

CHAPTER ELEVEN

—

While I was at Ash, I was summoned to Chatham for an army medical. This gave a gleam of hope. If you were found to be unfit or unsuitable, you escaped National Service. One heard of all sorts of ruses people adopted that proved more or less successful. Kenneth Tynan, the theatre critic, was said to have bought a pea-green silk suit and attempted to seduce the doctor, a ruse that had enabled him to escape completely – from National Service, whether he escaped from the doctor is not recorded.

I tried a more mundane ploy, limping in and complaining of flat feet. The doctor examined my feet carefully and looked up saying he could see nothing wrong with them. "You don't have to walk on them," I told him, but it was no good, I was passed A1. At some time in those months I had received a letter asking me which branch of the military I should prefer to serve in. Hearing that in the RAF you slept in sheets rather than blankets, I plumped for the RAF.

Then, at the end of August the letter arrived ordering me to report to Padgate in Lancashire. So it was back to Lancashire for the second time in eight months, but in what a different frame of mind I travelled.

I suppose, had England been threatened by an enemy, I might have reacted like my father in 1914. But in 1949 there was neither threat nor enemy; the war was over. It had cast its hateful shadow over our lives for the previous ten years and now the last thing we wanted to do was to put on uniforms and salute flags. Moreover the country was in ruins; people were fed up with the drabness of their surroundings and wanted cheering up; the theatre was needed – full houses in January on the pier at Southport had convinced me of that. If I were to be of any use to the community, it was more likely to be as an actor than an airman. It was in this frame of mind that I travelled north.

I remember almost nothing about the first few days in the RAF, except that on the first night a lot of the young men cried because they had never been away from home before. We were issued with uniforms and sent our civilian clothes home in sad little parcels, then after a few days, I was suddenly called by the sergeant and taken to see Flight Lieutenant Burton Gosling, the Entertainments Officer, who said that they were doing a play and someone had had to drop out. The play was in a few days' time and they had seen that I was an actor; could I learn a part in a short time? I said I could. The play was "See How They Run" by Philip King, a farce in which almost all the cast are, or pretend to be, clergymen. The part was that of the Bishop. I described events in a letter to my parents on the 8th September:

"From: 2443204 A/C2 Apps, Hut 138, 7 Flight B Squadron, Number (1) RTW S of RT, RAF Padgate, Near Warrington.

"Much has happened since I last wrote, and I shall probably phone you again to-night. I was posted yesterday to Padgate, the crowd I was with have been posted to Wilmslow near Manchester, but as I am doing this show I have been specially posted. Of course this is real HELL for the next 8 weeks. The N.C.O.s are of the very worst type (a mixture of prison warder, Joseph Kramer and a robot). Still 8 weeks can't last for ever, and I get a week's leave at the end! They have given me another hair cut (for which I paid 1/-) and my hair is no longer than 4" anywhere. I expect it will grow differently after this. On this job we get shouted at from daylight to dark, everything has to be cleaned, the coal box etc. everything has to be folded just so with cardboard in between the folds to make it look smart!! Sometimes I feel I could scream! At others I simply laugh. The one thing that keeps me going is this show in which I am play-ing the Bishop, a nice farce part, and considering the time I have had I am not making a bad job of it. They all seem very pleased and when they gave me the part on Monday and on Tuesday I arrived knowing the first Act they were suitably impressed."

My school friend Rhodes, whom I now knew as Gordon, had stayed on at school and passed the Higher Certificate. Now he was planning to train as a priest. This entailed a retreat at Cheltenham at which a Board of clergy judged the candidate's aptitude for the cloth. Gordon was turned down. This, he discovered later, was partly, due to the fact that Thoseby, with whom he had been on bad terms, had written a letter discouraging the board from accepting him.

Gordon had always seen his future in the Church, so it was a blow that left him disorientated. In the meantime he was called up. He, too, had plumped for the RAF and been ordered to go to Padgate, where on his first evening, Sunday 11th September, the recruits were marched off to see a play in the Gymnasium Theatre. His surprise was considerable when he recognised the bishop. There was no means of communicating in that situation, so it was sometime afterwards that I learned that he had been in the audience.

My contribution to the success of the play had apparently impressed Flight Lieutenant Gosling so that he now proposed that I stay at Padgate and help him organise the entertainment. To this end he took me to the Officer's Mess after the first performance to meet the Camp Commander. The officers welcomed me, they had apparently enjoyed the play and my performance and the Commanding Officer thought that my being posted to the camp to help with entertainment was a "damned good idea". Suddenly it seemed the RAF was not going to be such a bad thing after all. So it was arranged that I should do my initial 8 weeks' training and then have a permanent posting to Padgate.

During the training we were interviewed as to how we could best be employed during our 18 months service and what training we should receive. The first question was whether we wanted to try for a commission. As I had passed the Certificate "A" exam in the JTC, an exam that had largely depended on one's capacity to crawl in mud and stamp one's feet, I was eligible. But it meant signing on for two years. This was out of the question. If I hoped to get a place at the Old Vic School, I must be out of the RAF in 18 months. In any case, as I had the prospect of staying at Padgate and organizing entertainment I felt that this now hardly concerned me, so when the interviewer suggested that as I had "a nice speaking voice" I should go to the Wireless School and learn to tell aeroplanes when to take off and land, I agreed.

I did the eight weeks' training which proved predictably uncomfortable and a couple of days before the end, I was sent for by Flight Lieutenant Gosling. Supposing we were going to discuss plans for a first show, I took with me some notes I had made. But when I went into his office he greeted me with the news that he had suddenly been posted and that he was sorry, but the whole project was cancelled and there was nothing he could do for me. Two days later, I left for a week's leave at Gloucester to be followed by a posting to the Wireless School in Lincolnshire.

If ever in my life I have been a square peg in a round hole, it was at the RAF Wireless School. Telling aeroplanes when to take off and land, it seemed, included having to delve into the bowels of wireless and understand its mystery. I forget how long the course was, but at the end of it, as far as I was concerned, wireless had retained its mystery. In the exam at the end of the course, I got nought for technical knowledge and a hundred for speech. The officer, looking far from pleased, asked how I could explain my failure. "I imagine," I told him "it is because I do not have a technical mind". This seemed to upset him even more and he began to talk about my being sent to clean out lavatories, a fate that at that time seemed preferable to any more talk about waves, valves, condensers or printed circuits. In the end, however, it was decided that because of my nice speaking voice, I should be kept on. The question now, was where I should be sent to do all this talking to aeroplanes and it was here that my father played his card.

His office had recently been moved from the rather grand Victorian house in a park at the top of Alexandra Road, to a pre-fabricated building just outside Gloucester next to the offices of RAF Records. There, he had met and become friendly with a flight sergeant, who was interested in his First War flying experience. The flight sergeant happened to be in charge of posting recruits for their training. My father told him I was about to be posted and asked if it would be possible for me to be posted near Gloucester and the Flight sergeant said that it presented no problem. As a result I received a postcard, typed on my father's Remington portable. It is headed "Any Questions"

"The only question is, where shall we go next?

as Mr Pickwick paused in vain.

"Well, said that gentleman, "if you leave it to me to suggest our destination, I say...

"Are you going to ... ? said the strange man"

"I am, sir, said Mr Pickwick;

P.S. Where did Mr Pickwick go?"

I sent it back with the spaces filled in, "BATH". And a few days later I was posted to Colerne aerodrome near Bath where I remained for the rest of my sentence.

Bare and draughty, airfields are uncomfortable places to live and a tin hut with a tortoise stove that stinks of coke is not an agreeable environment. Colerne was an airfield built during the Battle of Britain (my father may very well have been responsible) Now it had outlived its usefulness and was being run down so that there were rarely more than two or three aeroplanes landing or taking off in the course of the day, But while there was a lack of aircraft, there was no lack of manpower. Six eighteen-year-old men, bursting with youth and vigour, had been engaged solely for the purpose of telling these planes when to take off and land. This meant that at any one time, five of these young men would be found lying on their beds in the hut we lived in.

It was in the RAF that I learned the full meaning of the word boredom.

Apart from the conscripts, the regulars, both officers and men, were a poor bunch, mainly people who, when the war ended, had lacked the courage to face civilian life. Some had tried it, but had signed on again, preferring being told what to do and grumbling about it to deciding for themselves and taking the consequences.

The conscripts were a heteroclite group; there was a very nice jazz trumpeter who was on drugs and kept going into the "ablutions" as the bathroom was called, to inject himself; his addiction passed totally unnoticed by the authorities. There was someone training to be a stockbroker, a future journalist with whom I became friendly and a good-looking young man who was hoping to make a career as a male prostitute. When I met him some years later, backstage after a London first night, it was clear that he was succeeding.

Life on the camp was very relaxed. Discipline was almost non-existent, I don't remember being bothered by kit inspections and there were no organized games or PT classes. The only parade was the pay parade on Fridays, when we lined up and two officers, sitting at a table covered with a blanket, doled out the pay. A sergeant shouted your name, you stamped up to the table; saluted, shouted the last three figures of your number, the officer handed you a pound note, you saluted, turned round and stamped back to your place.

We did have to do kitchen duty from time to time. On one occasion I arrived at the cookhouse at half-past five in the morning and found the cook sitting on the table, his white cook's jacket open revealing his bare stomach which he was holding obviously in pain. When I asked what the trouble was, he said "It's that fucking glass," explaining that in the pub, for a bet he used to drink a glass of beer and eat the glass. He had done it the night before and the glass was proving more indigestible than usual.

There were two pederasts in the hut; one was a scoutmaster who was forever telling anyone who would listen, his sordid adventures with boys when camping, and a man aged forty who had signed on for the third time and who used to go to London for weekends of a similarly doubtful nature. Another man, short and hairy and, one would have thought, far from attractive, used to go to Bath looking for women and come back and give loud, detailed descriptions of his sexual conquests.

From time to time it was my turn to be on duty in the Control Tower. There were two officers, a very pleasant flight lieutenant with a Battle of Britain moustache and another of slightly higher rank who was rather pompous. They took it in turns to be on duty, but the tower was run by the sergeant, a youngish boffin, with thick glasses and an unruly mop of hair. On these occasions I used to take my complete Shakespeare and sit in front of the microphone reading. For this I was nicknamed "Shakespeare". In fact the only positive thing that came out of my time in the RAF was that I managed to do quite a lot of reading, though it was difficult to concentrate in the hut where there was a loud speaker endlessly playing popular tunes;

"Put another nickel in,
In the Nickelodeon
All I want, is loving you
And music, music, music"

I had kept in touch with Jean after Southport and now she wrote that she was staying in Reading and suggested we meet. I got a day's leave and went to Reading. I was in civilian clothes, never willingly wearing uniform. Jean was disappointed. We had lunch and went into the park where we found a quiet corner and made love. A few days later I got a letter from her saying she had decided to marry a theatre manager, a man some years older than she. I wrote wishing her luck and never heard of her again. I have often wondered what became of her and remember her with affection.

A letter arrived from the Old Vic School inviting me to go for a final Scholarship Audition at Morley College at 4 p.m. of Tuesday May 23rd, so I wrote to George Benson to tell him and he kindly renewed his offer of a bed. He was living in a flat made out of the ground floor of Herbert Farjeon's house in St John's Wood. Herbert Farjeon had written a musical "The Two Bouquets" in which George had made his name in the 30s as well as "The Little Revue" in which George had starred with Hermione Baddeley. Farjeon had died during the war, but his widow was still living in their house and she had offered the flat to George when he returned from the States. He had just opened at the New Theatre in the Old Vic Season as Costard in "Love's Labour's Lost" so I was able to see the performance.

The play is set in the Court of King Ferdinand of Navarre (played in this production by Michael Redgrave), He and his friends have decided to devote themselves to study and forswear the company of women. Costard, a country bumpkin, who has got a girl into trouble, is at one point given a tip by Don Armado, a fantastical Spaniard, who says; "Here is your remuneration". Costard is very taken with the word "remuneration" which he has never heard before, and, after saying "Remuneration that must be the Latin for three farthings" continues mouthing the word "remuneration," "remuneration".

George was wonderfully funny; a leading critic said

"Nothing could be finer or funnier than Mr Benson, who mouths the words like mint humbugs",

he had a quality of almost child-like innocence and simplicity that made his performance as Costard unforgettable.

The following morning, he asked me to show him the pieces I had prepared for my audition and made some helpful comments. The audition went well. Glen Byam Shaw asked me what I had done. I was a little anxious telling him about Southport, as Theatre Schools did not generally like to take people who have had been in rep, fearing they might have picked up bad habits. Apparently it was not the case as I got a letter saying I had been accepted as a student for the forthcoming year beginning on the 5th October 1950.

If I could get an early "Class B Release" there would be no problem. The Old Vic School had a tremendous reputation and they auditioned hundreds of people, choosing barely twenty. At about that time the Young Vic Company came to Bath and I saw a production of "The Servant of Two Masters" by Goldone. It was a revelation of what team playing can be. Some months later it was announced in the press that the School would have to close after the end of the next year's course because Michel St Denis had to return to France and the other teachers, all well-known actors and producers, were committed elsewhere. So I had just scraped in to the last year. I could hardly believe my luck.

It was luck that did not hold; on the 15th September 1950 five months before I was due to be demobbed, the Prime Minister, Clement Attlee, broadcast to the nation to say that National Service had been extended to two years. It was devastating news as it meant I would not be free until the end of August 1951. I wrote to everyone I knew for help, Dorothy Sayers wrote a letter, as did Christopher Hassall, even Mr Thoseby wrote saying, "This man really does want to be an actor". But the Air Ministry was adamant; "There is no longer provision for National Service airmen to be given Class B release to take up vacancies in Universities or Schools." It was clear that without the valuable work I was doing at Colerne, the RAF would be unable to continue.

Most of us looked upon National Service as a milder form of prison sentence. A friend of mine, the actor Philip Guard, had decided to take the fast track. He refused to do it and went to gaol for six months instead. I had seriously considered doing so myself, but felt it would be unfair on my father. Now, having six months added to the sentence made it really seem like prison. It was very depressing and I count that autumn and winter as the most miserable of my life. In the spring, however, a chance meeting in a train brought a ray of light. Returning from Gloucester one Sunday night, I got into a carriage where there was a young man of my own age. He was instantly recognisable as a conscript because of his unusually short hair, but there was something in his manner that made me think he was an actor. We got talking and he told me he had just been called up after finishing his training at RADA. His name was Stuart Allen, his family lived in Birmingham and he was stationed at another RAF Camp some miles from Colerne. On his camp they had formed a theatre-group and they had some interesting people and were going to do "Now Barabbas" by William Douglas Home. Would I be interested in joining them? I said I certainly would, and the next evening borrowed a bicycle and rode over to see them. There was a young conscript officer, who gave the group status in the camp, a very beautiful young actor, Neil Christopherson, who had just trained at the Bradford Theatre School which had a good reputation, and an urbane Armenian just down from Oxford as well as an art student who had just left Art School who was to do the set.

William Douglas Home was a successful playwright who during the advance across Europe after the Normandy landing, refusing to shell a French town, was court marshalled and sent to gaol. "Now Barabbas" is the fruit of that experience and deals with the last hours of a condemned man and the effect of his execution on the other prisoners. It is a powerful play. Stuart wanted me to play the Irishman, not a part I would have chosen, as I am weak on accents. What is more the play opens with his singing "If you ever go across the sea to Ireland" I begged him to cut it, but he insisted, and my singing got us off to a bad start on the first night, with the Irishmen in the audience making their presence felt. However, the play pulled us through and we recovered. The song was cut and I learned two lessons, one was never again to sing in public and the other was never to let a director overrule my innate sense of what I can and cannot do.

Since I had been in the RAF, I had kept in touch with Rex, who was planning a summer season at Minehead. From the start I had thought it might be possible if I saved up all my leave, to manage to do a play somewhere. I had taken no leave except for the week after my initial training, weekends in Gloucester or London not counting as leave. Thus I had three weeks leave to come and Rex proposed the part of the Colonel in "Queen Elizabeth Slept Here" adding that, in the following play, in which he was to play the leading part, he had a problem as he had to go to Ireland after the first night. Would I, therefore, understudy the part and take over for the rest of the week?

Would I? You bet I would. I put in for the leave, which was granted and, wondering how the RAF would manage without me for so long, took the train to Minehead.

Rex greeted me warmly and that evening I went to see the current play. The company had changed and none of the Southport people were still with it, but it was a good company except for one actor who really made one wonder how he had ever got into the profession. Ungainly, with a disagreeable voice, he was slow and seemed not to have any idea of what the part he was playing was about. It would not be too much to say that he ruined the play.

During the days that followed, one by one the other members of the company took me aside and told how he had ruined play after play and how fed up they were with him. They had even complained to Rex, but the problem was that although he was a bad actor, he was a good husband and father who lived in a caravan with a nice wife and several children and Rex had not the heart to give him notice. Things came to head on the Thursday morning, when he did not turn up for rehearsal of the third Act and Rex explained that he had asked for the morning off as he had an audition at the Little Theatre Bristol. The Little at Bristol was a fortnightly company and the Mecca of all the actors in the weekly companies like Minehead. Everyone in the company longed to get into it, so the idea that someone who had ruined so many plays should imagine for a moment that he was good enough for Bristol made them laugh, when they were not raging with anger that he had dared miss a vital rehearsal in weekly rep.

Minehead Theatre was a typical nineteenth century country theatre, which had retained its rusticity to the point that the scenery was still delivered by a horse and cart. From the stage door you climbed up a short flight of stairs to stage level where there was a small landing from which all the dressing rooms led off. On the morning of the dress rehearsal, I was one of the first to arrive. At the top of the stairs was the company notice board and letter rack. As I looked to see if there was any mail for me, I could not help noticing a large envelope with the imprint of the Little Theatre Bristol. It was addressed to the actor. I went into the dressing room and through the open door I saw the others arrive one by one and as they did so, I saw that each of them looked at the envelope. No one said anything, everyone went into his dressing room, but there was tension in the air. The actor was the last to arrive and, running up the stairs, went to the notice board. As he did so, the doors of dressing-rooms appeared to open very slightly as people watched him open the letter and read the contents, then he gave a shout, "Rex, Rex!" Rex appeared rather too quickly from behind his dressing room door. "Rex, they want me at Bristol, it's a contract, may I go and 'phone?" Rex nodded and the actor rushed out of the theatre and as he did so, we all emerged from behind our dressing room doors and looked at Rex, who with a grand theatrical gesture, put his hand to his head and said "There is no God, there is no God!"

The three weeks at Minehead passed much too quickly and it was back to Colerne, lying on my bed and listening to "Put another nickel in" while trying to read. Some weeks later, feeling bitter about the loss of my place at the Old Vic School, and extremely bloody-minded as far as the RAF was concerned, it happened one Friday lunch time just before we were about to be paid that I was alone in the Control Tower and about to switch off the microphone and go, when a voice came over the speaker, "Colerne Tower, Colerne Tower, this is Fox Able, permission to land" This was bad news because it meant I would have to call out the crash crew and the ambulance – all of whom were about to be paid and we would miss the pay parade and have to wait a whole week before the next one.

I looked at the clock. It was five past one. I bent over the microphone and said "Fox Able, Fox Able, this is Colerne Tower. This Airfield is closed between the hours of one and two. You are however at liberty to circle the Airfield until that time." I heard a muffled exclamation of rage, switched off the microphone, walked downstairs, went out, closed the door, and joined the pay parade. As I waited for my name to be called I could see an aeroplane circling round and round the airfield. Under my breath, I said to my neighbour "You see that plane, it's staying up there until I've been paid!" I did not hurry back, and when I got there the two officers were already there and they did not look happy. Between them stood a purple-faced individual, covered in gold braid and with countless rings round his sleeve, who was uttering incoherent phrases like "Suppose I had no fuel? Who gave the order? A disgrace... won't hear the last of this!" As I approached the two officers turned on me,

"Apps, did you do this?"

"Do what, sir?"

"Did you tell the Air Vice-Marshall that we were closed?"

"Yes sir. It was five past one"

"But you might have thought."

"I'm sorry, sir, I understood it was orders."

I was untouchable and knew it for, as we were frequently reminded, we were not paid to think but to obey orders. It was one of those moments that life occasionally vouchsafes; a moment of complete satisfaction.

After the loss of my place at the Old Vic School, I had spent a weekend with George and the question had been where to look next for a theatre school. At the Old Vic he shared a dressing room with Walter Hudd, a well-known actor and passionate communist. Several of the actors of that generation at the Old Vic were communists. "Dickie" Hudd as he was known, had recently become head of Drama at the Central School of Speech Training and Dramatic Art, which had been founded by Elsie Fogerty, a celebrated voice specialist to whom almost all the great theatre actors had turned for help at one time or another. (Her remedies were sometimes unexpected; when John Gielgud lost his voice during the run of a play and turned to her in desperation, she made him stand in the corner of her office with a book on his head for half an hour. At the end of that time Gielgud found that his voice had completely recovered).

The general opinion was that the Central School was more serious and less showy than RADA and George and Christopher both advised me to try for it. I did so, auditioned, and was accepted. The year would begin in October and I would be free from the end of August.

My grant was from the Gloucester City Council and depended on the scale of my father's income. He and I were ordered to appear before their committee. To someone of my father's generation, the idea of discussing his income in public was very disagreeable, but for my sake he put a brave face on it and we went together. The committee members were very understanding and at the end one of them said to me, "If you develop such a splendid voice as your Father, you should go a long way," which made him blush with pleasure. He did in fact have a very well placed, musical voice, and clear articulation.

Each time I had stayed with George, I had noticed that Pamela White, the Fair Lady of the Canterbury Festival, was often present, and on one visit they announced that they had become engaged. Soon after they married, I got a letter from George saying that they had bought a house in Highgate, which had a spare room and suggesting I become their lodger. I did not have to think twice but wrote gratefully accepting.

The house that George and Pamela had bought was on Highgate West Hill. From the back of it, you looked out over London, and from the window of my bedroom I could pick out all the familiar landmarks. To get to it, you took the Northern Line to Kentish Town where you caught a trolley bus to Parliament Hill Fields. "Rumble under, rumble over ..." it was Betjeman country; the house where he grew up was on the other side of the road further up the hill. At the top of the hill was Highgate Village where Christopher Hassall lived at No 8, The Grove, a spectacular row of red brick Georgian houses. A blue plaque on one of them recalled that Coleridge had lived there. Christopher had converted the basement of No 8 into a big studio with a grand piano and it was there that he and Ivor Novello often worked.

Christopher encouraged me to go and see him when I was staying with George and Pamela. He and his wife, Eve, were very welcoming. He was working on a verse play about Perkin Warbeck and he told me that there was a part for me in it. It was a thought that I clung to during the dreary months at Colerne.

On one of my visits, Christopher told me how he had come to work with Novello. He had been engaged as Novello's understudy and when they were on a pre-London tour, playing at Oxford, at the end of the first Act, as the curtain came down, it struck a piece of furniture, the other end of which hit Novello in the crutch. Doubled up with pain he could not go on and Christopher was called to take over but had to admit he didn't know the part, with the result the audience had to wait until Novello had recovered sufficiently and could continue. After the performance, Novello took him out to supper and over the meal told him he was sacked. He then went on to say he had heard that Christopher wrote poetry and would he be interested in their working together.

Novello died suddenly, from a massive heart attack on the 6th March 1951, after the performance of "King's Rhapsody", aged fifty-one. That weekend I was at Highgate and went to see Christopher, who was trying to write a funeral oration. Novello was homosexual and had had many lovers including the First War poet, Siegfried Sasoon. His current lover was Bobby Andrews, who was devastated by his death and Christopher had been on the phone trying to console him. Writing a funeral oration for someone like Novello in the early fifties, when homosexuality was still illegal, presented a challenge. Christopher was Novello's executor and on a later occasion he showed me Novello's autograph collection. They were in several huge bound volumes, an extraordinary range of famous names through the centuries, but they were not in any recognisable order so, for example, there was the autograph of Leonardo da Vinci next to that of Owen Nares, a 1920s West end actor. Christopher also showed me his officer's pocket book (he had been a captain during the war) in which he had written the lyric of "We'll Gather Lilacs". He had been on leave and, as Novello played the tune to him, he had scribbled down the words on the first thing that came to hand.

At last the day of my release arrived and I walked out of the gates of Colerne and out of the RAF for the last time. As a special treat my Mother came to fetch me in the car and drove me back to Gloucester. It was the 30th August 1951 and each year since then I have celebrated the date.

I realised I was free, really free, free for the first time in my life. I was twenty years old and since the age of eight, except for the six months at Southport, I had been either at school or in the RAF, both situations where I had been ordered about and told what to do. That was, I decided, enough. From now on I would live my life as I wanted to. No one would ever again shout at me or tell me what to do. I would be; "The master of my fate, the captain of my soul".

It is a decision I have tried to stick to, even though it has not always been easy.

CHAPTER TWELVE

—

The Central School of Speech and Drama was housed in the Albert Hall. You went in through the pillars on the right of the building and climbed up to the first floor. The rooms backed on to the outside of the circular wall of the concert hall. The school was run by the Principal, Miss Thurburn; tall with a rather severe manner, she was a voice specialist and her book on the subject remains a classic. One of the main activities of the school was the training of Speech Therapists, and there seemed to be a great many earnest-looking girls about the place. The acting course was a three-year course (as opposed to RADA which was two) and the teaching, apart from Walter Hudd, was by Oliver Reynolds and Mrs Crossley. When I told George, he said that Reynolds had been at RADA with him and he was no actor, something that was not hard to imagine. Spare and bald, he looked the image of Mr Critchley of Southport memory, but he was an excellent teacher, thoughtful and analytical. With Reynolds we spent the time splitting hairs and with Mrs Crossley we did extempore scenes. I was happier in these last and found the Reynolds approach too dry for my taste. Voice was taught by Cecily Berry, an inspired teacher; young friendly and unstuffy, she immediately got the confidence of the most timid student and all the men fell in love with her. The other voice teacher was Clifford Turner, a huge man with a voice that, without the least effort, seemed to fill the room and make the walls shake. He taught at RADA at the same time and all the girls of both schools fell in love with him.

The first year students included a ravishingly pretty red headed girl from Yorkshire, Wendy Craig, a small and sexy girl, Mary Ure, and a seventeen-year-old Etonian called Jeremy Huggins. Whereas most of the students had had some sort of amateur experience, Jeremy Huggins had never been on a stage before; he had simply decided that he wanted to be an actor, done an audition and been accepted.

In the first few weeks, we did nothing but voice exercises, dance, movement and mime, but then we started to work on texts and went into the theatre for the first time.

One of the first of these texts was "A Winter's Tale" and Jeremy and I were to play the opening scene together. It is a conversational scene between the two characters, but Jeremy, walking on a stage for the first time in his life, stood looking and speaking straight out to the audience without once looking at me. When we went off, I asked him if he didn't think he should look at me from time to time as he would in life. He was staggered – the thought had never occurred to him.

I often think of this as I am painting, with the television on in the corner of the studio, and there is a repeat of the Sherlock Holmes series in which, having changed his name to Jeremy Brett, he starred as Holmes.

At the end of the first term we had to prepare a mime based on a dream. I carefully prepared a snappy, comic scenario where I was a King and my crown turned into a jerry-pot. When we did it in front of Walter Hudd, the others seemed to be doing mysterious dream-like movements which went on for a long time and seemed very dull, but when it came to my turn I got a lot of laughs and applause. Feeling pleased with myself I waited for Hudd's comments, only to be shot down in flames. I had, he said, understood nothing, learned nothing. This was mime, not a music-hall sketch. I felt very abashed.

I had found the first term very slow and began to feel I was wasting my time, so I determined to ask Walter Hudd if I could move into the second year. When I did so, he said, "You think a lot of yourself, don't you? No you can't," and took me to the pub for a drink. I explained that my father was very ill and I had to get going in the profession quickly, because he could die at any moment and I must start earning a living. He was sympathetic but adamant. So, disappointed, I went to Gloucester for the Christmas holidays. I had barely returned for the second term, when I was sent for by Mrs Crossley. It seemed that a student in the second year, called Harold Pinter, was leaving suddenly and they needed someone to make up the cast of "The Cherry Orchard" and she had suggested me. It didn't mean, she added that I was to be permanently in the second year, only for this one production. I could not believe my luck, "The Cherry Orchard" of all plays! Since my untimely reading of "An Actor Prepares", at Southport, I had read "My Life in Art" and, my reading at Colerne had included all the plays of Chekhov.

"The Cherry Orchard" is about a family of minor Russian aristocrats, headed by the feckless Madame Ranevska and her even more feckless brother Gaev, living on their run-down estate just before the 1917 revolution. The family is facing ruin and the only solution is to sell the cherry orchard for building land, a cherry orchard in that society being a status symbol appreciated simply for its beauty. They cannot bring themselves to take the decision and in the end it is sold at auction and bought by an entrepreneur who began life as a slave on their estate. With England being run-down after the war and in the process of selling off its empire, the play had great resonance.

The director was Hal Burton, who had a reputation as a theatre-designer. I had seen some of his sets at Stratford-on-Avon. He was a small, quiet man who encouraged rather than interfered, simply making helpful suggestions. I was to play the neighbour, Pistchik, another minor aristocrat. I found a photo of the original production and saw that Pistchik was played big and fat and dressed in a morning coat with a white apron and big riding boots. I decided to base him on my grandfather. Costume and make-up were not considered important in school productions, but I decided that if I wanted to stay in the second year, I had better pull out all the stops. I padded, found an apron and boots and frock coat did a make-up to resemble my grandfather. I had not even considered what the other second year students might think of someone being promoted from the first year to replace one of their friends, and when I presented myself in costume before the dress rehearsal I realised that not everyone was happy. Barry Foster, who was playing Gaev, said he refused to go on the stage with me like that. I pointed out that it was the traditional costume but he hardly seemed mollified.

However, when it came to Hudd giving his notes, I got almost unstinted praise, and although he said the make-up and costume were not necessary, he added that they showed I understood the character. From then on there was no more talk of my returning to the first year.

All this time I was living with George and Pamela at Highgate and going to Kensington and back each day from Parliament Hill Fields on the trolley bus to Kentish Town, then a tube to Piccadilly and then the No 19 through Knightsbridge to the Albert Hall. In the evening with more time, I would take the bus to Trafalgar Square and change for the 134 to Kentish Town. The stop where I changed buses was outside the National Gallery and evening after evening I would go into the Gallery and study the paintings. At the time this was not only because of my interest in painting, but also for the costumes. I would look to see how they were worn and try to get the feel of the period from how the figures stood or sat when wearing them.

George and Pamela were very happy. She had given birth to a son, Christopher, just before I was demobbed and I would baby-sit for them when they went out to parties. One of my happiest memories of that time is of the Sunday evenings, when George was not at the theatre and Pamela would make coffee and sandwiches and we would listen to Trollope's "Barchester Towers" on the wireless.

All this time George was playing in a very successful revue that had been put on for the Festival of Britain, "The Lyric Revue", at the Lyric Theatre in Shaftesbury Avenue. It was the hit of the season and he was starring in it with Dora Bryan, Noel Coward's companion, Graham Payne, and Ian Carmichael. George had had a success in a revue before going to the States with a sketch in which he showed husbands returning from the war how to do the washing up. It was topical because middle-class men of that generation had barely ever penetrated the kitchen before the war, let alone washed up. The sketch was very funny, with a lot about the "scritcher" and the "scratcher". Now, in the Lyric Revue, he had an equally successful sketch about stoking the boiler, where the unspoken comparison was trying to make love to a frigid woman. "And if she still won't have it, try filling her up with a bit more coke, and then gently rake her" etc. I would often on my way back go and meet him in his dressing room and we would go home together on the bus. If I arrived early I would watch the show and the boiler sketch never failed to make me laugh. George was a master of comic timing and I learned a lot from watching him.

When we had lived at the Vicarage, Aunty Peggy had organised a dancing class. My mother had played the piano. The dancing teacher was Jane Taylor, a friend of Aunty Peggy's. I hated dancing but I liked Jane. She was living with her family in Chatham, where her father was the admiral in charge of the dockyard, but at the end of the war they returned to London and now through Aunty Peggy, Jane invited me to tea one Sunday.

With the money I had earned at Minehead and some of my Southport savings, I had bought a ready-made suit. It was dark blue and made by Dax, a well-known make at that time. It didn't look too bad and almost fitted. So the following Sunday I put it on and went to tea with the Taylors.

1A, Holland Park, which has since been pulled down to make a public entrance to the park, stood behind a high wall. It was built in the style of an Italian villa in the early part of the nineteenth century. I rang the bell and Admiral Taylor answered it himself – butlers had become rare since the war. Jane came to greet me and introduced me to her mother a splendid figure in pale blue, wearing a hat and gloves to match.

We crossed the hall to the drawing room where there were thirty or forty guests, to whom I was introduced. I was struck by the fact that they all seemed to have names like the characters in Oscar Wilde's plays. The drawing room, with its period furniture and portraits that looked as though they were by Lely and Kneller –and I subsequently learned were – led to a terrace overlooking a magnificent garden which backed on to Holland Park. The Admiral regularly won the London Garden prize. There was a large conservatory filled by a camellia tree and a private chapel. After some time, we went down-stairs to the dining room where tea was laid on a long dining table surrounded by a set of tall, sculpted seventeenth-century Spanish silvered dining chairs. There were sandwiches, thin bread and butter and cream cakes. Some people sat at the table, others perched where they could.

In the middle of the table was an eighteenth-century silver centre-piece, which the Admiral, recently retired after 20 years as M.P. for South Paddington, had been given by the House of Commons "They wanted to give me a television set, but I drew the line at that. At least this won't hurt my eyes". We returned upstairs to the drawing room and later a glass of South African sherry was served, my neigh-bour whispering to me, "Such a pity we can't have real sherry, but of course we have to drink this stuff because of Ernest being for the Empire." She made a grimace as she sipped it.

When, at the end of the afternoon, I found myself again in the street, I felt like the hero of Alain Fournier's novel, Le Grand Meaulnes, who strays into an eighteenth-century party in a château. It had seemed unreal; a world I had read about in novels, but had hardly imagined still existed.

The Taylor tea parties, I was to learn, were an institution. They had begun in the 1930s because the Admiral, being in the House every evening, found he never saw his friends, so he decided to ask them to tea on Sundays. After that first afternoon, I was invited once a month and met all sorts of interesting and celebrated people. Frank O. Salisbury, the history painter, was often there, an impressive figure wearing a stock rather than the more usual tie. Ernest Thesiger (who had famously created the part of the Dauphin in Bernard Shaw's "Saint Joan"), was always introduced as "Mr Thesiger, who does such lovely needlework". He was a friend of Queen Mary's and they used to spend afternoons needle working together, so he usually had some royal story to tell which we all listened to eagerly. There was a story told of him that when he was in the army in France during the First World War, a General came across him sitting by the side of the road. "Who are you?" demanded the General. "I'm Captain Thesiger." "What are you doing here?" "I've lost me men". "And what do you do in civilian life?" "I knit."

Richard Goolden came on one occasion and as I talked to him in that elegant setting, I thought of Measday and our Monday-morning appreciations of his "Old Ebenezer" as we mixed the mash for the pigs.

There were a number of fashionable homosexuals including a well-known Vogue photographer and his friend (it was always said of them that they shared a flat) several elegant and witty women covered in furs and jewels and Mr Proctor, an elderly gentleman who was constantly bemoaning the fact that he had lost his villa in Florence, "with thirty thousand pounds worth of furniture, some of it given to me by Sir George Sitwell". At the time I was reading and enjoying Osbert Sitwell's "Left Hand Right Hand" and I mentioned it. "Osbert" he snorted, "he should be ashamed of himself writing like that about his father". On another occasion I asked him if he had known Edward Gordon Craig when he lived in Florence. He said that he had, but that nobody thought much of him "used to go about wearing a wide brimmed hat and a cloak – well, the Italians don't understand that sort of thing."

At one of my early tea parties, the talk was of Princess Margaret being in love with Captain Townsend.

"If" said the Admiral, solemnly, "If the King allows his daughter to marry a commoner, he is not the man I took him for," and everyone agreed

In June that year Guy Burgess and Donald Maclean, two diplomats, fled to Russia. At the tea party that Sunday, there was an air of stupefaction, because many of the guests knew them personally, and the idea that they could be Communist spies shook the group to its foundations.

It was about that time that I had my first contact with the BBC. It was, had I realised, a glimpse into the future and a warning. We were told that the BBC wanted us, and the equivalent class at RADA to record some crowd noises for them. It would, they suggested, be a helpful experience. We all trooped along to Broadcasting House on the next Sunday afternoon and were ushered into a studio where a military-style producer began giving orders; "cheer loudly", "scream with fright", "laugh madly" etc. The session began at two o'clock and at half-past six, we were still shouting, screaming and laughing. At this point it began to strike certain of us that the BBC was getting a lot of work out of us for nothing. In a short interval while they changed the tape, we asked if we were to be paid. "Oh, no" came the answer, "you see you are not members of Equity, so we can't pay you."

This was accompanied by such a satisfied, not to say smug expression, that it was clear that the producer had calculated that the BBC could get a stock of background noises that would serve for years to come without having to pay for them, and no doubt he also calculated that this would redound to his credit and perhaps lead to promotion.

Many of the students were extremely poor; one boy from Wales spent his evenings washing up in a restaurant to pay for his course, and it seemed particularly inappropriate for the BBC to exploit poor students for whom a pound or two would have meant so much. Discussing this with some of the RADA students, I mentioned that I was in fact a fully paid-up member of Equity and suggested that I ring the office the following morning. This was thought to be a good idea. So I duly rang, and told an official. "Leave it to me" he said grimly and in a very short time we were informed that because someone in the group was an Equity member, we were all to be paid at the going rate for the hours we had worked. I enjoyed a moment of popularity.

Most of the male students had done National Service and I found the prevailing atmosphere in many ways closer to the RAF hut at Colerne then the green rooms and dressing rooms of the theatre I knew. Several of them were abrasive; one in particular, Kenneth Haigh seemed particularly so. An exception was a nice and very funny cockney, Harry Landis. He had been working in the East End communist theatre and he brought a thoughtful and realistic approach to acting and the theatre. A student who joined us, and moved like me into the second year, was Michael David. A big Welshman, he had played rugger for the army. Passionately interested in art, theatre and philosophy, we became friends and would go to exhibitions and plays together.

The most exciting theatrical event while I was a student; or at least the event that we, the students, found most exciting, was a production of Ibsen's "The Father" at the Arts Theatre with Wilfred Lawson in the title role. Lawson was a great hulk of a man with a huge presence and a magnificent voice, whose career was marred by alcoholism, which made him unreliable so that managers were hesitant about employing him, but in "The Father" he gave the greatest performances I have ever seen. His playing was so fresh and spontaneous that it was impossible to believe that he had rehearsed, or was in any way subject to a written text, organized moves or actions. He seemed a natural force on the stage that moved and spoke totally by instinct. This impression was so overwhelming that several of us went to see the play again and again and were amazed to see that the moves, effects and intonations were always exactly the same: a remarkable example of the art that conceals art.

At the other end of the scale, George sent me to see the great Italian actor, Ruggero Ruggeri in Luigi Pirandello's "Enrico IV" at the St James's Theatre. Ruggeri was an old man at the time (George had seen him in the same play when he himself was a student twenty years earlier) and his acting style gave an idea of what Henry Irving must have been like. The play was in Italian and there were two invisible prompters, one at each side of the stage who spoke each line before he did, according to whether he was nearer one side or the other. This meant that the audience heard the line he was going to say before he said it. Whether this was due to his difficulty remembering the lines, or so that the audience, hearing the line in advance, could better appreciate his interpretation I did not discover, but the effect was made bizarre not to say comic by the fact that one prompter had a deep voice and the other a high voice, so that according to whether he moved left or right, the line would be bass or treble. It was altogether a curious evening.

Someone who taught occasionally at the Central School was Noel Iliffe. He was chiefly known as a radio producer and had produced Dorothy Sayers' "The Man Born to be King". He had, I knew, been at St Edmund's and when I heard he was producing the other half of our group of students I went to introduce myself. Noel Iliffe, in his middle to late fifties, in an old black overcoat and carrying a brown paper carrier, had a hint of the unfrocked clergyman about him. When I said I believed he had been at St Edmund's, he looked distant and, as though dragging a memory from the long past, said, yes he had been a long time ago. "Do you remember the early morning bathe?" I asked. It seemed to bring his memory back instantly. "Oh, don't" he said and shivered. We talked for a few minutes; it was the only time I met him.

It was the other group, though not in Noel Iliffe's production, which was playing a comedy in front of the school on the afternoon of February 6th. The first act went well and got a lot of laughs, but in the interval one of the staff came in front of the curtain to make an announcement. She said that it had just been announced that the King had died, "we thought we should tell you at once", adding that it had been decided to continue with the performance but not to inform the cast for fear of upsetting them. King George VI was a much-loved king. He had taken over the throne in difficult circumstances, struggled with an impediment in his speech, stayed in London during the blitz and the news of his unexpected death left everyone in shock. The curtain went up on the second Act, but there was not a laugh to be had and the poor actors could not imagine why they were suddenly playing to a totally silent audience. The general opinion afterwards was that it would have been wiser to tell the actors the news and not the audience.

I went to Paddington to watch the funeral procession. It was a moving spectacle, the silent crowd with only the sound of the horses' hooves, the jingling of the harness and the muffled drum approaching. Then, the gun carriage came into view, with the Royal Dukes walking in line behind the coffin, followed by the carriages with the heavily veiled women.

Soon after, at a Tea party, Ernest Thesiger told us that Queen Mary writing to her granddaughter now signed herself, "Your loving Grandmother and obedient subject".

One afternoon at Highgate the telephone rang and Pamela called me. It was the Admiral. "You're dining with us tomorrow tonight, dress in a suit of dittos." "Thank you, sir." I put the phone down wondering what a suit of dittos could possibly be. I asked George who had never heard of it either, but said he would ask Norman Hackforth that evening. Norman was best known to the general public as the Mystery Voice in the long running radio game, "Twenty Question" when, close to the microphone, he would announce quietly in his rich, dark voice "And the next object is a rubber duck" or something similar. As Noel Coward's accompanist, Norman had been with him throughout the war entertaining the troops. Now he was the musical director of the Lyric Revue. He and George were old friends and as he did not have a dressing room at the theatre, George let him share his. Norman's association with Coward, and through him with royal circles, led to his being something of an expert on etiquette. However, when George asked him what a suit of dittos might be, he too was at a loss, but he promised to find out. It was not until the following afternoon that he rang to say that a suit of dittos was a suit where the coat and trousers were of the same material, or what is generally called a lounge suit. I thanked him and, with a sigh of relief, put on my Dax suit and went to Holland Park.

Admiral Taylor had been captain of the *Renown*, the ship in which the then Prince of Wales, the future Edward VIII, had made his world tour. Mrs Taylor, or Rosabel, was a Campbell of the port-importing firm and on her mother's side she was descended from very grand Spanish aristocracy. Over dinner, as I sat beside her, she told me she had married Ernest because he was the most handsome man in London. It was not hard to believe; now in his seventies, the Admiral looked as if he was carved out of oak, slightly deaf and with a voice used to carrying in a force nine gale he was impressive, not to say a little intimidating for my twenty years. At the tea parties I had met several of Mrs Taylor's brothers, all of whom were old Etonians and colonels in the Guards. One was divorced and remarried, but naturally his new wife was never invited to the tea parties where he came alone with the air of a naughty schoolboy who had been caught pinching sweets.

The other guest that evening was Mrs Taylor's nephew, another

Colonel Campbell. "He is" she explained, "head of that underground railway" waving in the direction of Holland Park Underground and making it clear that she herself had no association with it and had certainly never been on it.

It was clear that had Edward VIII not abdicated, the Taylors would probably have had a place at court, and no doubt they suffered from the feeling of having been passed over by the new court of George VI.

When, in the birthday honours a couple of years later, the Admiral was made a Knight Bachelor and I called to congratulate him, Lady Taylor, as she had just become, said "Well I'm glad they've given Ernest something, not much, but something." She was no doubt thinking of the Victorian Order for services to the monarch, which might have been his, had Mrs Simpson stayed in America where she belonged.

The Taylors were extraordinarily kind to me, often inviting me to dinner and even suggesting I stay with them, an offer that would have been tempting had I not been with George and Pamela. Talking of theatre people he had known, the Admiral said he had visited the United States and been invited to dinner by Charlie Chaplin where they had eaten off gold plates. The noise of knives and forks grating on the gold, he said, was excruciating.

Each time I saw Christopher Hassall he talked of the play he was writing about Perkin Warbeck and repeated that there was a part in it for me. Then, as the summer approached, he told me that it was to be produced at the Edinburgh Festival by Henry Sherek. Sherek was a well-known producer who had produced T.S. Eliot's "The Birthday Party" at Edinburgh the year before. The play was to be directed by Norman Marshall and I was to meet them. At the interview Sherek, hugely fat, sat behind his desk smoking a cigar, while Christopher and Norman Marshall sat on each side. Norman Marshall was very erect, dapper and looked as if he had been in the Navy. He had a reputation as a director of interesting plays and had written a book "The Other Theatre" which I had read and enjoyed. They asked me what I had done and Sherek taunted Christopher, "So this is your great protégé" Norman Marshall looked at me in a dismissive way and I felt that I was on fragile ground. They asked me to read, which I did. The part was a peasant boy who had a scene with an old priest.

Later that day Christopher rang me: they had decided on an actor whom Norman Marshall wanted, but I could understudy the part and be assistant stage-manager for £10 a week. I accepted but it was a disappointment. All through the months at Colerne the thought of this play had buoyed me up and I had begun to see it as a launch into the professional theatre when I had finished at the Central School. Now all hope of that was over, but at least I had a well-paid job for the summer holidays and would not have to spend them at Gloucester sponging off my parents.

Rehearsals for "The Player King" were held in the Duke of York's Theatre in St Martin's Lane. I was interested watching Norman Marshall produce the play and noted how he never lost sight of the audience but kept repeating, "What is the audience thinking?"

The Stage director was a gentle Irishman, Roy Healey, and the Stage Manager, Peter Green who became a friend and latterly, my agent. Both were experienced West End stage managers and it was clear from the start that there was to be no question of not checking the cigarettes on this production.

Perkin Warbeck was a pretender to the throne during the reign of Henry VII, the first Tudor, and the play was based on recent research which suggested that he was not, as was generally thought, the son of a boatman on the Elbe, but the illegitimate son of the Duchess of Burgundy.

The leading part of Perkin Warbeck was to be played by a young actor getting his first chance, Tony Britton, and the Duchess of Burgundy, by Cathleen Nesbitt. Other members of the cast were Noel Howlett, as Henry VII, Ernest Clarke, Andrew Faulds and Milton Rosmer, who was to play the old priest with whom the peasant boy had his scene. Rosmer was in his seventies. He had begun his career in Miss Horniman's company in Manchester, where Ibsen had first been produced in England, indeed he had taken his stage name from the character in "Rosmerholm". Milton Rosmer was a piece of living theatre history.

During the rehearsals I had made friends with Andrew Faulds. Andrew was a big, bearded Scotsman who enjoyed the company of women.

The dress rehearsal was to be in Leeds on the Sunday. Several of us had booked digs from the Equity Digs List. This list included all the theatrical landladies in the British Isles, but there was no means of knowing what they were like and they varied greatly both in character and in what they offered. The only thing they had in common was a Visitors' Book, which they never let you escape without signing. They would bring it to the breakfast table on the last morning and stand over you while you signed it, so even after a dreadful week it was impossible to write the truth. The only actor who bucked the trend was George Arliss, famous for his rôle as Disraeli, who had toured England in the 1920s. In the 1950s looking through these books one could occasionally come across his signature and the enigmatic phrase "Quoth the raven". Arliss had obviously counted on landladies not being familiar with the works of Edgar Allan Poe and the line, "Quoth the raven, Nevermore!"

When we arrived on the Saturday evening in Leeds, we found ourselves in a strict Jewish household that was anything but welcoming. Because it was Saturday, we were informed, we could not have a meal and so we went to bed hungry. The following morning we were woken early by a furious landlady banging on our doors and shouting that we had not switched off the landing light. Clearly we were in for a bad week. Worse was to follow, for during the rehearsal, I was called to the stage door, where an attractive woman in her thirties showed me a letter I had written reserving a room. In other words I had double-booked digs. She was very distressed, telling me that she was the widow of a steeplejack with young children and dependent on letting her room. I apologised and explained that it was a mistake and paid her for the room. Going back to the stage, I ran into Andrew and told him of my misfortune. "You say she is young?" "Yes." "A widow?" "Yes." "Pretty?" "Yes." He moved in that afternoon, gave me back my money and when we left Leeds on the Sunday morning his landlady came to see him off. She thanked me with shining eyes for the wonderful week she had spent, and they had a long last embrace on the platform before the train pulled out.

My digs did not improve, the food was execrable and there was little of it. I began to regret that I had lacked Andrew's initiative. Altogether it was the worst week of the tour except for one afternoon when I went to York to meet Mrs Rhodes, Gordon's mother, who showed me round the city and the Minster and gave me tea. It was the only time I have ever been to York and it was interesting to compare it to Canterbury. They are, of course, the only two Anglican arch-bishoprics in England and the difference between them is expressed by one of those nuances beloved of the Church of England, for, while the Archbishop of York is the Primate of England, the Archbishop of Canterbury is the Primate of all England.

I liked Andrew; he was fun to be with, although difficult to keep up with. On our way to Liverpool he managed to become surpris-ingly intimate with a group of chorus girls who were on the same train.

Before leaving Leeds, he had told me that he knew a girl in Liverpool who had invited us to a party at her house. The girl's family were ship-owners with a big nineteenth-century merchant's house in a rich part of the city. The party was fun and went on late and the girl suggested that we stay the night if we wouldn't mind sharing a bed. We agreed, but I had the bed to myself most of the night, because Andrew went to find our hostess and did not return.

When, years later, Andrew became an M.P. during the Thatcher years, I often wondered whether Mrs Thatcher had been sensitive to his charms – or he to hers.

Up until now we had been on a try-out tour, but arriving in Edinburgh as the official play of the Festival was another matter. The first night was a major event with all the great and the good in the audience as well as the London Theatre critics. Many people had come up from London including Sir Edward Marsh.

"Eddy" Marsh, as everyone called him, was a polymath: he was at once Winston Churchill's private secretary and close friend, a scholar, translator of the Fables of La Fontaine and the Odes of Horace, a top civil servant and a social butterfly who went everywhere and knew everyone and never missed a London first night. Much in demand as a corrector of texts from Somerset Maugham, through Walter de la Mare, to Winston Churchill, he was the editor of "The Georgian Poets", encourager and patron of D.H. Lawrence, Stanley Spencer, Robert Graves, Siegfried Sassoon and many other painters and poets of whom Christopher Hassall was the last, but the first had been Rupert Brooke, the beautiful young poet who died in the First World War:

"If I should die, think only this of me;
That there's some corner of a foreign field
That is forever England".

Eddy had been Brooke's friend and patron and Cathleen Nesbitt had been his girlfriend and when Eddy came backstage and went into her dressing room, we all felt that we were close to history.

Unfortunately the critics were not impressed with the "The Player King" and their notices were lukewarm, but we all enjoyed visiting Edinburgh and free entry into the Festival Club, where we drank whisky late into the night. We were there a fortnight and then went to Aberdeen.

In the train we discussed digs and I said that I had booked with a certain landlady and, mentioning the address, asked if anyone knew it. One of the girls said, "I do. It is over Boots and there is no bath." This was worrying news and when the taxi stopped outside Boots, I became more worried. However, a fresh-looking, white-haired, motherly woman opened the door and showed me my room. Feeling reassured, I asked tentatively if I might see the bathroom. "Here" she said, opening the door to a spotlessly clean bathroom. The girl had been wrong.

The flat was comfortable, the food excellent and the landlady cheerful and friendly. On the Monday, I asked casually if it would be all right for me to have a bath. Her expression changed. "You want a bath?"

I said I did. "When would you be wanting it?" I said whenever it would be convenient. Would Thursday afternoon be all right?

I said yes. "What time?" I said it was up to her. "Would four o'clock be all right?" I said it would.

When I got back to the digs just after four on the Thursday afternoon, the landlady was red in the face and her face and hands were streaked with black. "I thought you'd forgotten" she reproached me.

I said I was sorry although it was only just after four. "It's ready," she said. I went into the bathroom; the geyser was hissing away, I turned on the tap and the water came out bright orange. I must have been the first person to have a bath in that household for a very, very long time.

On the Sunday morning, I had breakfast on the train with Cathleen Nesbitt. It was half-past eight in the morning, but she was beautifully dressed with a hat and elbow-length gloves. She was charming and funny, and I enjoyed the breakfast. It was said she had a difficult home-life with her husband, who was an alcoholic. The story was told that on one occasion she had taken his clothes away to keep him from going out to buy alcohol while she did the shopping, but on the way home she encountered him coming along the road, naked beneath an old mackintosh and holding a half-empty bottle of whisky. "You forgot the old Mack," he said as he staggered towards her.

The last week of the tour was at Brighton and as there was no offer of a London theatre, "The Player King" ended its days at the Royal Brighton and I went back to the Central School for the winter term that was the beginning of the third year of the course.

—

CHAPTER THIRTEEN

One of the plays we did that winter term was an Aldwych Farce. The Aldwych farces, begun in 1930, had been an institution throughout the thirties and forties. Tom Walls, Ralph Lynn, Yvonne Arnaud, Mary Brough and Robertson Hare were the stars, and the plays, which were written by Ben Travers and had titles like, "Plunder", "Cuckoo in the Nest", "Banana Ridge", "Thark" and "Rookery Nook," all dealt with infidelity and other forms of moral and social turpitude among the golf-playing, cocktail-drinking comfortably-off. Played at the Aldwych Theatre, they had long runs due to their resonance throughout the British Empire. From Poona to Bangkok, the administrators of Empire did not consider that their home leave was complete unless they had seen the current Aldwych farce and could return to their post able to describe the latest circumstances under which Robertson Hare had lost his trousers, been turned into a brown-paper parcel or hidden in a grandfather clock.

If comedy is the opposite of tragedy, farce is the opposite of melodrama, and if, as David Garrick said, "Comedy is a serious business", then farce is a deadly serious business. To play comedy one must suffer, but to play farce one must agonise. In the Aldwych farces it was Tom Walls and Ralph Lynn, with his monocle, who were the anarchic duo who caused the mayhem and Robertson Hare, small, bald and eminently respectable who, with his famous cry of "Oh, Calamity!" paid the price and did the agonising. The plays are beautifully constructed like pieces of fine-tuned engineering, but they were written expressly for the actors who played them and are almost impossible for others to play successfully.

I forget which of the plays we did, but the producer was Jack Allen who had toured in one of the later plays with Ralph Lynn and Roberson Hare and was full of stories about Ralph Lynn, his extraordinary sense of timing and his anarchic, dare-devil behaviour on the stage. How he would do almost anything to try to make Robertson

Hare laugh, even turning his back to the audience, undoing his fly buttons, taking out his penis and waving it at him, before returning it to its place for the next line, while poor Robertson Hare would be almost in tears, pleading under his breath, "No, Ralph, don't Ralph, please Ralph!" knowing that everything depended on his never, ever, laughing.

I found that I enjoyed playing farce and that the precision and the need for hair-trigger timing were something I had a talent for and wanted to do more of.

It was during that winter term of 1952 in early December that London suffered its last "smog", (a corruption of "smoke" and "fog") which brought the city to a standstill for nearly three weeks. London is built on a marsh and so is subject to fog, which the wind normally disperses. However on this occasion there was no wind. Moreover in the early fifties many houses and flats were still heated by open coal fires and a low cloud-base prevented the smoke from rising. The result was a thick, yellow, sulphurous atmosphere that clamped down on the city and penetrated every nook and cranny, making it impossible to see more than a few feet in front of you. One evening I went to the theatre and from my seat in the balcony could barely see the stage. On another occasion, when the other half of our group were doing a play in the school theatre and I set out to see it, I arrived at Piccadilly underground (the smog had penetrated even down there) and caught the bus along Piccadilly towards the Albert Hall. The bus advanced slowly and finally stopped, the driver announcing that he could go no further. I got out and began to walk along the pavement going from the faint glow of one street lamp to the next but unable to make out the shops I was passing, so that it was only when I found myself back at Piccadilly that I realised that the bus driver had turned the bus round before telling us to get out.

The smog had a devastating effect on people with breathing problems or who were in bad health and so many died that the city's stock of coffins became exhausted. When it was over, a law was passed forbidding open coal fires in private houses and there has never been a similar problem with smog since.

The money I had saved from the tour of "The Player King" allowed me to buy some clothes. In the Lyric Revue, George and all the actors had had matching suits made by a tailor who did a lot of work for H.M. Tennent, the leading play producing firm of that time. George had subsequently returned to the tailor and had a suit made. The price was reasonable and he offered to introduce me as a client.

H. and H. Larsson of 19, Wardour Street, were two brothers who had worked with their father, who had himself made jackets for King George V. They were installed over a sleazy-looking shop and you went up a narrow staircase to the bare room with a large window overlooking the street, where, helped by several women, they cut, sewed and steam-ironed. I ordered a tweed sports coat and a pair of grey flannel trousers and was fascinated to see how they were made, the collar of the jacket being shrunk into position with a steam iron, so that it fitted perfectly and would continue to do so until it fell to pieces, while the lapels and the shoulders were all sewn with hundreds of small hand stitches. That first jacket and the trousers the Larssons made me were a revelation. I discovered that clothes do indeed make the man. Lamentable as it may be, I defy anyone to put on a properly cut and made suit and not feel more pleased with himself and content with the world than he did before. I got to know the Larssons well, introduced several actors to them and, if I were in Soho, would often drop in and watch them work. Later I came to an arrangement where I paid so much a month and ordered clothes when I needed them. The Larssons made all my clothes from the age of twenty-one until I was forty-five and I still wear a suit they made in 1957 and a dinner-jacket made in 1961. When I wear them today, I think of great-uncle George's "Had this suit thirty years'. Only in my case, it is now nearly sixty years. I feel sure he would have approved.

Among the new intake of first year students was a beautiful, witty and original girl with whom I fell hopelessly in love. I had been careful to avoid any romantic involvement, having read Cyril Connolly's "Enemies of Promise" of which one of the first was "the pram in the hall". My situation was so fragile and my means so slender, (I was living on the £5 pounds a week that my father managed to allow me) that anything beyond fares, meals and the occasional theatre ticket was out of the question. In those days it was not the custom to ask girls to pay for themselves, however much richer they might be than you.

Cherry Seely came from Nottinghamshire. Her brother, Timmy, was at RADA. Anarchic and unpredictable, Cherry made me think of Sally Bowles in "Goodbye to Berlin". She shared a flat with another girl over a shop in Shepherd's Market, a fashionable enclave off Piccadilly full of up-market prostitutes.

Cherry's family background was very glamorous; her father rode his own horses in the Grand National and her mother had been a friend of the Prince of Wales, who had been a regular visitor to their house and played with Cherry and Timmy in their nursery. Timmy, it must be said, bore an uncanny resemblance to the Duke of Windsor. Cherry's elder brother was married to a very smart and dignified lady whom, Cherry insisted, had been a hostess at the "Bag of Nails", a fashionable nightclub. They lived in a small mews in Knightsbridge with a large dog whose tail seemed to be continually brushing ashtrays off tables. Altogether Cherry's was a new and fascinating world. I longed to make love to her, but didn't dare, feeling I had so little to offer. Like all frustrated love, it was seesaw of emotions; when I was not with her I thought of her all the time, and when I was with her I could not say what I wanted to. But we remained friends and spent afternoons and evenings together.

In the third year the history of the theatre was taught as a subject. While still at school it had been a hobby of mine; George was passionately interested in it and had a remarkable collection of books. I too had slowly been collecting books, especially about the lives of actors. One of the fascinating things about the history of the British Theatre is the line of great actors that stretches back to Burbage, the actor for whom Shakespeare wrote. The theatre is always a reflection of its time and the great actors like David Garrick, Edmund Kean, Macready and Henry Irving each reflected his period, its values and its aspirations. Today, our recently dead actors are recorded on film. We can still see John Gielgud and Laurence Olivier, but the only guide we have to how earlier actors played and their effect on the audience is from written criticism. This is sometimes tantalising, as when Byron, writing of Kean, says that seeing him play Hamlet was "like reading Shakespeare by flashes of lightning" or the critic who compared the acting of Munden to eating turtle; "the lean is like the lean of any other meat, but it has a quantity of green fat about it that is absolutely delicious".

When classes began I soon spotted that, although the teacher knew the general shape of theatre history, as far as the actors were concerned, he knew less than me and after I had asked one or two questions that put him on the spot, he came up to me after a lesson and suggested I give a short talk each week on a particular actor. I was delighted because it gave me a reason to research the subject properly. I had done several weeks of this and my talks had been a success, so much so, that they had got longer and longer and were taking up practically the whole lesson. When I reached Edmund Kean, whose life is one of the most romantic of all the great actors, I prepared the talk with particular care. But when I arrived in the classroom, the teacher said that the Inspector from London University was inspecting the Central School and he had chosen our class to sit in on. I immediately supposed that the teacher would cancel the talk, but he insisted I go ahead.

In reality I don't think anyone could recount the life of Edmund Kean without moving his hearers practically to tears in telling how an unimpressive little man with dark flashing eyes, after years struggling in the provinces in real poverty, was seen playing in a barn in Gloucestershire by one of the board members of Drury Lane and eventually offered a performance as Shylock, how he and his wife were so poor that they had to walk to London with their small son, Howard, who was ill through lack of food, and how on the night, Edmund walked to Drury Lane alone with a bundle of his costume and props under his arm, how none of the actors spoke to him and the curtain went up before an almost empty house, and how, as he began to play Shylock, the word got out and the theatre began to fill up so that by the end it was crammed full and there was a huge ovation such as had never been heard since the days of Garrick. How he walked back to their lodgings without speaking to anyone, opened the door and shouted to his wife, "Mary, you shall ride in your carriage and Howard shall go to Eton" but how Howard died a few days later.

The talk went well and the Inspector seemed genuinely moved by it. It may have been a trick of the light, but I had the impression his eyes were moist when he congratulated me.

By the time it came to the final term and the public show, many of the leading members of the group had already left. Harold Pinter, whose premature departure had allowed me to move up a year, had joined Anew McMaster who ran a fit-up company playing Shakespeare in Ireland. Pinter came back to the school and in the café where we used to go, held forth about his experiences so that several others, including Barry Foster, the Gaev of "The Cherry Orchard", left to join it too. This meant that there was less competition and more parts, so I got two parts in two different extracts.

The first was the young communist prison warder in a scene from "Now Barabbas" which was produced by a nice actor called John Kidd. John Kidd was a huge help for, although the young warder was close to me in age and appearance, it was the sort of part that I found difficult to identify with. John Kidd made me see that I was sitting outside the part and commenting on it. The truth was that the part reminded me of the people I had been with in the RAF, an experience I was busy trying to forget. He forced me to put all that aside and get right inside the character.

The second was Mr Justice Proudfoot, a fussy old husband, in Somerset Maugham's stage adaptation of Grenet-Dancourt's "The Noble Spaniard". This was produced by Stephen Joseph and was just the sort of part I revelled in. The play is set in the nineteenth century and the scene was a breakfast scene. We were allowed to go to the costumier's and dress the parts properly, and I found a magnificent quilted dressing gown, a wig with hair parted in the centre and Dundreary whiskers. For the character, the Taylor tea parties provided a rich mine to draw from.

Stephen Joseph was Hermione Gingold's son. His father was

Michael Joseph, the publisher. Stephen was a big ungainly figure. He had lived in America and wore jeans at a time when no one in England had seen them except in cowboy films. He was marvellous to work with, inventive and encouraging and I felt comfortable and secure with him.

The big event of the year was, of course, the coronation of Queen Elizabeth II on the second of June. George and Pamela and I went to some friends who had a television to watch it. It was a splendid spectacle and suddenly everyone was buying a television set and television began to be taken more seriously.

A week later, on the ninth, the Central School public show was held at the Strand Theatre in the afternoon. The judges were Gwen Ffrangçon-Davies, Alan Dent and Nigel Patrick. My mother came up from Gloucester and I met her at Paddington. She wanted to see St Martin's in the Fields where she had been married and afterwards I took her to the National Gallery, which she had never seen. Lady Taylor and Jane came, as did George and Pamela. The show went well and when it was over and I was undressing, someone came round to tell me I had been awarded the Elsie Fogerty prize for the best all-round performance. It had never occurred to me that there would be prizes. I had only been interested in the possibility of an agent seeing me.

The notice in the *Daily Telegraph* said that "The Noble Spaniard"; "turned out to be an amusing burlesque of the comedy of intrigue. Although played with spirit, it was rather beyond the talents of the students, only Edwin Apps seeming quite at home as a ridiculous old husband.

This actor also got well into the contrasting character of the young communistic prison warder in Now Barabbas"

The prize was £5 and I spent it on a new pair of shoes, thinking that I was likely to be doing a lot of walking round agents' offices in the next few months.

After the public show, the term was over for us. I went to the school for a last time and had lunch in the cafeteria with Cherry. She told me she was leaving, "I'm not dedicated like you," she said and told me she had decided to get married. He was rich and had an estate in the North. I never saw her again.

I received letters from three agents asking me to go and see them, Dorothy Mather of Film Rights, who was Nigel Patrick's agent (he had, she told me, insisted she see me), another agency, Fraser and Dunlop, (known among the actors as "Fraser and No hope") and a nice woman who was starting out and seemed really interested, Josephine Burton. She sent me for several jobs and thanks to her I found myself in a television studio for the first time. It was the 26th September at Alexandra Palace where the BBC had their first studios. I and another actor, Kim Grant, whom I was often to meet and work with later, were playing two guards sitting each side of the star, our prisoner, in the back of a car. The star was Catherine Lacey whom I had seen as the nun sitting beside the figure wrapped in bandages who had so terrified me in "The Lady Vanishes" (she later turns out not to be a nun and is given away by a typically Hitchcockian shot in which she is seen to be wearing high heeled shoes, but I had not stayed in the cinema long enough to see that.) At any rate, I was very impressed to be working with her even though I didn't have any lines.

The show was the Saturday night thriller, "A Place of Execution", a series in six parts by Alfred Shaughnessy, episode 1, "An Eye for an Eye" produced by Alvin Rakoff. The leading actor was Derek Bond and the cast included Ballard Berkeley, who was to become a friend some years later. It was live, as recording had not yet been invented. The studio was stiflingly hot with batteries of lights everywhere and we had had our faces painted bright yellow, which, it seemed, was what television cameras required. Shooting a scene in the back of a car was a major undertaking and we sat there for what seemed like hours during the rehearsal, with huge floodlights blazing at us, the yellow make-up running down our faces and four stagehands rocking the car with a back projection whirring away behind. Kim and I were both rather nervous, but Catherine Lacey soon put us at our ease and made us feel we were all in the same boat – or the same car – together. I don't remember what we were paid, only a few pounds, but it didn't matter. In future, in answer to the question, "Have you done television?" I could answer 'yes' without blushing.

Not that doing television was something to be proud of, it was considered a new-fangled, inferior sort of film, and filming itself was looked down upon as something that anyone could walk off the street and do. The theatre was what mattered and to do that you had to be a proper actor. This attitude continued well into the sixties. George Benson met Athene Seyler one day in the mid-sixties. She had recently been in several television plays. He asked her what she thought of it and she replied it was like being in a series of flops. To someone like Athene, used to running-in a play on tour and then playing it for many months in the West End, the idea of going to all the trouble of rehearsing a play for one performance must have seemed very frustrating.

I was beginning to think I had found an agent who was really interested in me, when one of Josephine Burton's actors was suddenly cast to replace Rex Harrison in the New York production of "My Fair Lady". Josephine was terribly excited and went to New York for his opening. The following morning she was found dead in her hotel room having suffered a massive heart attack. So it was back to the drawing board for me, as far as agents were concerned.

My investment in shoe-leather was paying off, as I went, afternoon after afternoon round the agents and sat with other actors in their waiting rooms. It was a depressing experience, not helped by the fact that when you did eventually get in to see the great man, he would lean back in his chair and say, "Tell me about your self". Then, before you could begin, the telephone would ring and he would have a long and relaxed chat with someone, all the time smiling at you as though you were in on it and knew who he was talking to – which of course you did not. When that was over, he would look at you and say, "You were saying?" And then the telephone would ring again and there would be another cosy chat.

In general the reaction of all the agents was the same: surprise that I looked so young. In vain I told them I could play old men. It was not what they wanted to hear. There were plenty of real old men about, they wanted young good-looking juveniles and that, I knew, was not me.

Some days after the public show, Stephen Joseph took me out to lunch. He must at that time have been in his early thirties and while in America, had been studying "dramaturgy", a subject that we in England, had not even heard of. Over lunch he asked me if I had ever thought of writing. I said no. He said that I should, and explained the theory of volition, which is that a character on the stage must want something. As long as he does, he is alive. What he wants can be something as simple as a light for his cigarette, but the moment the cigarette is lit, he is dead and of no further interest to the audience – unless he wants something else. That lunch with Stephen and that basic idea of volition set me on the path to writing. Stephen's real interest was in Theatre-in-the-Round and I was to work with him in several of his productions in the next few months and years as he gradually introduced the idea into the country.

When you win a prize as I had done, or give a good performance that gets noticed by the critics, everything hangs on what offers come up immediately. If something for which you are right comes up, you are away, if the offers are not right for you, or there are none, then in a very short time, someone else will win a prize or give a good performance or get noticed by the critics and your moment will have passed and you will have to join the queue.

My offer came from John Counsell at the Windsor rep. Windsor rep was very special; John Counsell and his wife, Mary Kerridge ran it, the Royal family often went to the plays and it was one of the best showcases for actors round London. During the holidays from the Central School, I had walked on in two productions at Windsor: "The First Gentleman", Robert Morley's play about George IV, and a production of George Bernard Shaw's "St Joan," in which Sir Lewis Casson, Sybil Thorndyke's husband, played his original part. Mary Kerridge played Joan. It was unkindly said that it was "a Miss Kerridge of casting" because she was too old for the part, but Sybil Thorndyke came to rehearsals and told her in front of us all, that she was splendid. One of my chief memories of the production was that during rehearsals Queen Mary, the widow of George V, died and that morning Sir Lewis came wearing a black tie which put us all to shame.

Now I got a letter from John Counsell offering me the part of Lord Goring in Oscar Wilde's "An Ideal Husband". It is a plum part, one of Wilde's witty, dandified bachelors. The play was to be produced by Jack Minster who had produced it in New York. It looked like being a real chance. But a few days before rehearsals were due to begin I got an embarrassed phone call from John Counsell, Jack Minster had insisted on playing the part of Lord Goring himself. Counsell was sorry, there was nothing he could do. He would find me another part later on. It was devastating news and meant that I joined the queue.

But work of a sort began to turn up. Hal Burton, who had produced "The Cherry Orchard", produced an "Elizabethan Evening" on television, in which scenes from Shakespeare and Ben Johnson were acted on an Elizabethan stage and I sat on the edge of the stage with a couple of others dressed in doublet and hose, smoking long clay pipes and heckling the actors. Soon after, I had a part in a play about George IV's going to Scotland for the first time called "The Honours of Scotland". Peter Bull played George IV and I carried one of the honours.

As Christmas approached, I was offered a part in Charles Hawtrey's "The Private Secretary" in the rep at Bromley. It was a play I had often heard about, because W.S. Penley had created the leading part. The Penleys were an old theatrical family who played the Kent circuit in the 18th and 19th centuries. W.S. Penley or "Willy" was born in Ramsgate and was related to the Mascalls and a first-cousin of my great-grandmother, Harriet Goodson, née Mascall. He had had a big success with "The Private Secretary" and an even bigger one with "Charley's Aunt". My grandmother had stayed with him at Dorking when she was a girl and had seen both plays and could quote lines from them. Spalding, the private secretary of the title, is a mild figure, a sort of curate who continually says "All I want is a glass of milk and a Bath bun" and who wears galoshes. The plot hangs on a mistaken identity when a major returning from India mistakes him for his nephew and tries to make him "go it." The cast includes two young men, the nephew and his friend, who Francis Matthews and I played. Michael Bilton played Spalding, but the returning major was played by a theatrical curiosity, Raymond Somerville, with whom I was to work often in the ensuing years. Raymond Somerville had been a major in the army who, when he retired in 1936, decided to go to theatre school. He was stout and rubicund and the very picture of a retired major. When he was not in rep, he lived in Oxford with his two sisters who were the pillars of Oxford's famous bookshop, Blackwells. His cousin was the Somerville of Somerville and Ross, the two ladies who wrote the books about fox hunting in Ireland, "Experiences of an Irish R.M." and another cousin was Professor Neville Coghill. The Somervilles had been a naval family and the family tree rustled with admirals. Raymond loved the atmosphere of the theatre and above all the company of young men. Some said he was rather too fond of it, but I saw no evidence of that. He was in his element standing at a bar drinking pink gin. "Gin", he would say, "as my friend Sir Otto Mundy, the head of Customs, used to say, is the purest spirit there is," and he would prove it by downing a couple of doubles before the show and a few more afterwards. When he made his first entrance in the play with the line "I'm just back from India!" no one could doubt it; he was the British Raj in person. And as he puffed his way across the stage after his supposed nephew, crying; "You shall go it, you shall go it!" it was the most perfect piece of casting one could imagine.

Finally at the end of the year I was given a small part in Clifford Bax's play, "The Rose without a Thorn" about Henry VIII's passion for Katheryn Howard. It was produced by Michael Barry, the B.B.C's senior producer, at Lime Grove studios and was a prestigious production: Basil Sydney played Henry, Barbara Jefford, Katheryn and Tony Britton, Thomas Culpepper. The cast included several experienced Shakespearean actors whom I had seen at Stratford and elsewhere, but my chief memory is the mortification of nearly walking in front of a live camera and being saved by Basil Sydney.

In those pre-recording days, we did the play on Sunday evening and returned to do it again on the following Thursday. After that I went to Gloucester for a week's holiday.

CHAPTER FOURTEEN

—

When I got back to London I got a call from Dorothy Mather of Film Rights. There was a company called the Elizabethan Theatre Company that was to do a spring tour of "Twelfth Night" and "The Merchant of Venice". The producers were looking for a Toby Belch, and would I go and see them? Hugh Goldie was producing Twelfth Night and a young man straight from Cambridge, Peter Hall, was to produce "The Merchant of Venice", his first professional production.

I met Hugh Goldie and read for him and soon after got a call from Dorothy Mather saying they wanted me to play Toby Belch in "Twelfth Night" and "The Prince of Arragon" and Old Gobbo in "The Merchant of Venice" for £12 a week. Stuart Allen had been demobbed and was looking for work, so I tipped him off that they were casting and he landed Lorenzo in "The Merchant" and Curio in "Twelfth Night" as well as assistant stage manager.

Rehearsals began for "The Merchant" which was to open at Cambridge and to be followed by "Twelfth Night" which was to open at Bedford. There would follow a tour of several months ending at the Playhouse, Oxford.

The Elizabethan Theatre Company was an experiment in bringing together people from the OUDS (Oxford University Dramatic Society) and the Cambridge "Footlights" with some additions from RADA and the Central School. It had the backing of the London Mask Theatre (an organization formed in 1938 by Thane Parker, Michael MacOwen, J.B. Priestley and Ronald Jeans at the Westminster Theatre, to encourage new talent in players, producers and authors) and had been founded by an ex-OUDS actor, Colin George, who had put his own money in it and normally played a leading part. From Oxford it had the blessing of Professor Neville Coghill and from Cambridge that of Professor George Rylands, the verse-speaking specialist who influenced a generation of directors and actors.

Rehearsals were at the Westminster Theatre, the cast was led by Tony Church as Shylock, Frank Windsor (who had been in the year ahead of me at the Central School) as Antonio, Josée Richards, (a founder member of the company) as Portia, Colin George as Bassanio, Peter Jeffrey as Gratiano, Deidre Doone as Jessica and John Nettleton as the Prince of Morocco and the Doge, with Roderick Cook as Launcelot Gobbo.

Peter Hall was tall, slim and baby-faced. He wore a blue Melton overcoat and thick rubber-soled suede shoes. He began by telling us his idea of the play, saying that Venice was masculine, hot and sweaty and Belmont feminine and cold. This simple, clear directive that set the context in which the actor's imaginations could begin to work immediately impressed me. When we left the rehearsal, Stuart said, "I don't think much of him." I replied, "On the contrary, he is going to go a long way." Stuart has often reminded me of this as we have watched Sir Peter Hall's vertiginous career.

Apart from Stuart, the actor with whom I got on best was John Nettleton. Recently out of RADA, he was suspicious of the OUDS and Footlights people who gave the impression they belonged to a club from which we were excluded, while to us they seemed to be amateurs.

The Prince of Arragon is one of the suitors come to woo Portia, and, as the name suggests, he is arrogant. I decided to base my character on Lady Taylor, with her "that underground railway" attitude to common mortals and I had a lot of fun with the part. Old Gobbo presented a problem, because he is blind and I felt that in the middle of the twentieth century one could not get much fun out of blindness. So I suggested to Peter Hall that I should have an ear trumpet as there seemed more mileage in that idea, with Young Gobbo obliged to shout down it and so on. Hall agreed and left us to our own devices and Roderick Cook and I built up a scene that was funny but not over the top.

During rehearsals I used to go into a coffee bar opposite the theatre and on several occasions Peter Hall came over and we chatted. I found him affable and pleasant, but at the same time his ambition seemed to get in the way of any real contact. All theatre people are ambitious, they have to be, it is part of the job, but usually people manage to hide it to some degree, Hall's ambition was almost indecently naked, not a fig-leaf in sight.

We opened at the Arts Theatre Cambridge and Stephen Haskell's criticism in The Cambridge Review found that

"Peter Hall's production had the great merit of speed and continuity, each scene melted into the next, and there was a sense of unrestricted space which enabled us to conjure up a solid three-dimensional background with a whole wealth of imaginative associations".

But he went on

"the clarity with which the actors spoke their lines made up for many deficiencies in the acting. Tony Church gave an oddly insensitive performance as Shylock... he never succeeded in turning Shylock into anything more than a hissing and melodramatic stage villain..

He praised Josée Richard's Portia, saying,

"she played the part beautifully".

And went on

"Peter Jeffrey as Gratiano was the best of the men; Bassanio was too assertive. Antonio tended towards ineffectual ranting and Launcelot Gobbo was rather too birdlike in his antics."

And he ended:

"But it was a joy to find a production which maintained such a consistently high level in the smaller parts: Old Gobbo and the two princes gave excellent character sketches without ever verging on the buffoonery which spoils many of the recent Old Vic productions",

which left John Nettleton and me feeling smug.

Once "The Merchant of Venice" had opened, work started seriously on "Twelfth Night". I had been reading the play and thinking about Toby Belch since accepting the part and wondering how to play it. Toby is the ne'er-do-well uncle of Olivia, living at her expense in her house and behaving badly. Talking to George Benson, he mentioned that there had been an actor in the Edwardian era of whom the critics said that he played Toby Belch as though he had been helped out of all the best clubs in London. This seemed an interesting line to follow. I talked to Hugh Goldie who thought it a good idea and we began work along those lines, but somehow it didn't take off. I found I was not getting the fun out of it I should, and my drunk scenes were laboured. Whether it was because I do not find drunkenness funny, perhaps because of my grandfather, I do not know, but for whatever reason, my Toby Belch was a flop. Certain scenes worked, but not the important ones and the audience's reaction told me I had failed. I kept working at it as we toured, but although it went better some nights, it still hung fire. I did not get any help from Hugh Goldie who seemed resentful that I was spoiling his production and our relations became increasingly strained.

John Nettleton played Sir Andrew Aguecheek and was excellent, it was a part that was perfect for him and Deirdre Doone was an enchanting Viola. I used to listen to her from the wings each evening in the "willow cabin" speech, which never ceased to move me. "Twelfth Night" is a magical play, perhaps the best of the comedies, and even though I was unsatisfied with my own performance it was a delight to be in the production.

We toured the South of England with the two plays playing Bedford, Plymouth, Exeter, Norwich, Worcester, Hereford, Barnstable, etc. At Plymouth we struck the worst digs I have ever encountered. Several of us found we had booked the same address and so shared a taxi from the station. When we arrived we found the landlady in bed in a room on the ground floor with her lover sitting on a chair beside her, holding her hand. She told us she had a weak heart and could not climb the stairs, so we must find our own rooms. We did and the state they were in showed that she certainly did not climb the stairs

Meals were in the basement and consisted of potatoes cooked, re-cooked and heated up. While we ate, the landlady walked round the table and talked, that is she repeated the same stories over and over again. One of them dealt with the fact that the garden gate had been repainted, had we noticed? It had been a major decision. The colour and the price the painter charged. This riveting tale played through meal after meal.

On the Tuesday when we got back after the show for supper, she said, "I've got you some fish". She had no need to tell us – the stink of elderly fish boiling reached halfway down the road. "Don't worry about bones", she said, "There aren't any" I took a mouthful and a fishbone stuck in my throat. I passed a sleepless night and the next morning went to find a doctor. Plymouth had been bombed flat and not yet rebuilt and I seemed to walk miles along roads with ruined houses on both sides. The doctor, when I got to see him, said he could do nothing. I must go to the hospital. This was another long walk. When I arrived at the hospital I was put in the waiting room, where I sat until the early afternoon, when someone came to say that I must go to the other hospital as the surgeon was there, but he would not be there long, so I must take a taxi. The taxi was expensive as the other hospital was on the other side of the town. When I did eventually get to see the surgeon and he examined my throat, he said that the bone had gone but that it had badly scratched the throat and that was what I could feel. I thanked him and made my way to the theatre where it was already time to begin making up for the evening performance.

The week passed slowly and we longed for Saturday. When it eventually came and we got back after the show we were in a state of euphoria as we went down for the last of these terrible meals. She served the potatoes and, suddenly I could not resist, I said, "Oh, by the way, am I right in thinking that you have had the garden door repainted?" All the heads bent down over their plates as the landlady replied "Yes, and do you know ..." and went straight into the story. I was sitting at the end of the table and had to keep looking at her and trying not to laugh as she went carefully through all the details, while the others spluttered over their food.

The management decided not to play Twelfth Night at Oxford,

which was an indication that it was not considered a success, but The Merchant of Venice was well received as it had been everywhere.

The Playhouse had its own staff and I made friends with a very pretty and witty ASM called Maggie Smith.

When the week came to an end, Hugh Goldie told me that my contract was not to be renewed which was a way of saying I had been sacked. The official reason was that one of the original OUDS people, the son of Henry Hall the bandleader, was returning from America and would take over the part, which he had played in a university production. It was a disappointment, but I knew I had failed in the part, so it was not unexpected, but it meant that I had messed up my chance of getting into the Old Vic/Stratford circle and henceforth I saw myself condemned to work in the commercial theatre. I felt it then and afterwards as a major setback and I still regret it.

Back in London, one of the places actors went when they were out of work was the bar of the Arts Theatre. It was a depressing under-ground coffee bar made more depressing by the presence of all the other out-of-work actors and actresses. A figure who always seemed to be sitting at the bar was Kenneth Haigh, the abrasive student from the Central School. I again tried to talk to him but found him as unforthcoming as ever. It was then that I ran into the pretty ASM from Oxford, Maggie Smith. She was in London looking for work and we began seeing each other and going to the cinema. One film we both enjoyed was "The Court Jester" with Danny Kaye and for days afterwards we were quoting: "The vessel with the pestle and the chalice from the palace" and laughing uproariously.

"Spotlight", the casting directory, in which we all advertised, buying either a quarter, half or full page with a photograph, also provided a casting service for repertory companies and I got a call from them inviting me to meet Ronald Russell and his wife Peggy Ann Wood who ran the Rapier Players, the fortnightly rep at Bristol which had been so coveted by the actors at Minehead. The Russells were in London casting their summer season of weekly rep. at Weston-Super-Mare. The interview went well and some days later I got a call offering me a contract.

Weekly rep at the seaside was a move in the wrong direction, but they had mentioned the possibility of going on to join their fortnightly company at Bristol when it was over, so I decided to accept. When I told Maggie she invited me to a party she was going to. It was an enjoyable party. Shortly afterwards she went to New York and our paths never crossed again.

When I arrived at Weston-super-Mare theatre, Ronald Russell showed me to my dressing room, but when I entered there was the most terrible stink. I returned to Russell and told him that there was a dead rat in the room, Afterwards, when it had been cleared up and the room made habitable, he told me he would not have been surprised if I had caught the next train back to London.

The summer season passed off well and the Russells invited me to join the parent company at Bristol.

Ronald Russell and Peggy-Ann Wood had run the Little Theatre for many years. The theatre was inside the Colston Hall, a large building, which housed Bristol's concert hall.

Ronnie was a heavily built, easy-going man in his early fifties and Peggy, who had begun life as a dancer, was small, bright and determined. They had no children and tended to treat the company as their family. They both acted and produced from time to time, but production for them meant copying as closely as possible the London production as described in French's Acting Edition. Any attempt at originality was frowned upon. In today's language, they produced a "product" rather than making any attempt to extend the boundaries of theatre. On the other side of the town was the Bristol Old Vic and the Russells left everything that they considered 'arty' to it.

I got on well with Ronnie, but had an uneasy relationship with Peggy, who had a school-mistress, "Come along now," manner that managed to rub me up the wrong way and made working with her difficult, although I recognised that they were a very nice, human couple who took a real interest in their actors.

One of the first questions I asked when I got to know them was what had happened to the actor they had engaged from the Minehead company four years earlier. They said he had not been a success but had only recently left because he had a nice wife and children and lived in a caravan and Ronnie didn't have the heart to sack him.

A pillar of the company was Paul Smythe or "Smithy" as he was called. He had been stage-manager to Barry Jackson at the Birmingham rep. and was considered something of an oracle, as he sat behind the scenes night after night listening to the play and telling stories of the young actors he had known at the Birmingham rep, and how Lawrence Olivier had asked him if he thought growing a Clark Gable moustache would further his career.

A peculiarity of Bristol is the local accent, which has an intrusive "l" at the end of words; the town was originally called Bristow and it was this "l" that changed it to Bristol. The Bristolians themselves seem unaware of it, for on one occasion I heard a member of the company doing a crossword puzzle with the stage-carpenter. The stage-carpenter suggested "ideal". "No" said the actor, "its four letters". "Yes", insisted the stage-carpenter, "ideal". It was sometime before the actor realised he meant "idea."

Bristol at that time was not exactly fun city. It was in the grip of Quaker chocolate makers who insisted that the pubs shut early and that the buses stopped running at 9p.m. The University existed and undergraduates occasionally gave cider parties, but from the time you arrived at the station you felt a provincial gloom descend that was as all pervading as the London smog.

While I was in Bristol it was recorded in the local paper that an old lady had died aged a hundred, who, as a young girl disappointed in love, had tried to commit suicide by throwing herself off the Clifton Suspension Bridge. Fashionably dressed in a crinoline, she had floated down unharmed, the crinoline acting as a parachute.

When I had been there about six months, I was walking in the city one afternoon when I bumped into Peter Jeffrey, who had been in the Elizabethan Theatre Company. Peter was out of work and with a wife to support was selling the Encyclopaedia Britannica. He asked me if I could help him to get into the Little Theatre Company. I said I would do what I could, so that evening I told Ronnie about him and asked if he would see him. Ronnie agreed and a meeting was arranged, but after it, Ronnie said he thought Peter looked as if he might be difficult. I managed to convince him that it was not the case, and finally Peter was engaged. A good and thoughtful actor, Peter was an asset to the company and went on to have quite a distinguished career. Then, at the end of my first year, the company was strengthened by the addition of two talented members, Sheila Keith and an Australian actor, Michael Blakemore. Michael and I became friends. He had been brought up in Sydney and had spent his youth surfing, so that he claimed he had never read a book until he found himself under the grey skies of England. Determined to be an actor against his father's wishes, he had worked his passage as steward on a ship to come to England to study at RADA. Since being in England he had made up for lost time and I have him to thank for the introduction to Marcel Proust and Simone de Beauvoir. Her book, "The Second Sex", we discovered together and it is probably not going too far to say that it was a life-changing experience, or at any rate an opinion changing one.

My own reading at that time included the autobiography of Augustus Hare, "The Story of My Life" which tells of his childhood at Herstmonceux in Sussex with his aunt by marriage who, widowed just before he was born, adopted him at birth from his real parents. (When she wrote, tentatively, asking if she might be allowed to adopt him, his mother's answer was brief, "My dear Maria, how very kind of you! Yes, certainly, the baby shall be sent to you as soon as he is weaned; and, if any-one else would like one, would you kindly recollect that we have others".) Augustus was subsequently brought up in a severe evangelical environment dominated by his uncle Julius Hare, the Archdeacon of Lewes, an over-serious and richly comic figure with a weakness for governesses. He had been a professor at Cambridge until the family living became vacant on his uncle's death, and continued to preach the same sort of highly intellectual sermons that he had at Cambridge to the country folk of Sussex who found them not only incomprehensible but too long – especially in winter when the church was unheated. They said of him that he was "not a good winter parson". Augustus grew up to write travel books and to become a popular Victorian weekend guest at house parties where he thrilled the company recounting ghost stories. His is an autobiography in five volumes because he said that if he liked a book he liked it to be long. It was and remains one of my favourite books.

While I was in Bristol, Jane Taylor married. Her husband, a retired District Commissioner, had been a regular at the tea parties. I could not go to the wedding. In all I spent eighteen months at Bristol, from June 1954 until Christmas 1955. It was a comfortable if unexciting time. A fortnight's rehearsal was adequate for the level of production aimed at. And the plays were in general well mounted, with one exception: a pair of double doors which, differently disguised, appeared in production after production and invariably swung open when you closed them. They had even had a bad notice in the press, but the Russells obstinately refused to change them. At one performance I made an entrance in a serious scene, closed them behind me; took a couple of paces forward, and heard them swing open. I stepped back and closed them again, but when I walked forward the same thing happened and the audience began to titter. I stepped back again, and this time shut the doors hard and began the scene. A little later, just before another actor was due to enter, I heard movement behind the doors and then the actor, entering unexpectedly from the bedroom, whispered that the doors were stuck. We played the scene at the end of which, I had to exit, but for reasons of the plot, I realized I could not possibly leave by the bedroom so, in desperation, I said, "I'll leave by the backdoor" and walked off the stage through the fireplace. After that the doors were changed.

My parents came to see the performance on the Saturday night of the first week and I went back with them spending the Sunday at Gloucester and returning to Bristol in the evening.

Although the atmosphere at the Little Theatre was unexciting, we did some good plays and I got the chance to play some good comedy and farce parts that helped convince me that it was the direction in which my future lay. But in rep I never lost sight of my objective, which was to save as much money as possible so that at the end I could stick it out in London long enough to establish myself there.

The temptation in rep was to settle for a pleasant life with good parts, a regular income and a local popularity. The Russells wanted their actors to stay and do this (one actor had only recently left after twenty years). But I saw this as a trap. If after twenty years I was popular in Bristol but unknown in the rest of the country, it might help the Russells but it would not help me. Moreover, with my father's experience before me, I was suspicious of employers and had long decided never to trust them or their promises. However nice or generous they might appear, they were in the last resort only interested in themselves and wanted what they could get out of you and would not hesitate to dump you the moment you were no longer useful. It was a lesson he had learned the hard way and I was determined to profit from it.

As Christmas 1955 approached, I felt I had got all there was to be got out of the Little Theatre, so I gave my notice. The Russells were not pleased and barely spoke to me during the last fortnight but that could not be helped.

The last play I did at Bristol was a curious piece that had been going the rounds of all the rep companies. It was written by Howard Bromley-Chapman and was called "The Blank Theatre Scandal" the name being adapted to the town where it was played; at the Little Theatre it was called "The Bristol Theatre Scandal". All the actors played themselves and there was a detective plot that I forget, the stage-manager found murdered or something of the sort. At first we all groaned and thought it was a silly stunt, but when we worked on it I found it one of the most useful exercises I had done, because it came at a time when I was trying to emerge from wigs and grease-paint and establish my own personality on the stage and the fact of appearing as "Edwin" was a real help. The critic John Bennet writing in the Bristol Evening World, said that it was the first time he had seen the present Little Theatre company and that he had enjoyed every moment of the brisk, entertaining production. Adding, "I liked particularly the Hulbertian comedy – Claude not Jack – of Edwin Apps". I found this encouraging and I was reassured by the fact that the audience seemed to accept me as I was.

When I got home for Christmas I developed quinsy and spent a painful fortnight in bed living from one swallow to the next, my throat on fire. During my convalescence I read Boswell's "Life of Johnson" for the first time. I have read it many times since and often return to it for its portrait of that most quintessential Englishman, who, while he was stubborn and often wrong-headed, remained lucid, and above all lucid about him self.

Back in London, independent television had started up and I began to get work with ABC and Rediffusion. The latter was housed in what had been Adastral House, the Air Ministry, where my father had worked as a Lands Officer before being appointed to the Aerodrome Board. There I made contact with a friend from St Edmunds, O.B.G. Fitz-Jones.

Now, as Bryan Fitz-Jones, he was producing talk shows. We used to lunch together. David Frost had begun his television career at Rediffusion and Bryan had been given the job of showing him round. He said that when, by the end of the first week, Frost had made a profit on the tea money he felt sure he would go a long way.

I was in a couple of Sunday night plays for Rediffusion and in a comedy series for ABC. These were all performed live in a studio in Manchester after rehearsals in London. The comedy series was about two unmarried girls sharing a flat, one of whom was Billy Whitelaw. I played a character that had to talk to a racehorse and persuaded it to win. Wondering how I could best get on terms with the racehorse, I rang my mother. "Pull its ears and blow up its nose," she said. When the horse appeared in the studio at the dress rehearsal, it seemed enormous. There was no doubt about its being a real racehorse, it exuded thorough breeding and the grooms could barely hold it. The scene in which I persuaded it to win the race on which the girls had put their savings, was a good one, and when I had rehearsed without the horse, everyone had laughed, but faced with this demonstration of starting-gate nervousness, W.C. Fields' advice, "never appear with children or animals", began to make sense. When the moment came for the scene, the floor assistant cued me and I approached the animal, but as soon as I went to whisper in its ear, it tossed its head and knocked me flying. I had another go with the same result. Next I had to fondle its muzzle and scratch its nose, but this went down very badly and it began rearing up. I said the dialogue as best I could, but the effect was ruined. On the sleeper back to London Billy Whitelaw gave me lessons in how to stand on your head in a moving train at which she was an expert but I'm afraid she did not find me a promising pupil.

Spending a few days in Gloucester, a conversation with my father led him to say that I didn't know London because I didn't know the City and he suggested coming to London to show it to me. So it was arranged that I meet him at Paddington and we spend a day together in the City. He took me to Dr Johnson's house, showed me the Mansion House and the Bank of England, several City churches and places he had known, where he and my grandfather had come to sell their hops each year, and then took me to lunch at Simpson's in the City. Not to be confused with Simpson's in the Strand and, alas no longer in existence, its site having been 'developed', it was an eighteenth-century building with a bow window. Inside there was a central aisle with time worn tables and high-backed benches on each side. The benches had brass rails above them for the diners' hats. The menu was steak and kidney pudding or pie, steamed puddings, served with draught beer. It was a Dickensian atmosphere where one would not have been surprised to see the Cheeryble brothers, or Ralph Nickleby. The clients were all city men and the hat-rails were full of bowlers and top hats. Afterwards, as we were walking along the Strand, he suddenly said he had had enough, and, hailing a taxi, told the driver to go to Paddington. I went with him and saw him off. He looked tired but said he had enjoyed it. I certainly had.

With the introduction of independent television came television commercials. Of course nobody who was anybody would have thought of appearing in them, but I was getting short of money so decided to put my pride in my pocket and earn £15.

The product to be puffed was a jelly to put on your hair called "Trugel.

At the time I had a full head of hair and when I went to see the sponsors, they approved and the shoot was scheduled for a few days later. It took place in a basement studio in Soho, which was a complex of several small studios built around the make-up and costume area, with different commercials being shot in each of them. The scenario for "Trugel" consisted of two scenes. In the first I returned tired after a hard day's work and slumped into an armchair leaning my head back on the cushion, only to have it whisked from under me by an angry wife because my hair was greasy. A whirling hand came out of the screen presenting a bottle of Trugel, while a voice vaunted its properties. In the second scene I came home again tired after another hard day, slumped in the same chair and the wife, all smiles, brought the cushion and put it lovingly under my head.

When I went into make-up, I found an elderly film make-up artist who was clearly slumming it. "What's this for?" he asked without enthusiasm. "Trugel", I replied. "Never heard of it." I explained what it was; "When it's hair I always use Brylcreem". The scenes were to be shot in reverse order, so that my hair could look immaculate to start with and be made greasy for the opening scene afterwards. He put a large dollop of Brylcreem on my hair, remarking that it was good because it reflected the light, and combed the hair carefully, at which point the sponsors came into the room and saw the open bottle of Brylcreem, their hated rival. It is not too much to say they went beserk, "Why haven't you used Trugel?" He explained that he had never heard of it, which did not improve matters. Angrier than ever, they produced a giant-sized pot of Trugel and gave it to him. He thanked them, but pointed out that it was too late because my hair already done. Still fuming, they left and I went to shoot the scene. When I had finished, I returned to the make-up room. "What is it now?" he asked. I explained that now my hair had to look as greasy and unattractive as possible. He looked round and seeing the giant-sized bottle of Trugel, said, "This'll do" and coated my hair with it.

I also did several small parts for the BBC. To keep fees low the BBC had hit on the clever idea of engaging several failed and bitter actors to negotiate contracts. These poachers-turned-gamekeepers enjoyed taking revenge on those more successful than themselves by grinding them down to the last halfpenny. A part in a BBC production with an audience of millions was paid scarcely more than one earned in a week of rep where the audience was in hundreds. This was an approach strictly in keeping with the BBC ethos.

The Corporation had been founded, at the end of the First World War, by men coming out of the forces. After four years during which the whole country had been mobilised, the structure to which everyone was accustomed was the military structure of officers, non-commissioned officers and cannon fodder. The new broadcasting project seemed to fit neatly into this pattern. The management were the officers, the producers and technical staff the non-commissioned officers and the writers and artists the cannon fodder.

This meant that the managers, had smart offices with their own dining room or officers' mess, and were rarely seen, the producers had smaller offices and their sergeants' mess, the BBC club, where artists and writers were not admitted, unless invited by a producer, and the artists and writers had the canteen. The managers, producers and technicians were well paid and well looked after while the writers and artist, in the line of fire, were exploited and thrown on the rubbish dump.

I had met several of the managers at the Taylor tea parties; they were elderly, charming, amusing men and the conversation invariably went like this;

"I'm with the BBC, you know, this broadcasting stunt. It was just after I was de-mobbed, looking for a job and I was walking down Piccadilly, ran into a chap I'd been with in the Mons show. Asked me what I was doing, told him I was looking for a job, he said he was with a new stunt doing broadcasting, said "Why don't you come and join us, some awfully decent chaps there," so I did; been there ever since."

They were awfully decent chaps, certainly, but one cannot help wondering what the result would have been if the structure had been reversed and the writers and artists had been in command and the managers, cannon fodder.

CHAPTER FIFTEEN

—

In the early Spring I was phoned by Spotlight and invited to meet the directors of the Pitlochry Festival who were in London casting their new season. Pitlochry is in Perthshire, and is a bottleneck through which one has to pass to visit the Highlands. It is a small town that consists almost exclusively of hotels (there were twenty in 1956), and where, apart from the salmon ladder, the Festival Theatre provided the main distraction by housing during six months of the year a resident company playing a repertoire of six plays, a different play each night. The repertoire in that 1956 season was interesting and the managers offered me a good line of parts, Young Marlowe in Goldsmith's "She Stoops to Conquer", Clive in "See How They Run", Beverley in Drinkwater's "Bird in Hand", Herrick in Stevenson's "Ebb Tide" and Gunner in Bernard Shaw's "Misalliance". The producer was Maxwell Jackson and we rehearsed in London.

The other actors were Arthur Howard, David Tearle, Enid Hewit, Jill Johnson, Geraldine Gwyther, William Moore, Graham Lines, Graham Rowe and his wife Jill Carey. Rehearsals went well, everyone seemed to get on and I found Maxwell Jackson's direction, which encouraged invention, refreshing after Bristol and the straitjacket of French's Acting Edition. With my newfound confidence in my own personality, the prospect of a line of leading juvenile parts was just what I needed.

Arthur Howard had an old Ford 8, known as "Miss Ford" and he invited me to drive to Pitlochry with him. Having just read Boswell's life of Johnson, I realised that we would be going through Lichfield and could visit Dr Johnson's birthplace, so jumped at the chance. Arthur was a kind, gentle, generous person whose career had been blighted by the shadow of his famous brother. Leslie Howard had been a cult figure in England in the late thirties and during the war and had died tragically when, returning on a civil flight from Lisbon in 1942 when Churchill was known by the Germans to be in North

Africa. An enemy agent saw a stout man smoking a cigar get on the plane and decided it was Churchill, whereupon the Germans shot it down killing all the civilian passengers including Leslie Howard.

Twenty years younger than Leslie and closely resembling him physically but with a very different temperament, Arthur had suffered throughout his career from the comparison and had never been allowed to be himself. He had married the actress Jean Compton, the niece of Compton Mackenzie and Fay Compton, who was also under the shadow of successful relatives. Arthur and Jean had a son at public school and the effort of paying the fees was telling on them both. They lived in rented rooms and rented another room during the school holidays. The prospect of six months' work, even if it were not particularly well paid, presented a welcome breathing space and we drove to Scotland in holiday mood. The journey took two days. We stopped at Lichfield and saw the Johnson museum, spent the night in a hotel near Wensleydale and arrived the following evening at Pitlochry.

The Pitlochry Festival Theatre was founded in 1951 by John Stewart, a Glasgow businessman, who built the theatre in the grounds of his own house and appointed his friend, Kenneth Ireland, as the Manager. They had made a success of it and the year before had played to a total of 40,000. Perthshire has many aristocratic castles and countryseats and the list of theatre patrons read like the Gotha. First nights were like the society pages of the "Tatler", with the audience in Highland dress; even the Queen Mother came to see the plays when she was in Scotland. All this had caused the two founders to become very socially conscious, not to say snobbish. When the Chairman, the Earl of Mansfield, came, we were lined up to be introduced, and Arthur was introduced proudly as Leslie Howard's brother, David Tearle equally proudly as Godfrey Tearle's cousin, Jill Carey as General Carey's daughter and when it came to me, "and this is Edwin Apps who has big parts." An unexpected, not to say undeserved encomium, which, I was pleased to think, might well improve my standing with the female members of the company.

The first play was "She Stoops to Conquer", in which I played opposite Jill Johnson who, when I said I had been to the Central School, told me that she was engaged to Harold Pinter.

The season had hardly got underway, when she got a letter from Pinter breaking off the engagement. The news, apparently quite unexpected, upset her and her performances suffered, which made our scenes together difficult and left me cursing the name of Pinter.

As most of the rehearsing had been done in London, we were able to open a new play each week. Thus, at the end of six weeks, all the plays were in repertory and we had our days free. During rehearsals I had digs with an old Scots lady which were comfortable, but I found the Scottish diet not only lacking in vegetables, but with all the various forms of bread, baps and cookies, a menace for the waistline that, as leading juvenile, I could not risk. So I decided to try to find a flat and cook for myself as I had at Bristol. What I found was a small cottage with three bedrooms, at a reasonable rent, attached to the back of a house called "Yeomans" near the theatre. The ASM was a tall red headed young man, Alan Wallace. He was looking for digs so I suggested we share and, as Arthur was finding the hotel they had put him in too expensive, we invited him to take the third room. Graham Lines, who was in digs without full board, came to lunch every day and Alan and I did the shopping and the cooking on an arranged budget. It worked well and we had a very enjoyable season, which greatly improved my cooking.

The second play was "See How They Run" in which I played Clive opposite Geraldine Gwyther. Gerry and I had got on well from the first and now we became close. It was still the fifties and discretion was the order of the day; love affairs in the nineteen fifties, especially in the land of John Knox, were conducted out of the limelight.

The nobility and gentry of Perthshire, all of whom, spent the summer in their castles and country houses, tended to get bored, and a company of actors from London made an agreeable distraction, so we began to receive invitations. It was then that "Miss Ford" came into her own making visits possible.

One invitation I remember particularly was from a Colonel Lyle. Arthur and I were invited to cocktails one Sunday morning. We drove up into the hills and a along a single-track road over cattle-grids until we saw, lying back about quarter of a mile from the road, a beautiful eighteenth-century shooting-lodge. We turned off along the drive and as we approached saw a group of people arranged on the terrace like a photo in the "Tatler". The Colonel greeted us warmly and introduced us to everyone. He told us that the house had been a twenty-first birthday present from his father. I remarked on the site and how very secluded it was. "You'd think so", he said "but would you believe it, the other day some tourists came along that road, stopped, got out and looked at us," He went on to say that there was no limit to what people would do now; a friend of his found a family from Glasgow who had climbed over the wall of his park and were having a picnic inside it. "Do you know what he did? Got his butler to pack up a picnic hamper and went and had a picnic on their front lawn."

On another occasion we were invited to the Ball of the Scottish Horse at Blair Castle, home of the Duke of Atholl, then elderly and un-married and known as "Lord James." For the Ball we decided we had better try to learn Scottish dancing, so we found someone to teach us. The Ball was a grand affair.

We had already been to Blair Castle for a picnic, invited by the mother of the heir and her husband (the heir's father had died in the war). It was a very elegant picnic served by footmen well trained in the art of being invisible. The family lived in a wing of the castle, which they referred to as "the museum".

One Sunday evening, a Mrs Fergusson invited us all to a country house. When we arrived we found the house was just a very ordinary nineteenth-century building, not at all what we had become used to. However, prepared to slum it, we went in and were taken into the drawing room, a long room with paintings in gilt frames round all the walls. As we moved about, talking to the other guests and the hostess, a sort of frisson of excitement rose among us as we began to realise, as we looked at one painting after another, that they were all Turners. There were over twenty. The owner's grandfather had been an early patron of the artist. A tall, fair-haired boy was there, too,

Mrs Fergusson's nephew. His name was Jocelyn Stevens, the heir to
the Hulton Press Empire.

I shared a dressing room with William Moore. Bill was a very
good actor who at that time was already engaged to Mollie Sugden
whom he afterwards married. Bill made a point before each performance of arriving early and carefully reading his part through. It is
something I have never done, preferring to leave it in the memory so
that when needed it comes up fresh and there is no risk of wondering, "Have I already said that?" It was a constant subject of debate
between us and if I fluffed a line, or had a dry, I would be sure to get
a lecture from Bill as we cleaned off our make-up: "if you had looked
through the text before, etc." One evening we were in the dressing room before the performance of Bernard Shaw's "Misalliance"
in which he played John Tarleton, the leading part, when a friend
arrived unexpectedly from London and came to see him. Bill broke
off his reading of the script to welcome his friend and afterwards
there was not time to continue. When, in the performance, he got to
the point when he had left off reading, he stopped and was unable to
continue. The prompter prompted, the other actors hissed the line;
nothing helped him. It was the worst dry I have ever seen on any
stage, it seemed minutes before he could continue. After that I had
no more reproaches about my not reading the part before the play.

Among the hotels in Pitlochry was one, which was kept by a
homesick London cockney who made us welcome every evening
after the show. In that part of Scotland the summer nights are very
short and we would spend them in his hotel drinking whisky, which
he generously provided, until dawn when the local poacher would
arrive at the backdoor with the salmon, and we would wend our way
back to the cottage and go to bed until lunchtime.

During the six months I spent in Scotland and in subsequent visits,
I found myself conscious all the time of being "abroad". Scotland
seemed far more like France than England. I have not returned since
the fifties and it may well have changed, but at that time there was no
middle class and society was divided between those who had high tea
and those who had dinner.

We had several visitors during the season, Jean Compton, Arthur's wife came to stay and on another occasion his son home from for the holidays. I went with Arthur to meet him at the station and my first memory of Alan Howard is of watching him cross the slender bridge over the railway line, aged sixteen, very much the public schoolboy in a tweed jacket and brown trilby hat.

Another visitor or rather two visitors were Alan Wallace's mother, a charming American, and his stepfather, Colonel Bobby Ingham Clark, who was the chairman of a family paint manufacturing company. A man who enjoyed the life-style of a millionaire, he had been a well-known playboy in the twenties. Having been brought up in the family castle in Scotland, he arrived wearing the kilt. On the Sunday he decided we should lunch at Gleneagles, the hotel, which is normally approached by the railway for which it was built. This involved a journey across that part of Scotland in a taxi during which he regaled us with a fascinating account of the history of the clans. Arriving at Gleneagles we went into the lobby and, going to the desk, he asked the clerk to cash a cheque for fifty pounds, a considerably sum at that time. "Do I know you, Sir?" asked the clerk, whereupon the doorman, in a strong Scottish accent, said, "I'll back it".

It was during the visit to England of Bulganin and Kruschev and they were spending the weekend in the hotel, so Borshch, the famous Russian beetroot soup, was on the menu. I have often eaten Borshch since, but it never comes up to my memory of the Gleneagles Borshch.

As Alan had told him about our cooking exploits, Bobby had brought with him a selection of wines and a book written by a friend of his, André Simon, "The Encyclopaedia of Gastronomy"; an extraordinary compilation that includes recipes for everything from elephants to rats. It revolutionised our cooking and on returning to London I got a copy, which I still have and still use.

As the time for the Edinburgh Festival approached, we discovered that we had a long weekend. Arthur wanted to go and see Compton Mackenzie in Edinburgh and I wanted to see George Benson who was playing in the Festival. Arthur invited me to go with him and as Alan Wallace had a long weekend too, and wanted to see some relations near Edinburgh, it was decided that we should all three make the trip in Miss Ford and have a picnic en route. For the picnic we found a recipe in André Simon for a ham and tongue pie. We managed to get the ingredients and a long time was spent on its construction, but that pie, eaten in a field on the way to Edinburgh, is a memory Alan and I share whenever we meet. It must be remembered that in 1956 rationing had only just ended and wine and good food were only just becoming accessible.

George met us in Edinburgh, and Arthur invited him to come with us to meet the great man.

Sir Edward Montague Compton Mackenzie, or "Monty" as everyone called him, lived in Drummond Place where he had the ground floor and basement of two adjoining large Georgian houses. His companion, hostess and secretary and later his wife was Chrissie McSween. Monty had a penchant for islands and at one point he had lived on the island of Barra in the Hebrides. There he had adopted the two daughters of a fisherman, Chrissie and her sister, Lillie whom he had sent to university.

When we arrived at the front door, two guests were leaving. One of them said to Arthur "Your brother played me in my film." It was Sir Robert Bruce Lockhart, who had worked for British Intelligence in the Great War and been implicated in a plot to assassinate Lenin. Tried, found guilty of espionage and sabotage and condemned to death, he had been exchanged for a Russian spy imprisoned in England.

We found Sir Compton in bed in a four-poster, smoking a pipe. He was suffering from nervous sciatica. Beside him was a syringe with which he injected himself from time to time, while sitting on chairs around the bed were several politicians and journalists to whom we added a theatrical dimension. His conversation ranged over all three subjects. Listening to him, I was fascinated by his accent, which was Edwardian and reminded me of great-uncle George. It is hard to describe accents, but the Edwardian accent of those who were young at the beginning of the twentieth century, with its dropped final "g"s as in "goin'" and "comin'" had a sort of world-weary charm and a racy quality that was unforgettable. It is curious how accents change with each generation and reflect the mood of the time. Recordings of Victorians such as Gladstone and Tennyson suggest that their speech was as ponderous as their architecture, while my father's generation, of the Great War, was clipped and sharp. The twenties and thirties was brittle and affected, and the accent of my generation is equally distinct from today's demotic "Estuary."

Monty was a brilliant conversationalist and raconteur. He came from a long line of actors and had come to public notice in the years just before the Great War with a novel, "Sinister Street", one of the first novels to take the lid off the public school system. A life-long friend of Winston Churchill, he used to say, "Both Winston and I had American mothers, that's where our energy comes from". He had many stories about Churchill, but one that I particularly remember he told me on another occasion; "Winston", he said "when he was young, was a passionate speaker but he spoke too fast, the words tumbled out and as a result he was ineffective. Then came pyorrhoea and he had to have all his teeth out and be fitted with false teeth. That slowed his speech down and made it much more effective, so you could say that dentures played a major part in winning the Second World War".

At that time Monty was in his late seventies. His daily regime was to get up at eleven o'clock, drink an egg-in-milk and go to work sitting in a special writing chair he had had made which resembled a dentists' chair. He worked in a big room, which had copies of Breugel's "The Four Seasons" round the walls. At 6 o'clock he would go for a short walk and dress for dinner. There were almost always guests and after dinner he would sit up drinking whisky with them until two or three in the morning. He did not believe in exercise, saying that more men died on the golf course than in their beds. He lived to be over ninety.

Every evening during the Festival, he kept open house for the artists where there was a constant supply of Grant's whisky. He had done a commercial for the firm and had been paid in whisky. He had a remarkable library and the dining room was built out of freestanding bookcases, which formed an inner room within a larger one. A feature of the flat was the Siamese cats, which climbed up and down the curtains in an alarming way. Monty was President of the Siamese Cat Society.

Chrissie MacSween, with her lilting gentle highland accent, was a countrywoman who exuded good sense and remained unimpressed by all the great and the good who visited Monty. She was a marvellous hostess and superb cook and she looked after Arthur and me royally.

Another weekend I went to Kirkintilloch, a village just north of Glasgow, to see Derrick Brown and his wife, Ray. Derrick was my mother's cousin, the son of Yaya, the baby she had abandoned and who had been brought up by his father's sister and her husband. During the war, he had been a colonel on General Montgomery's staff during the Africa campaign. Now he was the managing director of a company making packaging for whisky bottles. I asked him about his relations with Yaya and he told me that when he was twenty-one, he had inherited ten thousand pounds from G.M. Goodson, (Yaya's uncle who had disinherited her) and had bought a car and gone to visit great-uncle George at Frognal. Great-uncle George had said, "You must meet your mother," and a meeting had been arranged for the following weekend. Derek said he had arrived at the house, gone into the drawing room and great-uncle George had announced, "This is your mother." He looked across the room, saw a middle-aged woman and rushed out of the room to the lavatory and was violently sick.

He said he could never have any feeling for her.

He and Ray were kind and I enjoyed the weekend. Kirkintilloch was "dry", so on Saturday nights buses took almost the entire male population to the neighbouring village and they arrived home in the early hours of the morning gloriously drunk. In those days in Scotland, bars could not serve customers with alcohol on Sundays unless they were "bona fide" travellers, which meant that all the men walked to the next village to get a drink, so one saw a lot of men walking on Sundays.

Back in Pitlochry, we had more visitors including my parents who came for a week and were made much of by the company. They stayed in a hotel and during the day we visited the region.

As the Season drew to a close we all began to worry about our chances of finding work on our return after having been away for so long. Arthur, in particular, began to get depressed as bills started to accumulate for which no income was in sight. Every time the post came Alan and I would knock on his door, hand them to him and wait for the wail of misery as he opened them. Then, one morning, we handed him the letters, waited for the wail only to be surprised by a shriek of joy. "It's Frank Muir!" he said "they want me for a television series!" Arthur had often mentioned Frank Muir. He and Denis Norden were the BBC's leading scriptwriters responsible for the highly successful radio comedy series, "Take it From Here" which starred Jimmy Edwards. Frank Muir had been a protégé of Arthur's during the war when Arthur had been Entertainment Officer at RAF Warmwell and Frank Muir an airman. Arthur often grumbled that Frank Muir always said he would help him, but never did. Now he had written to say that he and Denis were to make their first television series. It was to be about a school, Jimmy Edwards was to play the headmaster and they wanted Arthur to play his Assistant.

Arthur's relief was evident and we opened one of the last of Bobby Ingham Clark's bottles of wine to celebrate.

CHAPTER SIXTEEN

B ack in London, George and Pamela needed my room for George's elder daughter, Caroline, who was coming to live with them, so I moved to a small basement flat in Tedworth Square, Chelsea. I had it on a sharing basis with Michael Blakemore; we shared the rent and calculated that we would not both be out of work at the same time. Michael was still in Bristol so I was in possession.

Determined now to stay in London, I decided to upgrade my quarter-page advertisement in Spotlight to a half-page with a new photograph. The problem was who to go to for the photograph. There was a great deal of snobbery about these photographs, with actors choosing famous photographers like Cecil Beaton or Anthony Armstrong-Jones, the husband of Princess Margaret. I had been to a well-known theatrical photographer for my quarter-page: I had rung him to make an appointment and gone to his studio where the walls were covered with his photos of stars. Looking at me as if I were something the cat had brought in, he had told his assistant to stick a light on me, done a quick click-click and charged me a week's salary. The resulting photo, in his famous style, while it was obviously by him, left me looking like everyone else.

Thinking about it, I was struck by the thought that to have a famous photographer's name on the photo was in any case a mistake, because the message it sent to potential employers was that if you looked interesting it was all down to the photographer, while if you did not, then if he had not managed to make you look interesting, what hope did anyone have?

With this idea in mind, I went to the passport photographer at Swan and Edgar, the department store on Piccadilly Circus. The photographer, a pleasant middle-aged woman, greeted me and when I told her what I wanted, she became very enthusiastic, saying what a pleasure it was to be asked to do something interesting for a change. She took great care with the lighting and the result was excellent. I

had it published with the acknowledgement; "Swan and Edgar passport photo". It caused quite a stir and years after I would meet people
who said "I remember you, you put a Swan and Edgar passport photo
in Spotlight."

While I had been in Scotland, Lady Taylor had died. Her death,
due to a heart attack, had been unexpected. I had written to the
Admiral and Jane, and now I went to see the Admiral who was living
alone at 1A Holland Park. I found him in the conservatory, repaint-
ing his garden furniture. He told me that he had decided to remarry
"Those fellows who have had unhappy marriages don't want to try
again, but I've had a happy marriage so I'm ready to try" We talked
and I found him less intimidating than of old, not that I think he ever
was, it was what he represented that had intimidated me. He told me
he was reading Dickens. I asked if he was enjoying it; "No", he said
"too many bounders. If there are any more bounders, I shall chuck it
in." It didn't look as though the project had much future.

Soon after my return from Scotland, my parents and I went to
Kent for the wedding of a friend and stayed the weekend in a hotel at
Deal. I knew that Carol Powers, who had retired from St Edmund's
in 1946, had settled in Deal to be near his favourite golf course, so I
rang him and asked if I might call.

Powers' father had been an American, the London representative of Singer Sewing machines. So unlike the other masters at St
Edmund's, he was relatively wealthy with a private income, which
had allowed him to dress better than the other masters, possess a
bigger car and be a member of the local golf clubs. It had also meant
that in retirement, he was able to buy a house and install a couple to
look after him.

I rang the bell and he answered it himself. He seemed pleased to
see me and led me into the living room, which was an almost perfect
replica of his study at school. The walls were covered with school
groups in their long black frames, intersected by individual photos of
good-looking boys who had been his favourites. The furniture was
the same even the smell was the same. It was uncanny and I could not
help wondering where the canes were kept.

We sat down and talked. He looked older and seemed depressed. He said he had given up golf because he could no longer keep up and could not bear the thought that he was keeping other players waiting. After a while his housekeeper brought in some tea. He said he did not go to the school any more because he no longer knew any of the boys. When it was time to go, he saw me to the door. We shook hands and I walked to the gate. Turning I looked back – he was standing at the door, a sad, lonely old man. He died two years later.

Living in Chelsea meant that each time I went into London the bus took me up the King's Road round Sloan Square in front of the Royal Court Theatre. The current play was the talk of London, "Look Back in Anger" by John Osborne. The leading rôle, Jimmy Porter, is a surly, abrasive character intent on sweeping away middle-class conventions. The play's eruption on the theatrical scene in 1956 launched the new "kitchen sink" realistic style and changed the focus of interest from the upper to the lower middle class.

The part of Jimmy was played brilliantly by my former fellow student, Kenneth Haigh, and each time I passed the theatre and saw his name in lights, it was brought home to me that the line of parts I had been developing was destined to disappear as the upper-middle-class young man was demoted from leading hero to small part-figure of fun.

It was, of course, a reflection of the revolution taking place in society, a very English form of revolution which was quite as sweeping as the French Revolution, but without the bloodshed. The middle and upper middle classes, instead of being guillotined, were held up to ridicule. The Queen's English, until then respected, even revered – including the accents employed by the Monarch herself – became a subject of mockery, and while erudition remained respected, from then on it was de rigueur to enunciate it in working-class and preferably regional working-class phonetics.

Someone told me that Jack Minster was producing a play, so I went to his office and when he came out, bearded him, reminding him that he had done me out of the part of Lord Goring in "An Ideal Husband" at Windsor. He acknowledged that he owed me something and offered me the understudy for Bryan Forbes in "A Touch of Fear", a thriller by the Christies, to be produced at the Aldwych. As there did not seem to be anything else on offer, I accepted.

I had met Bryan Forbes in the early fifties when I had done a play at Croydon with Nanette Newman, to whom he was engaged. Bryan had been a fixture at the stage door during rehearsals and the run of the play, and they had married shortly afterwards. The leading lady of "A Touch of Fear" was Jill Bennett, who had been the protégée some said the mistress, of Godfrey Tearle. In Pitlochry, David Tearle had never stopped cursing her, "That bitch, Godfrey left her all his money", adding a list of highly imaginative things he would like to do to her.

The other members of the cast were Colin Gordon and Nicholas Hannen. I had seen Colin Gordon in Peter Ustinov's play, "The Love of Four Colonels" in which he played the English Colonel, an unforgettable performance. Nicholas Hannen, known as "Beau" Hannen was the companion of Athene Seyler. In his seventies, and still very handsome, he and Athene, although unmarried were, with the Thorndykes, pillars of society.

Jack Minster was thin, bony and exuded an air of gloom. One day during rehearsals he showed Colin Gordon how he wanted a line played and when he had finished, Colin said quietly, "As miserably as that, Jack?"

Understudying is a nerve-racking occupation. You have to learn the part without rehearsing it yourself and copy the moves of your principal by watching him rehearse them. When the play opens, you have to be in the theatre half-an-hour before curtain up and stay until your principal has made his last entrance.

Once the play is on, you generally have an uninspiring rehearsal once a week with the stage-manager whose only interest is to see that you know the part and the moves. All your friends wish you luck and hope you get a chance to play the part, whereas it is the prospect you most dread and that keeps you awake at night. For me it was never more than a means of staying in London with my days free to make contacts and look for work in films, television and broadcasting.

The actress who was understudying Jill Bennett and I spent our evenings together. She had played the lead, as a young girl in a play that had been a big success and run for a long time in London. She left the cast after the first year to do other things and some long time later was asked if she would take over the part again in the number one post-London tour. As nothing much was happening, she accepted. The tour had been going on for over a year and the cast had changed several times.

The night before she was due to begin rehearsals she went to see the performance. Although it was a long time since she had played the part, everything came back except for one move when, suddenly in the middle of a scene, the girl playing her part jumped on to a low stool, touched her head with both hands, jumped down and continued with the scene. She had no memory of having done this and could see no reason for it in the text. The next morning at rehearsal, when she came to the line, she automatically jumped on the stool, looked towards the mirror to arrange her hair, but there was no mirror. At some point during the tour the mirror had disappeared, but actress after actress had continued to jump on the stool and touch their heads with both hands because that is what had been done in the London production.

Learning that I was living in Chelsea, Nicholas Hannen invited me to go home with him each evening in his taxi. I found his conversation fascinating, especially his memories of London. He said he remembered when Paddington was open fields. It was hard to imagine. As we went down Whitehall, he would raise his hat as we passed the Cenotaph and as we passed the Houses of Parliament, if the light was on to show that the house was sitting, he would say, "Our governors are governing." One evening Sir Malcolm Sargent came to see the play and came back in the taxi with us, getting out at the Albert Hall. I do not remember the conversation, only his enormous charm.

When the play closed, the management offered me the understudy of David Hutcheson in a new play by William Douglas Home, "The Iron Duchess" starring Athene Seyler and Ronald Squire. Other members of the cast were William Mervyn, Geoffrey Lumsden and Gladys Henson. I can't remember the plot, but it involved the cook, played by Gladys Henson, going on strike. Athene was the Duchess and Ronald Squire the Duke. I had often seen and admired Ronald Squire who was a master of that peculiarly English school of comedy of which du Maurier was the founder, which took comic underplaying to its limits. They delivered a comedy line so that each member of the audience believed himself to be the only person who had heard it. When a lady went to the stage-door after a performance of a play in which Wilfred Hyde-White, another exponent of the art, was starring, and complained that she could not hear what he said, he replied, "Madam, when I learned the trick of being inaudible, my salary went from fifteen pounds a week to two hundred and I don't intend to unlearn it."

Having heard so much about Athene Seyler, I was naturally fascinated to watch her rehearse. She was in her early seventies but remarkably fit. I walked with her along the Strand on one occasion and had to make an effort to keep up with her, even though she was talking all the time. "I don't know if you have ever spent a week-end with John Gielgud?" I admitted that I had not had that privilege; "Well with John, the sky becomes a backcloth. He thinks of nothing but theatre". She went on to say that it was important not to let it take over one's life entirely. She had a mischievous sense of humour, which she used very effectively on the stage and as effectively in private life. She and Nicholas Hannen were clearly still very much in love. She came to the theatre one evening heavily bandaged because he had embraced her and broken two of her ribs. "What is more," she said, "it's not the first time he's done it." She was clearly in pain but nevertheless played.

It was in this production that I got to know William Mervyn, who played a pompous politician, as did David Hutcheson, whom I was understudying. Feeling that I had not got a suit that was right for the part, I went to Mr Larsson and ordered a dark grey suit with a white stripe. When I went for the fitting, I noticed that there was another of the same material waiting to be fitted. I asked whose it was and discovered that it was for William Mervyn. Later, when he played Inspector Rose in a long running detective series for Granada, he always wore it and I used to remind him that I had the adjoining piece of cloth.

Geoffrey Lumsden was the member of the company I got on with best and we became friends. His father had been killed in the Great War and he had been brought up by his two uncles, the Salmond brothers, the two generals who had founded the RAF. He would describe how, when he was a young out-of-work actor, one of them would invite him to lunch at his club. "Well, now," he would ask, "what have you done today?" Geoffrey would explain that he had telephoned his agent.

"That's no good. You should get up each morning and go round every film studio." Geoffrey pointed out that the studios were several miles out of London in different directions and anyway they wouldn't let you in. "Right, so what do you do? You wait outside and Leslie Banks falls down and breaks a leg and they say here's a likely young chap, and you get the part."

Today when I see the repeats of "Dad's Army" in which Geoffrey played the pompous Captain Square, it is easy to see who was his model.

Geoffrey was in his forties but had never grown up. He was hopeless with money and always broke. What was more he had a wife and daughter in Salisbury and school fees to pay. The solution was Aunt Jane who lived in Edinburgh. She would always give him the money, but insisted that he go to Edinburgh to get it. On one occasion the bank manager in Salisbury refused to allow him any more over draft, so he borrowed the money for the fare to Edinburgh, went to see Aunt Jane who duly gave him the cheque, and returned to Salisbury. But when he took the cheque to the Bank, the Manager took it, thanked him and said that would help to pay off the overdraft, refusing to cash a cheque, Geoffrey sighed, borrowed some more money, went back to the station and caught the next train to Edinburgh.

He had been to school at Repton with the writer Denton Welch, and he figures in Welch's novel about his schooldays, "Maiden

Voyage" thinly disguised as "Geoffrey". Their headmaster was Geoffrey Fisher who became Archbishop of Canterbury (Canon Balmforth of St Edmund's had been a master there at the same time). Dr Fisher was the last of the Prince Archbishops and drove round Kent in a Rolls Royce with outriders. At that time, Geoffrey was doing a summer season in the little Leas Pavilion rep. at Folkstone and walking to the theatre one evening he noticed people putting out chairs and erecting a stage. Seeing the groundsman, Geoffrey asked if it was for the tennis prizes. "No" said the groundsman and explained that the Archbishop was to conduct an evening service. Geoffrey asked to see the vicar and explained that he was an old pupil, though very undistinguished, and would like to see him. The vicar said that the Archbishop had to be back in Canterbury at half past nine. As the curtain did not come down until ten o'clock it was not possible, but Geoffrey asked the vicar to remember him to the Archbishop.

When the curtain came down, Geoffrey was washing his face in the communal mens' dressing-room in vest and pants, when someone came in and said, "Geoffrey, there is someone to see you." "Who is it?" "Well, it looks like the Archbishop of Canterbury" "Cock!" said Geoffrey and a voice replied "It is not cock Lumsden, it is I!" He had delayed his return to Canterbury and spent half-an-hour with him walking on the Leas.

Michael Blakemore had left Bristol and he now took a flat in Carlyle Square which had two rooms, one of which he offered me. We were there alternately for a while, but there came a time when we were both there together out of work and we began to get on each other's nerves. Rather than lose a good friend, I decided to move. Chelsea was expensive, so I decided to look in unfashionable parts of London. To begin with I went further down the King's Road, beyond The World's End, which marks the limit of Chelsea and on to the New King's Road, which is in Fulham. (Fulham at that time was distinctly down-market) There, at Parson's Green, on the right hand side of the road was a tall building which stood alone, everything round it having been bombed. It was number 100.

The ground floor was a second-hand furniture shop; behind it was a car-breaker's yard, the first floor was occupied by the family of a cook who was in prison and the second floor by an ancient showgirl. The third floor was to let at a very low rent. It had one big square room and another smaller room. The cooking facilities were on the landing and the bathroom and lavatory, shared with the showgirl, were on the floor below. I liked the big room; its ceiling sloped down on the four corners and its window was of the opening inwards, cottage type and it was high enough above the other houses to have a view over the rooftops. I decided to take it. After Pitlochry, I had remained friends with Graham Rowe and his wife and had met a friend of theirs, Hamish Roughead, a Scottish actor who was looking for somewhere to live, so I offered him the second room. He accepted and we set up house together. He was a gentle, easy-going, pipe-smoking, bookworm and we got on very well. The bus to Piccadilly stopped outside the house and – apart from the night when the cook came out of prison and the party went on all night, and occasional worries about the old showgirl who used to get drunk and on one occasion, nearly set the house on fire – life was very peaceful.

All this time I had been in touch with Arthur and Jean. The "WhackO" series had been a success and Arthur liked Jimmy Edwards and got on well with him. Another series was planned and Arthur said he thought I would be right for one of the masters and would see what he could do. When I told them the tour of "The Iron Duchess" was going to Edinburgh, they told me to ring Chrissie and go and see Monty. When I rang, Chrissie told me to invite some of the company to dinner after the show, in particular Gladys Henson, who was an old friend of Monty's, and anyone else I would like to invite, so I invited Lumsden, who had borrowed a pair of my pyjamas to stay with Aunt Jane. We had a very enjoyable dinner but when it came time to leave and our taxi came, Monty told me to stay behind. Then he took me into his study, poured two large glasses of whisky and we sat in front of the fire talking until about three o'clock. His conversation was fascinating; I don't remember it all, I know at one point he told me how he had been walking with D.H. Lawrence on the shores of the Aegean one morning before breakfast and Lawrence had described a book he was thinking of writing, "I said to him, 'Don't do it, D.H., don't do it.'" The book was "Lady Chatterley's Lover".

He talked about the filming of his novel, "Whisky Galore"and how he admired Alexander Mackendrick, the director (it had been Mackendrick's first film). Then we got on to the history of the theatre. It was a subject that interested him, as his own family had been actors since the eighteenth century. When my taxi came at about three o'clock, he saw me to the door and, as we said good night, I asked him who he thought had been the greater actor, Garrick or Kean. He hesitated for a moment and then said, "Garrick, remember Partridge?" Partridge is the servant in Fielding's "Tom Jones" who goes to see Garrick play Hamlet and is unimpressed, saying that if he saw a ghost he was sure he would have behaved exactly like that.

"The Iron Duchess" opened at the Cambridge Theatre and got generally poor notices and a blistering one from Ken Tynan. Tynan was waging a war against all plays that had French doors at the back of the set – in other words that were middle class – so a play about dukes, duchesses and their cook, written by the brother of Lord Home, who was at that time a minister in a Conservative government, was fair game for him. A few days later I went into the pub opposite the stage door and found William Douglas Home sitting at a table, writing. "What do you think of this?" he asked and read what he had written;

"There once was a critic called Ken
Who wrote with a class-conscious pen.
To the plays that were "U"
He gave nought out of two
To the rest he gave nought out of ten;"
Tynan was an influential critic and the play did not run for long.

My third and last understudy was of Nigel Patrick in "The Egg", a translation of "L'Oeuf" by Félicien Marceau. During the run, news came that my grandmother, who had been in a nursing home for some time, was unwell and I was again deputed to represent my mother the following Sunday.

CHAPTER SEVENTEEN

I caught the train to Ramsgate where Yaya met me. It was several years since I had seen her, although we had written regularly. She was just the same in spite of living alone; OK had left her while I was in the RAF. He had got up one morning, packed his suitcase, said goodbye and walked out of her life. She had not heard from him since. He was forty and she was sixty; they had been together for twenty years. When we talked about it she was philosophical, "He was the best of them all," she said, "and, after all, twenty years' happiness is more than most women get."

She drove me to the nursing home in the Baby Austin. Nothing had changed; she still wore the sheep's wool backed gauntlets for driving and smoked with her eyes half-shut and the window open.

I asked after great-uncle George. I knew that Aunty Hilda had died some years before; they had been to a wedding where everyone had said how well she looked, but during the night, great uncle George woke and found her dead beside him. It was her sixty-second birthday. Now, Yaya told me, he had discovered that his bailiff, who had been with him for many years and whom he trusted implicitly, had been stealing from him. Shattered by the discovery, he had decided to sell Frognal and was now living in a wooden house in Wickhambreaux being looked after by Edie, the maid who had been with them since their marriage. Yaya said he was finding driving difficult and Edie was having driving lessons. An old friend of his who was in the same situation was having his butler taught to drive at the same time and he and Uncle George had a bet on as to who would qualify first. It seemed Edie was nudging ahead.

The nursing home, when we reached it, was typical of such institutions, a big characterless house in a garden that could just be classed as grounds. Yaya parked in the drive and said she would wait in the car. Relations between the sisters had not improved.

I went in through the swing doors and announced myself to the woman in charge. She said they were expecting me and would I come this way. I asked how my grandmother was. "Oh, we are holding our own," was the reply.

She was lying in bed and looked frail "Hullo, Lad." She seemed pleased to see me. We talked a little then she fell silent and looked tired. Suddenly she brightened and indicating the wall beside her said "Wenderton is over there." I asked after Uncle John. She said "Boy" had been to see her and lapsed into silence again. Suddenly she sat up and whispered ferociously, "I hate these bloody bitches!" indicating the nurses. I was shocked, never having heard her use bad language of even the mildest sort before. She sank back. I noticed that she kept plucking at the sheet with her fingers and was instantly reminded of Mistress Quickly in "Henry V", when she recounts the death of Falstaff: "For after I saw him fumble with the sheets, and play with flowers, and smile upon his finger ends, I knew there was but one way." We talked a little more, I told her what I was doing and she nodded approvingly. I stayed a little longer, then, seeing she was tired, left her.

As Yaya was driving me to her house for lunch, she suddenly said, "You know your grandmother was in love with your father" It was as though I was hearing something put into words that I had known for a long time but not wanted to know. "They used to go dancing together" "Yes, I know they did"; in fact various women friends of the family had told me this, and I had thought it amusing, imagining them as I knew them, two strait-laced elderly people dancing, not thinking of them as being much younger. Now, suddenly I let my imagination play on the situation for the first time; the children at boarding school, the drunken husband, the three of them living alone in the house in separate bedrooms: the frustrated wife, the returning hero. Why had I never thought, or rather, why had I never let myself think of it before? Then they were so prudish, both of them, so very conventional. Even now it was difficult if not impossible to imagine that they did anything other than dance, and yet it was the nineteen-twenties, and my father was barely thirty and my grandmother still under forty and an attractive woman. Perhaps, indeed, they were so prudish precisely because there was something to hide. One of my grandmother's favourite sayings, I remembered, was "Never let your left hand know what your right hand does" and at Gloucester I had frequently heard my father quote the adage "Hell knows no fury like a woman scorned". In any case, there must have been a lot of gossip at the idea of their going to dances together without my grandfather. Was that, perhaps the reason for my parents having married quietly in London? I had always thought it strange that my mother, the elder daughter, had not been married in the village church. The reason my parents gave was that farming was doing badly and it would have cost too much to invite everyone. Yet two years later, Aunty Peggy was married with full pomp and circumstance in the village church and farming was certainly not doing better.

And where did my mother stand in all this? Did she know? She must have done, and if so, what did she think about it? Her version of events had always been that she had intended to marry my father from the age of four and that one evening in 1930, she went into the office where he was working late and told him, "We are going to get married," while her explanation for the quarrel, was that, "everyone at Guilton was jealous because we were happy." "When you were born" Yaya continued, "your grandmother held you in her arms and said, 'He should have been mine, he should have been mine'"

Two days later my grandmother died. Aunty Peggy rang to tell me. The cremation was to be at the new crematorium at Barham. I met my mother at Paddington and we took the train from Charing Cross to Faversham, where Aunty Peggy and Uncle George met us. Relations, between the sisters and Uncle John, had been further exacerbated by his having recently sold the family furniture at auction. It had been put into store several months before when my grandmother had gone into the nursing home. Deciding that the storage was too expensive he wrote to Aunty Peggy and my mother saying that the sale would be on a certain date and if they wanted anything they should go to the sale, adding that the proceeds would be divided between the three of them according to the codicil. This move was seen as high-handed and not appreciated, and some very sharp letters had been exchanged, so now, when all of us were ushered into a small waiting room, the tension was considerable, with neither side accepting the other's presence. I suppose there was a religious service, there must have been, but I have no memory of it. All I remember is the poisonous atmosphere in that claustrophobic little waiting-room, and later, when we four had tea together in Faversham, before catching the train to London where I had to get to the theatre, Aunty Peggy's saying that Lady Harris had chosen the curtains herself and Uncle George's saying that it was a mistake to have built the crematorium in a valley, for when there was a low cloud base there tended to be a strong smell of roast meat.

It was at about this time that I joined the Greenroom Club. My proposers were Nigel Patrick, Austen Trevor and Jack Allen, and as nobody thought it worthwhile to blackball me, I became a member. The Green Room Club was a club for working actors, the backbone of the profession. It had recently moved into new premises in the basement of Adam Street, a small street off the Strand, and there at lunch time, sitting at the long table, you would see many of the faces that were currently appearing in the West end. The principle was that when you went to eat, you sat next to the last person seated, whoever it might be and whether you knew him or not, which made it very democratic. The whole atmosphere was friendly and unpretentious. There was a bar, a billiard-room and a writing-room. The membership fee was reasonable, the meals were cheap, cooking excellent and the staff welcoming and friendly, so that for many actors who lived alone or who were out of work the club was a home from home.

I made many friends there and enjoyed long evenings chatting in the bar drinking pink gin which had become my regular drink at the time. The reason for this was that pubs had suddenly started charging for the tonic water in gin-and-tonic, (up till then my preferred drink). It seemed to me an imposition and I remembered the pink gin I had drunk and enjoyed with Raymond Somerville. Deciding that not even the most bare-faced publican would dare charge for a couple of drops of Angostura, I had taken to drinking it regularly, to the surprise of many barmen for whom the making of it was a lost art. I would show them how to do it, putting the drops of Angostura in the glass, whirling the glass round between both hands to distribute the Angostura evenly, then throwing out all that I could, before putting in the gin and adding a little water.

In the early sixties, as television became increasingly the main employment for actors, fewer and fewer actors were to be found lunching at the club, a situation that endangered the finances and even existence of the club itself. By this time, I was on the committee and I was deputed to investigate the reasons and make a report. In "The Apps Report" I suggested that the problem lay in the fact that members of the club were expected to wear a suit and tie, whereas actors rehearsing for television were usually in jeans and sweaters. I went on to suggest that the cause of the problem lay in the fact that the theatre was a mirror of society and that the recent democratisation of society meant that plays were more often set among the lower than the upper middle class. All the London clubs, I went on, had been formed by gentlemen and up until now, actors had been expected to look like gentlemen, but that was no longer the case and the Green Room club had to make up its mind whether it was a club for gentlemen or a club for actors.

The report caused a stir but finally the point was taken and the wearing of ties and suits ceased to be obligatory.

Altogether, life was becoming easier and I was getting work, a day here and there on films and parts in television plays. My father's angina however, was getting worse, his attacks more frequent. He was still working, because he had joined the Civil Service too late to have a pension, but it looked as though he would be forcibly retired the following year when he would be sixty-eight. Then my grandmother's Will arrived. She had left everything equally to my mother and Aunty Peggy. This meant that my mother inherited about £7000, a helpful sum at that time. So, for the first time in many years, my parents were able to relax.

Among my grandmother's effects that my mother inherited were several pieces of jewellery, one of which was a carefully made copy of her own engagement ring which my grandmother had had made when my mother married my father.

CHAPTER EIGHTEEN

—

Early in 1958, Maxwell Jackson asked me to play the leading part in the try-out of a new play at Croydon where he was producing a season of rep. Trying out new plays in rep with a week's rehearsal is a foolhardy undertaking at best. The difference between a play on the page and a play on the stage is enormous.

A play may read well but when you come to play it you find whole passages that do not work and need re-writing. That is why plays for the West End have several weeks' rehearsal and a preliminary tour to get them right before the opening. On the other hand a play written as it is acted can seem incomprehensible on paper. Shakespeare and Molière, who were both actors, have stage-directions that are puzzling to read, such as that in Act III scene 3 of "The Winter's Tale", "Exit, pursued by a bear", but which work the moment you put them on the stage.

The Croydon play was a dud. We worked hard, but nothing could bring it to life and when it was mercifully over, I rang "Spotlight" and asked if there was anywhere I could go and do a good play. The answer came back: "Northampton is doing Hamlet" So I went to Northampton to play Horatio.

The Theatre Royal at Northampton was a typical nineteenth-century provincial theatre situated in a street with some very beautiful little Georgian houses. The stage door was in the street behind, and when you entered, you went down a short flight of stairs to the green-room area. On the first morning of rehearsal, I went down these steps and at the bottom saw a small group of actors, and an actress who was laughing. I looked at her and immediately felt I wanted to get to know her. Someone introduced us; her name was Pauline Devaney. She told me that she was playing in the current play, but was leaving at the end of the week.

The director was Lionel Hamilton, a dear, kind actor of the old school. He ran Northampton rep with flair and efficiency for many

years, living with his friend, a physiotherapist, in one of the pretty
Georgian houses beside the theatre. His production of "Hamlet" was
straightforward with Peter Wyatt, a good, sensitive actor, giving a
simple, clear interpretation of the part.

I went one evening to see the current production in which Pauline
Devaney was playing and thought her performance excellent. Then,
at the Saturday morning run-through of "Hamlet" she came to
watch and at one point when I was not on stage, I sat beside her and
was amused as she gave a pertinent and very funny criticism of the
production. I gathered she was leaving because she had not been
invited to play Ophelia.

I had been contracted to do two plays and the second was "The
Perfect Woman" which was to star the comedian, Frankie Howerd as
Ermyntrude, a robot invented by a professor who I was to play.

Frankie Howerd had had a very successful broadcasting career
in the forties and was a household name, but by 1958 his career was
in the doldrums and he was doing special weeks in reps around the
country. When I mentioned to friends that I was to do a play with
him, they all seemed to have horror stories of how he had behaved.
The problem was that Frankie, a brilliant music-hall comic, based his
comedy on establishing complicity with the audience by denigrat-
ing the other people on the stage, a "look at me up here with these
idiots" approach. In his stage-act, one of the funniest in the country, it was the lady pianist who was the butt, as he whispered to the
audience behind her back "Poor dear, she can't help it you know, we
mustn't mock the afflicted." But when he transferred this technique
to a play in which he was playing a character among other characters, it created difficulties for the other actors. An actor would say
a line and instead of saying his next line, Frankie would turn to the
audience and say "Didn't he say that nicely?" At Kettering, I was
told he had pulled off an actor's wig and said, "He's not really as old
as that, look!" I decided that it was best to be clear from the start,
so at the beginning of rehearsal I told him I had heard he was in the
habit of pulling people's wigs off and I hoped he didn't intend to do
it me. This cast a chill over the proceedings, but it paid off because

he behaved impeccably in our scenes. Off stage, we hardly spoke. He had a Rolls Royce and a small group of young men who filled the roles of chauffeur, dresser and much else besides.

Frankie was big and ungainly, and gave the impression he needed a bath. He wore a wig that, close to, resembled a gannet's nest, while from its edges, rivulets of the glue that held it in place could be seen running down his cheeks.

The play went well, Frankie was very funny, and at the end of the week our relationship thawed out sufficiently for him to offer me a lift back to London, which I accepted.

It was at about this time that I went to spend a few days with Yaya. She met me at Canterbury and we drove to her house in the Baby Austin with the window open, her cigarette in place as well as the sheep's wool backed gauntlets. On this occasion she took me to some of the places, I had heard about but never seen, including Upton, the home of the Goodsons at Broadstairs. When my great-grandfather had died in 1920, he had left a trust for his children and his eldest son, Teddy, had taken over the farm and moved into the house, but Teddy had died suddenly in 1929 leaving two daughters. And as Great-uncle George had daughters and their brother Frank was unmarried, there was no one to take over so, after more than three centuries, the property was broken up and sold.

Now, the farmland and even the former stack-yard were covered in bungalows, but a doctor had bought the house and he kindly showed us round. The following day we went to see great uncle George in his wooden house in Wickhambreaux. It was summer and he was sitting in the garden with Edie. Inside the house were many things that I remembered from Frognal, including the portraits of the family's horses. Suddenly, a small picture of a lady on a pony caught my eye; she was riding sidesaddle and was dressed in the period of the 1840s with a large hat. She looked as though she were in Hyde Park, but beneath the picture was written; "Lady Sale leading the retreat from Kabul in 1842". I asked Uncle George about it and he explained that she had been a Wynch and was a cousin of his grandmother's. Shaking his head, he added, "We've had too many women like that in our family." Back in London, I went to the British Museum and found that she had been a heroine at the time of the first Afghan war. The British had invaded Afghanistan to change the regime, expecting to be met with flowers and cheers, but it had been a major miscalculation and an early example of the folly of interfering in the affairs of a country whose complications you do not fully understand. It had ended with General Sale taking the army out of Kabul to quash a rebellion, leaving a few officers and men and all the women and camp followers in the town, which was immediately surrounded by the tribesmen. Lady Sale had taken the situation in hand and had led the retreat under enemy fire and in the snows of January – although probably not in the hat she wore in the picture. Hardly anyone survived the ordeal. She kept a journal of the events, which was published and makes fascinating reading. In 2003 I was tempted to send copies to George W. Bush and Tony Blair.

I asked great-uncle George some details about the family and he produced a large wooden chest full of documents, one of which was addressed to the Goodson of the time of the Napoleonic wars, when it was considered probable that Napoleon would invade England. The letter was from the mayor of Dover, with instructions as to what to do when Napoleon came. It was unopened. I pointed this out to great-uncle George and asked why it had not been opened. "Because he didn't come", he replied.

Not long after this I was called to do an audition for The Old Vic at the New Theatre in St Martin's Lane and among the actors and actresses waiting their turn, was the laughing girl from Northampton, Pauline Devaney. We said hullo and I suggested we have a coffee together afterwards. I had recently been sent a newspaper cutting by my parents saying that the basement of St Martin's in the Fields had been turned into a coffee-shop for out of work actors, so I suggested we go there, thus it was underneath the church in which my parents were married that I first got to know my future wife.

Neither of us heard any more from the audition, but within a week I had invited Pauline to dinner, asked her to marry me and she had accepted.

In those days, before the invention of the Pill, when young people's discovery of sex was haunted by the fear of unwanted pregnancy, marriage was the only sociably acceptable way to live together. You had to marry, not for yourselves, but for your parents.

At twenty-seven I was sexually very immature. The only girls I knew were actresses, and while I constantly imagined myself to be in love and had had affairs with several of them, marriage in any serious sense had hardly crossed my mind. I had in any case taken to heart Mrs Siddons advice to Macready as he records in his diaries (Mrs Siddons was the great star of the late eighteenth century who, it was claimed, was so imbued with the works of Shakespeare that the iambic pentameter had become her natural form of expression, and she had been overheard at an inn telling the pot boy; "You brought me porter, boy, I asked for ale".) Macready records that when as a young actor he first worked with her, she called him to her dressing room after the performance and said: "Young man, you are in the right way, but remember what I say, study, study, study – and don't marry until you are thirty."

But I was lonely and longed for someone with whom I could share my life. The marriage I knew best was that of my parents, which was rock-solid, but at the cost of my mother's total self-effacement. My father really believed that women were like overgrown children and had to be treated as such, and that it was up to the man to shoulder all responsibilities. My mother went along with this, but I could not help noticing that, for example, when the water-tank in the attic burst in the middle of the night, while he in his dressing gown marched up and down in a commanding manner repeating, "ruination, ruination", my mother got down on her knees and started clearing up the mess.

I was clear that I did not want that sort of marriage; I did not want to be totally responsible for another human being, I wanted a marriage of equals.

We had discussed this on our first evening together and decided that the decision to marry was ours and ours alone, that neither our parents nor anyone else should have a say in the matter. We were marrying not to found a family, children could not have been further from our thoughts, we were two dedicated actors who would combine forces and be the stronger for it.

Pauline was twenty-one. She had been at RADA, where she had had a scholarship from the founder of E.M.I. to pay her fees. On leaving the Academy, she had been taken on by Peter Crouch, an agent who had a stable of promising actors. He had got her a film test with 20th Century Fox, who had offered her a contract, but she had refused it, feeling that she needed experience in rep. It was a courageous, not to say quixotic decision, made more so by her family circumstances. Her father, Gerald Devaney, was a second-generation immigrant Irish Catholic, who did not go to church and, as a result, was haunted by a sense of guilt that perhaps only lapsed Irish Catholics can appreciate. A clever man and an inventor who had several inventions to his credit, including an aero-engine for which he had been invited to read a paper to the Royal Society, he was, in his personal life, totally unstructured, not to say chaotic. He had seduced and eloped with her mother, the sequestered only daughter of a retired Warwickshire schoolmaster, and their marriage had been a switchback. They had moved house over twenty times, as Gerald changed jobs or attempted to escape from creditors. When he was in the money, he smothered Marjorie in flowers and promises, but the flowers withered and the promises were broken and the debt collector knocked at the door. Marjorie insisted that Pauline be educated privately, so, out of respect for his religion, she was sent to a Catholic Convent, although she had had no religious upbringing whatever. The first day of term, Gerald took her to the Convent, but faced with the nuns, his guilt got the better of him and he told them that she was a naughty girl and although he had done everything he knew to make her go to Mass, she obstinately refused. Then he walked out and left her to the face the nuns.

When she went back for a second term, she was greeted by surprise, because he had not paid the fees. Thereafter she had no schooling, because her mother refused to let her go to a state school where she might "pick up a bad accent or catch something", so she spent her time evading the School Inspector until she was four-teen, when she got herself a job in a record shop. Her parents were delighted and felt she was launched for life, but she had other ideas, and applied to RADA for an audition and was accepted. Her parents were dumbfounded; "You? There must be some mistake." There was no mistake, but it was necessary for Gerald to declare his income so that her Living Grant could be assessed. Unable to admit the small-ness of his income, he tripled it, with the result Pauline had almost no money to live on as a student.

Pauline and I were not the only couple thinking of marriage, Stuart Allen had found a temporary job as stage-door keeper at the Duchess Theatre where the play was "The Bride and the Bachelor" starring Cicely Courtneidge, Jack Hulbert and Robertson Hare.

Stuart had fallen in love with Ann, the Stage Manager, and he asked me to be his Best Man. The wedding was in Croydon where Ann's parents lived. The night before the wedding we had a party at the Royal Automobile Club as guests of his friend Louis with whom he had shared a flat. We parted on the understanding that I would call for him the next morning.

Stuart was living in a flat near Paddington but when I went to get him, I found the door locked and nobody inside. It was the Best Man's worst nightmare. I waited and wondered what to do, until I saw a bedraggled figure at the end of the road coming slowly towards me. I hurried towards him and asked him what the hell he was playing at. "Don't go for me!" he said, "I've been up since five and I've been sick twice." He went on to explain how he had suddenly remembered there was no cat food. I hurried him into his morning suit, grabbed a taxi and we just made it to the church before the bride.

Ann was much appreciated as a stage-manager and the company had come to the wedding. I made a speech as Best Man and Robertson Hare made the speech for the bride. It was the first time I met "Bunny" as everyone called him.

Pauline and I had only been engaged for a couple of weeks when I found myself next to Stephen Joseph on the underground one morn-ing. He said that he was going to do a Theatre in the Round season

in the public library in Scarborough and would I like to do it. I was
of course tempted by the thought of working with him, but I was
getting television work and work in the plays produced in the reps
round London; Richmond, Leatherhead and so on, and I felt it would
be a bad time for me to leave London and said so. Stephen understood
and said he was also looking for a leading lady, "There" I said, "I
think I can help" and suggested Pauline. They met and he engaged
her, so the first thing I did to my future bride was to send her as far
away as possible.

However, before she left for Scarborough, we spent a few days
with my parents. It being the nineteen-fifties, because we were only
engaged, we slept in separate rooms. Pauline and my mother took
to each other immediately and it was the beginning of a very happy
relationship that developed into a real friendship.

CHAPTER NINETEEN

I had kept in touch with Arthur and Jean Howard and one day Jean rang to say that Jimmy Edwards had given them a brace of pheasants and announced he was coming to dinner the following evening as he wanted to watch Vera Lynn's "This is your life" on their television. Jean had no idea how to prepare and cook the pheasants, which were still in their feathers, Could I come and cook them and meet Jimmy?

I was of course delighted, but there was a problem. That evening I was due to play a policeman in Vera Lynn's "This is Your Life" It was only a short scene at the beginning, when she arrived at Lime Grove at 8 o'clock, so it should be possible to prepare the pheasants, start them off, rush round to Lime Grove and be a policeman, then rush back to Kensington to dish up. The plan worked perfectly, Arthur, Jean and Jimmy watched the show and I got back just as it was finishing. The pheasants were perfectly cooked and we had dinner.

Meeting Jimmy in the flesh after having seen and heard him so often, I was chiefly struck by his eyes, which looked out over that immense moustache with an unexpectedly gentle expression.

We got on immediately and, with hunting and farming had plenty to talk about. Arthur suggested that I could play one of the masters in the following series and Jimmy said he would speak to Douglas Moodie, the producer.

During the summer, I did a television play for Granada Television in Manchester and when it was over, I went to Scarborough for a few days to stay with Pauline who had taken a small flat for the season. I saw two plays and remember particularly a version of Marivaux's *"Le Jeu de l'amour et du hazard"*. The company was good, Stephen's direction lively and Pauline was enjoying working with him. There was a young ASM who was popular with everyone, Alan Aykbourne. At the Scarbrough rep theatre there was a fellow student of mine from the Central School, Jeffrey Dench. We invited him to dinner on the Sunday and he talked about his young sister, Judy, who had just started at the Central School.

My parents were now planning to build a bungalow in the country and were wondering what to do with their surplus furniture. In London, houses were beginning to be converted into flats and some of them were not very expensive. I found one, at Baron's Court in West Kensington that was for sale for £1500.

I asked my parents if they would lend me the money and they agreed. The flat was on the third and top floor of a house that, at the back, looked on to Queen's Club tennis lawns. It had a living room, a bedroom, a new bathroom with lavatory and a kitchen. It was freshly wired and decorated and seemed very cheap at the price. When I investigated; however, I discovered the problem was that while the first floor flat was vacant, the basement and second floor has sitting tenants, which was making it difficult to sell. What was more, the owner had run out of money and could not refurbish the first floor, the entrance or the stairs until the top flat was sold. I offered to buy it on condition that he gave an undertaking to decorate and carpet the entrance and stairs and fit an answer-phone at the front door. This was agreed to and written into the contract. So the top flat at 97 Comeragh Road W.14 became mine for the next ninety-nine years. I had become a man of property.

Jimmy Edwards was as good as his word and I was engaged for the spring series 1958 to play Mr Halliforth. The BBC booking department explained that, as the part would be small, they couldn't pay me my normal fee, but proposed £15 a show. "Make it guineas" I told my agent, which got me fifteen shillings extra.

Jimmy was paid £1000 a show.

Rehearsals were at the Sulgrave Boys Club in the Goldhawk Road. One of the hazards of working in television in those days was that the BBC had decided not to build rehearsal rooms, but to rent public halls in unlikely places all over London. The Sulgrave was one of the more accessible. We rehearsed downstairs, while "Dixon of Dock Green" rehearsed upstairs.

Douglas Moodie, who was the producer of both shows, (the word 'director' came in later.) moved between the two.

Today it hardly seems credible that the BBC should have entrusted to one producer, however talented, two of its most successful weekly shows, both of them live – recording having not yet come in.

Douglas Moodie was certainly an effective and resourceful producer but working with him was anything but a pleasure. He had been an actor when he was young, and like many producers who are disappointed actors, he seemed to enjoy humiliating other actors. This natural trait of character was made worse by the fact that he never seemed to eat anything, but lived on gin-and-tonic. After lunch, at which he consumed quantities of the stuff, we used to say that the gin turned to gall, for, purple in the face, he would become increasingly waspish, delighting in the cruel and biting shafts he would think up to launch at the actor or actress who was his current target. Only Jimmy was immune from this treatment. He was the star and Douglas had a respect bordering on veneration for stars.

We used to lunch at Oddie's Club on the Goldhawk Road in a basement under an Italian restaurant. There didn't seem to be any procedure for joining, but the clientele appeared to be restricted to the Light Entertainment Section of the BBC. The other company we lunched with regularly was "Hancock's Half hour" with Tony Hancock and Sid James. Billy Cotton the bandleader often ate with us, as did his son, young Bill, who was learning the trade.

The pattern was that the first person to arrive bought a round of gins-and-tonic, the second did the same, as did the third and so on. This meant that we each consumed at least four gins-and-tonic, more if there were guests that week. We then sat down to a hefty Italian lunch with several bottles of Beaujolais, after which we would stagger back to rehearsal.

In the club there was a fruit machine and during the rounds of gins and tonic, we would all try our luck. It never seemed to pay out except on one notable occasion when Jimmy came down the stairs, went straight to it, put in sixpence, pulled the handle and the jackpot fell out. Some minutes later, Tony Hancock came down, walked to the machine, put in sixpence, pulled the handle and the same thing happened.

A privilege of being in the series was the moment when the next week's Muir and Norden script arrived. They were a delight to read, carefully crafted, not a word wasted and full of the writers' unique humour. I have kept several of them and in spite of the yellowing pages of the 'roneoed' BBC typescripts, the dialogue leaps off the page, as alive and funny as it was when they were first written nearly sixty years ago.

Our work schedule did not vary greatly over the years. We met on Tuesday mornings to read the script. (If I had a good line, Jimmy would shout; "that will make a good cut; Jim does the funnies!") Then we would start plotting the moves.

This was followed by the usual convivial lunch, and the plotting continued afterwards in desultory fashion without Douglas, who was upstairs plotting "Dixon of Dock Green". Plotting in those days was complicated because, as each camera needed a team of men to push it around, the actor had to make up for its gymnastic shortcomings;

"Edwin, start the line on camera one, then lean back and turn your head to the right so that camera four can take the end of the line and bring Jimmy into shot, then, when you've said the line, take a step back quickly, so that Number Two can get the shot of Arthur entering."

Sometimes one felt more like a ballet dancer than an actor. Wednesday and Thursday followed a similar pattern. On Friday morning "the boys", as Douglas called Frank and Denis, arrived. Tall and elegant, towering above everyone, they gave the impression that they thought as one, with Frank starting a sentence and Denis completing it and vice versa. We did a run through for them after which they showered us with compliments interlaced with pertinent comments before rushing back to their office in Regent Street, where they were usually finishing next week's script, writing "Take it from here" and additional material for various other shows.

After they left, the technicians arrived and we went through it slowly with them, Douglas stopping us on every line to explain the shot. Saturday morning we did a run-through and on Sunday we were called at ten o'clock for the dress rehearsal in the Shepherd's Bush Empire, an old variety theatre that was used by the BBC for audience shows.

During all of Sunday morning and afternoon, we went slowly and painfully through the piece for the benefit of the cameras. Then at about 6 o'clock, we did a run-through. At the end of this, we all trooped up to a dressing-room with Douglas, Frank and Denis who would announce that we were running four or five minutes over time.

"So, Edwin, when you get to the bottom of page ten, cut to the middle of page eleven. Arthur, on page sixteen, cut the second and third speeches and go to line, etc."

There was no time to rehearse these changes; the audience was being let in. Frank and Denis did a warm-up to introduce Jimmy, then he did his warm-up, which never varied, the countdown began and we were on the air. In "A Kentish Lad", Frank Muir tells the story of the Tax Inspector's spectacles that Jimmy was supposed to break on purpose to prevent the Inspector reading the accounts and which, at the transmission, were accidentally replaced by a pair of unbreakable spectacles. How Jimmy coped, and how Douglas Moodie turned his back on the controls and said, "Tell me when it's over".

As I remember it, Jimmy, having tried every means to break the spectacles, threw them on the floor, jumped on them, picked up the remains and, turning to the inspector, asked politely whether he had accidentally broken his spectacles – to a round of applause.

This was by no means an isolated event. In one show, the School Inspector is coming and Jimmy, in a panic to find something positive to tell him, calls me:

JIMMY: Halliforth!
HALLIFORTH: (Entering). Yes, Headmaster?
JIMMY: What have the Lower Fourth woodwork class made this term?
(Halliforth shows him a plank)
HALLIFORTH: This, Headmaster.

JIMMY: (*Taking it.*) What is this meant to be?
HALLIFORTH: Well, it could be a shelf, or you could use it for
                        whatever you like.
JIMMY: Right, I will. (*Smashes plank over Halliforth's
                        head*).

During the transmission, as this scene approached, I looked for
the balsa wood plank and suddenly spotted it, lying on the desk in
front of Jimmy where it had ended up after the last rehearsal.

I gestured to the floor-assistant who realising, nodded and crept
in under a camera as it moved forward into close-up, so he could pull
it from the desk. Meanwhile, the scene was continuing and my cue to
enter fast approaching. I went to stand behind the door. Then I heard
Jimmy call:

"Mr Halliforth!

I opened the door "Yes, Headmaster".

I stood in the doorway holding out my hand behind me.

JIMMY: "What have the Lower Fourth woodwork class made this
term?"

I heard scuffling behind me and felt the plank put into my hand.
"This Headmaster...".

We were, of course, the last generation of pre-television actors. We
had all done several years of weekly repertory, learning and rehearsing a new three-act play week after week. So we were used to having
to invent an excuse for leaving the room through the fireplace – as I
had done at Bristol.

Nevertheless, a blunder of that sort in repertory in front of an
audience of a couple of hundred, was very different in scale from this
new experience of live television in front of millions.

During the autumn series of 1958, Jimmy got married to Valerie
and Pauline and I got married two days later, a coincidence which did
not escape the press.

We had thought long and hard about where and how to get married.
My problem was that knowing that any emotional upset could be

fatal to my father (he had already been very ill at the wedding of one of my childhood friends) I wanted it to be as simple and as unemotional as possible. I was also against the idea of a religious ceremony, feeling that for an unbeliever like me, it would be a farce. Pauline too was against a religious ceremony and as her parents were in no position to pay for a wedding, she too, was for keeping it simple. So we decided to invite nobody but our parents, to have the ceremony at Chelsea Register Office and to have a lunch at Grosvenor House afterwards, for which her mother would pay in advance, convinced that if Gerald got his hands on the money, it might well evaporate.

Arthur and Jean had moved to Gledhow Gardens in South Kensington and a Jaguar had replaced "Miss Ford". Arthur was a very endearing person, but totally impractical and in almost always submerged by minor, everyday problems. One result of this was that he was always late.

With so little rehearsal time this became a problem, so it was arranged that I should go and fetch him each morning. The pleasure of driving to rehearsal in a Jaguar was mitigated by the fact that if we were late – and Arthur nearly always had a reason for not leaving on time – Douglas invariably blamed me.

We frequently had guest stars, one of the most memorable being Vera Lynn. She joined in with everything, mothered us all and even made the tea. The episode was based on the fact that the Eton Boating Song was in the Top Ten, which give Jimmy the idea of writing a Chiselbury song and convincing Vera Lynn to sing it. The script begins with Jimmy holding auditions for Mr Dinwiddy's Benefit Concert. When it comes to Halliforth's turn:

Jimmy:	Mr Halliforth. And in what capacity do you hope to enthral the audience at the Village Institute Hall?
Halliforth:	(*Modestly*) I have been described as a lyric tenor, sir.
Jimmy:	You have been described as a lot of things. What are you going to do?

HALLIFORTH: Sing, sir. A song called "For Love Alone" made
              famous by Jan Kiepura. *(He nods off)*
HALLIFORTH: Thank you Mr Melhuish *(The intro starts)*.
JIMMY: *(stands right next to* HALLIFORTH, *who nervously
              holds the music before himsel.)*
HALLIFORTH: *(Sings)* "I have so little to give."
JIMMY: *(takes the music from him and tears it coldly in
              half.)*
HALLIFORTH: *(Bewildered)* Headmaster?
JIMMY: "Mr Halliforth, you have nothing to give! Next!"

As I have no ear for music and am incapable of holding a tune, I
decided that the way to play it was to try to sing correctly. The decision was evidently a good one, as Vera Lynn said to me;
"Edwin the way you do that, managing to change key on each word,
is absolutely brilliant"

Sometime in 1960, recording came in which made the show less
frenetic in that we could stop after each scene. It was the only advantage, because once the tape was rolling it couldn't be stopped and
retakes were out of the question. It meant, of course, that shows
could be prepared in advance and shown later, which, on one occasion at least, proved not to be such a good idea.

In 1960, Patrice Lumumba of the Congo was very much in the
news. So when I had to go into a classroom where the boys had put a
booby trap over the door, which fell and covered me in black ink, and
Jimmy said; "He's been Lumumbad!" it got a huge laugh.

However between the time of the recording and the transmission,
Poor Mr Lumumba was first arrested and then assassinated and the
Congo teetered on the brink of civil war. Questions were asked in the
UN and Jimmy's line became in the worst possible taste.

The only thing to do was to try to change it and record another
line over it. This meant trying to find the exact spot on the tape.
Douglas spent hours in the cutting room and eventually managed to
locate it and to record Jimmy saying "blacked out" over it. When it

was shown, the viewers must have wondered why such a banal line got such a huge laugh.

In the summer of 1960, a "WhackO" film was made. I was offered the part of Halliforth, but the fee offered was too low, so I turned it down. When we started the autumn series, Jimmy told me I had missed nothing and the film did not do well. I hasten to add that this was in no way due to my absence.

I saw a lot of Jimmy at that time and grew very fond of him. He was a most loveable character and great fun to be with, although women, especially actresses, used to find him difficult and he was clearly not at ease with them. He was essentially what used to be called a "man's man" and at his best in pubs and clubs; I remember a riotous evening with him at the Savile Club trying to play snooker.

All comics have grotesquely large personalities which often gives the impression of their being deformed, rather as one might have one leg longer than the other, or an unusually large head. Jimmy was no exception: his car horn played the "Take it from Here" theme-tune and at one point when the mini first appeared, he had a mini-van, on the side of which was painted, "Jas. Edwards, Purveyor of Family Humour".

His success was enormous and Arthur and I would often marvel at its universality. To the bloke on the building site, who would call out as we passed, "Wotcha, Jim!" to the city gent "A decent sort of fellow, Edwards. I hear he was at Cambridge", through the ex-service people who saw him as a war hero (he had been decorated with the D.F.C), to the intellectuals who found him "delightfully music-hall", there seemed no limit to his appeal.

Arthur used to criticise him for being lazy, saying that he had had it too easy and if only he would work harder he would be so much better. It was true. He tended not to know the script quite well enough and to repeat successful effects rather than attempting some-thing new. It was as if he preferred to be a brilliant amateur rather than a true professional and considered polo and fox hunting more important than the boring business of learning lines and rehearsing. It was a pity, because he had enormous talent.

Our rehearsals were programmed round his hunting, and during one series, when he was hunting twice a week we only had three days' rehearsal. As well as hunting, Jimmy played polo and played regularly with the Duke of Edinburgh – on one occasion calling to him, "Keep close to me, sir and you'll get your photo in the newspaper!"

Television had brought a noticeable change in the public's attitude to actors. Before, when we had only been seen on the stage or in films, people had paid for their seats and were, in a sense, our guests in our house. If we were recognised in the street, they might smile or even say a word, but their attitude was basically respectful of our privacy. With television, however, because we came into the sitting room and appeared in between the coalscuttle and the aspidistra under the photo of Aunty Mavis, we became part of the furniture. People felt they not only knew us, but they owned us, and they treated us accordingly. This complicated visits to pubs and restaurants, especially for someone like Jimmy who was so easily recognisable. He used to say that he dreamed of the day when he would shave off his moustache and pass unnoticed in a crowd.

Some years later I went into the club at the Television Centre one evening and several people told me that Jimmy was there and wanted to see me. We had not seen each other for some time and I went over delighted to see him. We chatted for a while and I saw he was looking at me rather oddly. After a moment he said, "Don't you notice anything?" It was only then I realised he'd shaved off his moustache.

Frank Muir has described the end of "WhackO" in "A Kentish Lad". It came several months after the death of Jean Compton, who died tragically of leukaemia. Arthur, who was typically late for her funeral, was bereft and we all rallied round him. His arrest for soliciting came as a surprise, but a bigger surprise was to learn that he was a recidivist and that it was something Jean had lived with for years. I went to the court with Frank and Denis. It was a sad business, with poor Arthur looking like Mr Toad in "The Wind in the Willows" between two burly policemen.

Although I knew him well, Arthur's homosexuality came as a surprise. I had accepted him as a married man and not thought beyond that. Homosexuality held no mysteries for me, I had encountered it at school, in the RAF, and in the theatre and my attitude to it had not changed since I was eighteen, when I had decided that it was infinitely preferable that men make love to each other rather than bring unwanted children into the world.

Jimmy's unforgiving attitude – he refused ever to see Arthur again or to have him mentioned – seemed at the time inexplicable, because they had been friends and Jimmy was naturally a generous person. It was only years later that it came to light that he, too, had a history of "the love that dare not speak its name". Frank told me that when he was young Jimmy had been in love with a young man who had died and that he had never got over his loss.

The last time I saw Jimmy was when Pauline and I were on the panel game, "Call My Bluff" with him. We had dinner together afterwards. He talked a lot about Valerie and reminded me of the time we had met by chance in St Martin's Lane and had a drink in the Salisbury. He had told me he was going to Australia and I had asked after Valerie. He had, I remembered, been rather evasive. Now he said he had been on the point of telling me he was leaving her, but had thought better of it. It was an enjoyable evening and, as usual we had a lot of laughs.

*

Pauline had often talked about her friend from RADA, Glenda Jackson. They had both been shy and had sat together at the back of the class knitting. Glenda was doing a summer season in a Butlins holiday camp and soon after we were married, Pauline got a letter from her saying that she too was married, to the stage manager of the company, Roy Hodges. At the end of the season they returned to London and came to see us. Glenda was the daughter of a bricklayer in a small seaside town near Liverpool. She had worked in Boots the Chemist, but had had a success in an amateur play and been advised to try for RADA, where she had won a scholarship. At twenty-one she bore an uncanny resemblance to Henri Toulouse-Lautrec's model,

Carmen Gauden, as he portrayed her in his *"La Blanchisseuse"*. Roy was tall and thin. He had trained at the Bradford Theatre School and had been in several reps as an actor and stage-manager. They were living in West Hampstead and we often visited them. Their situation was precarious they had two rooms with a tap on the landing. Roy worked as a barman in a pub and we would spend evenings sitting in the pub so we could chat to him when he was free. They looked upon us as being impossibly rich.

Soon after our marriage, Pauline and I had decided to try to write together and we embarked on a play. It was called "Our Father" and was about a respectable provincial family still living under the shadow of their dead father, mayor of the town, whose portrait dominates the scene. The play opens with preparations for the return of the ne'er-do-well brother who left home thirty years ago. He turns out to have been successful and contrasts with the others who have remained unchanged, dreaming impossible dreams rather than doing something concrete. We worked for years on this play, doing version after version, adapting it for television, for the radio, and although Frank Muir said it was the most boring play he had ever read, we learned a great deal from our efforts.

At the end of 1957 my father, now sixty-eight, had been forced to retire. I had hoped that he and my mother would return to Kent, thinking that they would be nearer their friends and Aunty Peggy, but they refused and bought a piece of land at Rudford, a village near Gloucester, and built a bungalow, stairs now being out of the question for him.

We went down to stay with them and saw the work in progress. My father was enthusiastic about the view across the fields to a distant wood. "Doesn't it make you want to reach for your brush?" I had done a painting of our cottage at Pitlochry, but nothing since. I told him painting was not on the agenda for the moment. They moved in at the beginning of October and their letters showed their pleasure in at last having a house of their own.

The 7th November 1959, a Saturday, was the first anniversary of our marriage and, money being short we celebrated with dinner at Lyons Corner House. The next day was the first rehearsal of a new series of "Whacko" at the Sulgrave Boys' Club. In the middle of rehearsal, Pauline arrived to say that my father had had a heart attack during the night and was in Gloucester hospital. Everyone was very understanding, Arthur drove me to Paddington and I got the next train to Gloucester. When I arrived, my mother said I must not go to see him, because it would worry him. So I stayed with her and returned to London on the Monday evening for rehearsal on the Tuesday to learn the moves. Douglas kindly agreed to my going back to Gloucester until the Friday, saying someone would read my part in the intervening rehearsals.

When I arrived on the Wednesday, my mother suggested we wait until Visiting Time at four o'clock so as not to worry him.

He did not seem surprised to see me. He had had a further heart attack and said he did not think he could withstand another. Although they had moved into the bungalow, they had not cleared the house in Alexandra Road, and in particular the attic. This was preying on his mind and he kept asking what we could do. I suggested that, after visiting, my mother should take me to see the problem and it was agreed. When it was time to leave, I touched his hand feeling he was too fragile to embrace. "Kiss me!" he said, urgently, "aren't you going to kiss me?" I kissed him and said we all wanted him to get better, and that Jimmy Edwards had sent him his best wishes. "Did he?" he said and seemed pleased.

My Mother bent down and kissed him tenderly on the lips. At that moment their love for each other seemed to irradiate them and had the effect of momentarily making them seem young again.

The attic did indeed present a problem; everything was there, from the boxes of stationery for Betteshanger Nurseries, to the toys from Beach House Tenterden, to the hand-basins and cupboard doors that he had installed at Wenderton which, when my grandfather, after agreeing to an independent valuation, had finally refused to pay for, my father had taken out. I suggested that they cut their losses and call in a dealer to clear it. We returned to the hospital to tell him of my suggestion. As we got out of the car, I followed my mother, but her way was barred by a Sister who said "We've been trying to ring you, I'm afraid you are too late." My mother let out a shriek. The Sister and I tried to comfort her, she wanted to go into the hospital, but the Sister said we should not see him, that it would be better to remember him as he was and finally my mother agreed. We got back in the car and she drove to the bungalow. It was Wednesday the eleventh of November, Armistice Day.

A friend of my mother's came to stay with her, as I had to return on the following day to do the show on the Sunday. Being the first of a new series, it was important, but it went well and I returned on the Monday morning to Gloucester to arrange the funeral. In his last letter only a few weeks earlier, my father wrote that he had seen a television programme about the waste of good agricultural land caused by building cemeteries, adding that it had convinced him of the advantages of cremation. So I knew what to do. The day of the funeral, my mother insisted on driving herself, saying she did not want to go in a gloomy funeral car. We arrived at the crematorium early and she decided to drive round so that her car was facing the right way afterwards. As we passed the back of the building, I noticed the stoker standing outside the back door with his shovel, having a smoke.

Uncle Harry, my father's eldest brother who lived near Oxford came, Uncle George represented Aunty Peggy who was too busy with some social event, and Mary, the daughter of his old Gloucester friend, Carey Pitt. I had talked to the officiating clergyman before, and had asked him to read the passage from the end of the second part of "The Pilgrim's Progress," where Mr Valiant-for-Truth crosses the river saying:

"I am going to my fathers and though with great difficulty I am got hither, yet now I do not repent me of all the trouble I have been at to arrive where I am. My sword, I give to him that shall succeed me in my pilgrimage, and my courage and skill, to him that can get it. My marks and scars I carry with me, to be a witness for me that I have fought his battles who now will be my rewarder, etc".

It ends;

 "So he passed over and all the trumpets sounded for him on the other side".

The clergyman demurred, saying it was not in the Bible and he only read from the Bible. However I insisted and he finally agreed. But when he came to the reading, could not forbear prefacing it by mentioning his reluctance to do so.

 During the next few weeks I alternated between "Whacko" and trips to Gloucester. As I expected, my Father's affairs were in perfect order; when all his debts were paid, he left £500.

CHAPTER TWENTY

—

At the end of the first series of "WhackO", I found that I was
now so associated with my part of Mr Halliforth, that other
television producers were reluctant to use me. Fortunately, I began
to get parts in films. There had been a spy scandal in London, which
had centred on a bungalow in Ruislip. One of the main figures was
a Russian double agent who worked for the foreign office called
George Blake, and in the film made from this affair, "Ring of Spies",
I was cast as George Blake. Blake had a beard and this meant I had to
get to the studio very early each morning, so that the make-up man
could create the beard out of yak's hair. It was a work of art and the
make-up man was justly proud of it, so proud in fact that he followed
me everywhere to see that I did not damage it by doing anything as
dangerous as eating. Throughout my meals he sat beside me and each
time I opened my mouth or chewed, a worried expression crossed his
face. It was this experience that persuaded me to grow a beard some
years later, thinking it would be easier to shave, than to go through
all that again should another part call for a beard. Not long after
the film was released, George Blake escaped from prison, which led
several of my friends to suggest that he had seen my performance and
was out to take revenge.

While television companies were unwilling to use me because of
"WhackO", repertory companies were glad to have a familiar face
from television, so I did quite a lot of special weeks at Northampton,
Oxford, Ipswich, Leatherhead, Croydon and Richmond. For most
of these weeks, I was able to commute and it was then that Gerald
Knight's geography lessons, when he had made us learn all the London
stations and the towns they served, came in extremely useful.

For as long as I could remember, my father had regularly drummed
it in to me that I must look after my mother when he died. Now
that the moment had arrived, I began to wonder what was to become
of her. She was fifty-five and had never worked or lived alone, and

during their marriage my father, who was fourteen years older, had been very much the dominant partner. Her situation was not encouraging; true she had a newly built house in the middle of a field and a car, but she had very little money and was miles away from her sister and from us. As one might have expected, she was totally lost without him. She had known and loved him since she was four years old and for the last thirteen years she had devoted her life entirely to him, watching over him night and day, driving him everywhere and doing everything in her power to see that he was not worried or stressed. When someone dies we have a tendency to think something has happened, but in reality it is quite the opposite; something has stopped happening, which is far more difficult to deal with. I could not be of much help because my work kept me in London and our only contact was by telephone.

One of the first things that happened was that the vicar called. She told me he had been very nice and had himself recently lost his wife. As the weeks went by, she mentioned him more and more, and she began going to church on Sundays. She told me that he had even invited her to the vicarage.

The question of what should be done with my father's ashes now arose and the vicar, to whom she now referred as Bill, suggested that they should be buried in the churchyard. Pauline was working, so I went down alone for the ceremony and met Bill, a stout, fleshy unctuous man who did not immediately inspire confidence. My mother and I went to matins on the Sunday where he preached the most rambling and confused sermon I had ever heard. He seemed very attentive to her, and there was talk of her taking over the playing of the organ. When we were alone, my mother said that he had suggested that they get together. I asked her what she thought about it and she said that she was considering it. I did not know what to say; on the one hand I felt she must be free to do what she wanted, but on the other, it seemed too early to think of such a thing and, while I wanted to avoid at all costs playing the heavy-handed male of the family, I was surprised that he, in his capacity as her priest, should have suggested such a thing to someone so recently widowed.

The Tuesday morning was scheduled for the burial of my father's ashes. My mother said she did not feel she could face it and wanted me to do it with Bill. At half past eleven, I walked to the church and found him waiting with the undertaker who was carrying a small box. Bill had chosen a spot opposite the door of the church among some of the older graves and the sexton had dug a small hole. The undertaker placed the box in the hole and Bill closed his eyes and said a prayer. As I watched him, I could not help thinking how macabre the situation was. Here was I with two men, neither of whom had known my father, one of whom was apparently hoping to "get together" with his widow, placing his ashes in their last resting-place, a place he had never known. At that moment my eye was caught by the name on the grave beside the hole, it was "Minchin", the name of the detested commanding officer of the 47th Squadron.

When they had finished, I thanked the undertaker and walked back to the bungalow. There were still matters to be dealt with and I sat down at my father's desk. Suddenly, sitting where he had so often sat, where he had written the cheques for my school fees, worried about bills and typed letters on his Remington portable, I sensed his presence and his loss, the fact that he no longer existed, that I should never see him again, never receive a letter written in that clear firm hand that had not altered since he was a schoolboy. For the first time since his death, I burst into tears.

At my following visit, I got the impression that it was now decided that Bill and my mother were to marry. He had suggested that she should move into the vicarage, but she drew the line at this and said they should live in the bungalow. I found the whole situation unreal. My father had not been dead for more than a few months and she was embarking on a new marriage with someone she hardly knew. I talked to her and tried to get at her real feelings, but all she would say was that she wanted just to go into this without thinking.

The difficulty was that Bill was a clergyman, albeit not like any clergyman I had ever known, and this made him respectable in my mother's eyes.

Bill had introduced my mother to two of his friends who lived in a neighbouring village. Originally from Manchester, they had lived in Africa where the husband had had a job as a representative. They had returned to England with the dream of keeping a pub, but it had not worked out and now he was representative for a small Welsh firm making carbon paper.

Bill suggested that he and my mother go to Lancashire to meet his family. She was a little hesitant, but finally agreed. When she returned we got the impression that it had been something of a shock.

Soon afterwards, Pauline and I met and got to know the couple to whom Bill had introduced my mother, and had a conversation with the wife. She told us that they did not know Bill very well, but that the rumour was he had not been the adoring husband that he had represented himself as being. On the contrary, he had treated his wife badly and since her death he had pursued two other widows who owned houses because he was soon to retire and, as he had gone into the Church late, he had hardly any pension and nowhere to live.

Soon after this he began to suggest that they should each make a Will leaving their possessions to the other. At this my mother began to react and her sense of survival reasserted itself. The problem was how to get rid of him, because he was extremely persistent.

At this point Yaya, who had been following the situation from afar, got into the baby Austin, lit a cigarette, opened the window, drew on the sheep's wool backed gauntlets and set out for Rudford. Once there, she soon summed up the situation and the next time Bill appeared she told him in no uncertain terms to leave and not to come back. She then began to sort out my mother.

The friend who represented a carbon paper company had found a better job and he suggested to my mother that she should take his place. She had often said that if anything happened to my father she would get a job and now she jumped at the chance. Her friend showed her what to do, took her round to meet the clients, introduced her to the management and negotiated her salary, so for the next ten years she went round offices, stayed in hotels and enjoyed the status of a being a business woman. She enjoyed it hugely, took a personal interest in the clients and their families and never stopped saying how much she appreciated earning her own living and being independent, always ending with, "What would Daddy have said?"

CHAPTER TWENTY-ONE

—

Now that we had bought the top flat at Comeragh Road, the owner of the house did up the first-floor flat and, according to the clause in our contract, installed an answer-phone, painted the hall and stairway and invited us to choose the carpet for the stairs. The first-floor flat finished, it was bought by a very jolly Irish lady; Mrs Murdoch, who had it painted bright pink throughout.

We decided to buy a fridge and as we did not have enough money, bought it on hire purchase. (It was the only thing in my life that I have ever bought on hire purchase, generally preferring to go without until I can afford things.) We bought it from a shop in West Kensington one Saturday afternoon, and the shop agreed to deliver it, but suggested that we should take the tray that fitted on top of it with us. As we had some shopping to do, I carried our purchases back on the tray. Arriving at the front door, we found a couple trying to get in, The woman was striking looking, but negligently dressed in an old mack'. When she saw me with the tray, she said, with a slight Irish accent, that it was the most original way of carrying shopping she had ever seen. She turned out to be Mrs Murdoch's daughter, Iris Murdoch, the novelist. We had both read "Under the Net" and "The Sandcastle" and had greatly admired them; but when we mentioned it to Mrs Murdoch she did not seem all that enthusiastic. "Yes," she said, "Iris is clever but she doesn't have to face Aunty." It seemed that she dreaded the publication of each of Iris' books because a major figure in their lives was an aunt who was very strait-laced, and when Iris's books appeared, it was Mrs Murdoch who had to do the explaining. We would meet her on the stairs and ask how she was and she would reply, "I don't know, Iris is having this new book published and she's given it me to read; frankly I don't know what I'm going to say to Aunty."

A little further along the road from our flat, there was a house that always seemed to have a white Rolls Royce parked outside and ravishingly beautiful girls going in and out. I was very intrigued, and Pauline accused me of walking more and more often to West Kensington Tube station, rather than Baron's Court which was nearer, in order to pass the house. When the Profumo scandal broke, we discovered that the Rolls belonged to Dr Stephen Ward and the beautiful girls were Christine Keeler and his other call girls whose activities led to the downfall of the Macmillan government.

Pauline and I both enjoyed walking and would often plan a walk to discover parts of London we did not know. On one of these occasions, we walked along the Thames to Greenwich to see the Naval College and the Queen's House, the first Palladian building in England. We then walked up through the park on to Blackheath, one of the finest open spaces near London. Opposite the main entrance to the park, across the heath, stood two pairs of large mid-Victorian houses. We crossed the heath towards them and when we got close saw that one of them was being converted into flats that were for sale.

The idea of living in the middle of this big open space and walking across the grass to Blackheath Village, where there was a regular train service to Charing Cross, twenty minutes away, was appealing. We took the telephone number of the company doing the conversion and rang them the following day. The ground floor and top floor were sold, but the basement was for sale. It had two bedrooms, a large living room, kitchen and bathroom and access to the garden. A garden! There was also a cellar, and a box-room on the second floor. The price was £3500.

A second bedroom meant that we could have my mother to stay. We decided to try to sell our flat. I was doing a play at Leatherhead at the time and mentioned I was selling the flat. The stage-manager was getting married and decided to buy it. The price was £3000; the flat's value had doubled in four years. We had, of course taken a risk buying it when the stairs and entrance were not decorated, but the risk had paid off. We took out a mortgage for £500 and moved to 2A Talbot Place, Blackheath, where we were to spend the next eleven years.

Stuart Allen and Ann were expecting a baby and they decided that

Stuart was not doing well enough as an actor to cope, and that something had to be done, so he decided to apply for a job at the BBC. Ann
wrote the letter, and he was offered a job as a television floor-assistant
and sent on a course. For a short time he was attached to "Whacko"
which we both enjoyed, and then he was posted to Manchester and
became floor manager for Light Entertainment, where they were
setting up a series with the comedian, Harry Worth. When they were
casting Stuart mentioned my name – and kept mentioning it, with
the result that I did many episodes in the series. One of these was
due to be shown on the 22nd November 1963. That evening we were
due to have dinner with George and Pamela and, as I had a good part
in the episode, I asked if they would mind if we watched it. They
agreed and we switched on the television just before it was due to
start – to hear the announcement of the assassination of President
Kennedy. Everyone was terribly shocked and "Here's Harry," transmitted immediately afterwards, did not play to a receptive audience.

Of all the comedians I worked with, Harry Worth was the nicest,
the most self-effacing and altogether the most normal. He had been
a ventriloquist and his act, which was based on self-denigration; ("I
don't mind when the audience walks out, it's when they walk towards
me I get worried') meant that he would say to the audience "If you
watch carefully you can see my lips move". He did a tour with Stan
Laurel, who, after Hardy's death, toured the music halls on his own.
He was an old man and it was his last tour. He watched Harry from
the wings and when he came off, said to him "Throw away the doll".
Harry took his advice and from then on his act developed into one of
the best stand up-comedy acts in the country.

Now, the BBC producer John Ammonds and the writers Vince
Powell and Harry Driver had devised a series for him. The basic joke
was that when he encountered people he engaged them in complicated explanations that they tried to follow but invariably got lost
and ended up in a state of total confusion.

We did the show in a converted church at Didsbury, a Victorian
suburb of Manchester, and rehearsed in the Didsbury Conservative
Club, a large Victorian house that stood in a park. John Ammonds

had been with the BBC all his working life, having started as a boy
on ITMA, the legendary wartime radio show that starred Tommy
Handley. One of the features of the show was the opening and closing
of the door as each character came and went. Its timing was central to
the comedy and it was John Ammonds who worked the door.

John radiated enthusiasm. He would watch the scenes he was
directing and roar with laughter, bouncing up and down on his heels.
He had only recently come to television and was like a child with a
new toy. His enthusiasm was infectious: up until then I had, like most
actors, sat at the back during rehearsal reading a paper or gossiping
with the other actors; now I started watching the rehearsal from the
front and taking an interest. After a time, John began asking me what
I thought and I began suggesting things.

During these weeks in Manchester, Harry and I would often spend
our evenings together. He loved the cinema and used to say that when
he died people would say that it was not drink or drugs that had got
him, but the cinema. A film we both enjoyed was "The Apartment"
with Jack Lemmon; we saw it a couple of times. Knowing we liked
films, the resident photographer approached us on one occasion,
saying he had made a pornographic film and would we like to see it?

Neither of us had seen anything of the sort before, so we agreed.
He took us to his house and in the front room with the curtains
drawn, the flickering images, so familiar today, even on television, of
detailed sexual intercourse appeared on the small screen. When it was
over we thanked him and left. As we got out into the street, Harry
turned to me and said in his northern accent, "I don't know about
you, but I feel really mucky".

Our recordings on Saturday evenings took place at the same time
that "Top of The Pops" was produced live in the adjoining studio.
There was a typically awful BBC canteen where we all had something to eat before the show. On one occasion I found myself beside
Herman of "The Hermits" and as he looked down unenthusiastically
at a greasy plate of bacon and eggs, I couldn't resist asking him if he
thought he was "into something good".

The scripts for "Here's Harry" tended to be a bit rough and

scenes often needed re-writing. One Monday during the first reading, the scene we had together clearly did not work, so afterwards
Harry took me aside and suggested I go off somewhere and see what
I could do to improve it. The plot involved Harry going to the BBC
to ask them to play a record for his aunt's birthday. I was to play
the BBC producer. I took the script and went outside into the park.
Suddenly remembering that I had written comedy sketches at school,
I turned the script over and began completely to rewrite the scene
on the back. I found that the dialogue came easily and that the scene
worked. I looked round me in that damp, gloomy Manchester, park
and thought to myself that writing comedy was something I could
do. I took the scene back in to the rehearsal room, showed it to Harry
who immediately started laughing. We began to act it and everyone
laughed. I had discovered a new talent and I suddenly saw possibilities opening up.

The BBC rang me to say that it was planning to make Harry the
subject of "This is Your Life", the popular programme with Eammon
Andrews, in which well-known people were taken by surprise
when they were having a haircut, or doing the Christmas shopping.
Suddenly Eammon would appear with a large book under his arm
and, pointing to it, would say; "So-and-so: this is your Life!" then
the scene would cut to studio, where Eammon would read out the
life, producing from behind a curtain forgotten friends and relatives
– sometimes flown in from half way across the world and not always,
it must be said, warmly welcomed by the subject.

I had, of course, been involved in a small way in Vera Lynn's "This
is your Life" the evening I first met Jimmy Edwards, and later Jimmy
himself had been the subject of the programme. He had not enjoyed
the experience, as he told me the following morning at rehearsal.
Jimmy came from a large family and the BBC had mustered all of
them behind the curtain, "A worse dressed bunch you never saw,"
he said, adding that afterwards the BBC had provided nothing more
than a bottle of Seagars gin to entertain them, so he had had to take
them all out to dinner which cost him a fortune.

Now the BBC wanted me to appear from behind the curtain to

surprise Harry and tell the story of how he had bought a new car, an Austin Princess, and invited me to drive back to London with him after the show. How coming into the London suburbs at two o'clock in the morning, we had had a puncture and Harry, not knowing where anything was, started to read the Instruction Book so that the situation began to resemble more and more a scene from the show, with me getting more and more confused.

At the time I was working on Galton and Simpson's film, "The Bargee", which was directed by Duncan Wood, who had produced "Hancock's Half Hour" (we had regularly lunched together at Oddie's club during the "WhackO" years). As he was a BBC producer, the BBC booker told me to explain the problem to him and ask if I could leave early, adding, "You'll have no trouble with Duncan, he'll understand immediately". The problem was that this was Duncan's first film and he was under far more pressure than usual, so when I asked if I could have a word with him, he said "Not now, later"; I made several attempts to speak to him during the morning, but each time he brushed me aside. He was not in the canteen at lunchtime, and when we started shooting in the afternoon I made a couple more attempts to speak to him, without success. Finally I went up to him and said, "Duncan, I must speak to you" He turned on me angrily and said, "Look, Edwin, you are doing it perfectly, please stop worrying me" and began to walk away. I shouted after him, "The BBC wants me to be in Harry Worth's "This Is Your Life" in Manchester this evening!" Duncan stopped dead, "But why didn't you say so?" "I've been trying to all day". He was very apologetic and arranged for a taxi and I got to the airport just in time. Harry's wife was on the plane looking very worried. She said the BBC had insisted she did not tell Harry about the programme and she did not know how he would take it.

In the end all was well, there were a lot of people who had known him, including the old Pit Manager who had employed him when he was a miner. Afterwards he and I flew back to London with Eammon Andrews. The plane was empty except for one other person whom Eammon knew and invited to join us. He turned out to be the representative of a Pools company, whose job it was to take the cheques to the big winners. The flight passed very quickly as we sat drinking the bottle of Irish whiskey that Eammon had thoughtfully brought with him, while we listened to stories of the unexpected reactions people had to winning large sums of money, including the family who barred the door and refused to let him in, shouting through the letter box, "Go away, we don't want it!"

By now I began to be known as a face, not a name, but a face on television. An article by Brad Ashton appeared in the Television Times headed "Oh Look, There's what's his name" which featured several of us who were in the same situation. For my part Ashton wrote:

"If a part calls for a helpful shop assistant who winds up with a nervous breakdown after trying to serve a fickle minded comic, 32-year-old Edwin Apps is a master of the art of controlled impatience"

Perhaps because of this, or because I was often seen working with comedians, I was asked to do another commercial. This one was for Flowers beer and starred Stanley Unwin, a comedian who had developed a nonsense language, which imitated speech so that the listener thought he was hearing normal speech and could not make out why he could not understand it. The scenario was set in the refreshment tent at a cricket match. We were supposedly discussing the match, but Stanley Unwin kept launching into his special language that left me more and more baffled. We were of course all the while drinking Flowers beer.

The shoot was again in a basement in Soho and this time the studio was converted into a tent with a bar, and at eight o'clock in the morning when we began, with me dressed in a striped blazer and white flannels, the tent flooded with sunlight, we were both handed pints of beer and began rehearsing. Stanley Unwin was a very nice, very funny man who told me he had been an engineer and had invented his language to amuse his friends. It had taken off and now he was a professional. It was not easy to work with him, because his nonsense was not scripted and he never said the same thing twice, so it was impossible to have a cue and know precisely when to speak. However, we rehearsed and the director who was very young, said we would do a take. As it was the beer that was the real star, we had to hold up our pints and they both had to have a large head of froth. Filming is a slow business with much attention to detail, the sound man has his say, the lighting man, the director, it all takes time and heads of froth do not last, so we would be told to sip some of the beer to make room for a new head to be added. Then the stage-manager or the director would sip some of the beer to save time. When it got to one o'clock and we broke for lunch, everyone had sipped or drunk a good deal of beer, nevertheless they all decided to go to the pub. I thought that after sipping beer for five hours it would be wiser not to go to the pub and sent someone out for a sandwich.

Everyone returned in a jovial mood and we started shooting again and to save time, the stage manager began to suck the beer out of our glasses with a straw. The director found that he was too slow and took over the sucking himself. He sat on the camera, working close to us, and before each take he would suck beer out of the two glasses, shout, "Fill them up, right, give it a burst, Stanley!" and Stanley Unwin would give one of his characteristic long phrases of nonsense. "Stop!" would cry the director, "The head's gone down!" and he would lean forward and suck some more beer out of the pint. He was doing this at five past four, when he suddenly toppled off the camera lay on the floor senseless and shooting came to an end.

I don't know what effect it had on the others, but I farted almost continually for two days, so that Pauline insisted that I sit on the window-cill with the window open.

CHAPTER TWENTY-TWO

During "WhackO," I had got to know Frank Muir and we had discovered that we had several interests in common. One day, when he and his wife, Polly, were having lunch with us, just as they were leaving, I mentioned my interest in the eighteenth-century theatre and my collection of books. Frank was immediately interested, and soon after decided to collect books himself. He had in the meantime had lunch with William Rees-Mogg, the editor of *The Times*, who had mentioned that antique books were about to become a good investment.

Thorough in everything he did, Frank was soon better informed about book collecting than I was. One day he rang me to say that there was an interesting sale of eighteenth-century books coming up at Sotheby's. He had recently done a television commercial and been paid in cash and wanted to invest it in books. He could not go to the sale, so would I go and buy for him? He had marked the catalogue for things he felt were interesting, but left it to my discretion. We met and he gave me the catalogue and the five hundred pounds and I went to the sale.

There were some splendid things, including a first edition of Dr Johnson's dictionary. I managed to get all the things he had marked and as there was some money over, saw that there was a first edition of 'Bewick's Birds', a book famous for its end-pieces, the small, beautifully drawn scenes from rural life at the end of each chapter.

When the sale was over, the auctioneer, obviously intrigued, came to me and said. "You have bought some nice things." I said I thought I had, paid and took the books to the Savile Club where we had lunch. Over lunch I told Frank that it was the first time I had bought anything at auction since I had bought my rabbits in Sittingbourne market when I was eleven. I could have added that it was also the first time I had had five hundred pounds in cash in my pocket.

Frank and Polly had become interested in canal boating an

unusual activity at the time, and Frank had had a boat built to go on the canals. The plan was to go down the Thames to Oxford and then up the Oxford Canal, one of the forgotten waterways dating from the Industrial Revolution. The canal had been made for the narrow boats, of which a few still survived and continued to work, moving cargoes slowly up and down central England. The narrow-boat people were a close-knit clan, born and bred in these boats, and the boats were decorated in a style similar to Gypsy caravans. For someone who normally worked under intense pressure like Frank, to be able to float along on a canal with fields of sheep and cows on both sides, and from time to time enter a lock and sit and smoke a pipe until the water had risen sufficiently, and then to wind down the other side of the lock to leave, was the ideal relaxation. The problem was that moving the boat about took time, which Frank rarely could spare, so he organized a group of friends to move the boat for him. He would ring and say, "Can you take Samantha from Staines to Oxford next week?" and if we were free we were only too pleased to do so. We had some wonderful holidays on the boat. But he made the mistake of talking about it on one of the many popular panel games he and Denis did on radio and television, and before long the canals began to get crowded. People would look out for Frank Muir's boat and want his autograph and it ceased to be a good way for him to relax. So, reluctantly, they decided to sell the boat.

One day in January 1962, he rang me and asked if I could speak French. I think the idea came from the fact that in one episode of "WhackO" a scene opened with the stage direction "Mr Halliforth is teaching French" but with no further indication. Feeling I had to do something, I told the class to recite after me the list of nouns, which in the plural end in *"X"; "bijoux, cailloux, choux, genoux, joujoux, hiboux, poux"*. This had made everyone laugh and I suppose Frank had remembered it. I told him I was far from fluent, but that I could get by and he said that he and Polly, who was half French and spoke the language fluently, had been on holiday to Corsica, where they had stayed in a hotel at Ile Rousse, and that one evening they had taken a taxi up to a village called Monticello in the hills. There they had seen a flat for sale, and decided to buy it. It was currently being modernised and he and Polly were supposed to go and see the masons this weekend, but Polly was ill. Would I go with him and talk to the masons?

We flew to Paris, had a late lunch of onion soup and a bottle of Beaujolais on the Champs Elysées stayed in one of those faded Second Empire hotels that had two bedrooms with a salon dividing them that seemed straight out of Feydeau, had dinner at La Reine Pédauge and went to the Lido. The following morning we took a plane to Nice and I experienced for the first time the shock of going suddenly from Northern Europe to the South of France in the middle of January. Another smaller plane took us to Bastia, where Frank had hired a car. As night was falling, he drove us up and down mountains on unlit narrow winding roads, crossing the island until we reached Monticello. The hotel had just been built by a family of shepherds and the following morning we got up early and watched the father and his two sons milk their flock of little ewes, picking each one up, giving a few squirts into the pail and pushing the animal behind them. The milk was to be sent to the mainland to make Roquefort cheese.

Corsica was a revelation. I knew, of course, that Boswell had been there as a young man to meet General Paoli, the Corsican hero, and had been instrumental in bringing him to London where he became a member of Dr Johnson's club. Boswell had written a book about the island, which I had read. It recounted its tragic history, continually invaded and occupied and at one moment sold to an Italian bank.

Boswell had been attracted to Corsica, seeing a similarity with his native Scotland, but it seemed to me much wilder than the Scotland I knew. The flat the Muirs were buying was made up of an old Genoese watchtower overlooking the sea, and several rooms at the top of a warren of a building that Frank described as being "like a bag of boiled sweets". It was approached from the village square by a long flight of stone steps. Next to it was a house that had seen better days, known as La Maison de Malaspina. The Malaspina family had been important in previous centuries and its members were buried in the chapel in the courtyard. Monsieur Malaspina, the present owner, was the village grocer. Napoleon had stayed in the house as a young man, but Monsieur Malaspina was loath to show the room where he had slept which was carefully preserved, or any part of the house, being ashamed of its dilapidated state.

A bar stood beside the church at the other end of the square. We went in and had a drink. In England Frank was tall, but here he towered above the Corsicans and immediately became the centre of interest. They asked him questions, which I interpreted as best I could, and watched, fascinated, as his professionalism came to the surface and, although he could not speak the language, he managed to make them laugh. This visibly pleased him and as we left he said, "Not bad, getting a laugh when you can't speak the language".

The trip had been made possible because Denis was in hospital having a major operation on his teeth. They had worked seven days a week for the last fifteen years, but now their scriptwriting partnership was running out of steam and Frank was wondering what to do, as he felt he was at a turning point in his career. Denis, who was a film buff, wanted to write films, but Frank did not feel it was for him. He wanted to write books, but for the moment could not see what to do or where to go. We talked about it till late into the night.

I managed to convey the necessary information to the mason and we returned to England. The weekend had been a revealing experience and was to have a far-reaching influence on the second half of my life.

Shortly after this, I was rehearsing a television play in a complex of rehearsal rooms in the middle of Soho, when one day after lunch, as I returned to rehearsal, the building seemed to be full of chorus girls who were coming in and out of a room on the first floor. As I passed it, I saw through the glass double doors, a row of people seated who were watching the girls audition. One of the people seated was fast asleep. Something about him seemed familiar; I looked again and realised it was Rex Deering. I went in and shook his shoulder; he looked up and an expression of panic crossed his face, no doubt a fear of debt collectors, but I quickly reassured him and we went into the corridor. He looked just the same. He told me he had written a play that was playing at the Chiswick Empire, an old music hall in West London, and invited me to see it that evening. He also explained that he was no longer Rex Deering, but had become Rex Howard, one of many name changes he practised throughout his life.

When I arrived at the Chiswick Empire that evening, the first thing I saw was a huge cut out of a woman with a colossal bosom that almost covered the front of the theatre. Underneath was the title, "Rochelle Lofting in 'Frying Tonight' by Rex Howard". I went to find Rex who was in the bar having a whisky before the performance. He took me to the box office and gave me a ticket and I went into the theatre. There was quite a large audience. The play was set in the living room behind a fish and chip shop. Rex played the owner of the shop and the plot concerned his daughter, whose over-developed mammary glands gave hope of her winning the Miss World Contest. Before the performance Rex had said, "I know she can't act, but when I saw that bosom, it didn't seem to matter". He was right; from her first entrance Miss Lofting quite literally carried all before her, as there did not seem to be a gag about her bosom that Rex had left unexploited. At one point he put a cup of coffee on it, as it might have been the mantelpiece – which it resembled. Then he turned, walked away to do something, before returning calmly to pick up his cup and continue the scene. The audience loved it and at the end I congratulated him, wished him luck and we parted.

I did not see him again, though I frequently met actors who had known him. One told me that he had been in one of his companies, which had toured Scotland. Arriving in Wick on a Sunday morning with the scenery and props, the stage-manager went to enquire about transport. When he returned, he told Rex that British Rail wanted eight pounds to take the scenery to the theatre. Rex, who was sitting on a skip, looked up and said, "If I had eight pounds I'd start another company." At the end of his career he was seen regularly sitting at the back of the bar room in "The Rovers Return", in Coronation Street.

For a short time Frank and Denis were installed in an office in the BBC as "comedy advisors", but Denis went off to write films and

Frank was appointed "Head of Comedy", a post specially created for him. He was looking for new material and knowing my interest in farce, asked if I would like to research old farces and write reports on them. The BBC paid me a small fee and, as I already had a reading ticket for the British Museum Reading Room, I was able to find several forgotten plays that had potential.

I had been looking for a better agent, and rang Spotlight and talked to Cary Ellison. Cary was a liaison man between the reps and the actors. He went everywhere and saw everything. He had seen me at Bristol and had told me to contact him when I returned to London. I had done so and since then he had been very helpful. On this occasion he took me out to lunch. He was full of a try-out of the most boring incomprehensible play he had seen the evening before. It was by someone called Harold Pinter. I said I knew him. It was called "The Birthday Party". On the subject of agents, he said there was an agent starting up who seemed to have good contacts and he would ring him. He was called Jimmy Laval. Jimmy was a small man in his forties with a nervous manner. He said he would like to work for me and I signed a contract. Jimmy turned out to be the most effective agent I ever had.

He had been born in South Africa. His father was Jewish and through him Jimmy was distantly related to several film producers and theatre managers. He had been to Blundells, the public school, and so had a foot in the old-boy network, and to crown all, he was a homosexual and so had entry into that society. For a theatrical agent, any of those three would have been helpful, but to have all three was the *nec plus ultra*. All the same, an agent needs means, and there again Jimmy was happily placed because his mother had remarried, and her husband was an elderly millionaire who had made his money by selling condoms by post under plain cover, discretion assured. He bought them for a farthing a gross and sold them at two shillings and sixpence for three.

Jimmy had begun as an impersonator on the music halls, where his imitation of Nellie Wallace had been a success. Unfortunately Nellie Wallace had died and his act had lost its appeal. He had produced

Beatrice Lillie at the Garrick Theatre in a revue, which had been a big success, but his calculations had been at fault and even when every seat in the house was sold, the show lost money. Added to these credentials, he was very funny and casting directors and producers enjoyed his company. He would take a casting director to see one of his clients in a play somewhere and end up in the bar drinking whisky with the members of the company and doing his Nellie Wallace act.

His agency got off to a good start when on the first day an actor went to see him and said that if he could guarantee him £3000 a year, he would sign with him. Jimmy looked at him and thought he looked a useful actor and decided to take the risk. When the actor left the office, Jimmy put a call through to Granada Television where they were setting up a new series about a Manchester street. The actor was engaged, became one of the stars of Coronation Street and then became the star of a spin-off series written round his character. With that one telephone call, Jimmy underwrote his agency for the rest of its existence. Ten per cent of Arthur Lowe's income throughout the sixties was enough to keep any agency comfortably afloat.

Peter Crouch did not seem to be doing much for Pauline since she had turned down the Twentieth Century contract, so she joined Jimmy too, and he got her several leading parts with Granada Television. Crouch was not doing much for Glenda at that time, either. She was working as a telephone switchboard operator and Roy was still being a barman. We would go to see them on a Sunday in the rooms at King Henry's Road. We would have lunch, which Glenda cooked, ending always with her speciality, Lemon Meringue Pie. I never see it on the menu today without thinking of her. She was very depressed at that time and we would go for walks and try to cheer her up. She would say that she could not see what she could play in the current theatre and I blush remembering telling her that I could see her playing one of those chirpy maids in Restoration comedy.

Pauline and I were both cast in a Granada production of Harley Granville-Barker's "The Madras House", whose cast included Veronica Turleigh. Veronica had been a star in the thirties when she had played in "The Laughing Woman" a play about Henri Gaudier

Brzeska, the Vorticist sculptor, with Stephen Haggard, a young actor who died in the war and who had written "The Craft of Comedy" with Athene Seyler. Since then, Veronica had starred in the film "The Horse's Mouth" with Alec Guinness whom she had converted to Catholicism – in between takes.

Veronica was married to James Laver, the well-known authority on the history of costume, and they had recently moved to a flat in Blackheath. James was away doing a lecture tour of American universities on the strength of having predicted the mini-skirt, a prediction based on his theory of the "moving erogenous zone", the notion that the centre of erogenous interest moves about, so that it was legs in the forties, breasts in the fifties and would be thighs in the sixties, Veronica suggested that when James returned we visit them in their new flat.

Graeme Muir, a BBC director with whom I had worked on several comedy shows, rang to say that Galton and Simpson had written a Comedy Playhouse for Frankie Howerd and they wanted me to do it with him. I told Graeme that I had worked with Frankie Howerd before, but that we had not hit it off. "Don't worry," he said, "it'll be different this time – he wants you too."

The script was set in an aeroplane with Frankie and me sitting side by side as passengers returning from holiday. He has bought a watch abroad and is worried about passing Customs. He behaves very suspiciously and begins asking me about it. I paint a discouraging picture but in the end offer to take the watch through for him. He gives it to me, but when we pass Customs I walk straight through with his watch and disappear, while the Customs officers make him undress and take his luggage to pieces.

The Galton and Simpson script was beautifully written and perfect for Frankie. He was on his best behaviour and we got on much better, Sitting next to him on two chairs in the rehearsal room at ten o'clock in the morning, I still felt it would be better if he had had a bath, he still wore his wig which looked as though the gannets had reared a couple more broods in it since I had last seen him, and glue was still running down his cheeks, but he was splendidly on form and very funny. That Comedy Playhouse was a turning point for Frankie, and after it his career really took off with "That Was the Week That Was," and a string of successes.

Graeme Muir also directed "Charley's Aunt" which Pauline and I had adapted for television. It had a very good cast, with Richard Briers as Babs, Colin Gorden as the colonel and Frank Pettingell as the Solicitor. There was not really a part for me, but Graeme insisted I play the Scout so that I could show them the traditional stage business and help with the comedy.

Soon after we had moved to Blackheath, my mother suggested we contact the Sandersons who lived there. Basil had been the recently qualified gynaecologist who had come to tea at Wenderton and spotted that Gladys was pregnant. Since those days his career had blossomed, with rooms in Harley Street. The family connection went back to his mother, Cecil, who was an old friend of my grandmother's and had the reputation of being equally difficult. So much so that the two families had from time to time packed both of them off to stay in a hotel somewhere so that everyone could have some peace. Basil, his wife Betty and their two children welcomed us warmly and we became close friends.

They had a house at Deal and one weekend we went down to stay with them. Basil had been a frequent visitor to Frognal when great-uncle George's daughters, Betty and Nina, were young and he was an eligible bachelor, so one afternoon I suggested we go to see Yaya. When we arrived at The Studio, we found Great-uncle George in his Morris 8 with the hood down and Edie at the wheel. He had bought the car in 1938 and true to his principles, had never considered changing it. The seats had been re-covered in red leather and the bodywork repainted and no doubt the engine had been renewed, but for him, it was the same car and he sat in it wearing his Burberry and check cap and smoking his pipe with an air of contentment, as he told us of Edie's triumph, of how she had outpaced his friend's butler in passing the driving test and how he had won his bet.

In the autumn of 1965, Stuart Allen was put on a Directors' Course. At the end of these courses, the student director had to direct a short piece and Stuart asked Pauline and me if we would write something and act in it for him.

A writer we both admired was N.F. Simpson. His "One-Way Pendulum" had starred George Benson at the Royal Court. Another of his plays, "A Resounding Tinkle" was set in the suburbs and featured a typical suburban couple, Bro and Middie Paradock, who dealt with life and events however outrageous and unexpected, with suburban phlegm. We decided to adapt part of it as a situation comedy; Pauline played Middie and I played Bro. Stuart with his several years of working on situation comedy directed it with a nice fluidity and it got a very good reaction in the studio.

Afterwards, the three of us had dinner in a Greek Cypriot restaurant in Soho and over dinner we told Stuart he really must become a director, as it was clear he had real talent. He said that to do so he needed a script to propose. Could we write something for him?

In fact, we had been trying to think of an idea for some time, but nothing had worked. The problem was that in the nineteen-sixties it was becoming almost impossible to write farce because farce has to do with transgression and in order to transgress there needs to be a clear set of rules. Feydeau in late nineteenth-century France and the Aldwych farces in England in the nineteen-thirties could both rely on a rigid set of rules that everyone in their societies subscribed to. But in the nineteen-sixties the sound of breaking rules was deafening: long accepted conventions were being dismantled one after another: in France the war cry of the *soixante-huitards: "Il est interdit d'interdire!"* was already being heard. True there remained institutions like the armed forces or hospitals, but they had all been exploited and did not appeal to us.

We turned to Stuart and asked if he had any ideas. He said he had been wondering about the old joke "As the actress said to the Bishop"; a Bishop who has a niece who is a stripper" Turning to me, he said, "You know about bishops." As soon as he said the word 'bishop', bells began to ring in my head. I realised that this was a world I knew about, and which no one had attempted. Moreover, if a society existed where there were still rules, and rules that everyone subscribed to, it was the church.

We agreed to go away and think about it.

However, when we began to examine the idea, it did not hold water. The niece was too lightweight; so we regretfully decided there was no mileage in it. But the idea of a bishop would not go away. I went to Lewisham library and looked up "Church of England" and found a book recently published by the Archdeacon of Hastings, Guy Mayfield, "Like Nothing on Earth", in which he explained the structure of the Church of England. How the Dean and the Bishop are both Crown appointments for life, how the Dean is responsible for the Cathedral and how the Bishop, whose throne is in the Cathedral, cannot in theory enter the building without the permission of the Dean. He, the Bishop, is responsible for the diocese and its clergy and his Archdeacon is responsible for the church buildings.

Reading "Like Nothing on Earth", I was back in Canterbury with Archbishop Fisher and the "Red" Dean, Dr Hewlett Johnson D.D., to whom Archbishop Fisher refused to speak. A bishop and a dean, who hate each other but are tied together for life and cannot escape, like some terrible married couple, is what is known in dramaturgy as "the unity of opposites" and is a perfect set-up for comedy. We began to picture them: the Bishop, easy going, fond of comfort in a beautiful eighteenth-century palace, the Dean, a humourless martinet, like Augustus Hare's Uncle, Julius Hare, in a stark gothic deanery. The Archdeacon, an older, worldlier character, former chaplain at Parkhurst, and the Bishop's chaplain, whom we based on my old school friend, Gordon Rhodes, and which I thought would be a perfect part for me. What was needed was a story. We racked our brains without success, then one night I went to bed but could not sleep as I turned the characters over and over. I had been re-reading Osbert Sitwell's autobiography, "Left Hand Right Hand" with its portrait of his father, Sir George Sitwell, and his passion for the middle Ages and its customs. Suppose, I thought, suppose a rich man like Sir George were to leave a large sum of money to the Cathedral on condition that the Dean and Chapter revive a mediaeval ceremony which forces the Bishop to do something he does not want to. As the night wore on the idea continued to take shape. The Bishop must find twenty virgins; he must ride round the diocese on a white horse dressed as a simple monk with his chaplain walking beside him and give twenty pairs of white stockings to twenty virgins. In 1965 girls were wearing miniskirts with white stockings and the advent of the Pill had greatly reduced the number of virgins. They would have to find a horse and buy the stockings, the Dean would insist the Bishop did it because the Norman tower was in bad shape and they desperately needed the money. The problem was how to end it, where to find the virgins? Morning light was filtering through the curtains; Pauline stirred, I said, "Listen, I've got it but I can't end it." I told her the plot and she said one word, "Novices" – and we were home and dry.

As Frank Muir was now head of comedy at the BBC, we did not want to embarrass him by putting him in the position of having to refuse it, so we sent the script, entitled "The Bequest" under the pen name of John Wraith. Some days passed and I got a call from Stuart. Nothing had come of his test no one had seen it and he would have to go back to floor managing in Manchester in two days. He was terribly depressed and said that the Director's Course was nothing more than a cynical device the BBC used to stop the staff getting impatient; – people were sent on a course, given a bit of hope and then sent back to get on with what they were doing.

We were shocked, because he had really done a good job on the piece and it seemed very unfair. After much hesitation I rang Frank and told him about it. "Leave it to me", he said. We heard no more for some time and then one day just before Christmas, Frank rang. He said they had seen Stuart's test and had invited N.F. Simpson to see it. Mr Simpson had liked it and liked us as Middie and Bro, so the BBC had commissioned him to write a series of three episodes for us to do on BBC 2, the new channel, recently opened and run by David Attenborough. Then Frank said he gathered we were *"Mr Wraith"* and that everyone had read "The Bequest" and liked it, and it had been decided to do it as a "Comedy Playhouse". Stuart, he added, would produce both shows.

  So it was party time.

—

CHAPTER TWENTY-THREE

Nineteen sixty-six was our year. It began with our meeting N.F. Simpson, or "Wally" as everyone called him, who proved to be one of the most endearing and original people we had known.

Wally never saw things as other people did, but had his own take on the world. On one occasion he told us how he had been called for jury service. "It was," he said, "obvious from the first that the accused was guilty, but the barristers went on nattering away for days about minor points of law before the judge summed up and we returned a verdict of Guilty. Then, he continued, "just when it got interesting, and when there really needed to be a discussion as to what was best to be done with him, the Judge said "six months" and the next case was called."

"Three Rousing Tinkles", the three scripts he wrote for us, were original and very funny. In one, Bro and Middie Paradock get a letter saying that their garden shed has been designated a building of historic interest and immediately begin to worry about the fuss it will be showing people round. In another, they have been feeding the dog on cat food and the cat on dog food, which causes the dog to become a cat and the cat to become a dog while the budgerigar and the canary suffer the same fate, as do the rabbit and the hamster. That evening in the studio was memorable for the quantity of animals on the set, almost all tied by one leg to a piece of furniture to stop them attacking another member of the cast, while an army of animal handlers hovered outside every opening, ready to pounce to save their livestock should it be attacked.

The press was generally good, Philip Purser in the "Sunday Times", while regretting the presence of a studio audience, found there were

"sheer felicities of misunderstanding and the playing of Miss Pauline Devaney and Mr Edwin Apps was everything it should be, accurate, disciplined, splendidly timed and quintessentially suburban ..."

The Telegraph headline was:

"Comedy which has a lot in common with the best silent films" and The Stage ended its criticism after the second episode with:

"Is there only one more rousing tinkle to come? Surely not, Mr. Simpson. We can't let Middie and Bro depart from our screens for good. Why not make it twenty or thirty Rousing Tinkles?"

In the event the BBC commissioned Wally to write four more, which we did the following year. But after that he felt he had had enough of writing to deadlines, so the project ended there.

In the meantime, plans were going ahead for the production of "The Bequest".

The first thing Frank said when it came to casting was that I could not play Noote, the chaplain. "You'll never do it", he said. In any case the BBC liked to have established stars and preferably those who were used to working together, so the first suggestion was Alastair Sim and George Cole as Noote. I was unhappy with the idea, feeling that Alastair Sim would be better cast as the Moderator of the Church of Scotland, than a Church of England Bishop. Fortunately, when he read it, he turned it down as being too funny, saying that he had to have scripts that were not funny so that he could make them funny. Frank's next suggestion was Robert Morley and Wilfred Hyde-White. I told him that we had to believe that these men pray and I could not imagine either of them praying except on the racecourse when their horse was being overtaken. Then someone came up with the name William Mervyn, which seemed a better idea and Stuart suggested Robertson Hare as the Archdeacon. For the Dean, we wanted John Barron. We had seen him in a play Geoffrey Lumsden had written in which he had been very funny as a manic headmaster and, if I could not play Noote, I told Frank the right person was Derek Nimmo. We had often been up for the same part and although I saw him as a rival, I admired him. So it was decided.

A short time before rehearsals began, Frank said he would like to go through the script with us and would we come in to the Television Centre one afternoon. It was arranged and he told his secretary that on no account were we to be disturbed. He then went through the script with us line by line.

It was a crash course in comedy writing, a distillation and the fruit of his long years writing with Denis. It was in the detail that he was so revealing, the principle of always having one more surprise up your sleeve and never letting a weak line pass. An example of the way he worked comes at the opening of the script. The Archdeacon arrives at the Palace and is greeted by Noote. He asks how the Bishop is, and Noote says he is very excited:

ARCHDEACON: I'm not surprised? Sixty thousand pounds would excite anyone. Mind you, he'll need it. The Norman tower is in a shocking state; death watch beetle.

NOOTE: Won't you come into the study?

ARCHDEACON: Thank you Noote. You know that noise they make is a love call?

NOOTE: The death watch beetles?

ARCHDEACON: Yes. They make it by raising themselves on their hind legs and beating their heads rhythmically against whatever they happen to be standing on.

NOOTE: How extraordinary. There doesn't seem much point.

ARCHDEACON: The females find it sexually attractive.

NOOTE: Really? This way, Archdeacon...

THE STUDY

NOOTE: (*ENTERING*) The Archdeacon, my Lord.

BISHOP: Morning Henry, How are you?

NOOTE: The Archdeacon has been telling me about the beetles, my Lord.

BISHOP: Really?

NOOTE: Yes. Did you know they make that noise by beating their heads against the floor?"

(We had written)

"BISHOP: I'm not surprised

ARCHDEACON: They do it to attract the females.

BISHOP: I was aware of that, Henry."

Frank pointed out that a line like "I'm not surprised" was dead weight, it did not add anything to the situation and he suggested changing it to;

"BISHOP: Really? My niece told me they use guitars and drums".

This makes it clear he is talking about the Beatles and we learn that the Bishop has a niece who is trying to keep him up to date for good measure.

During that afternoon we discussed the title and Frank suggested "The Bishop Rides Again" which we liked and agreed to, and it was under that title it was produced.

Just before the first reading, Stuart asked me to go with "Bunny" Hare to the costumiers and see him fitted for the Archdeacon. The costumier took him to a dressing room and when they emerged with Bunny in breeches and gaiters and the clerical morning coat of an Archdeacon, I felt certain we had a success on our hands.

At the first reading, several of the actors seeing me and Derek Nimmo both appear, thought the BBC had double-booked the part of Noote, and there were a lot of knowing looks. When they realised that Pauline and I were John Wraith, there was general surprise. The first thing Derek Nimmo said to me was, "You wrote this part for yourself, didn't you?" Thereafter, if ever I suggested something to him he would say, "You might play it like that, but I've got my own ideas." Pauline found a similar difficulty with William Mervyn who refused to listen to advice from a woman even if she were the author. Faced with their intransigence, we resorted to getting each other to give our notes. Pauline would say "Will you tell Bill ..." and I would say "Tell Derek ..." a ruse that worked perfectly

We went to the outside filming, where Stuart gave us the job of stopping the traffic. "What's this for?" asked the first motorist I stopped. I explained it was a Comedy Playhouse for the BBC. "Well I hope it's funnier than that load of shit they put out last night," was the disgruntled reply as I waved him on. It was a wet day, which enabled Stuart to get some very funny shots of Derek's sandalled feet splashing through puddles and the Bishop riding the horse while

holding up an umbrella. In the script the Archdeacon follows them
in his car and, with memories of great-uncle George, I had insisted
on an open Morris 8. Robertson Hare had never learned to drive ("I
never dared ... Suppose I were to run someone down? I could see the
headlines: "Oh Calamity!") So a team of men, out of shot, pushed
and pulled the car with ropes.

As soon as rehearsals began to shape up, it was clear that we had
the perfect cast. Bill Mervyn with his splendid appearance and solid
personality was the anchor, Bunny Hare his inimitable self and Derek
Nimmo endlessly inventive. I saw at once how right Frank had been
in not letting me play the part. Had I done so, I should have played
it as written, because, after all, I had written it. Derek, coming to it
from outside, brought another whole conception of the part which
I could never have done, and John Barron's Dean was the perfect
menace for the others to bounce off.

Rehearsals went well and the night of the recording a professional
entertainer did a warm up, Pauline and I introduced the actors and
then we went to sit behind Stuart in the box. The audience laughed
in all the right places and there was a crackle of electricity about
the evening as though everyone felt we had a success on our hands.
Afterwards, in the bar, Ray Galton and Alan Simpson and various
directors congratulated us and we went to Kensington with Frank
and Polly for dinner. As we crossed the road towards the restaurant, Frank asked if we felt we could do a series. We told him we felt
we could and the following day we had a meeting with the Head of
Light Entertainment, Tom Sloan. I had, of course, often met Tom
Sloan during "WhackO" when he was Assistant to the former Head
of Light Entertainment, Eric Maschwitz. Maschwitz was a rich and
colourful character, the author of many successful plays and musicals and two songs that marked a generation, "A Nightingale Sang
in Berkley Square" and "These Foolish Things". Sloan, a typical
ex-army BBC manager, had trotted along beside him. Now he had
replaced him and the style had changed. At the meeting, he treated us
as though we had just been promoted to the rank of corporal and told

us our responsibilities. We were to write six episodes in six months for £500 a script.

The question then arose as to what the series should be called, Stuart wanted "Oh, Bishop!" but I had in mind a biography I had read of Dean Inge, a famous Dean of St Paul's, in which he was quoted as saying that the trouble with the Church of England was that it was "all gas and gaiters". I suggested "Gas and Gaiters" as the title to Frank and Stuart, but they did not seem impressed until Frank, thinking about it said, "It will work if you keep the "all", so we decided on "All Gas and Gaiters".

"The Bishop Rides Again" was transmitted on the 17th May and in the event the press and public reaction was all we could have hoped for.

"Great triumph on TV for Robertson Hare"
was the Telegraph headline

"This first play in the 1966 Comedy Playhouse series was remarkable for the emergence of Mr Robertson Hare at 70 plus in his first real attempt at television comedy. In fact, Mr Hare found himself a contributor with William Mervyn and Derek Nimmo to one of the richest comedy trios TV has uncovered for some time. It was for him a complete and personal triumph"

Mary Crozier in *The Guardian*:
"Whoever he may be, John Wraith is fertile in invention and gave us a constant explosion of comic situations ...Robertson Hare's mischievous and plummy Archdeacon. His simplest phrases such as "Oh, thank you," are still pronounced inimitably. One might indeed echo, "Oh, thank you" for this proof that television can produce farce with such style and vigour".

So now we just had the problem of writing six more.

✳

The day after the showing, I was due to begin shooting an episode of "The Avengers", "The Correct Way to Kill". I played an umbrella salesman who tested the umbrellas in a shower dressed in a fisherman's bright yellow waterproof. At the end I was found dead in the shower skewered by an umbrella. Interestingly, I had to die twice, once with my eyes open for the European market and once with my eyes closed for the American – in 1966 the American public was too squeamish to accept a corpse with its eyes open. Most of the cast had seen "The Bishop Rides Again" on the previous evening and were very encouraging.

I liked Patrick McNee, who was great fun, and we had lunch together every day except one, when he said he had discovered that Christopher Lee was working on the next lot. They had been at prep school together and had not met since. It was amusing to think of Steed and Dracula having a quiet lunch together.

Pauline and I were not the only couple for whom things were happening. Since their marriage, Roy had always refused to let Glenda go out of London to work in rep, but, in 1965, seeing how depressed she was getting, he finally relented and allowed her to go to do a play in Perth. Quite by chance a director from the Royal Court Theatre was producing the next play and when he returned to London he met Peter Brook, who was forming an experimental company with a new approach and looking for promising people with whom he could work. The director mentioned that he had just seen a girl in Perth, Brook listened and Glenda was sent for and put under contract. At first they worked in private and then they gave a Saturday night performance to an invited audience in which Glenda played a sketch based on Christine Keeler, during which she stripped naked in front of the audience. It was the first time a serious actress had done such a thing.

The following day Pauline and I were going to do a play at Rotherham with the director Geoffrey Edwards and on the train he was full of how extraordinary it had been and how naturally Glenda had played it.

While we were in Rotherham, we were shown round a steel mill.

The visit was an eye-opener. The mill gave the impression of being a period piece; nothing had apparently changed since the nineteenth – one might almost say the eighteenth – century. Steel is rolled out between rollers while it is white-hot until the rods thin down to the right diameter. Modern requirements needed longer rolling mills than previously and continental firms had modernised their factories and elongated their mills, but the British manufacturers had not made the necessary investment, so the steel rods had to be turned round and sent back through a parallel mill. This involved catching the white hot rods, which were about fifteen feet in length, with tongs, swinging them round and aiming them so that they went in between the rollers on the return mill. The rods came out at considerable speed and had to be turned round and sent back in one movement before the next rod emerged. If the rod was badly aimed and did not go between the rollers but hit them and a moment was lost, the next rod of white hot metal emerged and went straight into the back of the operator. As we saw, boys did the work and we were told two had been killed in the last few months. In response to the question why boys accepted such a dangerous job, we were told it was well paid at twelve pounds a week.

The visit to the mill showed how run-down British manufacture was. There was a general feeling that we had won the war and no more effort was needed. In spite of tax benefits, the industrialists had made little or no effort to invest, preferring to pocket the money. I had met industrialists at Aunty Peggy and Uncle George's cocktail parties where I often heard it said that what the country needed was a good dose of unemployment to bring the working class to its senses.

*

As Glenda now had a regular income, she and Roy decided to buy a flat. They had come to see us often in Blackheath and decided to try and find a flat for sale near us. They found one in Coleraine Road and moved in. Soon after, Brook decided to do Peter Weiss's Marat/Sade, a play within a play based on the idea that the Marquis de Sade wrote and produced a play about Marat with the inmates of the Lunatic Asylum at Charenton while he himself was an inmate. Glenda was cast as the patient playing Charlotte Corday, the girl who assassinated Marat in his bath. It was produced at the Aldwych Theatre and we went to the dress rehearsal. Glenda, playing a role within a role in a play within a play, was brilliant and when we got home Pauline said, "I see. It is going to be, Dame Glenda." The play, and in particular Glenda's performance, took the town by storm.

As we often had to go to the Television Centre, it occurred to us that it would be a good idea to go by car so we could continue to talk on the journey. As neither of us could drive, we decided to take driving lessons. When it came to the test, I failed but Pauline passed.

Roy and Glenda had also just learned to drive and had bought an elderly Metropolitan, a curious vehicle, which felt more like being in a boat than a car. Now that the Marat/Sade was to transfer to New York, they offered to lend it to us while they were away.

The problem was that although she had a licence, Pauline felt she was not ready to drive while I, thanks to my father's lessons on the marshes near Sittingbourne, was able to drive but did not have a licence. So we decided I should drive with her sitting beside me and if stopped, we would say she was giving me lessons. We were stopped on one occasion when I had forgotten to put the lights on, and the policeman obviously thought the situation fishy, but he let us go. As soon as I could I took the test again and passed, while in the meantime Pauline gained confidence and we bought a second-hand Volkswagen Beetle, with which we drove triumphantly to the Television Centre and parked it in front of the building beside the expensive-looking cars belonging to the Heads of this and that.

Now that we were mobile, Frank and Polly offered to lend us the flat in Monticello so that we could write in peace, an offer we accepted gratefully. So, at the end of May, having just passed the driving test, we packed the car with everything including the ancient Underwood typewriter we had bought and set out for Corsica.

We spent a night with Armand Desenclos in Calais. Now married to Thérèse and with two growing children, he had taken over his mother's hat-shop and was selling wedding-dresses. From there we decided to take our time and follow the course of the Rhône.

It was a happy decision because we saw a France that was fast disappearing. We ate in small restaurants and stayed in little country hotels. We soon learned that the best guide was a television aerial. If the hotel or restaurant had one, it was to be avoided. If it did not, there was every chance you would find home-cured ham, vegetables from the garden, home-made *pâté*, a four-poster bed with a feather mattress and a real country welcome at a reasonable price. A television aerial usually meant that an attempt had been made to modernise both the establishment and the bill. In 1966 there were very few aerials to be seen as we went down the Rhône.

At Marseille we took the ferry for Bastia and from there, drove across the island to Monticello, where we installed ourselves in the Muirs' flat, now finished and comfortably furnished.

Writing comedy is very hard work and however beautiful the setting in which you do it, it remains very hard work. Although we had told Frank we felt capable of writing a series and we had a few ideas, we did not have anything as concrete as a plot. Moreover the fact that "The Bishop Rides Again" had met with such success made the prospect of following it extremely daunting. We slogged away as idea after idea bit the dust and proved to be unworkable. Our underlying anxiety is evident in a letter to my mother on June 18th 1966;

"We have been struggling on with the first script. It has been a bit heartbreaking – but at last we think we see a way we to make it work, – but if they're all going to be such a grind, we shall need another holiday before September. In fact this isn't really a holiday at all – I mean it's lovely to be here and we have a couple of hours on the beach each day and a nice swim – but the work has been so slow that we have felt guilty about spending any more time away from it – and being in such a lovely place, it is a bit tantalising. But we feel it was wise to come, because on the whole there are far fewer distractions than there would have been at home and we are getting an average of six or eight hours solid work every day – weekends and all - which must pay off and would be impossible at home with the 'phone, television, friends etc. ... This really is the most beautiful island. It has such wonderful variety. By the coast it is brown, sandy, with just the green grey olive trees and brown grey shrubs – gorse and that sort of thing and rocks. Then as you get up into the mountains, the scenery changes completely, becoming almost Swiss with Pine forests, blue grey mountains – some of which still have snow on them – and hay fields, orchards and an almost English green – with great chestnuts. Nobody seems to bother much about farming – but everywhere you are liable to hear tinkling bells and find a flock of the 'brebis' or ewes – little tiny delicate creatures milked to make Rocquefort cheese. They are always accompanied by a shepherd. The two most striking things are the light, which is extraordinarily bright and clear and the blue of the sea which is like no picture of it you have ever seen. Everywhere the wild flowers, honeysuckle, cyclamen and many, many species we don't know but which are not unlike garden flowers you see in England, grow wild – and the extraordinary smell of the maquis – a mixture of thyme, rosemary, myrtle and many others – which remind one very faintly of curry powder – is always in the air.

Everyone gets up very early – four or five o'clock. It is impossible to stay in bed after it gets hot – and all work is done by lunch time. Then they have their main meal and for the next two or three hours they sleep, here on the beach or sit outside the cafés under the trees. This mid-day heat is really a force to be reckoned with, and one simply cannot ignore it – it gets you. Then from four till six or seven they do a bit more work and then they begin to appear in the square again – the men play "boules" a sort of bowls and the women sit in their doorways and watch. People sit at the cafés drinking their Pastis and so it goes on – very restful.

Monday:

A marvellous day! We have really broken through with the script and got some really funny stuff – waves of relief – Just going to post..."

In fact an idea had emerged in which the Bishop returns to his old school each year to preach on Founder's Day. The preceding year, he had lost his sermon and had had to resort of communal hymn singing, a calamity that had left his old headmaster, Dr Pragnell, never his admirer, even less impressed. This time he takes enormous care over his sermon, and although it is not in the same league as the one on the Book of Daniel, that he lost, he is confident that he will at last win the approval of his old headmaster, but just as he is leaving, he finds he has lost this one too. He searches furiously while Noote and the Archdeacon make him relive every moment before the loss, until they discover he has put it in the lining of his top hat. What is more, the missing sermon on Daniel is there too. It took me a long time to convince Pauline that it was possible to put something inside the lining of a top hat and she remained doubtful until we returned to England and she could investigate the inside of a top hat for herself.

We enjoyed our stay in Monticello and got to know several of the villagers. They were friendly and hospitable. The village, like all the villages around, is perched on a hilltop, so getting from village to village without a car is a tedious business. On one occasion we took the daughter of a neighbouring family to the next village to see her aunt and uncle. It was the first time she had been out of Monticello in her life and her evident relief when we got back that evening was palpable; *"Monticello, Monticello!"* she kept intoning as we approached. Her aunt and uncle had given us a generous welcome which had begun with the thing they were most proud of, a glass of their well water.

One of the nicest things about Corsica, as I described in my letter to my mother, are the three climates and it was a great treat, when even Monticello became hotter than one could bear, to drive up into the mountains. On one occasion as we were walking in the forest following a mountain stream, we came across a French couple in great distress because the wife had dropped her new and very expensive spectacles in a pool. They were clearly visible at the bottom of the pool, but well out of reach. I offered to dive for them, but when I hit the water, it was icy cold and took my breath away. I missed the spectacles the first time, had another go and missed again and it was only on the third attempt that I managed to pick them up. I emerged blue with cold and they took me down the mountain to a bar and bought me a cognac.

Back in England we settled down seriously to write the remaining five scripts of the series. In writing Noote, we had based him on my friend Gordon Rhodes and had asked ourselves, how he would react, or what he would say. Now we turned to him for technical advice. Although he had been turned down by the Church, he was a mine of information on the subject and we sent him all the scripts for his comments. We did not dare tell him that he was Noote, though I suspect that he guessed.

At the same time, Frank put us in touch with Church House and we had a contact there we could ring at any time, fire questions at and test ideas on. On one occasion we wanted the Bishop to try to get rid of the Dean and asked how he might go about it. Our contact explained that the Ecclesiastical Appointments Secretary – whose job it is to spot the rising stars and keep the Prime Minister informed about problems in the Church – has an office in Number Ten Downing Street. He added that when, in 1956, at the height of the cold war the Russian leaders, Kruschev and Bulganin, came to London to meet the Macmillan government, at a delicate moment in the negotiations, the Russian leaders asked for a room where they could talk privately. Space, it seems, is in short supply in Number Ten, and the officials, looking desperately for a free room and finding the Ecclesiastical Appointments Secretary absent, ushered the two Russian leaders into his office. But the Ecclesiastical Appointments Secretary was not absent. He had had his customary excellent lunch at the Athenaeum Club, and was having a nap in his private lavatory. He woke to hear Russian being spoken and, realising what had happened, sat petrified for fear of being discovered. Had he been, the diplomatic repercussions might well have changed the course of history.

Our Church House contact was a great help; after all, neither of us had ever met a bishop or been in a bishop's palace. So it was very gratifying when we began getting letters from bishops saying, "How did you know that? It is exactly what happened to me yesterday". We also got quite a lot of letters from cranks, which the BBC replied to on our behalf.

The series was watched by between four-and-a-half million and five-and-a-half million viewers and warmly received by the public, although some critics thought the criticism of the Church was too mild. As we had never intended to write a biting satire, but rather a series of farces set in a Cathedral precinct, the criticism was beside the point. It took some time for the true nature of the series to sink in and it was not until the following series in December 1967 that Maurice Wiggin, the Sunday Times critic, showed that he had grasped it by saying;

> "The revival of All Gas And Gaiters" also revives arguments
> that it should be more stringently satirical, should knock the
> clergy harder. But how could it? Merely by perpetuating the
> image of useless, daffy parsons living in a dream-world it hits
> the Church about as hard as it could be hit"

When the series ended, it was repeated and again got excellent press and viewing figures.

In the meantime we were enjoying life in Blackheath. Since we had done the play in Manchester with Veronica Turleigh, James Laver had returned from his American lecture tour and we had been to see them.

Their flat was on the first floor of a large Victorian house. It had a large living-room with a dining-table at one end with a set of painted Regency dining-chairs. Veronica had the main bedroom and James a study in which he slept. On our first visit, he showed us this and, indicating a bookcase full of books, said, "My books." I was just beginning to think that I had more books than that, when I realised that he meant they were the books he had written. There were over a hundred.

The expression "an enquiring mind" might have been coined for James Laver. He was interested in everything and seemed to go to any lengths to find out about things. On one occasion he admitted to being a witch, "Don't tell Veronica!" (Veronica was a fervent Roman Catholic) He had gone through the process of becoming a witch because he wanted to attend a black mass to see what actually happened.

At Oxford he had won the Newdigate poetry prize for a poem on Cervantes. A second lieutenant in the Great War, he arrived in France on Armistice Day and burst into tears at the thought that he had missed the war. He joined the Victoria and Albert Museum where he had been head of the Engraving, Illustration, Design and Painting section, written a best seller, "Nymph Errant" which became a successful musical put on by Cochran with music by Cole Porter and starring Gertrude Lawrence. Deciding to read all the books on the Occult in the London Library, he became a specialist on the subject. He also wrote the lives of Oscar Wilde, Nostradamus and the painters James Tissot and James Whistler.

He said that just thinking of all he had done made him tired. We became friends with James and Veronica and saw a lot of them during the next few years. They were a remarkable couple who could not from all appearances have anything in common; Veronica an unbending Irish Catholic and James, if not a pagan – for the word pagan still has something of the country about it and James was essentially urban – a total unbeliever. "To think they call it a discipline!" he would exclaim with disgust whenever theology was mentioned. He had himself studied it at Oxford and had written a thesis on Wesley. For her part, Veronica disapproved of his writing books about fashion and claimed that she had not read any of them, adding, with a lofty air, "I married a poet."

At the time when we were settling down to write a second series of "All Gas And Gaiters", The Independent Television Authority was handing out new licences and various financial groups were looking forward to getting their snouts in the trough. In order to do so, they needed well-known people to front their demand. A group calling itself "London Weekend Television" approached Frank Muir and offered him money and shares to become its head of Light Entertainment. An innocent in the hands of such people and

believing their assurances that they were only interested in producing high-quality television, Frank accepted.

When he announced his decision to the BBC, Tom Sloan gave
him two hours to leave the building and from that moment his name
was no longer to be mentioned. (His position as an entertainer was,
of course not in question. As a household name, the BBC managers
could not afford to lose him, however cross they might be).

Frank asked us to go with him, but we could not take "All Gas
and Gaiters" and, not only were we enjoying writing it, but we felt
the series had a lot more life in it. Besides, we were not enthusiastic
about writing half-hour comedy for Independent Television with its
break in the middle for commercials that ruins the concentration of
the audience.

A new Head of Comedy was appointed, Michael Mills, a Light
Entertainment director.

At his first director's meeting, Stuart told us that one of his first
announcements was that "All Gas And Gaiters" would be dropped
after the current series and that the series would not, as planned, be
recorded in colour but in black and white. Stuart was worried by this,
as he said it would affect overseas sales, it seemed that Mr Mills was
sweeping with a new broom and did not want anything left by his
predecessor.

I knew Michael Mills quite well, although I was not particularly
drawn to him. He had been in the Navy and he directed in an author-
itative manner that I found inimical to creative invention. He had
been one of the instigators of the series based on P.G. Wodehouse's
"Bertie Wooster" stories and I had been involved in the early stages
when Frank had invited me to read the part of Bertie at a brain-storm-
ing session to decide how to do it. One of the problems had been how
to introduce the series and I had mentioned how much I admired
the opening credits of an American series about a family who had
found oil on their farm and become rich. The whole background
story had been covered quickly and amusingly behind the credits so
that anyone seeing an episode for the first time would understand
it. I suggested that Bertie should be seen driving through Mayfair

with Jeeves beside him, waving to his aunts etc. The suggestion was accepted and the credits were filmed along those lines.

Now, Pauline and I were summoned to meet Mr Mills. When we arrived in Frank's old office, Mills was sitting at the desk, while two men were busy laying an extra width of carpet round the perimeter of the room. Seeing our puzzlement, Mills explained that the post of Head of Comedy had been upgraded and he was therefore entitled to a bigger carpet.

The post of Head of Comedy had been created especially for Frank Muir so that writers like us could have the benefit of his advice and help in writing comedy scripts. Logically the post should have disappeared with him, but the BBC had decided not only to appoint a director – whose skills however great must essentially be interpretive rather than creative and unlikely to be helpful to writers – but also to upgrade it, or in other words, pay him more.

Our interview with Mills was short; he did not say that he was going to drop the show, but confined himself to a naval style lecture on how important it was to meet the deadlines for the scripts. We saluted and left.

After the news that Mills wanted to kill off the series and that it was not to be done in colour, came a further blow; John Barron was in a West-end play that was going to Broadway and he would not be available to play the Dean. We hunted round for a replacement and came up with Ernest Clark. Ernest had been in "The Player King" and we had remained friends. He was an excellent, thoughtful actor.

Looking for ideas, we had visited several cathedrals and had been to stay with Gordon, who was working on a newspaper in Norwich. Going round Norwich Cathedral, we noticed that the bishop's throne had been moved from the choir and placed behind the high altar. This gave us the idea for the first episode of the series, "The Dean Goes Primitive", in which the dean is preaching a long and boring sermon on the subject of the Primitive Church and the bishop, well concealed behind thick curtains on his throne in the choir, is heard snoring. The archdeacon in his stall at the back with his hearing aid in place listens intently – to the Beatles, the hearing aid being a transistor, "a present from my aunt."

The Dean, furious with the Bishop, decides to get his own back by moving the throne up behind the altar in full view of everyone so that the Bishop can no longer go to sleep.

Pauline left me to write the sermon, a pleasure I felt I had deserved after sitting through so many boring sermons during my schooldays:

"And so we see throughout the history of the Primitive Church, according not only to the testimony of Eusebius of Caesarea and to some extent Socrates Scholasticus, but also to the writings of such popular authors as Hermias, Sozomenus, Theodoret, not to mention Lactantius... Epiphanus, Hieronymus, Theodoret of Cyrus, Philostorgius, Nicephorus, Callistius, Lector, Paul Warnfried and the Venerable Bede. In all these authors we find the same emphasis on simplicity, stark, joyous simplicity. It was both the keynote and the watchword of the Primitive Church. Even in modern times, as recently as the year eleven hundred and seventy when the blessed Bishop Ogg built this cathedral, it too, was characterised by this same simplicity, stark, joyous simplicity. But where is this simplicity today? Alas, we find little evidence of it here – everywhere, comfort, luxury, opulence abound; we must renounce it, we must return to the stark joyous etc..."

Stuart built St Ogg's Cathedral for a thousand pounds at Denham film studios and, to our delight, we saw our characters in full canonicals processing with choir boys and vergers.

Learning the sermon with the list of Church Fathers was a baptism of fire for Ernest, but he did it splendidly and the episode got the series off to a good start.

According to the Stage on the 14th December 1967,

"The BBC's top audience for November was for Miss World 1967; it was seen by 26 million viewers. The highest Miss World audience so far recorded. ... The Steptoe repeats continued to attract audiences of about 14 million and the new series of All Gas and Gaiters opened with 10 million viewers."

On December 16th we crept for the first time into the Top Twenty, in 19th place, equal with Steptoe and Son and Petula Clark. By the 12th January we were at 6th place with 6.6 million homes viewing,, above the Ken Dodd show (6.45) Christmas Night with the stars (6.16) and even Morcambe and Wise (5.56)...

On the 10th January, the Daily Mail:

"BBC claims victory in viewing figures ... BBC TV average audience last month was 8,600,000 against ITV 7,550,000. Apart from special Christmas shows, BBC-1's top viewing programmes were the Val Doonican Show, which was seen by 16.5 million when it ended on Dec. 30th, Dixon of Dock Green (more than 13 million) and "All Gas and Gaiters" (10.5 million).

By the 25th January we were 2nd in the top 5 Comedy series still with 6.6 million homes viewing, ahead of Steptoe and Son with 6.1 million. It looked as though Mr Mills would have difficulty getting rid of us.

*

The series had made people aware that the dignitaries of the church were still wearing a form of eighteenth-century dress. It was as though everyone had known it, but no one had considered whether or not it was appropriate. Suddenly it became a subject for discussion and I was asked to be on the Sunday night religious programme, "Meeting Point", hosted by Derek Hart, to discuss the question. It was heavily puffed in advance;

"The News of the World":

"Edwin Apps who writes those delicately micky-taking scripts for the "All Gas and Gaiters" series, faces churchmen and a psychiatrist when he appears in BBC 1's "Meeting Point". The title for this religious programme sounds suspiciously like Mr Apps; "Bury the rev".

While the *Liverpool Echo* asked,

"So what will Edwin – also well-known as an actor – have to say about the revs?"

In the event, I went along to the BBC studio at about half-past five on the Sunday evening where I found Derek Hart suffering from a bad hangover. The other participants were a high-minded low churchman and a modest high-churchman. The low churchman had a teleprompter from which he read a long-winded, high-minded text, and then went on to monopolise the discussion so that the high-churchman and I had to battle to get a word in edgeways. Derek Hart was too busy with his hangover to be an effective chairman, so at the end the high-churchman and I got the impression that it was game, set and match to the low churchman. However, the *Church of England Newspaper*, which no one could accuse of being high church, put him in his place:

> "Then Daniel Jenkins D.D., who quite properly objects to being called "Reverend Jenkins" proceeded to inveigh against "the proliferation of grandiloquent titles" in the Church (I wonder if he minds being called Doctor Jenkins?) He described titles and distinctive dress as "impediments from the past" and declared that "any respect we have now, we have to earn". For the other side the Reverend Gerard Irving (who prefers to be called "Father") putting on the Eucharist vestments which preserve for him his continuity with first century worship, and wearing his cassock in the street. At this point an analytical psychiatrist put in a plea for a certain amount of discipline and restraint, for there is a danger of abolishing the essence by destroying titles and ritual. The rest of the programme was a discussion in which the two "revs" were joined by Edwin Apps, script writer of "All Gas And Gaiters" (of which a an extract was shown). Mr Apps pointed out that his characters are deliberately pretentious and all pretentiousness is funny.
>
> Both sides made some good points yet both used diametrically opposite arguments to get to the same result; all agree that ministers must be approachable and recognised as human beings; but Father Irving and Mr Apps rightly hold that in order to approach him, one must be able to recognise a minister as a minister – and how else other than by distinctive dress. On the

other hand Daniel Jenkins emphasised that first century dress was certainly contemporary in the first century but should we not be wearing twentieth century garments to celebrate mysteries which we claim to be relevant to the present day? This is a discussion which will no doubt continue in many vicarages – and not a few public houses for there is a lot more to be said on both sides."

It was surprising how quickly clerical dress disappeared after that. I felt it was a pity, because it was elegant and stylish, and I could not see why priests should be ashamed of being seen as priests; any more than soldiers and sailors and policemen are ashamed of being seen for what they are.

After the programme I drove Father Irvine back to his church in Kensington. He was very disgruntled; no doubt feeling that the Low Church had put one over on him, so to cheer him up I asked if I could see his vestments. This had the effect I intended and he whisked me up into the vestry and opened the sliding door of his wardrobe. There they hung exactly like a great lady's ball gowns, and as he took them out lovingly to show me, the simile was complete. I warmed to him and his enthusiasm, as I had not at all warmed to Dr Jenkins D.D.

CHAPTER TWENTY-FOUR

Derek Nimmo was invited to the "Man of the Year" luncheon and found himself sitting next to the Queen Mother's private secretary who told him that "All Gas and Gaiters" was the Queen Mother's favourite programme and that she insisted that her diary was arranged so that she could watch it each week. Never slow off the mark, Derek asked him if Her Majesty would like to come to see a recording. In the event she did not come, but sent her secretary and her household from Clarence House. The episode was one in which the Bishop, the Archdeacon and Noote go to dinner with the Dean who is very frugal and there is only a very small roast. When this appeared, a huge laugh went up from the Royal household who were heard to whisper, "Just like Clarence House!"

They came to the BBC Club afterwards and we met them. The equerries were all fresh-faced young men with Old Etonian ties, while the Queen Mother's Private Secretary was the very image of a courtier, standing always with a slight forward inclination from the waist that was almost a bow, but not quite. He was charm itself and I was fascinated to notice that without any apparent effort he managed never to turn his back on anyone.

Frank now invited Stuart to join him at London Weekend Television and, with a growing family, he agreed. This meant that we no longer had anyone at the BBC to fight our corner. Feeling that the show was good enough to defend itself, we did not worry too much. Later events were to prove how wrong we were.

Glenda's success had enabled them to sell their flat and buy a house. It was in Hervey Road, a comfortable family house built in the 1930s. Roy took us to see it before the sale was completed and we suggested that it might be a good idea to knock down the wall between the two downstairs rooms and make one big one with windows at both ends. Roy was very taken with the idea and said he would do it, but we were horrified next day when he told us he had knocked it down during the night. "But the sale is not complete!" "Oh, that's a detail," he replied. "But supposing it doesn't go through?" "It will." And of course it did, leaving us feeling very middle-class and cautious.

They now began to entertain and we were roped in to oversee the niceties of etiquette and help with conversation. Their first dinner party was memorable. I forget who the distinguished guests were, in fact I do not remember much about the evening nor, I suspect, do any of the other guests, because Roy, unused to drinking wine, had not bought enough. So when it ran out half way through the meal, with typical ingenuity, he refilled the bottles with neat gin and continued to top up everyone's glasses. Conversation was animated so no one noticed the change of beverage until speech became slurred and eyes out of focus. Next day, when we reproached him after a dreadful night, he shrugged his shoulders and said, "Well, it's all alcohol, isn't it?"

Two other actor friends we saw often at that time were Gwendoline Watts and her husband, Gertan Klauber. I had become friends with Gwen when we were in several of the Harry Worth shows together. Gertan had escaped from Czechoslovakia with his parents as a child, while many of his family had perished in the Nazi concentration camps. As a result, he was fiercely anti-German and when we went to dinner, we never dared park our Volkswagen Beetle in front of their house, but always left it in a side road. Often cast as a Nazi in the many Second World War films in vogue at the time, Gertan took pleasure in making his characters as monstrous as possible – until the day that a director took him aside and told him to tone it down. "Tone it down!" replied Gertan, indignantly, "This man is a Nazi!" "I know", said the director, "but there is German money in the film."

When it came to writing the third series in 1968, Frank and Polly again offered us their flat in Monticello. This time we decided to go for a holiday and enjoy Corsica and begin work when we got home

We left England in early March and drove south through France meeting the spring as it came towards us. But when we got to Marseille, the ferries were on strike. We waited several days at Cassis, a small fishing village beside Marseille, and drove in each day to see how things were progressing. When it got to Saturday and nothing had happened, someone told us that there was a ferry leaving from Genoa on Sunday afternoon for Alghero in Sardinia from where we could get another ferry to Bonifacio at the southernmost tip of Corsica.

It was already Saturday mid-day and we had not had lunch but there was no time to lose. We drove all along the coast to the Italian border, where we changed some money into lire. At that time petrol was still rationed in Italy and you needed coupons to buy it. There was no time for that, so we filled the car to the brim and hoped for the best. It was the first time either of us had been to Italy and when we stopped at a hotel in Bordighera to spend the night, we found the owner sitting outside, smartly dressed in suit and tie with a baby on his knee and all the staff standing round him in admiration.

We were shown to our room, but when we came down and asked for dinner, they explained that they had to put the baby to bed. This, we soon realized, was an operation that involved everyone including the cook and took a long time. Eventually it was accomplished and we were ushered into the dining room and ordered our dinner, mindful of the fact we had not had lunch. But when the first course was about to be served, suddenly everyone started rushing about. We asked what was happening and they explained that the baby had woken up. Everyone including the cook disappeared again, while we waited getting hungrier and hungrier. At last the baby decided to go to sleep and we got our dinner.

The next morning, a Sunday, we drove to Genoa along the coast road, which is narrow and winds up and down along the cliff edge. The Italians at that time had a small low-horsepower Fiat and the road was full of families in these little cars, which went at a snail's pace. We arrived just in time for the boat. The days waiting at Cassis plus the fact that we had had to drive all that way and spend another night on the road, made us decide to economise and travel second class. This meant sleeping in separate dormitories, one for men and one for women. I asked Pauline if she would mind, pointing out that she would have all the children in her dormitory. She said she could cope. In fact the children slept with the men. The man in the bunk above me had four children in bed with him. I was apprehensive I might be leaked on in the night, but the rain held off. Pauline had an old peasant woman beside her who, when she undressed, took off her skirt and another beneath it, then another and another, like a Russian doll.

The following morning we arrived at Alghero where the car was lifted off the boat by a crane and put down on the quay. There were a few houses and one or two people lounging about. I walked over to a small group of men and said *"Corsica?"* They all pointed in the same direction, which was reassuring, so we set off. It was a nerve wracking journey for two reasons, the first being that our petrol was getting low and we knew we could not buy any more in Sardinia without coupons, and the second, the fact that there had recently been a lot in the English papers about tourists being kidnapped in Sardinia. However, our luck and the petrol both held out and we arrived at the little port at the top of the island facing Bonifacio. As it was lunchtime we found a small restaurant run by an old man and his grandson, a boy of about thirteen whom he was teaching the trade. I gave him the rest of our Italian money and asked him to give us lunch. It was a memorable lunch, with fish, olives, tomatoes, fresh bread and delicious cheeses, with the old man teaching his grandson how to serve us.

We caught the ferry across the straits and then drove up the east side of Corsica, which is flat, to Bastia before the drive across the mountains to Monticello on the west coast.

This second visit was the first real holiday we had had since the beginning of "All Gas and Gaiters" and during it, driving round Cap Corse, the northern tip of the island, we visited the Cathedral of Nebbio, a beautiful small 12th-century cathedral which stands alone in the middle of a meadow, its episcopal city having been destroyed by the Saracens. The key was kept in the local café. Inside the cathedral, in a glass case, lay St Flor, a Roman soldier converted to Christianity. Dressed in a handsome eighteenth-century version of Roman military uniform and lying with one leg placed nonchalantly over the other, he had been found in the catacombs of Rome. The fact that his body was in a good state of preservation was the proof, if proof were needed, of his saintliness.

I had brought paints and canvases with me, and when we got back to Monticello, I began the first painting I had done for a long time. I set up my easel on the balcony of the tower, from where there was an interesting view of the Maison de Malaspina and began work.

It had been arranged that Frank and Polly would fly out and take over the flat from us in early May. We met them at the airport and asked if there was any news because we were completely out of touch. They said that the Vietnam peace talks were taking place in Paris and mentioned a few other things.

We left next morning and made good time reaching Châlon sur Saône that evening. This meant we had a day in hand before we were booked on to the ferry at Calais on Sunday, so we decided to spend a night in Paris. It was May 10th 1968.

We made for the Latin Quarter, intending to stay in the Hotel d'Angleterre in the rue Jacob. As we passed the Sorbonne we saw armed police lined up outside it and decided that it must be for the Vietnam peace talks that the Muirs had mentioned. When we arrived at the Hotel d'Angleterre, I went to the receptionist and said we wanted a room, adding that I would leave the car in the street for the night. "If you do," he said, "it will be burned." I asked him by whom and he said by the students who were rioting. I put the car in the hotel garage and we took our cases up to our room. Pauline was tired and wanted to rest, but I decided to go and buy *Le Monde* and find out what it was all about.

Le Monde was full of a confrontation between the police and the students scheduled for that evening. I went back to Pauline and told her we were in the hottest spot in Europe. She seemed unimpressed. We went to dinner in a little restaurant we knew in the Rue Seine and during dinner Pauline said she wanted to go to the drugstore after we had eaten, because the last time we had been there, she had seen a hideous doll she wanted to give to Glenda. I objected that, according to *Le Monde* that was exactly where the confrontation was to take place. "Oh", she said, "that won't be anything, just a few students."

When we arrived at St Germain des Prés, the square was empty. The Deux Magots was closed and the drugstore opposite was shut with the grill down. Over on the left side were a line of police and a row of police buses. Behind the grill of the drugstore were a lot of people looking out. Trying to make sense of the situation, we supposed that the people behind the grill had been arrested and the buses were prison vans waiting to take them to prison. I crossed over to the drugstore and asked a man behind the grill if he were a prisoner. He replied that he would rather be a prisoner than to be where we were. At that moment, from our right, a surge of students began advancing towards the police who started letting off tear gas. Journalists on motorbikes roared about and the police put up their shields and they, too, began advancing, so that we looked like becoming the filling in the sandwich. I grabbed Pauline and we bolted down a side street. When we reached the hotel, the receptionist was holding a club in his hand.

Back in London, everyone was agog to hear our story and we became popular dinner guests. The only person who was displeased by our account was James Laver; "All my life," he said, "I've wanted to see a revolution in France and you, you who don't in the least appreciate it, have had the luck to be there!"

Holly.

Front of house photo at Southport 1949
in the rather too loud check suit.

My grandmother in old age.

As Dr Kirby in *Eden
End*, Southport 1949.

As Weeks the butler in *High Temperature* at Bristol Little Theatre 1955 with Michael Blakemore and Sheila Fraser.

As Gunner in Bernard Shaw's *Misalliance* with William Moore. Pitlochry 1956.

As Young Marlowe in *She Stoops to Conquer* with Jill Johnson, Graham Lines and Geraldine Gwyther. Pitlochry 1956.

Pauline Devaney.

As Mr Halliforth in *WhackO*
with Arthur Howard and
Jimmy Edwards.

With Harry Worth as the
BBC producer in the scene
he asked me to rewrite.

Eammon Andrews
and Harry Worth in
This Is Your Life.

With N.F. (Wally) Simpson.

As Middie and Bro Paradock, 1967.

Pauline and me as Middie and Bro Paradock with Avis Bunnage and Geoffrey Hibbert in N.F. Simpson's *Tall Tinkles*.

Writing *All Gas and Gaiters* in our flat,
2A Talbot Place Blackheath, 1967

Robertson Hare, John Barron, Derek Nimmo and William Mervyn
in *All Gas and Gaiters (The Bishop Rides Again)*.

Robertson Hare, John Barron, Derek Nimmo and William Mervyn
in *The Bishop Rides Again*.

Finding the sermon, Robertson Hare, William Mervyn and Derek Nimmo.

The senior clergy of St Ogg (Ernest Clark as the Dean)
in procession, 1967.

William Mervyn and Robertson Hare in *All Gas and Gaiters*, 1966

Pauline with Barnaby in her (broken) arm.

Farm for sale in the West of France.

Cecil Swann.

The Swann's château.

Returning after thirty two years.

—

CHAPTER TWENTY-FIVE

Sometime in the early '60s, Pauline's grandfather had died and her mother had inherited enough money to buy a house. They found one in Richmond and decided to convert it into two flats and let the upper one.

We went to see them regularly to have dinner, but I found conversation with Gerald difficult. He knew everything about every subject mentioned and never stopped telling you so. I soon learned that the only way to make contact with him was to continually ask his advice, but it did not make for relaxed evenings.

When my parents had left the house in Gloucester I had recovered my bicycle and not having a place to house it at Blackheath, I asked Gerald and Marjorie if they would look after it for me and they agreed. Soon after, when we went to dinner, Gerald announced he was taking us all to a restaurant. It came as a great surprise because he had never done such a thing before, but we thanked him and walked to the restaurant.

Knowing he did not have much money, Pauline and I and Marjorie all chose the most modest menu, but Gerald chose everything that was expensive. After the meal, he tipped the staff generously and, as we returned to their house, said, "Oh, by the way, I sold your bicycle." It was then I realized we had just eaten my Raleigh.

Soon after our return from Corsica an example of the lengths to which he would go rather than admit that he did not know something occurred. He had been making a patio in the garden and Pauline had brought back some stones from the beach for him. When we next went to dinner, as we were sitting drinking a glass of sherry, Pauline told him about them and went to get them from the car. "No," he said, "I'll do it, give me the key." We gave him the key and he went out. He was a long time and we continued to sip our sherry. Then we heard him come into the house, go upstairs to the flat he was converting, come down and go out again. Marjorie began to despair of her shoulder of lamb in the oven. Time went on until, finally, he burst into the room, threw the keys at Pauline and said, "Those keys don't fit and anyway there are no stones in the car, I know because I've taken the door off"

There were two Volkswagen Beetles in the road outside the house and Gerald had mistaken the other one for ours. Unable to open the door and incapable of admitting it, he had gone upstairs to fetch his tool box, taken the door off the other car and, finding it empty, put the door back on again.

"If only," Pauline said afterwards, "if only the owner had come back in the middle."

As a result of the success of the second series, Michael Mills' attitude changed. Suddenly he adopted us and we became "*his*" series which made life easier and meant that the third series was to be done in colour. I had never been convinced by colour television because I like black and white and the black costumes of our characters were very well suited to it. However, a front-page photograph on the Radio Times with the Bishop in a purple cassock convinced me that going into colour would lose nothing.

The third series was no easier to write than the earlier ones and we were often behind our deadlines (on one occasion a BBC despatch rider waited outside the flat while I finished typing the script) for, as in the earlier series, we insisted on producing scripts that did not need to be rewritten. I had seen to my cost how scripts that did not work and had to be rewritten wasted the actors' rehearsal time and meant that the performance was less assured than it should be. We made it a principle that no script left the house until we were certain it worked, and it was a matter of pride that scarcely a word was altered during rehearsal. This policy might be inconvenient for the managers and their staff, but in our view that was what they were paid for, it was the actors that mattered and they were our chief, our only concern.

When Stuart had done the outside filming for "The Bishop Rides Again", we did not know how the Church would view the series. Previous attempts to write comedies about the Church had failed and the Church had let it be known that it had not appreciated them, so

Stuart had decided not to use English cathedrals but to use French ones instead. Now, the deans of Chichester, Winchester and several other cathedrals were falling over each other to have their cathedral become St Oggs.

The clergy's attitude to the series was summed up in a letter dated 29th December 1967 from a Canon Edwards writing from Bosley and Northrode Vicarage near Macclesfield,

"On this last night of the series of "All Gas And Gaiters", I would like to express deep appreciation of its clever, amusing themes... it has been so amusing and, if I may say so, so typically Anglican in style and predicament, it has been in no way hurtful to the image of the Church of England"

Robertson Hare had been seventy-six when the series began and he was now eighty. Learning a new part every week over a seven-week period with daily rehearsals and the stress of recording in front of an audience is tiring at any age, but now he was beginning to have difficulty learning the lines. This meant that we had to use him sparingly, keep his lines short and place a key word in the previous line to jog his memory. Both William Mervyn and Derek Nimmo, although they detested each other and never spoke unless it was absolutely necessary, were fond of Bunny and each in his way took care of him and nursed him.

He was an extraordinary mixture of respectability and anarchy. He lived with his wife in a block of flats in Kensington. Mrs Hare was a stately old lady with an impressive bosom covered with ropes of pearls in the Edwardian fashion. The flat and their life together were irreproachable. But it was an open secret that Bunny had long been having an affair with Constance Lorne with whom he had appeared in many plays. I had worked with Connie some years earlier in a television play in Manchester. She was slim, elegant and witty and wore small hats that could best be described as saucy. She had often talked about "Mr Hare" as she called him.

During the series, we used to take him home after the Sunday night recordings and I remember one night, as we were driving towards

Kensington, he suddenly said, "Oh, I do like a hungry woman!" and then after a pause, "I wonder what Constance Lorne is doing?"

He had some very funny stories about his time in the Aldwych farces with Ralph Lynn and Tom Walls and about the First World War. He had joined the Bicycle Brigade in 1914, which trained on Blackheath. "I was always a cocky little fellow," he said, "and when the sergeant shouted, "Mount!" I leapt on to the bike to be first and landed on my right testicle". The story continued with the testicle swelling to vast proportions, the doctor's advice and treatment, and ended "and if you were to see them today you would notice that they are still not in alignment."

At the beginning of 1969 we decided to take six months off and write a stage play based on the series. Several comedy series had been turned into plays with more or less success. The change from a half-hour format to two hours is rather like asking a 100-yard sprinter to run a long-distance race, but with our experience in rep we felt we were equipped to try and settled down to work out a plot.

We had hardly begun, when Pauline announced that she was pregnant. It was a shock, as children had never been part of our plan, but we recognised that if we were to have children, no time could be better than the present. We were better off financially than we had ever been and writing a play was less stressful than working to deadlines.

She went to see Basil Sanderson, who said everything was normal and she was to go for regular checks, which she did. He had been very involved in the building of a new hospital at Sidcup and had often talked about it and shown us the plans. Now he suggested that the birth should take place there, which seemed an ideal arrangement.

Living in the middle of Blackheath, we used often to go for a stroll after dinner at night. There was street lighting and it was nice to get some fresh air before going to bed. On the evening of her three months check-up, when, as she told me, Basil had said that, "unless Edwin kicks you in the stomach, nothing can go wrong" We went for a stroll after dinner.

We had just crossed the road leading up from Blackheath Village and were stepping on to the pavement on the other side, when I became aware of a car without lights approaching on my left which touched the back of my overcoat, I turned to Pauline on my right side to warn her, but it was too late; she was half a pace behind me and was hit by the car; an "E" Type Jaguar, and carried along the road on the bonnet before being thrown onto the road. It all happened so quickly that it took a moment to sink in. There was Pauline lying in the middle of the road, I hurried to her to see if she were still alive and heard her groaning.

My first thought was the danger of another car coming. The driver had stopped further along. I shouted, "Get help, she's pregnant". A man from a nearby house heard the noise and asked what he could do. I said ring an ambulance and ring Dr Sanderson and gave him the address. In a remarkably short time both the ambulance and Basil arrived. There was no sign of the police. Basil told the ambulance men not to wait and supervised Pauline being carefully put into the ambulance. I got in as well and, with Basil telling the driver to drive very carefully, we went to Greenwich hospital, Basil following in his car.

It was only later we learned that Basil had been operating on a woman whose womb had burst. It was only the second time in his career he had seen such a case and when he got home he told Betty he was too tired to eat supper and went straight to bed. When the telephone rang and a voice said that someone had been hurt and was asking for him, Betty told him not to go, saying that it was prob-ably someone from the Blackheath Rugby Club, of which he was Chairman, who had drunk too much. Basil Sanderson, like the dedi-cated doctor he was, said "No, you never know," got up, dressed and came to find us.

Pauline's injuries were all down her left side, her shoulder, her upper arm broken; her ankle with terrible bruising and the base of her spine where she had landed on the road.

The hospital did what they could for her, but Basil did not want her to have pain-killers because of the baby. While we were discov-ering all this, a nurse said the police had arrived and wanted to see me. There were two of them. They said they had talked to the driver of the car but that there was no case to answer because there were no witnesses.

I was in a state of shock and barely understood what they said. When all that could be done for Pauline had been, the nurses told me to go home and get some rest. I went back to the flat. The lights were still on, it was just as we had left it; I looked round and could hardly believe that in such a short time our lives had been completely transformed. We had left together talking about an idea for the play and here was I a few hours later, alone, with Pauline lying in hospital, broken and battered, having probably lost her baby. I stood in the middle of the room with tears streaming down my face.

In the following days and weeks I spent all day at her bedside. She suffered a lot of pain, but Basil was adamant about painkillers and the good news was that the baby seemed to be all right.

Pauline was in hospital for several weeks and when she came home her left leg and left arm were in plaster, which made movement difficult, added to which her pregnancy was becoming more and more visible and she was getting heavier. It was impossible to work.

We had become friends with a couple who lived in a flat above us, Christian and Pauline Adams. Christian was in the Foreign Office and they were away in South America and had let their flat. Their tenant came to see us about something. He was a pale-looking man and when he had gone Pauline said she was sure he had just come out of prison.

Sometime later, I was talking to the man who had the garage in Blackheath Village from whom we had bought our first Beetle and, as we talked, the tenant walked by. The garage man asked if I knew him and said he had run up a lot of debt in the village. I talked to Pauline and decided to write to the Adams, warning them that if their tenant was behind with the rent, they should not let it go on too long. They replied thanking me but saying that although he had been in arrears, he had suddenly paid up and all was well.

As the birth approached, Pauline became irritable. She was out of plaster but not out of pain. We had a large wooden chest that had been in my nursery at Wenderton. It was too large for the flat and we had put it in the bathroom, where it took up a lot of the space.

We had often talked about getting rid of it but had never done so. It had been made by great-uncle Frank in a fit of carpentry and had housed my toys and I was loath to part with it. But one morning Pauline suddenly flared up and said she was going out and when she came back she did not want the chest to be there. Under our lease, we had a share in the box-room on the second floor and I decided to take the chest up there. But I needed help, so I went to the Adams' tenant and asked if he would help me. He agreed and came into the flat. He showed interest in the layout of the flat, so I showed him round and then he helped me take the chest up to the box room. Pauline came back mollified and all was well.

It was hot in August and one day Pauline said she wanted to see the sea, so we decided to go to Pevensey in Sussex for the day. Everything went well, we walked on the beach and bought some fish from a fisherman, but on the way home she became tired and I began to feel we had overdone it. It was eight o'clock when we arrived and we decided to cook the fish and have a quick dinner, so she could get to bed. I laid the table and opened the drawer where we kept our table silver, only to find it was empty. I looked round and realized that we had been burgled, pictures were missing and the flat had been stripped of everything of value. I rang the police at Lewisham who sent two policemen round but said that the C.I.D. worked office hours and would not be able to see us until the next day. I pointed out that by the next day our things could very well be on the continent.

When the police left, Pauline said that I was in a state, which was true, and that she wanted me to take a sleeping pill. I had never taken a sleeping pill in my life – I am always reluctant even to take an aspirin – but she seemed very insistent, saying that she would need me the next day and I must have a good night's sleep, so I agreed and took a sleeping pill.

During the night I felt her shaking me and heard her voice as though at a great distance, saying, "The waters have broken, the waters have broken! Gradually I took in what she was saying and consciousness returned. I got up, dressed, and in a dreamlike state drove her to the hospital. Once there, the birth stopped and we spent the night waiting. Basil arrived at eight o'clock and the first thing I noticed was that he had a large bandage over his ear. He had, he explained, an infection of the ear. When he examined Pauline he decided to prepare for an eventual caesarean, but said he could not do it himself as his ear infection meant he could not go into the operating theatre. However, he had an excellent assistant, a Greek, and he introduced me to him. We talked about Greece and I mentioned the two Greeks I had been at school with. Time went on and when it got to lunchtime, the Greek said he would not be able to operate, as he had to take his wife to the dentist. Basil said it was a pity, but that he had another assistant, an African. He was not very experienced, but in any case he, Basil, would be standing by the door of the theatre and would oversee things. I had wanted to be present at the birth, but with a caesarean that was impossible and so Basil suggested I wait in his office. As I waited I noticed a book on Caesarean birth and opened it. The opening paragraph emphasised the fact that although people thought of Caesarean birth as a danger-free operation, it was far from being the case. It then went on to list all the things that could go wrong. I was in the middle of reading this and becoming more and more alarmed, when a nurse came in and said, "It's a boy."

They brought him in to show me, Basil came in and we had a cup of tea to celebrate.

I went home and rang my Mother. When she answered, I told her to sit down and then explained to her that we had been burgled and everything we had of value had been taken, but she now had a grandson. She said she was glad I had told her to sit down. I then rang Yaya. "Hullo, Baboo, I'm under the stairs, there is a storm." I knew how frightened she was of storms; her treatment for syphilis had included quantities of mercury and she had since been convinced she was a target for lightning. She was delighted about the baby, but in the circumstances did not want to prolong the conversation.

During the ensuing days tests were carried out to see if the baby was normal and he passed all of them with flying colours. Basil insisted that he had never doubted that all would be well, but Pauline told me that doctors never stopped coming into the room and peering into the cot and muttering words like, "miraculous", "extraordinary" or "fancy".

We had decided to call him Barnaby and we added the name Basil as we felt that Barnaby owed his life to him.

Barnaby's birth did not pass unnoticed by the press. The Mirror had a double page picture of Pauline in bed with the baby and a head-line "Barnaby Wins Through". The other papers mentioned it, if more discreetly.

Once back in the flat it became clear that we had a problem. We had a series to write and a baby to look after, and the two did not fit easily together. Moreover there was no question of one of us working while the other looked after the baby, because our work needed the total concentration of both of us at the same time. At this point our neighbour, Anita Bush, came to our rescue. David Bush was an archi-tect who specialized in churches (he later became a parson on the Isle of Man) and they had several children. They both loved babies and seeing our difficulty Anita took over and looked after Barnaby while we worked.

Glenda had given birth to a son, Daniel, a few months earlier and Roy was looking after him while she worked. We had always been friends and now, with the two boys, we saw more and more of each other as Roy looked after both boys while we worked. We would take Barnaby round to him in the morning and collect him in the evening. When Glenda won her first Oscar for "Women in Love", she refused to go to America to collect it and so it was sent by post. When I went to get Barnaby on the evening of its arrival I found both boys on the floor playing with "Oscar". Seeing the statue close to was interesting. It had very broad shoulders and a very small head, which struck me as being a perfect metaphor for Hollywood.

After her second Oscar, Glenda was much in demand and when I went to collect Barnaby one evening, she told me she had had an unexpected visit from a man in a Rolls Royce. "He sat there" she said, indicating the sofa opposite her, "and he was telling me that he would finance any film I wanted to do, I only had to choose, I looked at him and thought, here he is offering me all this, and I don't even know his name."

Meanwhile Frank had resigned from London Weekend Television. Predictably, the bankers and financiers who made up the board of directors, having used his name and the names of several other respected television figures to get their hands on a commercial television company, now decided that they no longer needed them. The idea that a show that did not generate money immediately should be given time to develop, was "off message". Revenue had fallen, so they sacked the managing director, Michael Peacock, the man who had persuaded everyone to join the project in the belief, as the prospectus had claimed, that the sole aim was to make quality programmes.

When Frank and the others asked to meet the board, the vice-chairman, a certain Lord Campbell, told them that although they might think that managing talented producers and performers raised special problems, he, who had "been in sugar all his life", could assure them that managing people in television was exactly the same as managing sugar workers. Whereupon they all resigned and, on principle, sold their shares back to the company at the price they had paid for them.

I congratulated Frank on his return to the real world and he seemed a lot happier. He now decided to write books and began with an anthology eventually published as "The Frank Muir Book" There was a section on the history of the theatre which I helped him with and enlisted George Benson's advice as back-up.

Pauline recovered from her injuries slowly, the series got written and things got back to normal. The Adams' tenant introduced us to his fiancée, a girl considerably younger than he. They were marrying and moving away, he explained, because the Adams were about to come home.

When the Adams arrived, they found their flat emptied of furniture (they had inherited some valuable eighteenth-century pieces). The tenant had sold it all to the antique dealer in Blackheath Village which explained how he had suddenly been able to pay the arrears of rent. When he was tracked down, it was discovered that Pauline had been right; he had indeed just come out of prison where he had served a sentence for bigamy (his new marriage was equally bigamous) yet the person who was most surprised, we were told, was the Chief Constable of Lewisham, with whom he had become fast friends.

When the Lewisham C.I.D had eventually investigated our burglary, they had found that the burglar had got in by means of a small window in the bathroom, which was left open for "Coopers", our marmalade cat. Now it occurred to us that as the Adams' tenant had been in the bathroom only two days earlier to help me carry out the wooden chest, he would have noticed the window. I had also let him see over the flat. If he had not burgled us himself, it was not unreasonable to suppose that he might have tipped off an old prison acquaintance. We mentioned this to the police, but they seemed uninterested.

After the accident I had been in touch with our solicitor, Michael Bruce. Michael had insisted I write a full account of what had happened immediately afterwards, which I had done. Now he was in negotiations with the car driver's insurance company, but pointed out that it was difficult because the driver claimed that we had walked off the pavement into the path of his car. I had explained that this was not so, but that we had crossed the road and were stepping on to the pavement when the car arrived without lights. The problem was that there were no witnesses so it was his word against ours. Moreover the driver was the son of an insurance agent and when the police had arrived at the scene of the accident, they had gone to the boy's home and seen the father before coming to find me.

After a while, I got an official letter from the clerk of the Greenwich court, telling me that it had been decided that there was no case to answer, as there were no witnesses. I thought carefully about it and finally wrote a short letter saying that I quite understood their point of view, however, if, as it was claimed, we had walked off the pavement into the path of the car, it seemed odd that the near headlight had been broken and Pauline's injuries were on her left side. I got a fresh letter saying they had decided to bring the case to court.

Michael Bruce was pleased at this, but each time a date for the hearing was announced, it was immediately cancelled because the police witness was not available. He was ill, or on a course, or on holiday; we got the impression he was unwilling to appear. It was not until two years later that the case eventually came to court with the policeman still mysteriously absent. I was summoned as a witness to Greenwich Crown Court and a duty solicitor was allotted to prosecute, a young man who began by saying he could not understand why the case had come to court, as without a witness there was no case to answer. I told him that, on the contrary, we were going to win and explained the evidence of the headlight and the injuries being both on the left side and we hurried into court. I was called and explained what had happened. Then the driver, Mr Alphonso, Lewis, Garth, Cheffins, was called.

He began by saying he had only had a few pints and admitted that putting on the car's headlights had "slipped his mind". Asked about the accident, he said he realized he had hit something and stopped. "I saw this bloke waving his arms about and shouting out about her being pregnant," he said, "He seemed very excited. At this point I caught the eye of the magistrate and we exchanged a look that made me think all would be well, and so it was; Mr Cheffins was found guilty. He had been charged with careless driving, but when the magistrate sentenced him to lose his licence for six months, he added that unfortunately it was the maximum sentence he could apply in the circumstances but that he could not understand why the police witness was not in court, and why the driver was not charged with a far more serious offence.

CHAPTER TWENTY-SIX

One day in June 1970 I read The Times more thoroughly than usual, including the personal column. My eye was caught by a small entry: "Farm for sale in western France, £2000." There was a London telephone number; I dialled it, a simple act that proved to be one of the most momentous of my life.

A girl's voice with a strong French accent answered. Her name, she told me was Monique Renou and the farm was at Liez. When I asked where Liez was, she said it was in the Vendée, near Fontenay-le-Comte. I was no wiser. Pauline and I had often thought of buying a cheap bolt-hole in France where we could go and work away from London, so now we looked at the map to see where the Vendée was. We found that it was between Nantes and Bordeaux and close to La Rochelle. Moreover it was near the sea and could probably be reached from England in a day. All points in its favour, so I decided to go and see what a two-thousand-pound farm was like. Before doing so, I rang Michael Bruce and told him I was going to visit a farm in western France and asked if he thought I had gone off my head.

"Not necessarily."

"Are there any questions I should ask?"

"Ask if it floods in winter."

I flew to Paris and caught the train to Niort, today a journey of two hours twenty minutes on the TGV, but then a five-hour journey on a *"rapide"*. When I went to have lunch, I found a dining car with tables and chairs and was waited on by waitresses wearing the traditional costume of Poitou with its white lace headdress. The lunch was excellent, consisting of traditional regional dishes. On subsequent trips I never again saw either the waitresses or the regional dishes and it was only years later I discovered that it had been a publicity-stunt, which had only lasted for that week

I was met at Niort station by the eldest of Monique's brothers, Jean-Michel, a boy of eighteen who spoke some English, and several of their younger brothers and sisters in a big old family Peugeot. They drove me through a flat countryside intersected by canals lined with overhanging ash trees until we came to a small village, where, down a lane, lying some thirty metres back from the road, stood a stone farmhouse with grey shutters surrounded by partially ruined farm buildings. Although it was July, it had begun to rain and, inside the house rain was coming through the roof in several places. The children began to laugh at the idea of anyone buying such a ruin. The house was built of a warm, yellow stone with dressed stone on the corners and a roof of Roman tiles. It had a central front door with a window on each side and three corresponding small windows above. Inside there was a central hall leading straight through to the barn, whose roof had fallen in. A closed staircase with a door led up to the floor above, which was a store for apples and potatoes, (several potato prize certificates were pinned to the beams) the roof tiles were laid on rushes.

The downstairs was divided into two very large rooms with big open stone fireplaces at each end. There were no ceilings, the wooden floor of the store above being laid directly on to the beams. The floors of the downstairs rooms were of cement, while that of the entrance hall was of old, worn tiles laid in sand. In front of the house were a well and two small buildings, one of which was a bake-house and the other a washhouse. A cowshed stood opposite across the front yard, while at the side of the house was the cart-lodge and behind that another cowshed and chicken-house. The house and farm buildings stood in a large meadow beside which, at a distance of some fifty metres, lay another similar small farm. The house, the outbuildings and those of the neighbouring farm were all built in the same stone and with the same dressed stone corners and Roman-tiled roofs.

Even in its abandoned state, the house had a nice feeling, the proportions were good; the big, generous rooms with their huge beams and big open fireplaces and the way the house and the outbuildings related to each other, making a unified whole. As a project it was daunting, frightening even, but somehow I felt we must try to buy it. I asked about local masons and was told that the neighbour, whose house stood on the road beside the entrance, was the village mason. I asked to meet him.

When I had looked round, they drove me to their home, a farm in another part of the village to meet their parents, Monsieur and Madame Renou and Monsieur Renou's sister, Marie, who was the owner of the house. M. Renou and his brothers and sisters had all been born in the house and at the death of their parents the boys had inherited the farmland, and Marie the house, which had been let since 1929. Few if any repairs had been done since that date.

Marie had never married, but lived with her brother and his wife and helped with their ten children. Their farmhouse did not possess a bathroom or indoor lavatory, and Marie had often repeated that if she could sell her house she would put in a bathroom. Now, Monique, the eldest daughter, was teaching French in London and she had had the idea of putting the advertisement in *The Times*. The Renous were very kind and hospitable. I had dinner with them, sitting at a large round table with all the children, and then Jean Michel took me to the neighbouring village of Maillezais to the Hôtel du Pélican which was kept by M. and Mme. Martin.

I went to bed and lay thinking about the day. Suddenly I had been plunged into a new world, a world I did not know but which was surprisingly familiar. It was the country, the country as I had known it in England in the nineteen-thirties.

The hotel was spotlessly clean but did not have indoor plumbing so the lavatory was a two-seater in the garden beside the rabbit hutches. I slept well and came down the following morning for breakfast to find my fellow guest, a hugely stout man, tucking in to ham and dried sausage to prepare him for a day's fishing on the canals. The Renous arrived and took me to see the eldest of the family, Jean Renou, a man in his early sixties, who farmed the biggest farm in the village. He acted for his sister and it was with him I had to negotiate. It must be remembered that women in France were not allowed to have bank accounts until after the Second World War. He told me that the only reason he had agreed to sell the house was because the roof of the barn had fallen in. Barns were, in his eyes, far more valuable than houses. For his generation houses were of little account and certainly not worth spending money on.

In the afternoon, Jean-Michel suggested taking me to see Maillezais Abbey, which he had already pointed out in the distance, where it dominated the skyline. Built on an eminence surrounded by marshland just outside the village, lay the west porch, the north wall and the transept – all that was left of a great cathedral. A few of the monastic buildings were still standing, and in the ruins of the clois-ters, sheep were grazing. Considering that it was a ruin, the ensemble had an extraordinary majesty and unity. I sat on a low stonewall hugging myself with pleasure as I took it all in.

The following morning early, before I left for home, I met Monsieur Larrignon the mason. I told him I was thinking of buying the house and wanted him to give me an estimate for repairing the roof, putting in a bathroom and lavatory and making it habitable. He was a pleasant, reassuring man in his sixties and he made several sensible suggestions. I gave him my address and he promised to send me his estimate.

I thanked the Renous for their hospitality, told them I was seri-ously thinking of buying the house but that I must see the mason's estimate first. Jean-Michel took me to Niort station and I arrived home late in the evening, having left my camera, with the photos I had taken, in the taxi from Heath Row to Charing Cross. Luckily the taxi driver handed it in to the lost property and the next day I recovered it and we took the film to be developed.

When the photos arrived, Pauline thought them interesting and when M. Larrignon's estimate arrived it was more than reasonable so I wrote to him accepting it. However, before going any further; we decided to enlist the help of my cousin Christopher Apps (the son of Uncle Stuart), who is an architect. He came with us to see the house but when we arrived we were greeted with the news that M. Larrignon had died suddenly. It was a sad disappointment. However his son, Yvon Larrignon, was taking over the business so we now turned to him. Young and just married, with a baby daughter, he was eager for work. Christopher spent a morning in the house after which he suggested I offer £1500, which I did and it was accepted. On returning to England he did a plan which we had translated into French and sent to M. Larrignon, who, with the local carpenter, the local plumber, the electrician and the painter (most of whom were in some way related to him) each gave us an estimate. Building firms as such were almost unknown in France and, in the country, are still quite rare. You have to treat with the individual tradesmen. Their estimates were all very reasonable.

The problem now was to get the money out of England, which was not yet in the Common Market. We had to apply to the Bank of England, which made the process as difficult as possible with endless forms to be filled. Once permission was given, we then had to buy the money on the foreign exchange market on which there was an unpredictable tax which varied from day to day and could be as little as 10% or as much as 70% or 80%. All one could do was to watch its course daily and when it was falling, take the plunge and just hope the tax would not shoot up between the time you applied for the money and the time of the actual purchase. We were reasonably lucky and, as I remember; only paid about 25%.

I sent money to the mason to distribute among the others as the work progressed, but at one point, just when I was about to send him £1000, the Wilson Government announced that no money was to leave England. It is the sort of order that politicians enjoy issuing. It solves a problem at a stroke and they can go off to their clubs and enjoy a good lunch with a feeling of self-satisfaction, safe in the knowledge that the difficulty and distress that such a blanket order may cause is no concern of theirs. In our case we were aware that Yvon Larrignon, just setting out on his own account, needed our money to continue and that without it he would be in very real difficulty.

Desperate to get the money to him, I turned to Peter Crouch, the theatre agent, for help. He made enquiries and advised me that the brother of the millionaire, Jimmy Goldsmith, was a gambler and that if I took a thousand pounds in cash, in an envelope with his name on it, to his gambling club, Yvon Larrignon would be paid in francs in France where Mr Goldsmith had interests. I duly drew the money from the bank, put it in an envelope and went to the address I had been given, a smart gambling club in Mayfair. I went to the reception desk and asked to see Mr Goldsmith but was told he had not arrived. "I have something for him," I said. Hardly looking up from his work, the desk clerk said, "Put it there," indicating the end of the counter. I took out the envelope and muttered something about money and a receipt. "Oh, no need," said the desk clerk, casually, "Just stick it there." I did so, reluctantly, and left imagining Mr Goldsmith arriving, finding the money, losing it in the first five minutes and forgetting all about it. In the event, Yvon Larrignon was paid a week later.

The work took six months and when we went out in the April of 1971 the house was finished and ready to live in. We bought furniture at local auctions and when we did our final accounts, the whole cost including our visits, paying my cousin, furniture and household equipment, came to £8500. The BBC was now paying us £1000 a script plus an agreed repeat paid in advance, so for each script we received £2000 which meant that the house had cost us a little over four scripts.

During the 1950s, we had been staying with Aunty Peggy and Uncle George Stevens, when Uncle George had suggested we go to see a new neighbour of theirs, a Captain Swann. Uncle George was secretary to the local hunt and Captain Swann and his family had moved into the dower-house at Belmont and become members of the hunt. "The amusing thing," said Uncle George, "is that he was a captain in the French army."

That afternoon they drove us to Belmont. The dower-house proved to be a typical Kentish farmhouse, but once inside we found ourselves in the Paris of the Second Empire. The furniture and decoration was all of that period. The walls were painted dark green; at the end of the hall was a large portrait of a lady sitting under a tree, dressed in the costume of the 1890s, with a small boy in a sailor suit at her knee. Our host, Cecil Swann, the little boy of the painting, was a burly tweed-clad figure in his early sixties who spoke with a French accent. His wife, Doris, was American. They introduced their daughter, who curtsied. Cecil was a larger-than-life character, witty and astute, who had a publicity firm in London and was making a film about the local hunt. We took to him immediately. Over the years we kept in touch with the Swanns and when, in 1966, they moved to France, they sent us a change of address. It was a château near Tours.

Our road to Liez took us by Tours, so before our first visit, we wrote to the Swanns and suggested calling on them. They replied inviting us to stay overnight and we accepted. The Château de Breuil at St Paterne Racan lay in a small park. The château was eighteenth-century, of moderate size, elegant and welcoming. The Swanns had rented it from the Baron Alexandre de la Bouillerie, who lived at the neighbouring Château d'Hodebert, on a lease that allowed them several years rent-free on condition that they renovated the château. This Cecil had done with great flair and taste. He was immediately interested in our new house and proposed coming to see it. When he came, in his large Mercedes, his visit caused a stir in Liez. He met everyone, talked to them and did a great deal to help us to be accepted in the village. For years afterwards neighbours remembered *"Monsieur Swann"*.

He had moved to the château at the age of sixty-nine with his family, his horses and "the Smiths". Some twenty years earlier, a Mr Smith, his wife and two baby daughters had arrived in an old van and asked if they could rent a broken-down cottage at the bottom of the garden. Cecil had been unimpressed by Mr Smith but had liked the look of Mrs Smith and suggested she work in the house in lieu of rent. Soon after, Mr Smith disappeared leaving his wife and daughters in the cottage and, as it was ill adapted for babies in winter, Cecil suggested they move into the house. From that moment he set about training Mrs Smith to be the perfect servant, a sort of female Jeeves and Mrs Smith responded so well that, like Jeeves, she had become the envy of all their friends. The babies had grown into attractive girls who now looked after the horses, ran the château and drove the car. Since they had been in France the girls had learned French by watching television and were now fluent. The Smiths had their own quarters and seemed to relish their new life as much as the Swanns.

As we got to know him better, we learned Cecil's history. His grandfather had been a medical student in Edinburgh sometime in the eighteen-fifties or sixties and had met Thomas Cook, the tour operator, at dinner one evening. Cook had mentioned that he was about to send English tourists to Paris in large numbers, adding that they would all over-eat and make themselves ill and that the first person to open an English chemist's shop in Paris, where they could buy the remedies they were used to, would make a fortune. Cecil's grandfather did not hesitate; he gave up studying medicine, moved to Paris and opened the Pharmacie Swann in the rue Castiglione, (round the corner from the Hôtel Meurice.) It is still there. He installed a mineral-water fountain and it became the fashion to take a glass of mineral water with "Docteur" Swann, as he was known. He became a favourite with the Empress Eugenie and when the Prince Imperial was born, while the official doctors entered the Elysée Palace by the front door, "Docteur" Swann came in by the backdoor and waved chloroform under her nose a short time before Queen Victoria enjoyed the same relief.

The Pharmacie Swann prospered. After his father's death, Cecil's father sold it for a huge sum with which he bought a château in Normandy. He had been at the Lycée Condorcet at the same time as Marcel Proust and Cecil claimed that Proust had asked permission to use their name for the character in his novel. A letter from him had existed, he said, but had been sold or had disappeared. His parents certainly frequented the same fashionable world as Proust. On one occasion I showed him an article about Sarah Bernhard, the great French actress, which had a photo of her salon. He pointed to a small stool and said that he used to sit on it when his father took him to see her. The life-style at the Château de Cantepie, was very grand, with many servants and gardeners and a great deal of entertaining. Cecil's father regularly sent his shirts to be laundered in England but when Cecil was ten, bad investments in the Russian railway and similar projects led to disaster. The château was sold and the family found themselves in a small flat in Paris. His father became the editor of the review, "La Semaine de Suzette" where he worked for the rest of his life, dying at his desk some years later. To Cecil he said that while he had wanted a future in the Diplomatic Service for him, now he must make his own way and this Cecil proceeded to do. After serving in the French army in the First World War, he moved to America, where he founded the first French newspaper in Hollywood and involved himself in many more or less successful projects until he married Doris, an heiress, and they moved to England.

On one occasion when we were staying with them, they took us to meet a neighbour, the owner of a magnificent château surrounded by a moat. Entering the hall we saw a swarm of footmen cleaning a chandelier. The *"chatelaine"* arrived having been mushrooming and showed us round. In the basement, at the level of the moat, was a big modern kitchen where a couple; who had had a restaurant in Paris, were installed and were preparing partridges for dinner that night. In the stables were seven hunters, but the memory that stays in my mind is of the Visitors' Book. During the war the château had been commandeered by the German the High Command. These high-ranking officers: – the *"Über"* this, and the *"Uber"* that – had signed their names on a page of the book. When the family had recovered the château after the war, the page had been ripped out, but a little later, wiser counsels had suggested its historic value and it had been carefully stuck back.

The owner told us that she had been visiting Scotland a couple of years earlier and had met the Queen Mother informally. They had had a pleasant chat and she had invited her, should she be in France, to visit her at the château. Sometime later she got a telephone call saying that Her Majesty was in France on a private visit and would like to see her, so she invited her for lunch. The Queen Mother had arrived with a party of thirty.

Cecil was revealing about his time in America and about his mother-in-law, an old lady from the South who, if they were short of money, would invariably suggest they sell some slaves.

He had an impish sense of humour; I remember him at dinner, telling a story about a neighbour of his father's in Normandy who had given a dinner where an ox had been roasted whole. It was brought in on a pole carried on their shoulders by two men one of whom tripped

and fell and the ox fell on the ground and broke into pieces, whereupon the host clapped his hands and two more men came in bearing
a second ox. As he told the story, Cecil clapped his hands and Mrs
Smith came in carrying an omelette.

CHAPTER TWENTY-SEVEN

As I approached my fortieth birthday, I felt it was time to take stock: I had the feeling that I had arrived somewhere; though I was not sure exactly where. I was neither the classical actor that I had hoped to be, nor was my name in lights over any of the west-end theatres. Indeed, my acting career had all but collapsed, for since we began writing the series I had been obliged to turn down offers of parts because of the pressure of working to deadlines.

It was not that I felt that writing the series was not worthwhile. Making ten million people laugh weekly could be said to be a positive contribution to society; it was just that I had a nagging feeling I was not living, as I should.

On the other hand, we had recovered from the trauma of Pauline's accident; we had a healthy son, a flat in London and a bolt-hole in France. Everything seemed to be for the best in the best of all possible worlds

I decided that a celebration was called for, so we gave a dinner party for George and Pamela, Stuart and Ann, Frank and Polly, Wally and Joyce Simpson, Glenda and Roy and our solicitor friend Michael Bruce and his wife, Joyce. We had a private room in the "Escargot" restaurant in Soho and it was an enjoyable and lively evening.

At about that time, Mrs Hare died. I went to the funeral at a church in Kensington High Street, Bunny sat, a lonely figure, in the front pew, "The balloon's gone up," he said when I spoke to him afterwards. There did not seem to be many theatre people, Frankie Howerd was the only other person I knew. It was typical of Frankie Howerd; beneath his baroque façade, there lay a very warm human heart. Frank Muir told me that when Jimmy Edwards was dying, Frankie went to see him. Obviously distressed by Jimmy's diminished appearance, as he left, he turned at the door and said, "Jim, is there anything I can do for you?" "Yes," said Jimmy "You can change your shirt."

All his friends hoped that after a decent interval Bunny would marry Constance Lorne, but Connie developed cancer of the lungs shortly after and died a few months later.

Bunny was very lost and his memory got worse so we had to use him very sparingly. But a great addition to the team was Joan Sanderson as Mrs Pugh Critchley, the Dean's wife. Her presence allowed us to develop the home life of the Dean and with her behind him (and sometimes in front) the Dean became a more human, interesting and credible opponent for the Bishop. The fifth series was very well received by press and public however, after the last recording, Michael Mills congratulated us but at the same time told us that the BBC did not want any more.

As Pauline drove us home, I sat slumped beside her as it sunk in that this was the death knell for St Oggs and its senior clergy. We had invented them but they had taken on a life of their own and, in doing so, had taken us over. For the last seven years we had thought about them night and day and life without them was going to take some getting used to.

Our period of mourning had a short reprieve when we were invited to Broadcasting House for lunch to discuss the possibility of adapting the scripts for the radio. When we arrived, the Head of Light Entertainment, Charles Maxwell, who had produced many of the most successful radio shows including "Take it From Here", came to the foyer to receive us. Once in his office, he called in the Assistant Head of Light Entertainment, then, together, they both took out their key chains, went to a cupboard in the corner and simultaneously unlocking two locks, opened the cupboard and took out a bottle of gin from which they poured four drinks before returning the bottle to the cupboard and ceremoniously re-locking the two locks. Gin in hand, we discussed the problems of adapting television scripts for radio and then lunch arrived on a trolley from the canteen. This, we gathered, was a huge compliment to us and to our stature as successful television scriptwriters. We tried to show how appreciative we were.

Over the next three years we adapted all the scripts for radio and they were successfully broadcast. The producer was David Hatch.

We now had to decide what to do next; we needed a new idea. We tried several, first a Comedy Playhouse called "Sitting Pretty." about a couple of sitting tenants harassed by a landlord who wants to get rid of them so he can sell the house. John Howard Davies produced it and we had good actors, but somehow the magic was not there. Another idea came from reading about a woman top civil servant who was private secretary to a minister. The idea of a pompous politician being told what to do by a woman seemed to have some mileage in it, but somehow we lacked the enthusiasm and the energy that had launched "All Gas and Gaiters". Fifteen years later, the success of the series "Yes Minister" proved that the idea was sound. Finally we settled for an idea based on the fact that Britain had recently joined the Common Market. We imagined a small British firm teaming up with a small French firm. The idea was to use Derek Nimmo.

We researched traditional British products for a model, and came up with "Gentlemen's Relish" a product with a secret ingredient. The makers were very helpful, the BBC commissioned the idea and we wrote a script, but it did not take wing. There were some nice lines, such as the Englishman talking proudly of the Dunkirk spirit and his French counterpart replying, "Ah, yes, Dunkirk, when the French army held back the Germans so the British could escape." But one line does not make a script and it came to nothing. It was clear that our enthusiasm was not what it had been.

When we had written "The Bishop Rides Again", television comedy had felt like an adventure, something dangerous and fun and worth doing. Now the mood was different; the obsession with profit that had led to Frank Muir and his colleagues leaving Independent Television was beginning to infect the BBC. Accountants, formerly kept out of sight, began to appear in public and force their views on programme-makers, with the result that where it had been the policy to encourage writers to go away and develop an idea and write three or four or six scripts, produce them and, even if they were not an immediate success, give them time to shape up, now the accountants decreed that a series must succeed immediately and consist of twenty-five episodes to make it marketable.

To the argument that no two writers could write twenty-five episodes in the time, they replied that in that case there must be a team of writers. But when a team of writers are employed, they have to keep strictly to the basic formula, which means there can be no natural development of character and the series ceases to be a handmade article and becomes a factory product.

Someone suggested that we take the "All Gas and Gaiters" plots and re-hash them round another group in a different context. There was money to be made without much effort.

Of all the influences on me none had been stronger than that of St Edmund's School. There, the example of the dedicated staff and the whole ethos of the place had underlined the belief that to spend one's life amassing money was to waste it. Money was necessary but of no interest beyond that. The important thing was to develop one's talents to the full, to do something worth doing and try to make a positive contribution to society. Coming from a mercantile background and seeing, as I had at close quarters, that the pursuit of wealth did not lead to happiness, this message had resonated strongly with me.

The notion of re-hashing "All Gas and Gaiters" to make a quick buck, even were it possible, did not appeal.

In our private life, the landscape was changing too, great-uncle George died in 1970. He had bought The Studio for Yaya and had probably helped her financially, for after he died she became short of money. When I went to see her she said she must sell something, but did not know what. I found that she had kept all her dresses from the 1920s and 30s and her shoes. She had been smart and fashionable at the time and they were in mint condition so I packed them up and took them back to London. It was the moment when filmmakers were beginning to insist on clothes being of their period and Glenda put me onto a small firm in North London that was specialising in that period so I took them to the director with the shoes. He was delighted, especially with the shoes, which he said had rarely survived. The result was I was able to give her quite a large cheque.

But soon after, she became ill and moved into a nursing home where she died. Pauline and I went to her cremation where we found Uncle John. He was indignant because she had left her furniture to two neighbours who had looked after her. "It should have been kept in the family" I felt grateful to the neighbours who had looked after her, which we had failed to do.

At the beginning of 1973 my mother was taken ill and rushed to Gloucester Hospital where cancer was diagnosed. We drove down to see her, determined to tell her the diagnosis, but when we got there we found her smiling cheerfully, the surgeon having just told her that her condition was benign and there was nothing to worry about. I went to see him and he confirmed that it was cancer. I asked him why he had lied to her and he replied that, "no one can live with the truth" and added that he was sending her to the newly opened chemo-therapy unit at Cheltenham.

The surgeon's lie put us in the position of having to lie too. From then until she died in the following October we had to keep up the pretence that her illness was nothing and that she would soon be better. This meant that any serious conversation about the future was denied us and that our relationship, which might have deepened, remained superficial and basically false. I regretted it then and have never ceased to do so.

Chemotherapy was in its infancy and not only was the dosage too strong, but the entire body was treated so all the vital organs were irradiated and damaged by it. Obviously she could no longer live alone, so we engaged a housekeeper to look after her while we sold both our flat and her bungalow and bought a large house in Greenwich where we adapted part of the first floor for her. She arrived in September, but was there only a few weeks before going into hospital where she died.

A few days before her death, she told me that her happiness had ended at the age of four with the birth of her brother. "Until then" she said, "I was the centre of attention but I can remember sitting on the step outside my mother's bedroom where he had just been born, and seeing everyone walk past me without a glance as though I no longer existed." She also said that in nineteen forty-seven, when my father was diagnosed with *angina pectoris*, the specialist had forbidden them ever again to make love. She had been forty-three at the time.

In those last days, I was tempted to ask her about the relationship between my father and my grandmother and what she had felt about it, but somehow I could not bring myself to the point. She was ill and frail and I did not want to upset her.

She had not wanted to talk about her funeral and said she left it entirely to me. Looking through family papers, I discovered a grave ticket from St Peter's Thanet. It seems that when her second child was crushed at birth, she and my father had bought a grave there, where all the Goodsons are buried, so I decided to bury her there with the baby she had lost. St Peter's Church was in the news at the time, because the Prime minister, Edward Heath, whose father had been the local builder, was a native. (Yaya had told me that Mr Heath's mother had been the cook at Upton for a while).

Mr Heath still kept contact with the village and returned from time to time to play the organ in the church. I contacted the local undertaker who found the grave. He told me that his father, then over ninety, remembered that when my great-grandfather died, he was buried in the family vault but that, soon afterwards, Harriet Goodson, his widow, became concerned that he must be feeling the cold there and insisted he be taken out and buried in the earth. As her concern was preventing her from sleeping and destroying her health, special permission was obtained from the Archbishop of Canterbury to take the body out of the vault and rebury it. The Archbishop's permission stipulated that the transfer had to be effected at night, so the vault was opened and everyone descended by candlelight to remove the coffin. I knew about the event because Yaya had been present and had often spoken of it. It has always reminded me of the scene in Wilkie Collins' "The Woman in White".

The vicar had asked me if we wanted organ music and it had been agreed that the music master from a local prep school should play the organ. However when we were all seated with Pauline and me in the front pew beside the coffin, there was a long silence, followed by a whispered discussion at the back of the church after which the vicar came up to me and said the organ was not working. I asked him what he suggested, and he said there were two alternatives, either we had no music or we must get the piano out of the vestry but that would require people to move it. I stood up and turning round, explained the situation to the congregation and asked for volunteers. My cousin Arthur Stevens, a captain in the marines, and a few other men volunteered and we went with the vicar and brought the piano out of the vestry. As we did so, Arthur whispered to me that my mother had always been better at playing the piano than the organ. The piano was hopelessly out of tune, but we managed a hymn or two and then the coffin was pushed to the graveside on an ancient bier that let out a series of mournful squeaks on the way. Afterwards we had arranged a buffet lunch for all her friends in the Albion, the local hotel, something that was unusual at that time but very much appreciated and everyone agreed that, had she been there, my Mother would have thoroughly enjoyed the informal nature of the ceremony.

My relations with my mother had been complex. As people, we had almost nothing in common. Apart from horses, her chief interest was in cars, and there too, I could not join her, but she was a warm and very loveable person and she loved me, as only mothers do, totally and without reserve. What I did, did not interest her intrinsically, as it had interested my father, but that did not matter; if I was interested in it, she was too. As a child, and through adolescence, our relations had been strained, but as time went on, and with the help of Pauline who really appreciated her, we came to have a warm and frank relationship that was only spoiled at the end by the lie about her illness.

My mother had never suffered as I had from doubts about her identity; she knew exactly who she was and had an easy relationship with people. This was partly due to the fact that she had a particularly warm and disarming smile. An example of this was when she "took things back to the shop", a practice she was much given to; if anything she bought did not meet her standard, she would immediately return it. Returning things to shops is something I hate doing and which, in my case, always seems to end in sharp words and my never being able to return to the shop.

It was never like that with my mother; she would go to the shopkeeper, give him the benefit of her smile and say that she was sure he would not want her to have the object in question. Smiling, he would agree and replace it and she would leave the shop convinced she had done him a good turn.

In middle life she put on a lot of weight and took to wearing corsets. There was a particularly substantial corset that she wore that was not unlike mediaeval body armour and equally indestructible. However on one occasion she bought a new one and barely a month later noticed it was already showing signs of wear: the steel retaining struts were beginning to emerge from their canvas casing and the edges were looking frayed. True to her principles, she straightaway took it back to the shop. The shopkeeper was extremely surprised and said he would send it back to the makers and shortly after she received a letter from the makers.

They were clearly devastated by what they had seen. Never, they said, had one of their corsets worn so badly in such a short time. They could find no explanation and were recalling the entire batch and would investigate further in their laboratory. In the meantime, with many apologies they enclosed a replacement.

My mother took the new corset in its packet and put it in her wardrobe; as she did so, she noticed another similar packet and realised that it contained the corset she had bought. She then realised that the corset she had taken back to the shop, was one that she had worn regularly for the past ten years.

*

Among the people who came to her funeral were Uncle John and Aunty Betty and I had the first conversation I had had with him for many years. They talked about their daughter, my cousin Anne, then aged eighteen, whom I had of course never met and who was currently a hippy living in the caves of Crete, and they invited us to go to see them.

While my mother was alive, I had avoided any contact with my uncle, but now I saw no reason to continue a quarrel that had not been mine. Moreover I felt drawn to him: he reminded me of my mother; they were very alike. I also hoped eventually to hear the other side of the family quarrel. So I thanked them for their invitation and it was decided that Pauline and I should drive down and have lunch with them the following week.

And so, after thirty-two years' absence, I returned to the only place I had ever thought of as home. From the moment we drove through Wingham village, up Preston Hill and down Wenderton Lane and the house came into view, I felt an extraordinary wave of emotion. Over the years the house had continually played and replayed in my memory and in my dreams. The manner in which I had left it, being told by letter that my parents had moved, meant that I had never had a proper period of mourning such as one has when seeing furniture carried out and the house empty. For me it remained furnished as it always had been and I could remember where each and every item of furniture stood. For years I had had a recurring dream in which I returned and replaced everything as it was. Now I was face to face with reality.

It is generally said that when you return to the home of your child-hood, everything seems smaller. It was not the case, – if anything the house was bigger than I remembered it. The garden had changed: gone were the weeping ash, the big old yew, and the clipped yew hedges. The garden now lay open surrounded by a hedge of horn-beam. John and Betty welcomed us warmly and showed us round. When we went into the nursery, something was missing and without thinking I said, "There used to be a hand basin here that I floated my boats in." before I remembered that my Father had had all the basins taken out – but it passed off. We had lunch in the breakfast-room, now the dining-room, as the dining-room had become a drawing-room. Frances, not our Frances but another, who had come to work for them when they were married, did the cooking. She had lunch with us and it was easy to see that she was part of the family.

After lunch, Uncle John showed me the farm. He had given up Guilton and the other farms and was now only farming Wenderton. It was unrecognisable. The hop-garden had become a field of onions and the oast was gone, a metal shed had replaced the wooden thatched barn and the cottages were empty; where twelve or fifteen men had been employed and brought up their families, now two tractor-drivers were all that was needed. I asked if he had any sheep, he said not since he had had two hundred and fifty ewes on the point of lambing when the shepherd got a better job. It was clear that farming had changed.

A few days later I realised that I could no longer remember where our furniture had stood. At a stroke, the visit had wiped away a memory that had remained intact for thirty-two years.

After that we returned several times and my cousin Anne came to see us at Greenwich. We got on from the first and my only regret was that we had not known each other earlier and were denied the shared memories that might have been ours.

In 1986 I got a letter from Uncle John saying that he had sold Wenderton farm. Anne did not want it, as she was making a successful career for herself as an antique dealer specialising in antique kitchen equipment.

He added that the day his prize herd of Sussex cattle was sold, had been one of the worst of his life. The following year, he had a stroke. He was taken to Canterbury Hospital in a coma and died some days later. He had been preparing for his eightieth birthday and had even ordered the marquee. I went to Wenderton for the funeral. Anne took me to the funeral parlour where he lay, and left me alone with him. As I stood beside him, I thought of all that had passed between him and my parents, of the family quarrel, how it had changed my life.

After the funeral, I stayed several days with Aunty Betty and Anne, I had always hoped to be able to talk to John about the quarrel, but it had never been possible, but now, with Aunty Betty, we discussed it. I asked why John had so resented my father and she confirmed that it was because he believed him to have been his mother's lover.

While I was at Wenderton, I went into Wingham village and into the Red Lion. To my surprise the painting of it that I had done all those years before, was still hanging there. Smoke from the open hearth had darkened it, but it was still visible with my twelve-year-old signature, *"B.E.G. Apps"*. The pub had changed hands several times in the previous forty-six years and the painting had presumably changed hands as part of the furniture and fittings. I bought a beer and mentioned casually to the landlord that I had painted it. His jaw dropped and his disappointment was evident. Apparently he had believed it to be eighteenth-century and very valuable.

CHAPTER TWENTY-EIGHT

In 1974 we spent most of the summer at Liez and Glenda and Roy came for a holiday while we were there. Yvon Larrignon's widowed mother was our neighbour and she agreed to rent them the house that adjoined hers so that Glenda's mother and sisters could come out. We knew that their marriage was rocky, Roy had wanted Glenda to give up her career and spend more time with Daniel (when she won her second Oscar, the phone rang in the middle of the night. Roy answered it, listened, and shouted, "That's all we need you have won another fucking Oscar!" and slammed it down). Nevertheless, when they arrived all seemed well and we spent the first week or so pleasantly together.

Madame Larrignon was a dedicated television viewer and one afternoon when I went to see her, I found her watching the BBC series, dubbed into French, about Queen Elizabeth 1 in which Glenda played Elizabeth. She was enjoying it hugely and kept saying how good she thought Queen Elizabeth was, so that I could not resist pointing out that Queen Elizabeth was her next-door neighbour. After the first shock, she took the news calmly and behaved as though she had been in the habit of having Oscar-winning film stars next door all her life. Glenda used to go and sit with her and practise her French and they built up quite a friendship. Afterwards she followed Glenda's career enthusiastically and would say, *"Je vois que Madame Hodges joue à Londres en ce moment"*. Or *"Madame Hodges tourne en Amérique dans un nouveau film"*. But when Glenda went into politics, Madame Larrignon's opinion of politicians made her unable to follow, and from then on she would shake her head when Glenda was mentioned.

There is a scandalous newspaper called "France Dimanche" that resembles "The News of the World" in its search for salacity. Published on Sundays, it arrived in Maillezais on Mondays and Glenda and Roy enjoyed reading it to see who among their acquaintances in the film world was pilloried each week. Roy used to insist each Monday morning that I went with him to buy it. On one particular Monday we bought it and as we were driving back, he said eagerly "Who is it this week?" I looked to see and replied "You". There was a scandalous article about their marriage. He swerved and we nearly went into the ditch.

Hopes that a holiday would help the marriage get back on track began to fade and Roy asked if he could sleep in our house. Finally, Glenda and her family left by train and Roy stayed on to take the car back. He asked me to go with him to the post office in Maillezais to ring the hotel in Paris where they were staying. I did so and when I got through asked for Mrs Hodges, only to be told that no one of that name was staying there. I asked for Miss Jackson and was put through. I saw the look on Roy's face. Nothing was said between us, but I felt sure from that moment that the marriage was over. In fact it limped on for another year and ended when they were in America.

After their divorce many unkind things were written in the press about Roy; that he was a passenger and a dead weight on Glenda's career. Pauline and I, who saw them daily over a long period and knew them as well as anyone, were always convinced that it was far from the case. Roy was a tower of strength for her at the beginning of her career and his individual and uninhibited approach to life, combined with an easy contact with people, allowed him to give her sound advice and help her to overcome her original shyness. It is one thing to be invited to the White House by the Kennedys, or to Number Ten Downing Street by the British Prime Minister because you are a great actress, but it is quite another to find yourself in that situation simply because you are a husband and carry it off with aplomb as Roy managed to do. As a couple they were ahead of their time and journalists, who are always by their nature hidebound by the opinion of the day, while they would have been vociferous in his praise had he been a wife, were unable to accept his contribution because he was a husband. It was, of course, years later that Mr Thatcher gained a grudging respect for supportive husbands.

We enjoyed the summer in Liez and got to know the village and its inhabitants. The village consisted of a cluster of small farms lived in by families who had lived in the same farms or, in some cases, played a sort of musical chairs, beginning in one farm then inheriting another as people died and families inter-married. When the village was mentioned in the surrounding country, there were two reactions; people would say, "Liez is a village tied at both ends" (*lier* in French means to tie), by which they meant that no one ever entered and no one ever left. A statement endorsed by the names on the graves in the churchyard, which were the same as those of the inhabitants. The other reaction was "Ah, le curé of Liez!" There had been a famous curé, the Abbé Migné, who had died in the fifties and was buried in the churchyard. He had had the gift of healing and people had come from great distances across France to consult him. He was very tall and impressive and ruled the village with a rod of iron. No one dared miss Mass on Sundays, where he would not hesitate to name and shame anyone who had been up to no good.

The Bishop of Luçon had become uneasy about his healing activities and from time to time would come to remonstrate with him. On one of these occasions, as they walked together in the Curé's garden, the Bishop's eye was caught by a huge pile of empty wine-bottles, gifts from grateful patients. The Bishop shook his head and said, "All these dead men!" to which the Curé replied "Yes, Monseigneur, but I can assure you that not one of them died without first seeing the priest." It seems he had learned the art of healing during the First World War when he was in the Ambulance Brigade, or so a lady in Maillezais told me, adding that her father had known him at the time having first met him in a brothel.

No one in the village was rich: they milked cows, raised crops on small fields, had goats, rabbits and poultry and a pig or two that they killed, salting the meat and making hams. They caught eels and fish in the canals, and, beside their kitchen gardens, they almost all had vineyards from which they made wine for annual consumption. The first tractors had appeared just after the Second World War and were rarely recent models. Many farmers still ploughed with horses or oxen. Cars were either the Citroen 2cv or the Renault 4L. Nevertheless, the standard of living in all essentials was high; they had clean, drinkable well water, plenty of cheap firewood from pollarding the ash trees that bordered the canals, good fresh vegetables and fruit. Moreover, their farms being mixed, they could ride out a bad harvest or an epidemic of foot-and-mouth disease or similar disaster.

Suddenly finding ourselves in this society after London, the chief difference that struck us was that, while in London we had everything anyone could ask for (there was, for example, a shop in Soho where you could buy fresh figs picked that morning in Greece) here you could only find things that were in season, but oh, the difference! The figs from Greece tasted nothing like the figs we picked off the old fig tree in the garden and the same went for vegetables and everything else. Then, too, at home values seemed to be changing; money was becoming more and more an acceptable subject of conversation; people were changing their kitchens almost as regularly as they changed their underclothes, bathrooms were constantly being redecorated to have the latest colour scheme and while the "shopping experience" still lay in the future, people were already buying things they did not need and they no longer repaired anything, they threw away and bought new.

In Liez, people only bought what they needed and nothing was thrown away, everything was repaired and conserved as long as possible and the ingenuity with which some items, such as doors and windows, had their usefulness extended, amounted almost to an art. It seemed a more sensible way to live.

Barnaby was at a school in Blackheath. When I had taken him on the first day, I had chatted to a mother who told me she had five children and she had come with the last of them for his first day at school. "I hope he can read and write," she said, indicating Barnaby "because he won't learn to here." In fact we had made no effort to teach him as friends had advised against it on the grounds that if children can read already, they get bored at school. The teacher was a nice young girl who looked eighteen and cannot have been much older, but although she was cheerful and encouraging, we felt that she did not seem to have much of a grip on her pupils. The impression was confirmed when we went to Open Day to see what the pupils had done at the end of the first year, Barnaby's work consisted of a few scribbled pages. He was now seven years old and could not even form the letters of the alphabet. Clearly something had to be done.

One option that appealed to us increasingly was to let the house in Blackheath and move to France for two or three years. The schools in France had a good reputation, it would allow him to learn French and it would take the pressure off us to earn money, as the rent from the London house would be sufficient to live on and we could take our time to develop a new idea.

In any case, "All Gas and Gaiters" had not been repeated since 1972 and it was bound to be shown soon. After all, everyone kept telling us it was a classic and with its thirty-three episodes would guarantee us an income for the future.

In January 1976, Hubert Gregg invited me to play the Commander in a production of "French without Tears" he was doing at Farnham. I did not realise it at the time, but it was to be the last time I was to act on the stage.

In fact my interest in acting was waning. Being an actor is a state of mind, the pleasure of getting away from your self to become some-one else. Acting had been a therapy for me at a time when I was not sure who I was. One of the worst aspects of being out of work had always been the lack of identity. When I had a character to play, I had known who I was: I was that character throughout rehearsals and the run of the play. When the play ended the crisis of identy returned until I was cast as another character. Now I felt less the need to become someone else. I was beginning to be resigned to being the person I had become.

While I was doing the play at Farnham, Pauline found a tenant for our Greenwich house, a commander in the Australian Navy who was at the Greenwich Naval College. He rented it for two years. So we packed up our things and early in February 1976, Roy lent us his van and we set out for Liez, Roy following with our car a few days later. And so began the second part of my life, with a new country, a new language, new loves and a new profession – but that is another story.

When I told Michael Bruce our solicitor friend that I was moving to France, he said; "You will never come back."

Shortly after we arrived in France, William Mervyn died suddenly at the age of sixty-two. Soon after, we got a letter from his widow saying that the family had approached the BBC to ask if they might buy copies of some of the episodes of "All Gas and Gaiters" only to be told that they had all been wiped so the tapes could be used again. Did we, she asked, know anything about it?

We told her we did not and that it was difficult to believe that a responsible television company would destroy a comedy series that had cost many thousands of pounds to make, consisted of thirty-three viable episodes, had had an enormous success in Britain and had been equally successful in Australia, New Zealand, South Africa and elsewhere, simply to economise on recording tape. We decided that it was more likely that the BBC could not be bothered to make copies. We had had difficulty persuading it to do so when we had bought two copies, which we had tried to sell in America.

However, the series remained off the screen and when, in the 1990s, nostalgic BBC programmes began to be broadcast about the successful comedy series of the nineteen sixties, it was never mentioned. Nevertheless, the press continued to mention it. Whenever there was a crisis in the church, the headline would be "All Gas and Gaiters" and it was always described as "the 1960s classic comedy series about the Church". It was not until 1995 that, exasperated by the BBC's silence, I wrote to the then Director-General, Mr Birt, to ask for clarification, I said that we had heard rumours to the effect that the tapes had been cleaned to use again, but had not believed them, as we felt sure that, had the BBC intended to destroy our work, it would have informed us and, at the very least, given us the possibility of buying the tapes. A month later, I got a letter from a Mr Hemsley, who styled himself "Assistant to the Secretary's Office for the Director-General"

"I have made enquiries about the existence of the "All Gas and Gaiters" tapes and I am afraid I have to tell you that of the thirty-three programmes originally transmitted, only eight remain in the BBC's Broadcasting Archives at Brentford – two from 1970 and six from 1971. I understand that before 1975, it was up to individual departments to decide which of their output material should be retained in the library – and what should not. Sadly it appears that the majority of "All Gas and Gaiters" tapes fell into the latter category".

There followed a list of the episodes in question. When we examined the list, they turned out to be some of the least successful as far as both viewing figures and audience appreciation were concerned, so the reason why they were selected to escape the holocaust remains a mystery.

While Derek Nimmo was in Australia (where he had a considerable success) he asked the local BBC what had happened to the set of tapes that had been shown there. He was told that London had insisted they be sent back to be cleaned.

———

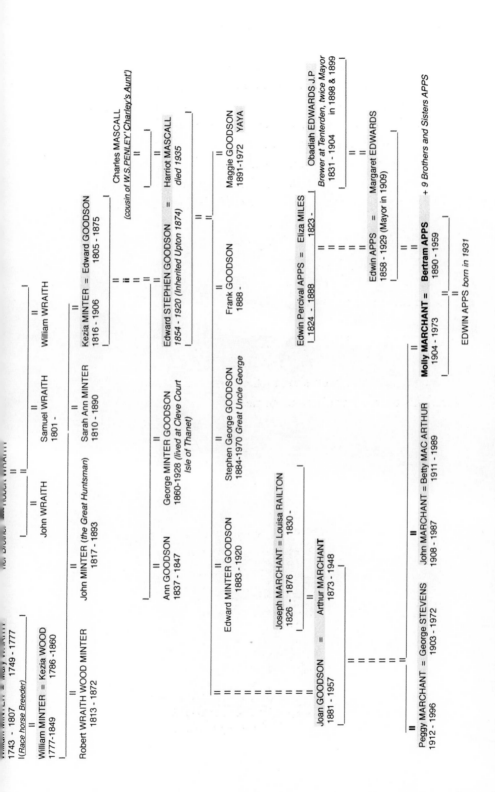

William MINTER = Mary WRAITH
1743 - 1807   1749 - 1777
(Race horse Breeder)

William MINTER = Kezia WOOD
1777-1849   1786 -1860

John WRAITH

Samuel WRAITH
1801 -

William WRAITH

Robert WRAITH WOOD MINTER
1813 - 1872

John MINTER (the Great Huntsman)
1817 - 1893

Sarah Ann MINTER
1810 - 1890

Kezia MINTER = Edward GOODSON
1816 - 1906   1805 - 1875

Charles MASCALL
(cousin of W.S.PENLEY 'Charley's Aunt')

Harriot MASCALL
died 1935

Edward STEPHEN GOODSON =
1854 - 1920 (Inherited Upton 1874)

Maggie GOODSON
1891-1972   YAYA

Frank GOODSON
1888 -

Ann GOODSON
1837 - 1847

George MINTER GOODSON
1860-1928 (lived at Cleve Court
Isle of Thanet)

Stephen George GOODSON
1884-1970 Great Uncle George

Edward MINTER GOODSON
1883 - 1920

Joseph MARCHANT = Louisa RAILTON
1826 - 1876   1830 -

Arthur MARCHANT
1873 - 1948

Joan GOODSON   =
1881 - 1957

Edwin Percival APPS = Eliza MILES
1824 - 1888   1823 -

Obadiah EDWARDS J.P
Brewer at Tenterden, twice Mayor
1831 - 1904   in 1898 & 1899

Edwin APPS   =   Margaret EDWARDS
1858 - 1929 (Mayor in 1909)

Molly MARCHANT =   Bertram APPS   + 9 Brothers and Sisters APPS
1904 - 1973   1890 - 1959

EDWIN APPS born in 1931

John MARCHANT = Betty MAC ARTHUR
1908 - 1987   1911 - 1989

Peggy MARCHANT = George STEVENS
1912 - 1996   1903 - 1972

ACKNOWLEDGEMENTS

———

I wish to thank all those friends, especially Florent Bourdeau, Sylvia and Humphrey Gyde, Roy Hodges, Christine Scott and Mark Urry who had the patience to read early drafts of this book and the courage frankly to tell me what they thought of it.

My particular thanks go to Pauline Devaney, whose memories of our shared adventure have amplified and corrected mine; to Gordon Rhodes, whose pertinent criticisms have been, as always, invaluable; to Peter Leek, who brought the experience of a lifetime in publishing to bear on the problem and whose belief in the project acted as an umbrella over my head when the rejection slips from publishers rained down; to Alan Wallace who corrected the text; to Stuart Allen who plunged into his archives to furnish the photos of "All Gas And Gaiters" and "The Tinkles": to my publisher, Patrick Durand-Peyroles, and, last but by no means least, to Josette Jaud, my companion, without whose help, encouragement and computing skills the book would simply not exist."

INDEX

Photos

—

Lightning Source UK Ltd.
Milton Keynes UK
UKOW05f0620040813

214806UK00002B/70/P